D0622393

NEGOTIATING FOR PEACE IN THE MIDDLE EAST

Negotiating for Peace in the Middle East

ISMAIL FAHMY

THE JOHNS HOPKINS UNIVERSITY PRESS
Baltimore, Maryland

First published in Great Britain, 1983, by
Croom Helm Ltd, Provident House, Burrell Row,
Beckenham, Kent BR3 1AT

Published in the United States of America, 1983,
by the Johns Hopkins University Press,
Baltimore, Maryland 21218

Library of Congress Catalog Card Number: 82-49057
ISBN 0-8018-3016-8

Printed and bound in Great Britain

CONTENTS

LIST OF PLATES

To the Egyptian people.

ACKNOWLEDGEMENTS

It has been my privilege and burden to be a participant in all the events discussed in this book. My problem thus has not been to find out what happened, but to sort out and organize my recollections so as to let the reader gain an insight into the important historical events of the period.

Memoirs are intensely personal, and the author can only receive limited help, but I was fortunate in having all the support I could hope for. My wife Afaf lived with me all the historical events contained in this book. She not only inspired me on many occasions but also provided the peaceful domestic atmosphere in which I could work undisturbed. My daughter Randa spent long months transferring on to paper what had just been ideas in her father's head. My sons Hamed and Nabil provided many suggestions and constant critical comment: their day-to-day interest in my project greatly encouraged me to see it through to the end. Marina Ottaway arrived in the final stage to assist me in editing the manuscript and certainly she arrived at the proper moment. Yasmine Abdool, my Mauritian secretary, took dictation and typed innumerable drafts of the manuscript with unfailing patience, and she valiantly struggled to finish the final copy in the days immediately preceding and following the birth of her son, Muhammad Ali. To all of them I want to express my most heart-felt thanks.

Cairo, June 1982

INTRODUCTION

Many Egyptian, Arab and foreign friends have expressed interest in reading my story concerning Sadat's decision to fly to Jerusalem on 19 November 1977. They argue that this was a major historical event and that, as Deputy Prime Minister and Foreign Minister of Egypt up to 17 November 1977, I was under special obligation to break the silence I had voluntarily imposed on myself. The story of what really happened between Sadat and myself prior to his final decision to go to Jerusalem has to be told. They continue to argue that, while it is true that Sadat's visit was acclaimed world-wide, on the other hand there remain many major questions and serious doubts as to the wisdom of the initiative itself.

How did Sadat decide to get to Jerusalem? Why did he keep the decision secret? Why did the Egyptian President not consult his own government? Was he sure of unanimous rejection by his own cabinet and the country's institutions? Why did Sadat choose not to consult anyone in Egypt except his Foreign Minister, as he personally admitted? What were the reasons behind President Sadat's decision to keep his friend President Carter ignorant about the bilateral contacts which took place between Egypt and Israel in Rabat in September 1977 and particularly concerning Sadat's final decision to visit Jerusalem? It certainly seems strange that, if President Sadat really believed that the solution to the Middle East crisis lay in the hands of the United States alone, he would hide such a major initiative from President Carter. Was Sadat's secrecy his own decision or did the Israelis persuade him to keep quiet?

I have now decided to write about these events because I am increasingly concerned about the many statements made and the many articles and books published on this matter. My final decision to go ahead was triggered by the incorrect versions of events presented in books such as Ezer Weizman's *The Battle for Peace*, Moshe Dayan's *Breakthrough*, *The Year of the Dove*, written by three Israelii journalists, and above all Sadat's own *In Search of Identity*.[1]

For obvious reasons, everyone has claimed that their story was the correct version. The discrepancies in the accounts are natural because those who have written or are writing about Sadat's trip to

1

Jerusalem differ greatly in terms of their access to information. In fact they can be divided into two groups: firstly there are a very few senior government officials like Dayan who were well informed of what was taking place by virtue of their official position. The second group comprises those journalists who did not have any direct access to primary sources; their stories were compiled on the basis of second-hand or even third-hand information to which they added bits and pieces from their imagination. Neither Sadat nor Begin, the main actors in the drama, have shed any serious light on events. Begin until now has been almost silent. Sadat, on the other hand, has given several different explanations of how, why and when he took the decision to visit Jerusalem. The explanation of these contradictions resides in Sadat's own personality and the complexity of the events and circumstances he faced in Egypt and the Arab world.

The contradictory versions of events leading up to Sadat's trip have inevitably given rise to heated debate. Israeli Foreign Minister Moshe Dayan and Sadat's advisor Hassan Tuhami, who represented Begin and Sadat in the early bilateral contacts at Rabat, have been particularly vehement in defending their versions of events. However, neither knew the whole story, because their functions were limited to arranging a meeting between Begin and Sadat. In fact, Dayan admitted in his book that he was completely taken by surprise when he learned, through the media, of Sadat's statement in the Egyptian Assembly that he was ready to go anywhere in the world, including Jerusalem.

Irrespective of what has been published or said by various sources, the main protagonists were Begin and Sadat. Ultimately, the story can only be told by those participating in and familiar with the events involving the two leaders. On that basis, I believe that my own version should have special significance because it reveals for the first time Sadat's thinking concerning his trip to Jerusalem. These ideas unfolded in a series of meetings between Sadat and myself devoted entirely to his decision to go to Jerusalem. Our discussions had special importance because at no time did Sadat discuss his intentions with anybody else as his own book, *In Search of Identity*, admits.

Throughout these sessions with President Sadat I was resolutely opposed to his going to Jerusalem. My rejection of the trip was based on very specific criteria. I believed it would harm Egypt's national security, damage our relations with the other Arab countries, and destroy our leadership of the Arab world. Sadat did not consider any of these issues. Furthermore he could not demonstrate any proof that the Israelis would respond to his move with comparable good will. He was unable to produce any justification that such a completely new approach would lead to a comprehensive and just peace settlement in harmony with the decisions already adopted by the Arab heads of state.

Many of my assertions will contradict statements made by Sadat on many occasions. Without realising it, he had the habit of regularly making contradictory statements. Disregarding the fact that to any international problem there is more than one party, Sadat had a penchant for storytelling and some bore little resemblance to reality. What he said changed with the occasion and the audience. This was especially true concerning his trip to Jerusalem, because he was afraid to tell his counterparts in the Arab world and his compatriots in Egypt what had really happened and the concessions he had made.

Sadat's trip to Jerusalem, my decision to resign rather than to go along with this step, and the catastrophic consequences of Sadat's sudden move for the Arab world cannot be understood without taking into consideration the events of the previous years. The trip to Jerusalem was not the beginning of an attempt to bring about a permanent peace in the Middle East. On the contrary, it was a misguided move that aborted a peace process which had been going on for a long time. The re-evaluation of Egypt's foreign policy and of its relations with the great powers which took place after Nasser's death and Sadat's rise to power were part of this process. The October War in 1973 gave it greater momentum, because it made clear to the outside world that the Middle East conflict could not be dismissed as a purely regional concern; a new flare-up in the region could easily lead to direct confrontation between the United States and the Soviet Union. Years of careful diplomacy ever since the 1973 war had brought us closer to a final solution, and by late 1977 these efforts appeared likely to be crowned by success at the Geneva Conference scheduled to take place in December.

Sadat's sudden decision to go to Jerusalem cannot be understood and evaluated unless the preceding steps are also discussed. For this reason, my assessment will start not with 1977, but five years earlier, with the convening of a symposium by the Centre for Political and Strategic Studies of *Al-Ahram*, the major Egyptian daily newspaper. This symposium, held in May 1972, was an unprecedented public discussion of Egypt's foreign policy and it greatly influenced Sadat's views, providing a major incentive for change. I will then consider the other major events, which are in my view, essential to an understanding of Sadat's move: the 1973 war and its impact on the prospects for peace in the Middle East; the effort to negotiate disengagements on the war front and consolidate the cease-fire; the evolution in Egypt's relations with the great powers; the enormous progress made by the Arab countries to reach a unified position toward Israel and the Palestinian problem; and the very concrete steps taken toward the convening of the Geneva conference after President Carter's election. I will also consider the role played by a number of major participants: three American presidents, Nixon, Ford and Carter, put their own imprints on the peace process; Kissinger dominated the scene for years. Brezhnev, Gromyko and other Soviet officials appeared and disappeared from the peace process, trying to make their presence felt or sulking on the sidelines, watching Kissinger's performance and swallowing Sadat's rejection. And finally, Sadat himself occupied centre stage, with his strengths and weaknesses, determination and fickleness, dreams of grandeur and fears of another war.

It was my lot in this period to be not just an observer but an actor as well, shaping Egypt's policy alongside Sadat. As Egypt's Foreign Minister, I was very closely involved with the events discussed in this book and I cannot look back on them and analyse them as a neutral observer. There would be little point in feigning detachment; I had a deep commitment to certain policies and outcomes, and I can only assess these matters in light of what I thought Egypt should do. As a result, this book not only narrates events, it judges them too. But the facts presented here are the facts, as I know them from my direct participation.

Notes

1. Ezer Weizman, *The Battle for Peace* (New York: Bantam Books, 1981); Moshe Dayan, *Breakthrough* (New York: Alfred Knopf, 1981); Eitan Haber, Zeev Schiff, Ehud Yaari, *The Year of the Dove* (New York: Bantam Books, 1979); Anwar El-Sadat, *In Search of Identity* (New York: Harper and Row, 1977).

1 SADAT AND I

The beginning of 1972 had brought heightened tension and internal crisis to Egypt. President Sadat, having failed to fulfill his promise that 1971 would be the 'year of decision', was faced with an increasingly rapid drop in his already low domestic popularity. Students and blue collar workers, faced with the dismal economic situation, challenged his authority. Egypt's internal problems, coupled with the war situation on the Israeli front, gave no hope for optimism. Israeli intransigence prevented progress toward peace. The Soviet Union's hesitancy in providing Egypt with sufficient armaments for the liberation of the occupied territory in Sinai damaged Sadat even more. A new initiative in Egypt's internal and international policies and priorities was necessary. However, in the international arena at that time the highest priorities were Vietnam and the scheduled summit meeting between Nixon and Brezhnev; the Middle East was dismissed as a secondary, if troublesome, area of the world.

The Symposium at *Al-Ahram*

The Centre for Political and Strategic Studies at *Al-Ahram* organised a symposium in May 1972 to discuss the forthcoming USA–USSR summit meeting in the light of the sudden United States decision to block and mine the port of Haiphong in Vietnam. Egyptian intellectuals from different governmental and non-governmental institutions were invited to participate. I attended in my capacity as Under-Secretary of State at the Ministry of Foreign Affairs.

President Nixon had decided to mine Haiphong harbour just a few days before the scheduled opening of the summit meeting in Moscow. The decision was extremely provocative, and presented an unprecedented challenge to the Soviet Union both in form and timing. The participants at the symposium were of the view that the summit meeting, as a result of the United States decision, would either be cancelled or postponed. I was the only one to hold a contrary opinion, arguing that the summit meeting would take place as scheduled because of the superpowers' desire for détente.

The discussion inevitably led us to an extensive appraisal of the Middle East crisis and to a reassessment of Egypt's relations with the superpowers, especially with the Soviet Union, relations with the United States being almost non-existent. At this point the discussion focused exclusively on our foreign policy. I had given much thought to these issues and I took advantage of the opportunity to make my ideas public. I pointed out that the overall situation in the Middle East had to be reappraised and that Egypt could not continue to vacillate in a precarious state of 'no peace, no war'. This term was later picked up by others and used to describe the situation in the Middle East. Internal as well as external pressures made change imperative, but any new move would have to be planned carefully and take into account our relationship with both superpowers. I argued that it was high time we examined our relationship with the Soviet Union and then confronted the Soviet leadership with our own idea of how our relations should be reshaped and redirected. I suggested that the superpowers were contributing to the maintenance of 'no peace, no war', because a permanent settlement in the Middle East had low priority for them. Détente was likely to make this priority even lower, as the two superpowers would now be preoccupied with safeguarding their new rapprochement. As a consequence, the Soviets would become even more reluctant to provide Egypt with the arms it needed for a new confrontation with Israel. I made it clear that without such confrontation there would be no incentive for the superpowers to work for a comprehensive peace in the Middle East. I suggested that the symposium should concentrate on analysing the causes of the state of 'no peace, no war' and how it had been perpetuated by the conflicting interests of the superpowers. The Soviets must understand that we wanted their friendship, but were not prepared to accept indefinitely the state of 'no peace, no war'. I argued that if the Soviets were actually unaware that Egypt, backed by the Arab world, was rejecting the stalemate of the state of 'no war, no peace' and that it had no alternative but a new confrontation with Israel, they were making a colossal mistake in their calculations. I was convinced that in Moscow they were aware of the implications of their policy.

Whereas the Soviets policy objective was intentionally to limit the Egyptian military option, on the other hand they grossly miscalculated the effect that policy had in discrediting them with the Egyptians and thereby the negative impact it had on their interests in the region. Moreover, it was clear that the Soviet advice to the Egyptian side not to start military operations was due to Moscow's fear that once a war started events might lead to a greater confrontation between the two superpowers in the Middle East. The state of 'no peace, no war' was causing a gradual haemorrhage of Egypt's resources.

Egypt therefore had to take a military initiative to revitalise the crisis, but before embarking on such a course of action, Egypt had to mobilize all her resources and those of the entire Arab world. In particular I expanded on the importance of using oil as a major political weapon.

This symposium was the first frank and public discussion of Egyptian foreign policy and the options open to us since 1952. The discussion was not meant specifically as a criticism of the Soviet Union. Rather, it was an attempt to re-examine Egypt's own interests and to invite the Soviet Union to review its attitude and policy toward Egypt, so that our relationship might serve the interests of both countries and thus be strengthened. But in the course of the discussion it also became clear to us that we should seek to re-establish relations with the United States. Egypt simply could not afford to ignore one superpower, becoming totally dependent on the other.

The discussion which had taken place at the symposium was published on 19 May 1972 in *Al-Ahram* and was the first serious evaluation of the situation to appear in print in Egypt. We expected that the publication of the symposium would create much interest, but we also expected problems, for President Sadat, in an address to the People's Assembly in early May had proclaimed: 'I shall take strong measures against people who criticise Egypt's major ally, Russia, rather than Cairo's enemy, the United States.'

The report of the meeting was greeted with all the more interest because it was widely assumed that my intervention represented an official government position. Nobody could quite believe that statements deviating from the government position could have been made in public without Sadat's consent. As a result, it was thought that the symposium had been conceived by Sadat as a trial balloon. In fact, I had never even met Sadat at that time. In addition, I had been invited to participate in the symposium just three hours before it was to start, and I had hardly had time to prepare myself, let alone clear my comments with anybody.

The Soviets, too, assumed that the symposium had been inspired by the government, and formally protested. As a result the Foreign

Minister, Dr Mourad Ghaleb, decided to submit for Sadat's signature a presidential decree to the effect that I should be relieved of my duties as Under-Secretary of State for Foreign Affairs but should remain in the Ministry of Foreign Affairs as ambassador. Ghaleb's position was understandable in view of his personal status: after many years as Egyptian ambassador to Moscow, he regarded himself as a pillar of Soviet-Egyptian relations. When the Soviet Union protested about the symposium, he felt compelled to remove me as the principal offender. In private, however, he praised my evaluation: 'This is the best analysis I have come across in a long time,' he told me. When Ghaleb presented the decree to remove me for Sadat's signature, however, the President refused to sign it. By this time Sadat had read my statement and had apparently been impressed by the ideas I had set forth; he started implementing some of the suggestions made at the symposium. This at least was the assessment of Dr Mahmoud Fawzi, at that time Vice-President of Egypt. 'Sadat,' he told me a month later, 'has started implementing the policies you outlined at the symposium.' I have no way of knowing whether this was in fact the case, because I did not yet belong to Sadat's inner circle. However, there was no reason why Fawzi should invent this and Sadat's foreign policy certainly started changing in the direction I had suggested.

There was a reevaluation of Egypt's relation with the great powers. Undoubtedly, this was facilitated by the fact that Sadat had had problems with the Soviets ever since he came to power. The Soviets had originally preferred Ali Sabri to Sadat. After Sabri's defeat, they appeared to accept Sadat, but he always doubted whether the acceptance was real. He remained extremely distrustful of the Soviets although he had rushed to sign the Treaty of Friendship and Cooperation with them in May 1971. The problems with the Soviets had led Sadat to establish contacts with the United States. All exchanges remained covert, but they were numerous. The most important intermediary between Egypt and the United States at this point was a highly-placed Saudi official whom Sadat had known for a long time. The conclusions of the symposium thus struck a chord with Sadat. While it did not cause him to move in a completely new direction, it did provide a much clearer focus and strategic underpinning for his foreign policy.

By way of first blood, Sadat expelled the Soviet military experts from the Egyptian army on 18 July 1972. Inevitably, the decision angered the Soviet Union, and a delegation sent by Sadat to

Moscow in October met with an icy reception. However, one member of the Egyptian delegation, General Ahmed Ismail, had fruitful exchanges with KGB representatives. Later, in March 1973, General Ismail, now Minister of War, led a further delegation to Moscow and successfully negotiated a very large arms deal. Clearly, the Soviets had got the message that they could not take Egypt for granted and had to take positive measures to maintain good relations. Although only a third of the promised arms were actually delivered, this was enough for Egypt to launch the war with Israel in October 1973. The remaining arms were not delivered until two years after, as we shall see later. Another positive effect of the expulsion of the Soviet experts was that it made it possible for Egypt to establish its credentials as a military power capable of challenging Israel on its own during the October War. Had the Soviet experts remained with the Egyptian army, our successes would have undoubtedly been attributed to the USSR.

Sadat also took some steps to broaden his contacts with the United States. Hafez Ismail, his national security advisor, travelled to the United States to meet with Henry Kissinger and Richard Nixon in February 1973 and saw Kissinger again in France in May. An official CIA representative also came to Cairo with Sadat's consent and approval in July 1972. However, the main 'back channel' between the United States and Egypt still passed through the Saudi Arabian counsellor.

The symposium also had considerable impact on my personal career, because it caught Sadat's attention, eventually leading to my appointment as Foreign Minister. Until that time, I had not been an insider within either the Nassar or the Sadat régime. As a career diplomat, I had been posted abroad during most of the Nasser era and I had never met him personally, although I was occasionally recalled to Cairo for consultations by one or another member of the Revolutionary Council. In fact, one of them, upon assuming a new important post, asked me to come back to Cairo and become his personal assistant for foreign affairs. The offer was attractive in terms of the rank and other prerogatives of the post itself, but I decided not to accept it because I had reservations about the system prevailing under Nasser and did not want to become closely associated with it.

I also turned down another assignment during the Nasser years, which was quite revealing of the policies Nasser was following in this period. In late 1960 I was recalled to Cairo for consultations.

When I arrived I was told that Nasser had agreed to a request by Patrice Lumumba, then Prime Minister of the Republic of the Congo, that Egypt provide him with a foreign policy advisor, and had chosen me for that post. It will be recalled that Egypt at this point had decided to throw its weight behind Lumumba in his struggle for control of the country, and had established a large diplomatic and military mission in Brazzaville. Furthermore, Nasser had also contributed Egyptian troops to the United Nations forces in the Congo. I was both surprised and irritated by this appointment. Nasser did not know me personally, and I found it surprising that he should have chosen me for a delicate post; when I commented about this, it was explained to me that the President 'knew everybody'. But I was also very irritated by Nasser's methods, because he had informed Lumumba of the appointment without knowing my reaction. In addition, it was clear that it had not occurred to Nasser or those around him to check whether the advisor they sent to Lumumba agreed that the policy favoured by Nasser, namely to build up Lumumba into a radical, anti-Western leader, was in the Congo's best interest. I was convinced that Nasser was encouraging Lumumba on a disastrous course. If I had served as Lumumba's advisor, I would have felt compelled to suggest that he follow a more moderate policy. I explained this to the government official who had conveyed Nasser's message to me, but I had a very hard time: he had never considered the possibility that an advisor appointed by Nasser might support policies other than those favoured by Nasser. In the end the President cancelled my appointment, which was most fortunate because shortly afterwards the Congo fell into total shambles and Lumumba was deposed and later assassinated.

Anwar el Sadat was not one of the members of the Revolutionary Council with whom I dealt in this period. In fact, I had seen him only once in 1967 at a formal luncheon given by the Soviet ambassador in Cairo. This was supposedly a purely social event, but Sadat was most unsociable, sitting silently picking at his food and ignoring his neighbours. At the end of the lunch, the Soviet ambassador and the Egyptian Foreign Minister said a few polite words about the relations between their countries. Just then, when everybody assumed that the social event was over, Sadat stood up and delivered a long rambling speech about Soviet-Egyptian relations, hailing the help the Soviets had given Egypt and concluding that indeed the USSR and the Eastern European countries were Egypt's only friends. It was a strange performance, particularly since the occasion did not demand that a speech be made. I was also rather surprised by the fact that Sadat had been the only member of the Revolutionary Council at the lunch. I inquired about this, and was told that in this period Nasser had delegated Sadat to maintain close contacts with the Soviets, meeting with them on a weekly basis. These close contacts in Nasser's time did not smooth Sadat's relations with the Soviets later; he never understood, liked or trusted them, and this attitude was amply reciprocated by the Soviets.

After Nasser's death, I remained for several years outside Sadat's inner circle. I was serving as ambassador to Austria when Nasser died, and stayed on in that post until I was recalled in 1971, at the request of Mahmoud Riad, then Foreign Minister and later Secretary-General of the Arab League. Riad wanted me to take the post of Under-Secretary of State for Foreign Affairs in order to help him reorganise the ministry. Sadat had to approve the nomination, a rather delicate matter because it meant that I would be promoted ahead of colleagues with greater seniority. However, he accepted Riad's recommendation, and I had to leave the Austrian capital quickly and return to Cairo.

I was thus serving in Cairo at the time of the symposium, still as a career diplomat and not as a confidant of the President. But the symposium changed the situation. Initially, to be sure, it caused me problems, including the new Foreign Minister's attempt to relieve me of my post. But gradually Sadat started consulting me on some decisions, although through third parties, rather than personally. In particular, he sought my opinion on a decision to revoke Egypt's support of Security Council Resolution 242 which he had taken but not made public. Such revocation would have represented a hardening of the Egyptian position, since Resolution 242 called for recognition of the right of all states in the Middle East to live in peace. As requested, I prepared a memo for the President outlining the overall situation, spelling out the various options open to us and their probable consequences, and finally making my recommendation that Egypt's support of Resolution 242 should not be revoked. He accepted my recommendation and often cited this episode to prove he was open minded and a real democrat. I believe that what impressed Sadat was not only the logic of my opinion, but also the fact that somebody had dared to disagree openly with him. The tendency in Egypt has unfortunately always been to find arguments to support and glorify the President and his decision.

In April 1973, Sadat decided to reestablish diplomatic relations with Bonn, which had been severed seven years earlier because West Germany had shipped arms to Israel. He designated me to be ambassador to that country. The post, I was led to understand, was doubly important because Sadat intended to strengthen his relations with the United States through Germany. I never found out whether in fact Sadat had this intention because I never took up my new post. By this time, Sadat was in the midst of reshuffling his cabinet in preparation for the war with Israel. When I requested a meeting with the President to take my leave before going to Bonn, I was initially told he was too busy, so I decided to leave without the customary ceremonial meeting. However, Sadat unexpectedly decided to receive me. I went to see him at the residence near the Barrage outside Cairo, where he often stayed, and spent with him not the customary few minutes but two and a half hours.

This was my first meeting with Sadat, and it was marked by extreme frankness on both sides. I was astonished by the openness with which he talked to me, expounding his views and asking for my opinion on a very wide range of topics. However I also surprised him by putting my cards on the table from the outset. I told him that I had greatly appreciated what he had done for me in the past, by agreeing to my appointment as Under-Secretary of State, refusing to sign the presidential decree relieving me from that post, and finally appointing me as ambassador to Bonn. But I also warned him that he should not expect that my gratitude would result in my agreeing with him all the time. If our relationship continued, I made clear, I would always tell him exactly what I thought, in line with my convictions and my conscience. President Sadat listened to me in surprise. 'Ismail, it is very strange,' he said. 'Not many people would tell me what you just said.'

The most important part of our discussion centred on the possibility of a new war with Israel. Sadat told me that he saw no way out of the impasse with Israel other than by initiating a war. Strangely, he justified his decision to go to war by declaring, 'I want to awaken the Egyptian people.' I have to admit that I was rather shocked by this statement, not because I was against military action, but because I thought it too drastic a step merely to awaken Egypt. Furthermore, Sadat did not have any convincing answers when I asked him whether politically Egypt was ready for war. On the contrary, he was very critical of the internal situation. He astonished me by systematically attacking every high official in his cabinet, making belittling comments about their ability and performance. Only at the very end of the meeting did he refer to the purpose for which I had come, namely my appointment as ambassador to Bonn. Instead of giving me instructions, however, he asked me to postpone my departure until the new cabinet was formed.

I left Sadat with rather mixed and confused impressions. He seemed to be a natural and sincere man, somewhat complex but not sophisticated, willing to say what he thought. But he also seemed to be very isolated, with no special relationship with anybody, in fact distrustful and contemptuous of those around him. He did not appear to have any clear ideas about long-term policies, but rather to be inclined to live from one day to the next, in fact from moment to moment, dealing piecemeal with problems as they arose. I was much more impressed by his human qualities than by his genius, and was rather apprehensive about what might happen to Egypt with Sadat at the helm.

Shortly after this meeting, the new cabinet was announced and to my surprise I discovered I had been appointed Minister of Tourism. As a career diplomat, I was dismayed. Tourism was not a field in which I had any particular interest. I made up my mind to decline the appointment and sought another audience with Sadat. It was granted, but when I arrived there I discovered that I was not alone: Sadat had convened the entire new cabinet at the same time. I was in a very awkward situation, because it would be very difficult to decline the appointment in front of everybody. Sadat exchanged a few words with every minister, talking about their new duties. When he came to me, he said nothing about tourism, only that I would be his advisor and trouble-shooter on special missions. He kept me on briefly after the meeting and explained further that the appointment to the Ministry of Tourism was just a cover, an excuse to keep me in Cairo. He could not appoint me Foreign Minister, he explained, because the incumbent minister was at the time in New York, and he never dismissed people when they were abroad.

Between April and October 1973, as a result, I served in a double capacity as Minister of Tourism and advisor to President Sadat. A month before the October War, I became acting Foreign Minister and a member of the inner war cabinet, standing in for the Foreign Minister who was attending the UN General Assembly in New York. In my new capacity, I was sent by President Sadat to confer with Kissinger and Nixon in late October, for the first crucial meetings in the aftermath of the war. While I was on my way to Washington Sadat appointed me Foreign Minister.

I was to be Foreign Minister of Egypt, and later Deputy Prime Minister until I decided to resign over Sadat's decision to go to Jerusalem in November 1977. The four years between my appointment and resignation were crucial ones for Egypt and the Middle East, years of great opportunities and great changes. The events in this book will show that working with Sadat was both fulfilling and frustrating. His penchant for change augured well for my determination to shift Egypt's foreign policy from an over-dependence on the Soviet Union towards a more middle-of-the-road, nonaligned political posture. I was able in this period to establish solid relations between Egypt and the Western world. To my dismay, Sadat's change of course was from one end of the political spectrum to the other. I enjoyed the long strategy sessions in which we seemed to agree on the course Egypt would pursue. Yet he lacked the patience and tenacity to follow through till the end, often making split-second decisions out of frustration, thereby wrecking a delicate balance achieved during delicate, painstaking negotiations, if not totally reversing direction. I had always believed that the easier part was conceptualising foreign policy strategy, the more difficult resolutely staying on course as all the intricate pieces are slowly put together. While our minds met on certain points, our differences were numerous and sometimes quite acute, particularly concerning the second Egyptian–Israeli disengagement agreement and the abrogation of the Soviet–Egyptian Friendship Treaty. We were always able, however, to agree to reset our bearings and steady our course. Our personal relations were strong. We shared a mutual respect which allowed for a candid exchange of views on all issues. Ultimately, however, we were bound to part, our aspirations for Egypt and its role in the Middle East becoming increasingly divergent. On Sadat's decision to go to Jerusalem we found no common ground. It constituted for me a change of course too drastic to remedy, with dangerous repercussions for Egypt. On an event with immense implications for Egypt and its people our personal friendship could not bridge the gap between us. I chose to resign, and while I would have been glad to be proven wrong, Israel's actions since then have vindicated my decision.

I have chosen the symposium as a starting point for my analysis because it was an event of major importance in Egypt. This statement may leave some foreign readers sceptical, and this is understandable. In many countries, symposia and seminars on all aspects of foreign and domestic policies, with the participation of government officials, intellectuals and experts of all kinds, are a very frequent event. The publication of the papers of these symposia is also normal. As a result, these events rarely have much impact. But this is not so in Egypt and in most Third World countries. There, once a policy is decided upon it is seldom discussed again, and certainly not questioned in public. To be sure, there were many problems in our relations with the Soviet Union at this time, and Egyptians from all walks of life were aware of it, from the soldiers trained by Soviet experts contemptuous of their religion and traditions to high government officials whose requests for concrete military aid rather than rhetorical support for the Arab cause fell on deaf ears. What had never been done, however, was to draw overall conclusions on the basis of all problems marring our relations with the Soviet Union. This is what the symposium did, providing a focus for the discontent and the will to change the situation.

For these reasons, the symposium was truly a historic event in Egypt. Its conclusions challenged the policy we had been following ever since Nasser's time and influenced the course of Egyptian foreign policy for years to come. It is therefore worthwhile summarising these conclusions:

a) Egypt should completely reappraise the international situation and the role of the superpowers in relations to the Middle East. It should realise that the superpowers accorded very low priority to the Middle East problems and that détente would distract their attention from the Middle East even more. Egypt had to shape its policy so as to force the superpowers to become more involved in solving the conflict in the Middle East.
b) International diplomacy was not sufficient to push Israel towards a final and just peace.
c) Consequently, military action should be initiated by Egypt to convince Israel and international public opinion that it was high time to solve the chronic problem of the Middle East.
d) Oil should be used as a weapon in the coming conflict, for this was a major resource in Arab hands.
e) The Soviet-Egyptian relationship should be reevaluated and

discussed with the Russians in a candid way, to create a new confidence and understanding and overcome the problems which had featured for almost eighteen years.

f) Egypt should also have closer contacts with the United States, which was bound to continue playing a crucial role in the Middle East.

2 OCTOBER VICTORY

A large part of my first conversation with Sadat was devoted to a discussion of the possibility of war with Israel, of the goals of such a war and of the form the military operations might take. Sadat, as I have already mentioned, saw war above all as a means of awakening the Egyptian people. I had reservations about that idea, but I told the President that I was not opposed to a war aiming at liberating the territories Israel had occupied in 1967. As for the type of military operations Egypt could consider at the time, it was my impression that Sadat and those around him were still quite vague about how to proceed.

Preparing for War

At the President's request, I expounded at some length on the type of military operations Egypt might consider undertaking. We had three options, I argued. The first, which I favoured, was total war, launched in a coordinated action by all Arab confrontation states with a preemptive strike on all fronts. This military offensive should be supplemented by political steps on the part of the Arab countries, with the imposition of an oil embargo being a major component of the strategy. Egypt should not embark on this course of action, I argued, unless it was ready to continue military operations for at least four consecutive weeks. Israel would suffer colossal damage from such protracted fighting, not only militarily, but economically as well. The economy of Israel simply cannot sustain a prolonged conflict: because of the small size of its population, mobilisation for war causes production to grind to a virtual halt. The Arab countries should take advantage of this situation and be prepared to prolong the conflict. Such protracted military confrontation, I further pointed out, entailed some risks of international reaction. Both our political and military moves should thus be very measured. There should also be close cooperation with the other Arab states, but each should be solely responsible in its own area. Finally, this total war option required a very high level of preparedness on the part of our armed forces. We should be ready not only to launch the preemptive strike, but also to react to the Israeli counteroffensive.

The second option open to Egypt was to undertake a limited military operation, not to recover our territory, but simply to move things on the ground, so as to arouse international public opinion enough to lead to a renewed peace effort in the Middle East. Even such a limited military operation required that Egyptian troops cross the Suez Canal and advance into Sinai, preferably up to the Giddi and Mitla passes, and be prepared to stay there even when faced with an Israeli counteroffensive. It also required cooperation with other Arab countries and could only succeed if the Israelis were taken by surprise. In fact, the only difference between the first two options was that in the first Egypt should aim at prolonging the fighting, while in the second it should encourage and welcome international political intervention to push the parties toward an early ceasefire and later a settlement.

The third option was a very limited attack against a specific military target in Sinai. Here, we would simply hit hard at an Israeli installation, then withdraw to the West Bank of the Suez Canal. Israel would undoubtedly retaliate, forcing Egypt to strike again and thus creating a vicious circle of attacks and retaliations. I made it clear to Sadat that this type of action would cause some movement on the international scene, but mostly in the form of attempts to stop the fighting and to renew the ceasefire, rather than efforts to push the parties toward serious peace negotiations. Sadat listened very attentively, but he did not say anything until the very end, when he commented that he would never consider the third option, because it would simply lead to a replay of the 1967–70 war of attrition.

Although Sadat had refrained from commenting on my arguments, he must have continued brooding over them and he must have discussed them with his Minister of War. For soon after the Minister of War, General Ahmed Ismail, called me to discuss the various war options open to Egypt. I repeated to him what I had told Sadat, but tried to simplify things because I thought he was unclear about the various alternatives and the probable Israeli reaction to each of them. He also seemed very confused about my own position. 'It seems you do not want us to fight,' he told me suddenly. 'No,' I explained, 'my position is that Egypt must go to war, but not before its leadership understands what it wants to do, and analyses the probable reactions and counterreactions to every move. Another military setback at this time would have extremely serious consequences.'

The lack of thorough planning and analysis of the consequences of various choices was a problem that had plagued Egyptian policy before, contributing seriously to the 1967 defeat; unfortunately, it continued to cause problems in the preparation of the 1973 War. In 1967, Egypt had stumbled into the war without any coordination between its military command and the people in charge of foreign relations, with disastrous consequences. I had an opportunity to witness this unfortunate state of affairs directly, because a few weeks before the 1967 War broke out I had been hurriedly given the task of setting up a 'political operations room' in the Foreign Ministry. I felt that the creation of this new institution was a very positive step, because we needed a department capable of analysing political events and recommending alternative courses of action on the basis of an accurate assessment of the results of each move. However, foreign policy decisions remained centred in the hands of Nasser and of his inner circle. The Foreign Ministry was at that time, in the awkward position of being the last to be informed, and was thus unable to make recommendations.

The consequences of this situation were apparent at the beginning of the 1967 War. Nasser had taken the decision to request the UN forces to leave Sinai without consulting anybody in the Foreign Ministry. In fact, he had simply instructed the Minister of War to pass the request on to General Rikki, the chief United Nations observer. General Rikki refused to comply with the Egyptian demand unless it was transmitted to him by the Secretary-General of the United Nations. Then Nasser decided to ask instead that the UN forces be withdrawn only from specific locations.

It was only at this point that the Ministry of Foreign Affairs was contacted; however, it was not consulted, but only instructed to transmit the request to the United Nations. As the director of the office responsible for political operations, I instead submitted to the Foreign Minister a memorandum analysing the situation. I argued that if we asked for the withdrawal of the UN forces from certain locations in Sinai, we were likely to be answered instead by a complete withdrawal from the area. The result would be that the UN forces would leave Sharm el-Sheikh, and the Egyptian government would be forced to station a garrison there. This garrison would have no option but to block the navigation in the Gulf of Aqaba, and Israel was bound to react to this move with a surprise attack on Egypt. My memo was totally disregarded. For reasons known only to him, Nasser single-handedly dismissed all rational analysis of the situation and took a series of irrational decisions. The compounded effect of these decisions was that events acquired a momentum of their own, and it became impossible for Nasser to slow down or back out. The result was that war broke out with the Israeli preemptive strike on 5 June, leading to a quick Egyptian debacle. Nasser's decline as an Egyptian and Arab leader started then, and it was really only a matter of time before his political career came to an end.

Therefore, it was encouraging indeed when Sadat for the first time summond his full cabinet in an extraordinary session. Inaugurating the meeting, Sadat informed his ministers of his intention to consult his colleagues on a very major step. He wanted everybody's opinion concerning what he called 'a battle or no battle'. He made it clear that he was personally in favour of a battle, but failed to explain what sort of a battle he had in mind. None of the ministers attending the meeting knew whether Sadat was talking about a protracted major war, a limited advance across the Canal followed by a quick ceasefire, or a simple incursion against a selected target. Most of the ministers had no real knowledge of Sadat's specific plan and certainly not of the state of preparedness of the Egyptian army. While Sadat was justified in not revealing details about the war plans to the entire cabinet, he had not provided enough information for anybody to express a considered judgement.

The ministers spoke one after the other in support of Sadat's decision – yet they had no idea what the decision really was. With great emotion all participants declared their support for the President: 'We are behind you, Ya Rayes, we are in favour of a battle.' When my turn came, I reiterated in detail what I had already told Sadat concerning this major issue, during our first encounter at his residence at the Barrage. I, too, was in favour of fighting and explained that I would stand behind the President, if his choice was going to war with Israel for the specific purpose of liberating Sinai. After a lengthy discussion there was a unanimous decision to go to war. To Sadat's credit this was the first time that any Egyptian President had seen fit to discuss such a momentous decision with his cabinet colleagues.

The preparations for the war with Israel did not begin at this time, but had been underway ever since the 1967 defeat. That catastrophe occurred not only because Israel had struck first, catching Egypt by surprise, but above all because the Egyptian army was not prepared. Nasser had always been very wary of a strong army, fearing he might not be able to control it. As a result, he encouraged internal rivalries and created many centres of power in the military. This may have helped Nasser stay in power, but the result was that by 1967 the Egyptian army was a political organisation rather than a professional war machine. In addition, ever since 1956 Egypt had basked in the illusion of having won a war against Israel, Britain and France, thus demonstrating the high quality of its military establishment. The propaganda machine had successfully convinced all Egyptians of this, including people within the army itself who should have known better. In fact, Egypt had not won a military victory in 1956. Egypt's great victory had come later, when it demonstrated to the world that it could keep the Suez Canal open and functioning smoothly; but that battle was won by the Canal pilots and workers, not by the army. The myth of the Egyptian military victory was kept alive, however, with the result that the military rested on imaginary laurels instead of working seriously to improve its level of preparedness and training. The result was the 1967 debacle.

Fortunately, after 1967 some lessons were learned. To be sure, the propaganda machine had initially tried to hide the truth from the Egyptians, but the magnitude of the defeat was such that it could not be kept hidden for long. Nasser realised that he had to abandon his old policy of weakening the army and keeping it divided, and that he must instead concentrate on building a professional fighting force of high calibre. Nasser had to start virtually from scratch in this endeavour and he had to reactivate his contacts with the Soviet Union to obtain both the sophisticated weapons Egypt needed to stand up to Israel and help in retraining and restructuring the military. Sadat continued Nasser's policy of rebuilding the army, knowing that there could not be a political solution in the Middle East until Egypt had an army capable of standing up to the Israeli armed forces. The policy paid off, because the army which attacked on 6 October 1973 demonstrated the high professional calibre of its officers and men, and the adequate level of its equipment. Quickly, this army managed to cross the Canal, destroying the fortifications which the Israelis had been building up for six years, breaching the Bar-Lev Line.

The Course of the October War

Three aspects of Egypt's performance in the 1973 War were remarkable: firstly the level of preparedness of the army and the coordination among the various branches of the armed forces. A second factor was the determination of officers and men in the Egyptian armed forces to prove themselves and redress the humiliations suffered in previous wars, and as a result they fought with fanatical determination.

The third remarkable factor was that an operation of this magnitude, involving so many people and branches of the government and of the armed forces, was prepared without any leaks. Total secrecy was vital to the success of the preemptive strike and of the Canal crossing, and it was maintained until the attack actually started.

The performance of the armed forces was such that the Egyptian government did not have to lie to its people about the real course of events; we did not have to be afraid of the truth, on the contrary we could be proud of it. In fact, this time it was the Israeli government that had to lie to its population. 'We have taught the Egyptians how to fight, and they have taught our radio announcers how to lie,' an Israeli soldier is supposed to have declared with grim humour in the aftermath of the war.[1]

It is not my intention to engage here in a detailed analysis of the military operations, particularly since many accounts have already been published, some of them very good and accurate.[2] However, I must comment on some of the distorted versions of the military aspects of the war, and also explain the political implications and repercussions of what happened in the period of heavy fighting. Israeli Major General Chaim Herzog presents an especially distorted and objectionable version of events in his book *The War of Atonement*.[3] His main argument is that the initial Egyptian success, up to the Israeli counteroffensive and crossing of the Canal on 15 October, was simply due to the fact that the Israeli army was caught by surprise and that the front was defended only by semi-trained reservists. In other words, Herzog refuses to admit that the Israeli defeat was due to the fact that the Egyptian army at this point was well trained, well equipped and well led and thus capable of inflicting serious losses on the Israelis. Herzog's excuses are extremely unconvincing and do not stand up to close examination. While there was an element of surprise which initially facilitated the

Egyptian advance, surprise did not last that long. The Israeli army is rightly famous for the speed with which it can mobilise, and it undoubtedly could have pulled itself together and replaced the untrained reservists on the Egyptian front with professional soldiers well before October 15. The truth of the matter is that the Egyptian army performed brilliantly, and that the Israelis could not stand up to it on their own. In Dupuy's words:

> The single most important element of the Israeli defeat [on 8 October] was the fighting quality of the Egyptian army, and its performance in accordance with carefully prepared plans to deal with anticipated Israeli counterattacks. The integration of infantry; anti-tank missiles, rockets and guns; and an effective air defense system had brilliantly achieved General Ismail's major pre-war objective: the neutralization of Israeli superiority in the air and in mobile armored warfare.[4]

In fact, as even Israeli commentators more honest than Herzog have admitted, the Egyptian attack had created a very difficult situation for Israel, driving even Dayan to the edge of despair. Shlomo Aronson, for example, clearly admitted that Israel immediately launched a counteroffensive, but that it failed to push back the Egyptian army, although it managed to stabilise the front. This situation was very threatening for Israel, since it opened up the possibility of a large-scale war of attrition under circumstances which Israel found very difficult to face: total mobilisation and high losses due to the Arab advantages in firepower and the static character of the operations.[5] In fact, Aronson argues on the basis of a report which appeared in *Time* that the fear of a Syrian breakthrough may even have driven Dayan to consider the use of their 'basement bomb', the nuclear warheads Israel possessed but had always kept in storage, rather than mounted on missiles. The nuclear warheads may have been mounted at this time.[6] All this certainly does not indicate that the problem faced by the Israeli army was merely one caused by initial surprise.

What changed the course of the fighting and allowed the Israelis to mount a counteroffensive, was the massive amount of military equipment the United States airlifted into Israel. It was the sophisticated weapons provided by the United States at this time – weapons for which the Egyptians did not have any equivalent –

which made it possible for the Israelis to change the course of the war. Egypt and Syria received some weapons from the Soviet Union at this time, but the quantities shipped were very small in comparison to what the United States was pouring into Israel. Most importantly, the Soviet Union did not send any sophisticated equipment to counteract the new weapons Israel was being equipped with. Among these weapons were TOW anti-tank missiles, laser-guided bombs, air-to-ground guided missiles or 'smart bombs', and advanced radar equipment. In addition, the United States also supplied Israel with vast amounts of intelligence information, including satellite pictures of the positions of the Egyptian army, particularly in the Deversoir area where the Israelis carried out their crossing. It was these weapons that changed the military situation, allowing the Israelis to destroy the massive concentration of Egyptian missiles around the Suez Canal. These missiles had succeeded in neutralising the Israeli air force for a time, providing the Egyptian army with a very effective umbrella.

The Syrian Front

Before we discuss the latter part of the war, we need to go back and look at events on the Syrian front. The attack launched on 6 October was, as is well known, a joint Syrian–Egyptian operation. This had an enormous political significance and very important military consequences. Politically, President Assad's willingness to work with Sadat in preparing for war indicated the fundamental unity of interests and purpose between Egypt and Syria. The formal union between Egypt and Syria in Nasser's time had not lasted, but the political affinity and psychological closeness between the two countries remained deep. Thus, there was no obstacle to close cooperation between Sadat and Assad in preparing for war with Israel.

The joint planning for the war was totally successful, and complete secrecy was maintained. This was a real breakthrough in the Arab world, that two countries could cooperate for a long time and on such a complex issue without any fear of leaks which would destroy the possibility of a surprise attack. In fact, the success of this cooperation gives reasons for optimism concerning future relations between Syria and Egypt. I am sure that once the present difficulties are overcome, cooperation will resume and the joint political weight of Damascus and Cairo will be felt again.

Military operations started simultaneously on the Egyptian and the Syrian fronts, but while the Egyptian army scored success after success for several days, the Syrian army quickly ran into difficulties, because the Israelis concentrated their efforts against Syria. This could have been predicted, because Israel has no strategic depth on the Syrian front, and a Syrian breakthrough would have had immediate and devastating consequences. On the other hand, the breakthrough of the Egyptian army on the Canal still left it 300 kilometres away from Israeli territory.

The military planning on the Syrian front was, in my opinion, defective. Although the Syrian army performed quite well it did not receive sufficient help against the massive Israeli counteroffensive. Jordan and Iraq sent some aid, but this was not adequate. Even Egypt could not do much to relieve the pressure on Syria: after the initial crossing of the Canal the Egyptian armed forces could not advance rapidly toward the Sinai passes without losing the protection of the missiles on the Canal bank and thus becoming exposed to Israeli air attacks.

President Assad had apparently foreseen a difficult fight for Syria, and prepared his political plans accordingly: even before the attack was launched he had requested the Soviet Union to propose formally a ceasefire as soon as the war broke out. The problem was that Assad never informed Sadat that he had made this request, and denied that this was the case when the Soviets informed Egypt. Since this issue had considerable impact on the efforts to secure a ceasefire and created difficulties between Brezhnev and Sadat, I will discuss it here in some detail.

On 4 October the Soviet ambassador in Cairo told General Ahmed Ismail that Damascus had informed Moscow that an attack on Israel would be launched on 6 October. Assad had also requested the Soviets to propose formally a ceasefire on 8 October. Only a few hours after the fighting started on 6 October, the Soviet ambassador conveyed a message from Brezhnev to Sadat, which explained that Assad, fearing a prolonged conflict would not serve Arab interests, favoured immediate intervention by the superpowers. Assad was convinced, Brezhnev wrote, that such intervention by the superpowers would lead to positive results.

On 8 October, the Soviets again informed Sadat that Assad was putting enormous pressure on them to obtain a ceasefire, because the situation on the Syrian front had become very difficult. Assad wanted the Soviet Union to propose either to the UN Security Council or to the General Assembly a resolution asking for an immediate ceasefire and for the withdrawal of Israel from all territories occupied in 1967. The Soviet ambassador also added that Assad was ready to send Sadat a message informing him of these requests, if Sadat so asked.

Sadat expressed his astonishment; he pointed out that Assad had not informed him at all, and that he would certainly request a direct confirmation from the Syrian President. He also added that a ceasefire in place at this time would only be to Israel's advantage. Things would go back to where they were before the operations started, and the Middle East situation would again become dormant for many years to come.

Sadat informed Assad of all the communications he had received from the Soviet Union, asking for confirmation. Assad denied everything. On 9 October Sadat thus called in the Soviet ambassador, informing him that Assad had denied ever requesting a ceasefire. Furthermore, Assad had declared that the military situation on the Syrian front was satisfactory. Cairo would thus not accept a ceasefire at this time and Moscow should inform Damascus of this choice. Sadat's refusal to believe that Assad had requested a ceasefire angered the Soviet Union greatly. Both Gromyko and Brezhnev were later to bring up this issue with me, declaring that they were appalled by Assad's denial that he had requested a ceasefire and by Sadat's decision to believe Damascus rather than Moscow. Both pointed out that the Soviet Union had documents proving that Assad had requested a ceasefire, not once but three times.

While this exchange of messages was going on at the diplomatic level, the war continued. The Egyptian army continued to score successes and even the Syrian front stabilised. In fact, it was Israel that was in a difficult position. Although the first American arms shipment reached it on 10 October, it took several more days before the quantity received became massive enough to change the course of the war. On 12 October the situation was so bad for Israel that Prime Minister Golda Meir informed the United States that her government was ready to accept the American and British proposal for a ceasefire in place. Sadat, however, made overly confident by his army's victories, and Assad's assurances that Syria had no problem, refused to accept the ceasefire in place. This was a mistake. Although under normal circumstances a prolonged war would have been in Egypt's interests, the US decision to send arms to Israel changed the situation and made an early ceasefire preferable.

Sadat personally informed me that he had conveyed the Egyptian refusal to accept the ceasefire to the British ambassador in Egypt, who was pressing him to accept it. I was very upset by this decision and could not hide my distress. 'But what can I do?' he replied, 'the Israelis normally accept a ceasefire and never respect it, but continue to violate it.' I answered: 'It is true that they have always behaved that way in the past and will probably do so now. But it is still better that they violate the ceasefire now, when they are still on the East Bank of the Suez Canal, than later, because they might succeed in crossing it.' Sadat just kept silent, trying to digest the implications of what I had told him.

Ceasefire

My prediction was unfortunately correct. A few days later the American arms shipments had reached the point where the Israelis were able to cross the Suez Canal. This created a situation of near panic within both the military and the political leadership of Egypt. There was confusion and fear in the military high command, although on the ground the army continued to fight bravely. One example of the high command's attitude after the Israeli crossing is a telephone call I received at 3 a.m. one morning from Minister of War Ahmed Ismail, who was almost yelling as he described the latest manoeuvers of the Israeli tanks on the west side of the Canal. They were following tactics totally unconventional, he complained: first a few tanks would appear, then a much greater number would follow, then they would all disappear as if the fighting had been taking place in a jungle rather than in the open desert. I advised him to deploy Egyptian paratroopers to take the Israeli tanks by surprise, using the anti-tanks weapons which had proved very effective earlier in the war. 'No, no,' he argued, 'we cannot do that. There are too many of them, they appear and disappear, and we are not used to this kind of war. We follow the Soviet tactics, and move our army on the entire front in a massive, coordinated way.' What Ismail wanted from me, it appeared, was not advice on how to fight back against the Israeli tanks, but an effort to negotiate a ceasefire quickly. While their men fought on, the high command was distraught when they encountered the first Israeli counteroffensive after the American military shipments.

On the political front, the reaction to the Israeli breakthrough into the Suez area was even worse. There was a situation of near-panic among even normally responsible politicians. For example, some argued that the government should withdraw to Assyut, some 230 miles south of Cairo, and get ready to organise popular resistance against the Israeli invasion, fighting if needed from street to street and from house to house in our major cities.

President Sadat was aware of the psychological impact of the Israeli counteroffensive. On 21 October 21 he summoned the military high command and asked for a thorough briefing on the military situation. He then contacted Brezhnev and informed him that Egypt was now ready to accept a ceasefire. Unknown to Sadat, the United States and the Soviet Union had already agreed on a new ceasefire resolution during Kissinger's brief trip to Moscow. When Sadat informed Brezhnev that he would accept the ceasefire, the Soviet leader wasted no time informing the Americans. The result was that a ceasefire resolution, known as Resolution 338, was approved by the United Nations Security Council on 22 October.

When Sadat decided to accept the ceasefire, he immediately sent Assad a cable explaining his position:

We have fought Israel to the 15th day. In the first four days Israel was alone, so we were able to expose her position on both fronts. On their admission the enemy have lost 800 tanks and 200 planes. But during the last 10 days I have, on the Egyptian front, been fighting the United States as well, through the arms it is sending. To put it bluntly, I cannot fight the United States or accept the responsibility before history for the destruction of our armed forces for the second time. I have therefore informed the Soviet Union that I am prepared to accept a ceasefire on existing positions, subject to the following conditions:

1) The Soviet Union and the United States guarantee an Israeli withdrawal, as proposed by the Soviet Union.

2) The convening of the peace conference under United Nations auspices to achieve an overall settlement, as proposed by the Soviet Union.

My heart bleeds to tell you this, but I feel that my office compels me to take this decision. I am ready to face our nation at a suitable moment and am prepared to give a full account to it of the decision.

Assad's answer to Sadat's cable was astonishing. Pretending he had not been putting pressure on the Soviet Union to bring about a ceasefire even before the war began, Assad presented himself as the hard-liner determined to continue fighting:

> I beg you to look again at the military situation on the northern front and on both sides of the canal. We see no cause for pessimism. We can continue the struggle against enemy forces, whether they have crossed the canal or are still fighting east of the canal. I am convinced that by continuing and intensifying the battle it will be possible to ensure the destruction of those enemy units that have crossed the canal. My brother Sadat, for the sake of the morale of the fighting troops it is necessary to emphasise that although the enemy have as the result of an accident been able to break our front, this does not mean that they will be able to achieve victory. The enemy succeeded in penetrating the northern front several days ago, but the stand we then made and the subsequent heavy fighting have given us greater ground for optimism. Most points of enemy penetration have been sealed off and I am confident that we shall be able to deal with those remaining in the course of the next few days. I consider it imperative that our armies should maintain their fighting spirit.

Despite the brave façade put up by Assad, both Syria and Egypt were ready to accept a ceasefire, although Israel then continued to violate it for several days with the United States' tacit approval. Already before leaving Washington for Moscow on 20 October, Kissinger had hinted to the Israelis that a reason for the trip was to give them more time to consolidate their position. After visiting Moscow, he stopped in Tel Aviv at Golda Meir's request, again providing the Israelis with time to advance on the West Bank of the Canal. Even after the Security Council passed Resolution 338 Kissinger made no real effort to force the Israelis into respecting the ceasefire. In fact, it was only after the Soviets started threatening to intervene on behalf of Egypt, especially to liberate the Egyptian Third Army, that Kissinger started putting pressure on Israel to respect the ceasefire.[7] The Israeli advance finally ceased, but by this time the Israelis were well entrenched on the West Bank of the Suez

Canal, the Third Army was encircled and the city of Suez cut off. There is no doubt that Egypt would have been in a much stronger position if Sadat had accepted the ceasefire in place on 12 October, before the Israeli counteroffensive.

After the guns fell silent, a few steps were taken to consolidate the ceasefire. The UN observers who were already in Cairo resumed their function, despite the attempts by the Israelis to prevent this from happening. When we first asked UN Secretary-General Kurt Waldheim to reactivate the observers, he agreed promptly and sent instructions to that effect. The head of the UN observers, General Ensio Siilasvuo was for his part ready to act immediately. Yet, for several days nothing happened. The reason, it turned out, was that the UN cables to Cairo were routinely sent through Jerusalem, and the Israelis had intercepted the orders so as to be able to continue to violate the ceasefire without the presence of UN observers. A direct phone call by Waldheim finally solved the problem.

While there was an unwelcome delay before the UN observers took up their posts, we were confronted with an influx of eager but unwanted Soviet observers. Moscow had suggested that both Soviet and American observers come to Cairo to monitor the ceasefire, but the Americans procrastinated, while the Soviet personnel arrived quickly. I greeted these observers in my office, but informed the Soviet ambassador that they could not be deployed unless the Americans sent counterparts. The result was that they remained in Cairo for a few days, and then went back home.

The Soviet–American understanding reached when Kissinger visited Moscow included not only the ceasefire proper, but also a broad strategy on how to proceed towards a political solution after the fighting stopped. In particular, the Soviets and the Americans had agreed that there should be negotiations between the two parties under appropriate auspices; if an international conference was convened in order to pursue the negotiations, the United States and the Soviet Union would act as co-chairmen. Finally, the two superpowers agreed that there should be an exchange of prisoners among the parties as soon as the ceasefire went into effect.

Before we discuss the process of negotiating a political solution, we need to consider here three issues which were to have considerable impact on those negotiations: how important was the role played by the United States in support of Israel during the war, and whose game did Kissinger play? How significant was Soviet aid to Egypt? And finally, did the October 1973 War constitute a victory or a defeat for Egypt?

We have already partially answered the first question: it was the sophisticated equipment sent by the Americans which allowed the Israelis to mount their counteroffensive. I will add here that in my opinion the possibility that American personnel also were sent to Israel cannot be dismissed. My conclusion is based on the fact that all the new equipment which was suddenly included in the battle – the TOW, the laser-guided bombs, the 'smart' bombs – cannot have been used by the Israelis alone, because they had never had it before and thus could not have known how to operate it. Such training takes a long time, and the Israelis had only a few days in which to score their victory. According to Dupuy,

A number of Israeli students attending colleges in the United States were mobilized late on 6 October, and ordered to the US Army Infantry School at Fort Benning, Georgia, to take a crash course in the use and maintenance of the TOW. But by the time these eager young students were able to bring their new training and knowledge back to Israel, and to teach Israeli soldiers how to use the new weapons, it was October 24, and a ceasefire was finally settling over the fighting front.[8]

However, Dupuy also concludes that there is evidence that 'the Israelis had TOWs and trained crews for these weapons, available for employment by October 14 and 15'.[9] Dupuy does not dare draw the obvious conclusion, and he leaves the question open where the crews came from. But the obvious conclusion is that the Americans provided not only the weapons, but also the personnel to operate them.

Another aspect of the American role which we need to discuss here is the part played by Henry Kissinger personally. This question is important not only in relation to the war period, but also to the years of negotiation which ensued. Kissinger was free to act on behalf of the United States during the war, because Nixon was at a particularly difficult stage of the Watergate scandal and had little time for foreign policy issues. As a result, Kissinger started to show his true colors. Pretending to be the peace-maker and the go-between, he was in fact always acting on behalf of Israel; this is not surprising considering that he is a Jew himself and that, as he personally told me, his parents were 'extremist, fanatic Jews'.

There is no doubt that he did manage to give Israel considerable assistance not only during the war but during the ensuing negotiations as well. At the same time, Kissinger was seldom straightforward in all his dealings, at times even with the Israelis. For example, whenever he did not satisfy an Israeli request for more weapons, he put the blame on Secretary of Defense James Schlesinger and on the Pentagon, and always claimed that whatever Israel received, had been sent because of his efforts to overcome the Pentagon's reluctance. In fact, as James H. Noyes, the then Deputy Assistant Secretary of Defense for International Security Affairs, told me, the Pentagon executed to the letter all the instructions Kissinger issued in the name of President Nixon. Although Kissinger may have at times used delaying tactics, the amount of weapons he had dispatched was enormous; Noyes also told me that 'the truth is that we had to disarm some of our active units and ships in order to respond to the continuous Israeli requests for more arms and spare parts'.

The help given by the Soviet Union to Egypt was not remotely comparable to that provided by the United States to Israel. There were many stories about the Soviet build-up in Egypt, and the Americans even claimed that it was this build-up that had forced them to send aid to Israel. The Americans also claimed that during the last days of the fighting the Soviet Union increased the level of alert of its own armed forces in preparation for intervention in Egypt and Syria. I do not know whether or not this is true. Certainly, the Soviet Union could not have sent any troops to Egypt or Syria without the specific request of the leaders of those countries. It is conceivable that President Sadat, worried about the effect of the Israeli crossing on his army, asked the Soviet for help, or at least considered the idea of doing so. I do know that the United States was informed through Saudi intelligence that Sadat had requested Soviet aid. This occurred because of a very curious and very disturbing incident involving a very young and inexperienced aide in Sadat's secretariat. The incident was recounted to me personally by this individual, who came to ask me whether in my opinion his behaviour had been justifiable or not. Apparently this young man had overheard Sadat say something which could be interpreted as meaning that he had requested Soviet aid. Upset by what he heard, and despite his total lack of experience he had taken upon himself the responsibility of informing King Feisal that Sadat was seeking Soviet intervention. He had relayed the message to

Feisal through the usual channel in the Saudi intelligence apparatus. Since Saudi intelligence was in close contact with the CIA, there is no doubt that Washington was also informed of this purported step taken by Sadat. This may be the origin of the idea that the Soviets were about to intervene in Egypt. To complete the story, I will add here that Sadat's aide was later seized by a fit of doubt and repentance about his action, and went to see Sadat, carrying his revolver. He presented the weapon to the President, recounted what he had done, and rather theatrically asked to be shot if he had acted wrongly. President Sadat understandably was furious, but he declined to shoot the aide. After hearing this story from the principal protagonist, I checked with Sadat, who confirmed it.

The last issue we must discuss here is whether the War of October 1973 was a victory or a defeat for Egypt. The facts are simple enough. The war started with a series of successes on the part of the Egyptian army, which crossed the Canal and consolidated its position on the East Bank. It ended, however, with the Israeli army on the west side of the Canal, the Third Army encircled and the town of Suez cut off from Egypt. Militarily, it could be argued, Israel had proved once again its superiority and Egypt had been defeated. Such a conclusion is far too simplistic for several reasons. First, as I have already argued, the Israelis succeeded in their counteroffensive not because of their own superiority but because of American aid; while they obviously could not admit this in public, the leaders were aware of this, and badly shaken as a result. Secondly, the war had clearly demonstrated that the Egyptian army now had the capacity to inflict heavy casualties on Israel, and above all to engage Israel in the kind of prolonged war it cannot withstand. Thirdly, while the Israeli counteroffensive had been successful and the Israeli army was now on the West Bank of the Canal, the fact remained that the Egyptian army stayed on the East Bank of the Canal. In other words, the Israelis had not succeeded in erasing the effect of the Egyptian attack and the situation on the ground after the ceasefire finally took hold was quite different from what it had been before 6 October. To be sure, the situation had been even more favourable to Egypt on 12 October, when Sadat took the unfortunate decision to reject the ceasefire in place; this does not mean, however, that all of Egypt's victories had been obliterated in the following ten days.

Egypt had not won the war in the sense of pushing the Israelis out of Sinai, freeing the occupied territories but Egypt had scored a valuable political victory. The Egyptian assault had demonstrated to Israel and to the United States that Egypt was now in a position to inflict heavy damage on Israel, making it pay very highly for the continued occupation of Sinai. It provided for the first time an incentive for Israel to negotiate and for the United States to push Israel seriously towards negotiations. The task of finding a lasting solution to the Middle East conflict acquired a new urgency because of the war, and negotiations resumed in a totally different political climate.

Notes

1. Quoted in Trevor N. Dupuy, *Elusive Victory, the Arab–Israeli Wars 1947–1974* (New York: Harper & Row, 1978), p. 421.
2. See, for example, Trevor N. Depuy, *Elusive Victory, The Arab–Israeli Wars 1947–1974*.
3. Boston: Little, Brown and Co., 1975.
4. Dupuy, p. 433–4.
5. Shlomo Aronson, 'Israel's Nuclear Options', ACTS Working Paper No. 7, Center for Arms Control and International Security, University of California, Los Angeles, November 1977, p. 13.
6. Ibid., p. 14.
7. See William Quandt, *A Decade of Decisions*, (Berkeley: University of California Press, 1977), pp. 194–8.
8. Dupuy, p. 502.
9. *Ibid*.

3 MY FIRST ENCOUNTER WITH NIXON

My first major mission on behalf of peace in the Middle East took place in late October 1973, when the guns of the October War had barely been silenced by an uneasy ceasefire. I had only been Foreign Minister for a few weeks when President Anwar Sadat asked me to go to the United States as his special envoy to President Nixon.

President Sadat's decision to send me to Washington was made during an extraordinary meeting in Tahra Palace on 28 October 1973. The meeting was attended by Vice-President Hussein El Shafei, Minister of War Ahmed Ismail, National Security Advisor Hafez Ismail, Minister of State at the Presidency Abdel Fattah Abdullah, myself and some advisors. Sadat explained his views on the ceasefire and on the necessity of taking certain steps to separate the Israeli and Egyptian armed forces. Then, as usual, he took everyone by surprise, informing us that he had decided to despatch a special envoy to President Nixon immediately. Addressing me directly, he added, 'My envoy will be Ismail Fahmy.' He asked me to take a special plane and leave at 6 p.m. local time.

Almost everyone took notes while the President was talking. When he had finished, I told him that I needed a little more time to prepare myself for this sudden trip. I wanted to write down his ideas as clearly and accurately as possible in the form of a 'master framework' and leave a copy with him. This would serve as a basic reference to facilitate our communications during my stay in Washington. He agreed that the framework was a good idea, but nevertheless insisted I leave that very day. I tried to postpone my departure saying that I had to see my family and pack my luggage. President Sadat replied that I could see my family on my return; as for the luggage, I could buy whatever I needed in Washington.

I had no choice but to agree. I went to my office in the Foreign Ministry and dictated a memo organising the President's ideas concisely, in the form of a framework outlining a series of steps to be implemented in sequence. This did not take long, except for the choice of the proper English term to describe Sadat's idea of separating the belligerent armies. My staff and I finally agreed on the word 'disengagement' as the most suitable.

The framework for negotiations envisaged the following steps: Israel would withdraw to the October 22 lines; all prisoners of war would be released; Israel would then withdraw to a line inside Sinai east of the passes, while Egypt's forces remained in place; UN forces would be deployed between the Egyptian and Israeli forces; after Israel started withdrawing to the disengagement line, Egypt would lift the blockade of the Straits of Bab el-Mandeb; once the disengagement was completed, Egypt would start clearing the Suez Canal; within an agreed period of time, Israel would withdraw to the international frontier; at this point belligerency would end. We also included in the framework an outline of the steps which should be taken to obtain a disengagement on the Syrian front, to convene an international peace conference, and finally to restore diplomatic relations between Egypt and the United States.

A copy of the framework was sent to President Sadat who approved it in detail. In the meantime, a special plane was being prepared for my departure. The flight was a unique experience because the Boeing 707 which brought me to Paris had been made ready in a hurry, and was completely bare except for four seats installed for the trip. It had been previously used to transfer military equipment from various parts of the world before and during the military operations and there had been no time to restore it to its normal condition.

After a night's stop-over in Paris I reached Washington in the afternoon of 29 October. At Dulles Airport, I was met by Assistant Secretary of State for Near Eastern and South Asian Affairs Joseph Sisco, Deputy Assistant-Secretary Alfred Atherton and their colleagues. Sisco conveyed to me Henry Kissinger's greetings and added that the Secretary of State would receive me the following day. I insisted that we should meet the same day and Sisco was forced to contact Kissinger from the airport, arranging an appointment for 6 p.m. I wanted to see Kissinger immediately in order to do something quickly about the precarious situation of the Egyptian Third Army. I also wanted a preliminary encounter with him to gain a first-hand impression of his operating style and to find out which problems he considered most important.

Sparring with Kissinger

I was received by Kissinger at the State Department at 6 p.m. The meeting lasted one hour and forty minutes and was attended only by Kissinger and Sisco on the American side, myself and Dr Abdullah El Eryan, a senior legal counsellor on the Egyptian side. Welcoming me to the State Department, Kissinger routinely enough expressed his hope that this visit would be a fruitful step towards a long and lasting cooperation between our respective countries. Then he unexpectedly added that he hoped that direct contacts would be established between Cairo and Washington, rather than passing through Moscow. He kept emphasising the importance of establishing a direct channel of communication apparently because he was tired of the repeated Soviet claims that they spoke for Egypt. The Soviets had been Egypt's spokesmen in Washington since 1970, when President Nasser had concluded that there was no possibility for an understanding or even for communication between Cairo and Washington. He had thus authorised the Soviets to speak on Egypt's behalf, on the assumption that the Soviet Union and the United States, as superpowers, could at least understand each other.

When Sadat came to power, the Soviets continued to claim they spoke for Egypt, although the Egyptian President had sent his National Security Advisor, Hafez Ismail, to meet Kissinger in the United States on 20 May 1973 and later in Paris. These first contacts led nowhere. By his own admission, Kissinger was not ready to switch his attention from other international problems to the Middle East situation, which he believed would be dormant for a long time to come. In my opinion, Kissinger had come to that conclusion precisely because there had been no regular communication between Cairo and Washington. The 'back channel' exchanges through Egypt or Saudi Arabia, and those established in 1972 with Sadat's approval through the CIA in Cairo, were not sufficient. Kissinger had also been misled, he admitted to me, by the poor intelligence provided by the CIA regarding the military preparedness and capabilities of both Israel and its Arab neighbours. He had come to the conclusion that there was no chance of armed conflict in the foreseeable future. The October War had therefore come as a considerable surprise and forced the Nixon Administration to take the Middle East seriously. In fact it was a turning point in the history of the Middle East crisis: after

1973 all American administrations automatically played an active role in the peace process.

My talks with Kissinger were cordial and fruitful. I emphasised the Egyptian and Arab conviction that Israel would never have been able to score military successes in the second phase of the October War without the huge American airlift of sophisticated weapons. I also added that the war had demonstrated that the Arabs were capable of a good fight against all odds. Kissinger agreed, admitting that the outbreak of the fighting and especially the swift crossing of the Suez Canal by the Egyptian army had taken everyone by surprise. However, the key issue in our discussion was that the situation in the Middle East had reached a cross-road: it was no longer a regional crisis but had repercussions at the global level. There was an unusual state of alertness and military preparedness both in Moscow and in Washington, and this could lead to a confrontation between the superpowers, if one of them went too far in backing its client in the area. Kissinger agreed fully with my analysis and I then made it clear that we were ready to establish relations between Washington and Cairo, but that we needed reassurance about American commitment.

I outlined for Kissinger the issues to which I granted top priority:

a) that supplies of a non-military nature should be provided on a permanent basis to the Third Army
b) that the ceasefire must be fully honoured and the Israelis must withdraw to their positions of 22 October 1973, as requested by Security Council Resolution 339.

I also brought to Kissinger's attention the fact that the Israelis were proving very uncooperative in the Kilometer 101 military talks. These talks, so called because they took place in a tent at Kilometer 101 of the Suez–Cairo road, had brought together Egyptian and Israeli representatives with General Ensio Siilasvuo, the commander of the UN force in the Middle East, in an attempt to define the respective positions of the two armies on 22 October or at least to agree on a ceasefire line. Kissinger replied he was aware of the problems and that, upon being informed that the Israelis had tried to prevent the Egyptian delegation from reaching Kilometer 101, he had personally intervened with Prime Minister Golda Meir.

He then promised he would continue to do his best on all these issues.

At this point Kissinger digressed saying that he wanted to be very candid with me on a major issue: Washington did not appreciate the Arab pressure and ultimatum resulting from the use of oil as a weapon. The US and the Western powers were facing and would be facing serious difficulties because of the oil embargo. If it continued, he said, panic would spread in Western Europe and later in the United States, particularly if the governments were forced to ration petrol. Kissinger also underlined that the Israelis would not easily accept American pressures concerning the ceasefire or a final settlement. Israel did not want to relinquish the land it had occupied, and it would require a great deal of American influence to force it to change its attitude. Kissinger then added that he understood Egypt was not happy about American military assistance to Israel during the war, but claimed that he had kept it to a minimum, resisting the pressures of the Jewish lobby in the United States; as a result, he had personally come under attack by Senator Henry Jackson and many prominent American Jews.

To prove the sincerity of the Nixon administration, he stressed that the United States had refused to send any assistance to Israel during the first seven days of the war, and that it had favoured the adoption of a ceasefire resolution by the Security Council when Egypt's victory was at its peak on 12 October. Washington had asked the British to present the resolution to the Security Council and had guaranteed the nine votes necessary for its adoption. The United States and the Soviet Union had agreed to abstain. This procedure had been followed because the Soviets had argued that Sadat would refuse a resolution put forward by the United States or the Soviet Union, but might support it if it came from another member of the Security Council. The failure to have an early ceasefire, Kissinger argued, was due to the intransigence of Egypt. The United States had succeeded in forcing Israel to accept the ceasefire in place on 12 October, but Sadat refused without justification. The British had informed him, Kissinger said, that Egypt had insisted that the ceasefire draft resolution should embody a paragraph requesting Israel to withdraw to the lines of 5 June 1967, a request which Israel would not have accepted at that time.

Kissinger went on to expound on his personal role as peace-maker:

The problem with the Arabs is that they expect me to accomplish what I have accomplished in other areas of crisis. But they forget the four long years of negotiations that were consumed before the final settlement of the Vietnamese problem. Regarding China, I consumed two years before reaching any concrete results. My way of tackling things is to have a long period of preparation and to move after the atmosphere is ready for the solution. I don't want to move hurriedly and propose a new American initiative in the Middle East. I fear its fate would be similar to that of the 1970 initiative. But I do not want to be misunderstood: I am not saying that the Middle East crisis should take years to solve. I believe it could be solved in three to six months, if everybody cooperates.

I could not help smiling when Kissinger said that the solution might take three to six months. I reminded him that the Israeli representatives had already started going back on their promises during the talks at Kilometer 101: first they argued that they were not authorised to discuss the ceasefire problem; later they proposed that the Egyptian forces withdraw ten kilometres west of the Suez Canal and the Israeli forces ten kilometres east of the Canal, but this was exactly what the British and the French had proposed in collusion with Israel in 1956. Egypt completely rejected the Israeli proposal for the withdrawal of the Second and Third Egyptian Armies from the East Bank of the Canal.

Smiling, Kissinger said, 'You know how the Israelis function. Frankly, they think that you in Egypt intend to send military equipment to the Third Army under cover of the ceasefire.' I argued we would not do that, and that the Third Army did not need weapons but food and water. I also made it clear that the Third Army would not surrender. Kissinger hastened to say that the United States did not want the Third Army to surrender or the withdrawal of the Egyptian army to the west of the Canal. Kissinger merely inquired whether Egypt was ready to guarantee that no military supplies would be sent to the Third Army even after Israeli forces withdrew to the line of 22 October. I confirmed this and insisted that non-military material should be sent immediately and continue permanently, adding that the only alternative was to break the blockade around the Third Army. I pressed Kissinger to approach the Israelis promptly and forcefully as he had promised.

Kissinger said that he would speak to Nixon that night and inform me at our meeting on the following morning of the President's decision.

Then Kissinger astonished me by bringing up the issue of the prisoners of war. He announced that the United States and the Soviet Union had agreed that there should be an immediate exchange. Brezhnev himself had given the Americans the guarantee that the Egyptians would agree to exchange all the prisoners of war as soon as possible after the ceasefire became completely effective. It was the first time that I heard of this guarantee and I told Kissinger that we had never given Moscow any such assurance. Kissinger commented that it would be very difficult to achieve any progress towards the negotiations for peace if the exchange of prisoners was not completed. I simply replied that we were ready to exchange a full list of the prisoners' names with the Israelis through the International Red Cross, but that the actual exchange of prisoners would have to wait until a more comprehensive settlement was negotiated.

Having temporarily concluded that point, I explained to Kissinger the circumstances leading to the arrival of fifty Soviet military officers and twenty interpreters in Egypt. The officers were expected to act as observers and the Soviets had told us that an equivalent number would arrive from the United States. Kissinger denied that there was an agreement with Brezhnev on this point. Rather, the Soviets had presented the USA with a/*fait accompli*, informing Washington only after the Soviet observers had arrived in Cairo. Kissinger stated that the Americans did not believe that the presence of US and Soviet observers would be in anybody's interests. However, because of Soviet insistence the Americans were ready to send thirty-two observers, with the Soviets providing an equivalent number, if Waldheim officially requested it. 'I ask you to communicate with President Sadat, urging him to convince the Soviets to take eighteen of those who have already arrived in Cairo back to Moscow,' he said, adding: 'At any rate, it would be better if there were no Soviet observers in Egypt at all.'

Concluding the conversation, Kissinger repeated that the United States was determined to open a new chapter with Egypt and promote a lasting friendship. He also informed me that President Nixon had decided that the situation in the Middle East should never return to what it was before the 1973 War; therefore it was imperative to convert the precarious ceasefire into permanent peace. 'Nixon has decided to exercise the necessary pressure on Israel,' he assured me.

I have to add here that Kissinger constantly referred to the President's decisions. He never tried to give the impression that he was the policy maker. On the contrary, he used the President's name more than necessary: 'President Nixon has decided . . .' 'President Nixon thinks. . .' 'President Nixon is determined to . . .' Henry Kissinger had enormous powers, being head of both the State Department and National Security Council, positions which no former Secretary of State had ever managed to combine. No Secretary but Foster Dulles had been as strong as Kissinger. Yet he was always very careful with President Nixon. As it will appear later, he was also very wary, fearing that the President might take independent decisions or overrule his recommendations. Kissinger was very sensitive about Nixon's prestige and public image. He clearly was in awe of the President to some degree.

Kissinger was also very conscious of his own dignity. At the end of our meeting he insisted on accompanying me to my car and since he did not usually escort his visitors that far the move caused a stir among his aides and the press. Surrounded by reporters and cameramen, Kissinger immediately became jubilant. I also saw a more sly streak in Kissinger's personality during that short walk to the car. He informed me that he was planning to meet with the Syrian Deputy Foreign Minister, who was also in the United States at that time. I just looked at him and made him understand that I knew what game he was playing. It was well known that Kissinger liked to hint to his interlocutor that the relation between the two of them was very special and that together they had the upper hand against a third party. I have to admit that sometimes this worked, but he played it too often. In the end, it became common knowledge and in certain cases led to great misunderstanding and even pushed things to crisis level. At any rate, on this occasion I disappointed Kissinger and told him that, on the contrary, I welcomed his meeting with the Syrians, since our relations with them were basically good.

Back at the hotel, I cabled President Sadat about my first meeting with Kissinger and about my impressions of him. I decided to be very cautious with Kissinger and to try, if possible, to meet directly with President Nixon after every talk with Kissinger or at least often. I wanted to be sure that what Kissinger said to me reflected exactly Nixon's position and that Nixon had full knowledge of what I told Kissinger. At any rate, I was satisfied with the first meeting, and felt justified in having insisted on seeing the Secretary of State immediately upon my arrival in Washington. The first contact established a basis for understanding and certainly paved the way for cooperation later on.

Round Two with Kissinger

The following morning, I had a four-hour meeting with Kissinger at the State Department. Joseph Sisco tried to attend, but Kissinger jokingly said, 'I am not Rogers and Joe is Rogers' boy.' Everybody laughed and as the meeting was tête-à-tête, Sisco had to leave. After he had withdrawn, Kissinger again stressed that Sisco had been very close to Rogers (the previous Secretary of State), and that the famous Rogers plan had in reality been a Sisco plan. I may add here that this shows that the rumours that Sisco was Kissinger's man sent to keep an eye on Rogers were unfounded.

Kissinger, it was clear, had thoroughly reviewed all the issues we had discussed with President Nixon and spoke with the President's support. President Nixon had only reluctantly agreed to let Golda Meir come to Washington, Kissinger informed me. Nixon had ultimately consented so that he could confront her and particularly make her feel the new atmosphere prevailing in Washington. He would only receive 'the old lady' two days after her arrival and not straight away, as he used to do. Moreover, Kissinger told me, President Nixon had directed him to cable Mrs Meir informing her of the Egyptian requests so she would have enough time to consult the Israeli Cabinet before leaving; in such way an agreement could be reached and implemented even before Kissinger's planned trip to Cairo.

I drew Kissinger's attention to the fact that Israel had always feared close contacts between Washington and Cairo. In this connection, I referred to the famous 'Lavon Affair', when the Israeli minister arranged to send agents to Cairo in 1954 to blow up American institutions in the city centre. He hoped Washington would conclude that the Egyptians were committing acts of sabotage against American interests and that Egyptian–American relations would deteriorate. Fortunately, the Egyptian police had caught two of the Israeli agents and uncovered the whole plot. As a result, Ben Gurion dismissed Lavon, although he had personally authorised the operation. Kissinger told me that he and his colleagues were aware of the Israeli determination to drive a wedge between Washington and Cairo, but wanted nevertheless to improve and consolidate the American–Egyptian relationship.

From there on, the dialogue developed in a constructive direction. I brought up all the items included in the Egyptian framework, but refrained from informing Kissinger that such a document existed. Kissinger told me that Israel had agreed to let a second convoy composed of fifty trucks go through to the Third Army but that they were not prepared to withdraw to the lines of 22 October. Firstly, a withdrawal was a tacit admission that they had violated the ceasefire. Secondly, they wanted to extract major concessions from Egypt: they would withdraw completely from the West Bank of the Suez Canal if Egypt withdrew the Second and Third Armies from the East Bank. This meant a return to the situation existing before the Egyptian forces crossed the Canal and attacked the Bar-Lev Line on 6 October. Officially, the Israelis argued that they could not move back to the 22 October lines because they did not know exactly where their forces were located on that date. In reality, there were numerous satellite reconnaissance pictures taken by the USA and the USSR that showed the respective positions of both armies.

I also told Kissinger in the course of this meeting that Egypt wanted a guarantee in writing from the United States that it would do everything possible to keep the Israelis from conducting military operations west of the Canal. Without such a guarantee, Egypt might have to take military action to destroy the Israeli force. Kissinger simply replied that he would inform President Nixon of the request.

Kissinger then raised once again the problem of the exchange of prisoners of war. I repeated that we were ready to exchange the lists of the prisoners to assure the Israelis of our good intentions, but that the actual return of the men could only be part of an overall agreement to consolidate the ceasefire. Unfortunately, while we were talking I was informed from Cairo that our military delegation at Kilometer 101 had, on Sadat's instructions, told the Israeli team that we were ready to exchange prisoners. Kissinger received the same information from the Israelis. The Egyptian government had also informed the Soviet ambassador in Cairo, and Kissinger told me that Anatoly Dobrynin, Soviet ambassador to Washington, had already requested a meeting with President Nixon. It was to take place during the weekend at Camp David.

I was appalled by this early and unnecessary disclosure of our readiness to exchange prisoners, knowing it would lead the Israelis to ask for more concessions before they agreed to move on other issues. The prisoners' exchange was a very important card in our hands because the Israeli government was under great pressure from the families to get the men back, but Sadat had given it away. The decision also encouraged the Americans to believe that the Russians indeed made decisions on Egypt's behalf. The Soviet Union had earlier guaranteed that Egypt would accept an early exchange, and now Sadat appeared to be complying with the Soviet decision.

As I expected, after we agreed to exchange the prisoners immediately, the Israelis came straight back with a new request. Kissinger told me that they were asking us to guarantee free passage in the Straits of Bab el-Mandeb at the south end of the Red Sea, which they believed we and the Russians were blockading. Sadat's concessions had only whetted the Israeli appetite. In fact Egypt did not have full control of Bab el-Mandeb. Although we had ships there the Soviets and South Yemenis really controlled this waterway. I later learnt from the Russian ambassador Dobrynin that there was never any real blockade of the Straits anyway.

During the second meeting, Kissinger again brought up the issue of the oil embargo. He tried to appear composed but it was clear that the Arab decision to use oil as a weapon presented Washington with enormous difficulties internally and internationally. Although the US dependency on Middle East oil was still limited in 1973, energy experts predicted a sharp increase in consumption and this would mean greater dependency and a sharp price increase. Kissinger, however, wanted to give me the impression that only the Europeans were affected. He belittled the Europeans' reaction and repeatedly mentioned that Washington was under great pressure from them to obtain the lifting of the embargo. But, above all, Kissinger employed the classic superpower argument: as a superpower the United States could never accept ultimata or even strong pressure from small countries like the Gulf states.

Kissinger's arguments only served to reinforce my opinion that the embargo was a most appropriate measure and that the oil weapon should continue to be used; its psychological and political impact was enormous. I cabled President Sadat to this effect, making specific recommendations which were followed despite

Kissinger's incessant efforts to convince the Gulf countries to lift the embargo. The oil weapon should not be used again except in extraordinary circumstances, but in 1973 the conditions were right. Unfortunately, the embargo was lifted too soon, in March 1974, as we shall see later.

These early meetings with Kissinger were primarily concerned with solving the most immediate problems of the ceasefire, but they were also important in opening the way to a better relationship with the Americans. Kissinger and I came to understand and respect each other. He tried hard from the beginning to be friendly. Already at the second meeting he surprised me by saying: 'Mr Minister, we have only met twice but I already feel we have known each other for a long time. I have known Abba Eban for six years and I still call him "Mr. Minister". In your case, I feel we can call each other by our first names. May I call you Ismail?' So it was Henry and Ismail from then on, without formalities.

These first encounters demonstrated that it was vital that Egypt speak directly with the United States, without allowing the Soviets to act as intermediaries. Letting Moscow speak for us had always been a mistake. Nasser's difficulties with the United States were not helped by having Moscow interpret for him. The problems were a function of basic differences in political principle between Nasser and the United States and no amount of Soviet interpreting could change that fact. As Foreign Minister, I changed this policy and spoke directly to the United States but not without resistance from the Soviet Union and even some circles in Egypt, and the Soviets still tried to speak for us either through Ambassador Dobrynin in Washington or directly with Kissinger in Moscow.

In his discussions of these early meetings in *Years of Upheaval*, Kissinger presents a distorted view of the Egyptian position.[1] He argues that I made it clear that Egypt wanted a lasting solution to its problems with Israel, and would not allow anybody to stand in the way, least of all the Palestinians. The implication here is quite false. What is true is that we never discussed the Palestinian issue at this time, for the simple reason that we were only dealing with the urgent issues of the ceasefire and not with a comprehensive solution to the problems of the Middle East. This is no evidence that Egypt was ready to betray the Palestinians.

I was scheduled to see President Nixon on 31 October at 3 p.m., shortly after the second meeting with Kissinger, but a new complication arose: I was informed from Cairo that General

Gamasy, the Egyptian representative at the Kilometer 101 talks, had given his Israeli counterpart, General Abaron Yariv, a copy of the framework I had prepared. Sadat had ordered him to do so, apparently hoping that Yariv, as a member of the Israeli cabinet, might convince Golda Meir to accept our framework. It was a misguided move, and the damage was compounded by the fact that officials in Cairo had then distributed the document to Soviet, British and French diplomats. I found myself in an absurd position because Sadat had shown all our cards to the enemy without receiving anything in return.

I had to give a copy of the framework to the Americans before my meeting with Nixon, and I arranged to see Kissinger at the White House at 2 p.m. He arrived with Brent Snowcroft, his deputy in the National Security Council. I gave a copy of the framework to Kissinger, who read it and commented: 'It is reasonable,' adding that it could even be adopted as an American proposal. Fearing he might do exactly that, I hastened to inform him that Gamasy had given a copy to Yariv, apparently by mistake. Kissinger shouted: 'That would be a catastrophe!' I added that both the British and the French had also been given copies. He said: 'That would be a second catastrophe!' Kissinger then checked with the CIA about information they had received that morning that a document had been given by the Egyptians to the Israelis at Kilometer 101. When he hung up, he told me that it was the same document.

I was intrigued by Kissinger's comment that it was a catastrophe if the British and the French should know of the framework. When I suggested that they might play an influential role in the solution, Kissinger answered that neither the British nor the French had the political or economic potential to be of any use. Rather, their interference might complicate things. The only country which had any influence on Israel was the United States, while the French and the British could do nothing but would later claim that they had been important. Kissinger was particularly hostile towards the French.

First Encounter with Nixon

At 3 o'clock Kissinger and I were ushered into the Oval Room and there I met President Nixon. It was the first encounter between an American president and an Egyptian Foreign Minister since the severing of diplomatic relations between the two countries during the 1967 War. He welcomed me and we both stood in front of the fireplace, as was the custom, so that photographers could record this first official meeting. President Nixon was smiling all the time and said that he wanted to be the first to congratulate me on my appointment as Foreign Minister. (I had been confirmed in that position that morning.)

President Nixon, Kissinger and I then met for one hour. I have to confess that I was deeply touched by the President's first statement. 'As President of the United States, as an American, and as Richard Nixon, I respect those who fight well and sacrifice themselves. You fought well, like the Vietnamese, and we respect this. Please don't misunderstand me – the Vietnamese are communists – I only meant the fighting and fighting well – the spirit itself. I have to admit in my three capacities that you have done all this well.' As a result, Nixon continued, the whole picture had changed and the US and his own position were now different. He also expressed his desire to meet President Sadat, not immediately but in the near future. Then Nixon went straight to the point, informing me that Kissinger had shown him the framework for the disengagement of forces and that he had found it 'constructive'. The United States could very easily adopt it as a basis for future action.

The difference between President Nixon and Kissinger was immediately obvious. President Nixon described the framework as 'constructive', Kissinger had only called it 'reasonable'. This was not an accidental choice of words, but revealed a difference between the two personalities. Nixon was more straightforward; Kissinger always remained cagey and evasive. For this reason, I made it a point always to sum up the gist of discussions which took place between Kissinger and myself with Nixon, and later followed the same policy with Ford. The difference between the two was shown again in the course of the meeting. I referred to my request to Kissinger that the United States should give a guarantee to Egypt that the Israeli troops stationed on the West Bank of the Suez Canal would not initiate any military action. President Nixon looked at Kissinger asking 'Which guarantee?' Kissinger apologised to the President, saying he had forgotten to inform him and explained the purpose of my request. The minute Kissinger had finished, President Nixon, in a rather loud voice and unhesitatingly pointing his finger at Kissinger, ordered: 'Give him the guarantee.' This was typical of Nixon. Once he was convinced of a point, he made the decision straight away. He was a man of decision and thus was much more effective than his two successors – Ford and Carter. At any rate, I seized the opportunity to explain to President Nixon that this American guarantee was of vital importance because there was a high concentration of tanks and troops around the Canal. If any military operation were to start, a chain reaction would turn the area into a ball of fire, and the superpowers might find themselves automatically involved. The American President agreed entirely with me.

Nixon then told me that Mrs Golda Meir had asked to come to Washington but that he had postponed giving his approval until my arrival. He added that he had declined her request to see him right away and that he would meet with her only the following day. President Nixon stressed that, 'In the history of the United States, there was never a president who could make decisions against Israel or displeasing to Israel, except Eisenhower and Nixon. No president of the United States has been able to resist the various forms of Israeli pressure and harassment. I don't want you to misunderstand me, I am not against minorities and I do not belittle the influence of Congress, but when the supreme US national interest calls upon me to make the necessary decisions, I will make them unhesitatingly irrespective of the Israeli pressure. On this basis, I have instructed Kissinger to proceed with the discussions with you and the Israelis, and to prepare himself to go to Cairo as you have requested.' Then President Nixon suggested that the Egyptian framework should be implemented in stages and that he would bring pressure to bear on the Israelis to comply with the first stage.

President Nixon also openly stated his desire to see diplomatic relations reestablished between the United States and Egypt in the near future. When I reciprocated, he inquired where I was staying and upon hearing that I was staying at a hotel, he expressed the hope that next time I came to Washington I would be able to reside at the Egyptian embassy.

Like Kissinger, President Nixon brought up the issue of the Arab oil embargo and he expressed his personal concern about the consequences of that policy. Gently rather than excitedly like Kissinger, he talked about the problems he faced because of the mounting pressure from Western European countries and some groups in the United States. I told Nixon I appreciated his difficulties, but the embargo would only be lifted gradually as progress was made towards a peaceful solution of the crisis. Nixon was worried enough about this problem to return to it again during this conversation.

Before the meeting ended, I wanted to be sure that the meeting between Nixon and Golda Meir the following day would not produce unpleasant surprises. I told Nixon that while I was completely satisfied with what I had heard from him, I was still somewhat worried. He insisted that I speak frankly, so I told him that rumours were circulating to the effect that his meeting with Golda Meir would result in a new American military aid commitment to Israel. 'This was true in the past,' Nixon replied, 'but the Prime Minister of Israel will find a new Nixon this time and no such statement about new arms for Israel will be issued.' I thanked him for his assurance but warned him that if Golda Meir got new arms at this stage, there would certainly be extremely adverse reaction from the Arab countries. He assured me that there would not be new arms. I then inquired about other rumours to the effect that Mrs Meir had been meeting with members of Congress and influential leaders of the Jewish community, so that when she met President Nixon she could argue that Israel enjoyed much support in the United States. President Nixon smiled and said, 'I am aware of this and in fact I encouraged certain Jewish leaders and congressmen to see her. But I repeat again, she will find a new atmosphere in the White House.'

Speaking about the US attitude towards Egypt, President Nixon made a point of telling me that he and his administration were convinced that Egypt, the biggest Arab country, had a special role to play and could exert great influence on the newly independent countries. 'US policy in the future will be formulated with all this in mind. Egypt has great potential although it does not own large quantities of oil like other Arab countries. It has an enormous human potential, it has people with great skills and exports them to all the Arab countries. I myself have witnessed this when I visited many of the Arab countries. Wherever I went, I met Egyptian experts, teachers, instructors and technicians. I am aware of the difficulties Egypt faces at present in its development program and of the help it needs. I believe that something should be done, and positively, in this regard,' he concluded. Nixon also praised Sadat, comparing him favourably to his Arab brothers. He was pleased that the relations between Sadat and King Faisal were improving despite the pressures exerted on Egypt by President Muammar

Qaddafi of Libya. Moreover, Nixon expressed the opinion that Nasser had lacked the flexibility of Sadat in the sense that he only maintained contacts with the radical leaders in the area.

At the end of the meeting President Nixon insisted on accompanying me to my car, explaining 'Normally, I accompany foreign ministers only as far as the Rose Garden, where my daughter Patricia got engaged. But to show the press and everybody my interest and the new US position towards Egypt, I shall escort you to your car.' The next day, Nixon met with Mrs Meir and when she left the newsmen addressed many questions to President Nixon about their meeting. He only replied, 'My meeting with the Prime Minister of Israel was as constructive as my meeting with Fahmy yesterday.' This was an unprecedented remark: never before had an American President put Israel and Egypt on the same level. This was not lost on the newsmen, and the next day the incident was prominently reported in the media.

I left President Nixon with a real sense of accomplishment. It was clear that the October War had drastically changed the US position towards Egypt. The Americans now appreciated that the confrontation states in the Middle East could no longer be ignored, because the crisis could lead to a confrontation between the superpowers. As a result US interests were no longer identical with those of Israel. Washington saw that Egypt had a crucial role to play in the peace process.

These first meetings in Washington had also led to some very concrete steps. In particular, I had obtained a US guarantee that Israel would not undertake any military action on the West Bank of the Suez Canal. This written guarantee made the possibility of a new flare-up of fighting remote, and allowed Egypt to concentrate its efforts on reaching a peace settlement, rather than preparing for a new war. To be sure, we still had to take military precautions in case Israel should not agree to the American request and guarantee, but the danger was much reduced. It is important to note here that Sadat never acknowledged the existence of this American guarantee. Resorting to his usual rhetoric, he threatened to order his army to wipe out the Israeli pocket on the West Bank if Israel should renew the fighting. He even claimed that he informed Kissinger of this plan during their first meeting in Cairo, but that the Secretary of State had warned him that if Egypt attacked it might find itself 'fighting the Pentagon'. Sadat thus abandoned the plan. The fact that Nixon signed the guarantee bears heavily against such a conversation having taken place. The Pentagon itself denied it had ever planned operations in Egypt. I must add that Kissinger never mentioned the existence of the guarantee either, probably fearing an adverse reaction by the Israelis and the Jewish lobby in the United States if it was publicised.

These early meetings gave me an understanding of the working of the Nixon administration. Nixon was clearly the boss in foreign affairs, despite Kissinger's reputation and flamboyance. During the first meeting with Nixon, Kissinger never spoke unless the President specifically asked him a question. He just sat there, meticulously wiping his glasses with a large handkerchief. It was also clear that Nixon had a thorough knowledge and understanding of international affairs, a rare quality among American presidents. He listened to his aides but ultimately he was the one who made the decisions. I was convinced from the very beginning that Nixon was the only American president who could bring about a comprehensive solution in the Middle East. He was forceful, decisive, and willing to stand up to the Jewish lobby. But he needed time, and the Watergate scandal unfortunately deprived him of the time.

The importance of Nixon's personal role in shaping US foreign policy led me to follow the Watergate affair with interest and anxiety. By the time that story leaked I was able to talk very openly with President Nixon on almost every issue. So I chose the right moment and asked him how he intended to react to the mounting Watergate crisis. As usual, he was very blunt and told me that he would fight it to the very end. Knowing Nixon, I believed he would fight, although I was not confident he would win. On later visits, when the campaign against him was almost at its peak, I found that he was using his bold moves on the international plane to bolster his position and restore his image at home. It was while the pressure of Watergate increased that he expressed his desire to visit Egypt.

Israeli Influence at Work

After my first meeting with Nixon I stayed on in Washington a few more days at his request and saw Kissinger repeatedly. These encounters brought to light the extent and effectiveness of the Israeli lobby. Kissinger himself was clearly in touch with the Israeli mechanism, since he almost invariably embraced the Israeli position. On the few occasions when he did not, the Israelis brought him quickly into line. At this time, for example, Mrs Meir at first refused to see Kissinger, whom she held directly responsible for the delay in starting the US airlift of military equipment to Israel during the war. The Israelis were convinced that this delay had allowed the Egyptian army to fortify its positions on the East Bank of the Suez Canal after the initial crossing. In fact, Kissinger claimed that both Nelson Rockefeller and President Nixon had to intervene with Golda Meir before she agreed to see him. Despite these interventions, the first meeting between Kissinger and Mrs Meir lasted only a few minutes. A second meeting continued for several hours over dinner at Blair House but was bitter and acrimonious. Kissinger, whom I saw the following day, was acutely aware of the limits of American influence on Israel, although he insisted that the USA would honour its guarantee to Egypt.

During a later meeting with Kissinger, I could see that the Israeli pressure was beginning to affect him, and that he was becoming worried about his future. As a result, he appeared willing to embrace the Israeli position on the issue of withdrawal to the 22 October lines. Meir, Kissinger reported, claimed that by insisting on such withdrawal the US was only playing the Soviets' game. Moscow wanted the Israelis to withdraw so that the blockade of the Third Army would be lifted. Kissinger had replied that the USA, too, wanted the blockade to be lifted because it might lead to a physical intervention by the Soviets, which was not in the USA's or Israel's interests. If the Soviets intervened to resupply the Third Army with food, Kissinger had told the Israelis, the Americans could do nothing about it.

With me, however, Kissinger started arguing that because of the Israelis' intransigence concerning withdrawal to the 22 October lines it might be better to concentrate US efforts on achieving a broader, more permanent solution, namely the withdrawal of the Israelis to the East Bank and of the Egyptians to the West Bank of the Canal. Mrs Meir, Kissinger said, would agree to that. In fact, this had been the Israeli request all along, since it would have wiped out all of the Egyptian gains, restoring the status quo before 6 October. Kissinger knew Egypt could not accept such a solution, but he was caving in to the Israelis.

The Israelis raised problems and quibbled all along. Mrs Meir finally agreed to allow the resupplying of the Third Army with non-military items on a permanent basis. Yet she and Yariv, who had left the military talks at Kilometer 101 to accompany her to Washington, continued to raise a host of problems about trivial details such as whether the supplies would be inspected just by UN observers or by the Israelis as well. It is worth recalling here that the Israelis' hand had been greatly strengthened on this score by President Sadat when he had agreed to an unconditional exchange of prisoners. Had he made the exchange of prisoners conditional on an Israeli withdrawal to the 22 October lines, he could automatically have freed the Third Army and lifted the blockade on Suez.

Even after they had agreed to the resupplying of the Third Army, the Israelis raised further obstacles. I vividly remember that, after my return to Cairo, General Ahmed Ismail, the Minister of War, called me in the middle of the night very worried bcause the Israelis had refused to let a load of pullovers through to the Third Army. I was surprised and told Ismail that there must be a mistake because pullovers are certainly not a military item. When I asked why the Israelis were doing this he said that they contended that if the Egyptian soldiers got the pullovers, they would be warm and therefore fit for fighting. Despite the comedy in the situation Ismail was dead serious, arguing that if the Americans could do nothing to solve the problem, he would have no choice but to initiate some military action to break the blockade. I assured him that he should not worry and that the pullovers would reach his troops. I then immediately contacted Kissinger, who was similarly surprised, and UN Secretary-General Waldheim, who instructed General Silasvuo to solve this stupid and childish problem.

I stayed on in Washington after Mrs Meir departed to finalise our agreements with the USA and prepare Kissinger's trip to Cairo. Although we had not reached a full agreement on the disengagement of forces at this point, we had laid the foundations for it. We had also solved the urgent problem of resupplying the Third Army, which could so easily have led to renewed fighting. But the most important achievement, in the long run, was Nixon's written guarantee that the USA would prevent any military action by Israel on the West Bank of the Canal. This constituted a turning point in Egyptian–US relations and forced the USA to become and remain directly involved in the peace-making process in the Middle East.

In *The Secret Conversations of Henry Kissinger*, Matti Golan concluded that the crucial early decisions were all taken in

Washington during the meetings I have just discussed, and that nothing new happened during Kissinger's trip to Cairo and Tel Aviv.[2] This is certainly true. The six points later announced during Kissinger's first visit to the Middle East had all been agreed upon in Washington:

1) Egypt and Israel would observe the ceasefire called for by the UN Security Council.

2) Discussions between the two countries would begin immediately in order to settle the question of the return to the 22 October positions in the framework of an agreement on the disengagement and separation of forces under the auspices of the UN.

3) The town of Suez was to receive daily supplies of food, water and medicine. All wounded civilians in the town of Suez were to be evacuated.

4) There would be no impediment to the movement of non-military supplies to the East Bank of the Canal.

5) The Israeli checkpoints on the Cairo–Suez road would be replaced by UN checkpoints. At the Suez end of the road Israeli officers would verify with UN representatives the non-military nature of the cargo.

6) As soon as the UN checkpoints were established on the Cairo–Suez road there would be an exchange of all prisoners of war, including the wounded.

It is important to stress that the six points were the culmination of long discussion between the Egyptians and the Americans, and not the solution proposed by Golda Meir as Abba Eban claims in his book *An Autobiography*[3]. In fact, Abba Eban could not know because he was not in Washington. Perhaps he wanted to create the impression that, as Mrs. Meir's Foreign Minister, he had suggested these six points in absentia.

Certainly, the main results of this stay in Washington emanated from my negotiations with the Americans and could only come from them. Nevertheless, I did make a point of talking to representatives of other countries as well, not only to discuss bilateral issues but also to inform them about Egypt's position in the talks with the Americans. I believed that the Middle East crisis required a real international solution, not just the involvement of the superpowers. For this reason, I had talks with the Canadian Foreign

Minister and received the ambassadors of the Soviet Union, France, Kuwait, and Saudi Arabia, as well as the Syrian Deputy Minister of Foreign Affairs. I put all of them in the picture as far as possible. To the French ambassador I conveyed Egypt's desire, or rather insistence, that France take an active part in the overall peace talks. I told him that I would never agree to the convening of the proposed peace conference at Geneva unless it was under the auspices of the UN and in accordance with a decision approved by the Security Council in its entirety. The French ambassador appreciated this very much, informing me that Paris held identical views, and that the French delegate would make a policy statement supporting this position at the next meeting of the Security Council.

Before returning to Cairo I had a meeting with Dr Kurt Waldheim in New York. I exchanged information with him on the Middle East question and tried to put him in the picture concerning my talks in Washington and above all what we expected from the UN observers and forces. I had known Kurt Waldheim a long time as he had been the permanent representative of Austria at the UN when I served in the Egyptian delegation there, and later Foreign Minister of Austria while I was ambassador to that country. I thanked him particularly for his tireless efforts during the cease-fire period and his vigilance in seeing that General Silasvuo was always at hand to help when something went wrong. I apologised for having, on many occasions, woken him up in the middle of the night because of the six hours time difference between Cairo and New York. Before leaving New York, I invited the Secretary General to come and meet President Sadat, and he later did.

Kissinger Visits Cairo

Kissinger arrived in Cairo on 6 November, after stopping in Morocco and Tunisia. He had expressed great qualms about this visit to Cairo earlier, not for political reasons but because he was worried about his personal security. He even told me that his parents had advised him against the trip. I assured him that we would take all necessary security measures, and added that he could walk the streets of Cairo without anybody bothering or even noticing him. He was rather upset at the idea that nobody would even notice him.

I arranged for Kissinger and Sadat to meet alone, not only

because Kissinger enjoyed dealing directly with heads of state but also to give the two of them an opportunity to talk freely. The meeting did not last long, however, and Kissinger just gave Sadat the paper outlining the six principles. These were not new to us and neither this first meeting nor a second one led to new developments. Diplomatic relations between the United States and Egypt were formally re-established during Kissinger's visit. A brief ceremony was held in the garden of the American embassy; the Spanish flag, which had flown there while Spain took care of American interests in Egypt, was lowered and the American flag raised. Kissinger was beaming, although he had not been the one to insist on resumption of diplomatic relations. But he knew President Nixon would be happy and above all he was enjoying being the centre of attraction. Before the end of the visit it was announced that Hermann Eilts had been nominated US ambassador to Cairo and Ashraf Ghorbal, Egyptian ambassador to Washington.

I had some meetings with Kissinger in the course of his visit and brought up again the issue of Soviet–American dealings on the Middle East question. The two superpowers were still talking behind Egypt's back, particularly concerning the issue of the convening of a peace conference in Geneva. Prior to Kissinger's arrival, I had been informed by Vladimir Vinogradov, the Soviet ambassador to Cairo, that the two superpowers had agreed on a formula for convening the Geneva Conference without the involvement of the UN Security Council but simply under the auspices of the US and USSR as co-chairmen. When I heard this, I summoned to my office both Vinogradov and Hermann Eilts, then head of the American interests section and later ambassador. It is very unusual diplomatic procedure to summon Soviet and American diplomats at the same time. Once both ambassadors were in my office, I started to dictate the Egyptian position concerning the Geneva conference, stressing above all that we would not participate unless the Security Council was involved. The Soviet ambassador, used to playing a more important and influential role in Egypt than even Lord Cromer had during the early years of British Colonial rule, was appalled. I still remember the expression on his face. He protested that the Soviets and the Americans had already agreed on a common position and refused to write down the Egyptian position. However, Ambassador Eilts wrote down what I was dictating without complaint and Vinogradov finally realised that he had missed the boat and asked me to repeat myself because he had not been writing. I suggested that he could get a copy from his American friend.

When I saw Kissinger in Cairo I asked him bluntly whether he was concocting something with the Russians behind my back. When he denied this, I faced him with some statements he had made to Ambassador Dobrynin about the arrangements for the Geneva Peace Conference. Kissinger apologised and said that he thought that the Russians had informed us on these points. I also informed Kissinger about the phone call I had received from Vinogradov, explaining that I had summoned the US and Russian ambassadors to my office simultaneously and raised serious objections to their agreement that the Geneva Conference would not be put under the auspices of the UN. I told Kissinger that we would fight any such agreement and insisted that the Secretary-General of the UN should preside at the Geneva Conference. I added that I would never accept that the two superpowers attend only the first meeting and then absent themselves, as they were planning to do, because this would have changed the meeting from an international conference into direct negotiation between Israel and the Arab countries.

Kissinger's reaction was swift. The agreement that the superpowers only attend the first meeting was a manoeuver to get the Soviets out of the picture, he explained. What counted were the behind-the-scenes and direct contacts between the United States and all parties to the Middle East conflict. He added, 'No country can play the American role or in fact deliver the goods.' I was amazed that the Russians had fallen into this American trap of only attending the first meeting and then absenting themselves. In fact, the Russians insisted on this procedure even during the first days of the Geneva Conference in December 1973 when Ambassador Vinogradov, the Soviet representative at the conference, informed me that the Soviets intended to absent themselves after the first meeting. I objected strongly, and conveyed my opinion directly to Foreign Minister Andrei Gromyko, who agreed with me.

Before leaving Cairo, Kissinger sent two of his aides, Joseph Sisco and Harold Saunders, to Israel to show Golda Meir the six points in their final form and give her ample time to present them to the Israeli Cabinet before he arrived in Tel Aviv. He then went on to Saudi Arabia, as Nixon had asked him to do, in order to inform King Faisal of the new developments and also to discuss with him the problem of the oil embargo. Initially King Faisal did not want to receive Kissinger, but ultimately a meeting was arranged. The King, aware of the fact that Kissinger is a Jew, lectured him on the Zionist movement, stressing that Zionism and Communism were, in his view, identical. Kissinger later told me that King Faisal had expounded his views for almost two hours without giving him any chance to utter a single word.

Furthermore, the King lent a deaf ear to Kissinger's arguments on the necessity of lifting the oil embargo, repeating that it was necessary for the Israelis to withdraw from all Arab territory, including Jerusalem, before he would agree to such move. Kissinger told me that he said to Faisal that he was very moved, being a Jew and being allowed to see the King of the Holy Places who never allowed any Jew to come to his court. Although the meeting did not bear any fruit, Kissinger was very impressed by the King's firmness and determination as to the future of Jerusalem. He was also very impressed by the way the King expressed himself and the precise wording on every issue he tackled. Kissinger rightly described King Faisal as 'a man of his word'.

Notes

1. Henry Kissinger, *Year of Upheaval*, (Boston: Little, Brown & Co, 1982), p. 618.
2. Matti Golan, *The Secret Conversations of Henry Kissinger* (New York: Quadrangle, 1976).
3. Abba Eban, *An Autobiography* (New York: Random House, 1977), p. 538.

4   KISSINGER STARTS HIS ADVENTURES IN THE MIDDLE EAST

Planning the Geneva Conference

The six-point agreement formalised during Kissinger's visit to the Middle East solved the first, urgent problems on the ground. By ensuring a steady flow of supplies for the Third Army and the town of Suez, it removed the risk of an immediate resumption of warfare, giving all parties a breather and time to deliberate on what the next step should be. There were essentially two approaches. The first, officially favoured by both superpowers, was that an international conference should be convened in Geneva in order to negotiate a comprehensive solution to the Middle East problem. This strategy had been agreed upon between the United States and the Soviet Union during Kissinger's visit to Moscow on 21 October 1973. The second solution, the one Kissinger really favoured, was to pursue a 'step-by-step' approach, aiming at incremental progress, beginning with military disengagement between Egypt and Israel as well as Syria and Israel.

Kissinger probably agreed to the idea of the Geneva Conference because of pressure by the Soviets, but he must later have hoped to find an excuse for retreating from the commitment. An international conference convened by the two superpowers would have given the Soviet Union an unprecedented opportunity to play a central role in the Middle East negotiations, and it would even have entailed American admission that the Soviet Union had a legitimate interest in the area. Furthermore, Moscow would have been encouraged to claim a similar role in other troubled areas of the world.

Egypt favoured the convening of the Geneva Conference as long as it was placed under auspices of the United Nations and included a Palestinian delegation. Our insistence that the conference be held under UN auspices was based on our conviction that the crisis in the Middle East required a truly international effort and not just the involvement of the great powers. The United States and the Soviet Union had already agreed on a formula for convening the conference without UN sponsorship as Soviet Ambassador

Dobrynin had told me in Washington. Despite my argument he refused to budge from what had been agreed. I then discussed the issue with Kissinger. At first, he did not want to talk about the conference at all, in fact he had deliberately avoided mentioning it. However, eventually he agreed to seek a compromise and after much haggling it was agreed that the UN Secretary-General would act as convener of the conference, thus making the role of the United Nations official.

Concerning the Palestinians, our position was adamant: a Palestinian delegation must participate in the conference, because there could be no solution of the Middle East problem without the Palestinians. However, Egypt was willing to attend the opening session of the conference without a Palestinian delegation, and then to discuss the modalities of Palestinian participation during the conference itself.

Israel accepted the Geneva Conference, but without enthusiasm. It is always opposed to international conferences for fear of facing a united Arab front. Similarly, Israel prefers to exclude the Soviet Union, relying instead on the United States with its certain support. However, this time the United States put great pressure on the Israelis to attend the conference and they were forced to comply, although half-heartedly.

Both Jordan and Syria had initially agreed to attend the conference, but after all was set Syria withdrew. It tried to justify its decision by claiming that Egypt was planning to sign a separate disengagement or even a peace treaty with Israel at the conference. In fact the conference convened and adjourned without a single document being signed by Egypt and Israel.

The conference finally opened on 21 December amid worldwide attention, despite a last-minute snag about seating arrangements. First, although the Syrians were not there, I insisted that their chairs be placed around the table, to underline that their absence was only temporary. Then the Israelis demanded to sit next to the Egyptians. I refused, insisting instead that we follow standard United Nations practice and seat the delegations in alphabetical order. This upset the Israelis because it would have left them sitting next to the empty Syrian chairs. The compromise finally suggested by the UN Secretary-General was to place Egypt and Israel to the right and left of the chairman, the United States next to Egypt and the Soviet Union next to Israel, followed by the Jordanians. The empty Syrian chairs would be between the Jordanian and the US delegations. As agreed, the Palestinians were not present at this time as a separate delegation, but some were incorporated in the Jordanian delegation.

It had been agreed beforehand that every delegation would present a moderate and balanced opening speech, and that all delegations would speak on the first day, except for the Israelis, who had expressly asked to speak on the second. Everything went according to plan, but just as we were getting ready to adjourn the Israeli Foreign Minister, Abba Eban, changed his mind. Realising that the media would report the Arab position but not the Israeli view, unless he too delivered his speech, he asked to be allowed to speak immediately. We agreed.

The speech Eban delivered that afternoon did not comply with the agreed guidelines of moderation. He launched into a long tirade against the Arab countries, presenting them as the aggressors, while suggesting that Israel had never had anything but peaceful intentions. The reason for Eban's vehemence was soon explained by a note sent through an usher by a journalist: Eban's speech was being carried live on the Israeli television. Israel was in the middle of an election campaign and Eban's speech was clearly a party address aimed at the domestic audience. I decided to spoil his attack and asked for the floor again, delivering extemporaneously a firm rebuttal of all his points. While I was speaking, I was watching the Israeli delegation and could see they were quite upset, and that Eban's aides were whispering excitedly to each other. It was obvious that they wantĕd Eban to reply, but at the end of my speech he remained silent. For once, he resisted the Israeli urge to have the last word.

When the conference resumed the next day, we were supposed to start discussing the substantive issues, but I refused to do so until both the Syrian and the Palestinian delegations were present. We were thus forced to turn to procedure. We created various subcommittees, including an Egyptian–Israeli military sub-committee where all issues pertaining to military disengagement could be discussed and agreements signed. The Israelis were requested to send military representatives immediately, so that some points agreed upon during the talks at Kilometer 101 could be finalised. Apparently Golda Meir did not want to send military representatives immediately, but finally gave in at Eban's insistence.

After the initial session, the Geneva Conference never

reconvened. There were several reasons, but most important was the problem of Palestinian representation and the attitude of the Syrians, which remained extremely negative. Still, the very fact that the conference was convened and that most of the parties sat together around the same table was a step forward.

During my stay in Geneva, I had private meetings with both Gromyko and Kissinger, which were very revealing about the attitude of the superpowers and their indifference towards a comprehensive solution at this time. I was in fact struck by the similarity in the positions of the United States and the Soviet Union towards the conference. The Soviets were delighted to act as co-chairmen alongside the Americans, because this gave them legitimacy in the Middle East. To my amazement and disappointment I found that Gromyko was ready to accept the United States proposal that after the initial session the United States and the Soviet Union would absent themselves from all serious deliberations. The discussion would then take place in the various subcommittees, in which only two delegations – one from Israel and one from an Arab country – would be represented. This meant that the negotiations would be bilateral, and that the Arabs would be talking directly to the Israelis, without the mediation of the great powers. This was of course the procedure favoured by Israel. While I was not surprised that the Americans were willing to go along with it, I was amazed at the Soviet willingness to accept this. At any rate, I firmly objected to this procedure, insisting that the two co-chairmen of the conference be represented in each subcommittee. Gromyko simply argued that this was unnecessary, since the great powers would be ready to intervene if problems arose. Interestingly enough, this was the same argument used by Kissinger when I discussed the issue with him. I made it clear to both of them that there would be no point in reconvening the conference if they insisted on forcing direct negotiation between Israel and each Arab country.

While Kissinger's official position was no different from Gromyko's, he was more conciliatory in private. However, this did not hide his determination to drive a wedge between Egypt and the Soviet Union and to relegate the latter to a very minor role in the negotiations. During dinner in my hotel suite, he promised to find a compromise solution concerning the great powers' representation in the subcommittees, and then suggested that the United States and Egypt should cooperate closely during the conference, without putting the Soviets into the picture. It was quite clear what Kissinger had in mind: the exclusion of the Soviet Union from all serious negotiations, thus making the United States the arbiter of a Middle East solution.

This particular meeting with Kissinger was very revealing of his concept of the role the United States should play in the world. In the course of the discussion, I asked him why American companies, with government support, had made a last-minute effort to win the contract for the SUMED pipeline away from the French companies which appeared likely to get it. (This pipeline was to carry oil from the Red Sea to a port west of Alexandria, to allow supertankers which cannot use the Suez Canal to load in the Mediterranean, and avoid the long trip around the Cape of Good Hope.) 'Nobody can beat the United States, politically or economically,' Kissinger answered; 'France? No Way!' I reminded him that France was a US ally, but that seemed to make no difference to him. 'We cannot allow any country, even a Western European country, to compete with us on major projects.' He also added that in any case France would not be in a position to take any major decisions for at least a year, because President Pompidou was seriously ill with a terminal disease, and was not expected to survive for more than six months to a year. Clearly American intelligence in French medical circles was sharper than their coverage of Israeli and Egyptian military matters prior to the October War.

The Geneva Conference adjourned without having accomplished anything concrete, because the parties could not even agree on procedure. We returned to the step-by-step diplomacy favoured by Kissinger, and specifically to the attempt to secure a disengagement of forces on the ground. The original plan had been to secure the simultaneous disengagement of forces on both the Egyptian and the Syrian fronts, but it had to be abandoned, primarily because the problem of exchange of prisoners between Israel and Syria had not been solved at this stage. President Hafiz Asad of Syria had refused to accept the Israeli position that the release of the prisoners was a precondition to all other negotiations. I finally helped to solve this problem during my second trip to Washington, in February 1974 after the four-power Arab summit meeting in Algiers. By that time, the agreement on disengagement on the Egyptian front had already been signed.

The Egyptian–Israeli prisoner of war exchange, on the other hand, had taken place in November 1973, opening the way for further negotiations. It should be noted here that the Egyptian prisoners were five times as numerous as the 276 Israeli prisoners. The reason was that the Israelis had captured and deported to the Israeli-occupied Sinai a large number of civilians from Suez, hoping to strengthen their bargaining position. In reality, the prisoners were a much greater psychological and political problem in Israel than in Egypt. In the past we had never attached major urgency to the return of our prisoners and although after the success scored in the October War we were more interested in carrying out an early exchange, the great number of Egyptian prisoners did not significantly enhance Israel's bargaining power.

The negotiations leading to the disengagement of forces on the Egyptian–Israeli front got under way in earnest in January 1974, with Kissinger acting as the go-between. It was decided that Sadat and I would receive him in Aswan, far from the pressures of Cairo. Three days before Kissinger's arrival on 10 January, President Sadat and I went to Aswan to review the situation and prepare our strategy in the forthcoming disengagement negotiations. We met in the garden of the presidential rest house, a beautiful spot overlooking the first British-built Aswan Dam. Aswan is not only a beautiful place, but also one of great symbolic value, linking the remote Egypt of the pharaonic age to modern Egypt. Meeting in this unique spot was of great inspiration to everybody, both psychologically and politically.

Egypt at the Crossroads

President Sadat insisted that I present my own appraisal of the situation and my perception of how it would unfold. It was clear, I told him, that Egypt and the Arab world had come to a crossroad and were entering a delicate period. This new phase required evaluation of the long-term and short-term effects of every move on Egypt and the entire Middle East. Any Egyptian strategy therefore should take account of the following major issues:

1) The American position, with particular attention to the relationship between the United States and Israel.
2) The Soviet position.
3) The rivalry between the United States and the Soviet Union and their immediate and long-term strategy for influence

and dominance in the Middle East.
4) The military and political situation on the Egyptian and Arab fronts.
5) The oil embargo.
6) Domestic and international public opinion after the October War.
7) Last but not least, the Israeli strategems with all their intricacies and their style of negotiating.

The American position had undergone major changes since 6 October. The war had created a new military and psychological situation, and the oil embargo had put new pressures on the Americans. Washington had no option but to move quickly to defuse the crisis, but it could not do this without improving its relationship with the Arab world and particularly Egypt. The direct contacts the US had established with Egypt and other Arab countries since October would make this task easier. We had to be careful, however: the US goal was to change its image within the Arab world without making major concessions or commitments which might jeopardise its special relationship with Israel. During the early stages, I told President Sadat, the Americans would give the impression that they were neutral and full of good intentions, and that there had been a genuine change in their position. In reality, however, there would be little change and the American moves would largely be window-dressing.

We should expect Washington to continue giving first priority to lifting the oil embargo, thus stripping the Arabs of their most powerful new weapon. Simultaneously, Kissinger would be working very hard to weaken the Soviet position in Egypt and Syria. This was not just because of the overall rivalry between the US and USSR, but because Kissinger wanted to be the sole arbiter of progress in the Middle East. For this reason, he would also undoubtedly try to undermine Arab unity through his manoeuvres, creating a mood of competition, jealousy, suspicison and distrust among the Arab leaders.

We should expect the United States to concentrate on Egypt in order to attain all these goals, weakening the Soviet position in our country and establishing a special relation with us that would separate us from the rest of the Arab world. However, the United States would avoid making substantive commitments on important issues, offering instead only concessions of symbolic and psychological value. To be specific, in January 1974 the United States was not ready to fill the vacuum left by the deterioration in the Soviet–Egyptian relationship and to back Egypt politically and militarily. From the American point of view, such a commitment could have led to a breakthrough in the Middle East crisis, and destroyed or at least weakened the growing unity of the Arab world, but they were not ready to make it. As a consequence, I repeatedly warned President Sadat, we should not make any major concessions or move unnecessarily quickly. We should also remember that the United States did not normally submit proposals to the Arab side, including Egypt, unless it knew beforehand that the Israelis would accept them. The enormous Jewish influence and pressure on decision-making in Washington would belie any soft-talking by Kissinger.

As to the Egyptian–Soviet relationship, it was not in the best interests of Egypt to provoke the Soviet Union and its leadership, either on the bilateral level or on the international plane. We should not abruptly shift away from Moscow, and our communication lines with the Soviets should be kept intact. I thus advised President Sadat to avoid open and violent criticism of the Soviet leadership. There was no purpose in eliminating the Soviet Union from the peace process and giving the United States the monopoly it sought.

I retraced the evolution of our relationship with the Soviet Union since the first arms deal concluded by President Nasser in 1954, stressing that the October War presented the first challenge to it in twenty years. The Soviets knew that their investment in Egypt was endangered and that the USA might suddenly inherit their primacy. The Soviet Union would undoubtedly be upset and it would try to strengthen its presence and influence in the surrounding Arab countries, hoping to offset the damage. The only countries where the Soviet Union could hope to increase its influence were Syria, Iraq, Southern Yemen, Sudan and later on Libya. The Soviet Union would also try to increase its influence in some African countries, particularly in the Horn of Africa. Therefore any drastic and sudden change in our policy towards the Soviet Union, without prior progress on the long road to peace and without a major US commitment to Egypt, would be a serious mistake. The Soviet leaders would take a long time to digest a major change, but in the long run they would not tolerate their loss in Egypt. Even in the short run, Moscow would react by withholding the military equipment and spare parts which we desperately needed to offset our losses in the October War.

I therefore advised Sadat, to play the game of nations, maintaining a balanced relationship with both superpowers. Egypt could play this game and benefit from it because of its political and strategic position. The main idea was that Egypt should not completely destroy its bridges with either superpower – submission to either the United States or the Soviet Union was not in Egypt's interest.

The Military Situation

The new military situation in the Middle East, I argued, was also favourable to Egypt. The Egyptian–Syrian first strike on 6 October had been well prepared and had taken Israel and the United States by surprise, proving that Egypt and Syria, could put up a good fight and, in the initial stages, do so without help. It is the initial stage, rather than the final military victory, which really counts in the Arab–Israeli wars because the final results do not depend on Israel and the Arab states, but on outside intervention. Neither side can afford to sustain a major conflict on its own for very long and after a few days, outside powers always intervene, with arms and diplomatic efforts. In the October War, the Arabs won the initial stage and this was bound to affect the diplomatic efforts from which a long-term solution would emerge. To be sure, after 14 October Israel had been able to carry out a counteroffensive, but only with a massive airlift of American arms and the introduction of new sophisticated weapons. In this sense, the Israeli victories later in the war were a foreign element and not purely Israeli. Egypt should draw maximum benefit from the excellent show of the Egyptian armed forces during the early days of the war. We should not minimise this at all, but rather capitalise on the political and psychological effects of the Egyptian crossing of the Suez Canal and the successful swift advances of the Syrian army during the first two days. We should not forget that these victories had convinced Golda Meir to accept the American inspired British proposal for a ceasefire in place on 12 October.

The psychological impact of the initial Arab victory in the war had been compounded by the oil embargo, which greatly worried the United States. But, I suggested to Sadat, we should not base our policy on any one of the factors I had discussed. There were linkages among them, and together they provided excellent cards in any negotiations with the Americans or, at a later stage, with the Israelis.

President Sadat seemed to approve everything I had said thus far, and so, taking advantage of this, I put forth an explicit proposal: we should be very strict and rigid in dealing with Kissinger. Kissinger would probably not bring a genuine American compromise proposal, but only Israeli demands disguised as American suggestions. In such a case, we should receive Kissinger cordially and with all the fanfare he relished, but refrain from discussing any substantive political questions with him. Instead, President Sadat should be firm, telling Kissinger to go back to Washington and return in a month after spending more time digesting the situation. He should come back to Egypt only when he was ready to tackle the Middle East crisis in its totality and in a more substantive way. As soon as Kissinger left Aswan empty-handed, President Sadat should go to Syria and to all other Arab countries and come back to Aswan and just wait for Kissinger. The Secretary of State, I assured President Sadat, would return with substantive proposals. In the meantime, President Sadat would have mobilised Arab opinion behind him, and when we resumed negotiations with the USA in a month or so, we would be doing so from a position of strength. President Sadat was happy and so utterly convinced that he insisted that I submit a memo outlining my proposal. I argued this was not necessary, but he insisted: 'No, Ismail. This is a historic day and we need a full strategy and in writing.'

I had no choice but to comply. I returned to my hotel and started to dictate exactly what I had told him to Mohamed Riad, the Under-Secretary of State for Foreign Affairs. Having completed the dictation, I went down to the garden of the hotel to relax a little. I was enjoying the beautiful weather and scenery of Aswan and chatting with the newspapermen when Said Marei, secretary of the Arab Socialist Union and later speaker of the house, came running to me. He had just seen Sadat and was worried because the President was planning to take 'the intransigent position you have suggested to him'. President Sadat was so impressed by my exposé, Marei told me, that he was going to implement it to the letter. I was not as confident as Marei that Sadat would follow that strategy. I knew him to be a very unpredictable person, always impressed by the last person he saw. I told Marei: 'If President Sadat was so impressed, I hope he will abide by fifty per cent of what we have agreed upon.' I was, alas, far too optimistic.

Negotiating the First Disengagement Agreement

As I had expected, Kissinger did not come to Aswan with a genuine American plan, but rather carried Israeli proposals, trying to pass them off as his own. This, I should add, remained true throughout Kissinger's shuttle-diplomacy. He brought us a string of Israeli proposals or at best American ones already accepted by Israel, always presenting them as his own. The Israeli demands presented by Kissinger on 10 January were as follows:– there should not be a mere military agreement confined to the separation of forces, but a contractual agreement with political implications; Egypt should withdraw all its armed forces from the east side of the Suez Canal – this of course would humiliate Egypt and restore the status quo before 6 October 1973; in addition, the area separating the two armies should be demilitarised; in order to discourage the Egyptian side from taking any new military adventures, Sadat should agree to reopen the Suez Canal, start the rehabilitation of the hard-hit area west of the waterway and guarantee the Israelis free passage through the Straits of Bab el-Mandeb.

If Sadat had stuck to his brief and acted as agreed, he would have kept all his strong cards and prevented the Israelis from achieving their goals. Kissinger would have been forced to return a month later with a genuine compromise rather than a proposal tilted toward Israel. At the first Aswan meetings, Sadat's political position was strong: he had the support of the Arab world and internally, Egypt was completely mobilised behind him. World public opinion was for the first time impressed by the military prowess of the Egyptian army crossing the Suez Canal against all odds. Western Europe and the United States were beginning to feel the pinch of the oil embargo, and Israel's image had suffered from its first military defeat. Moreover, a delay in the negotiations would have imposed further strain on Israel. To keep their troops on the west side of the Canal, the Israelis would have had to maintain their military mobilisation, with negative economic repercussions. Egypt could also have surrounded the Israeli forces west of the Canal with strong fortifications and a considerable force of artillery, tanks and armed vehicles, all without firing one single shot. There was no fear that the Israelis might start firing again because the resumption of military operations would be self-defeating.

However in his eagerness to sign with the Americans Sadat put aside his most important cards. This not only damaged Egypt but the entire Arab cause, and weakened Syria's capacity to bargain at a later stage in a more complex situation. It is beyond comprehension that Sadat should have conceded every point after agreeing with my evaluation of the situation. But this he did, yielding to Kissinger who knew a delay was not in Israel's interest. Kissinger also wanted a quick settlement to prevent the Soviet Union from participating and he put pressure on Sadat to get rid of the Soviet presence in Egypt.

Detailed accounts of Kissinger's shuttle-diplomacy between the first meeting in Aswan and the signing of the first disengagement agreement on 16 January 1974 have already been published. Rather than elaborate on what is known, I will discuss here some important incidents in the course of the negotiations. These episodes illustrate how Kissinger and the Israelis tried to put one over on Sadat by inserting, into the disengagement agreement, clauses or expressions of political significance which could have direct bearing on the final Arab–Israeli settlement. The problem was compounded by Sadat's state of mind at this time. He had been very badly affected by the success of the Israeli counteroffensive in the last part of the war, and his early confidence had gone. As a result, he entered the negotiations ready to make concessions. After it became clear that Sadat was not abiding by our agreed strategy, I made sure that at least he did not sign anything with serious political implications, and particularly nothing that departed from the basic Arab position concerning peace with Israel.

The military aspects of the agreement, I may add here, were the exclusive responsibility of President Sadat and General Gamasy who was at that time Chief of Staff. The Minister of War, General Mohamed Ahmad Ismail, was not at Aswan, because Sadat had not wanted him to be present. Sadat himself explained to me that he preferred to put the responsibility on Gamasy, because he was more professional in his attitude and easier to work with; in fact, Sadat was planning to appoint Gamasy Minister of War in the near future.

The Israelis were truly devious in their efforts to extract politically significant agreements from Sadat. One major incident took place during Kissinger's second trip to Aswan. He submitted an innocently-phrased Israeli formula which in reality contained an agreement to end belligerency, the one thing we could not countenance. The document appeared logical enough at first sight and it was carefully drafted, with a very precise choice of words. As usual, Sadat looked at it and gave it his consent. Then he passed it to me, but I realised that in a proposal of barely five lines, the Israelis had managed to use enough different expressions to end belligerency between Egypt and Israel at least five times, without saying so. I drew Sadat's attention to this. He looked at Kissinger sorrowfully and reversed his previous decision to accept that formula, complaining 'Oh, Henry, I thought you were my friend. Fahmy is correct. This ends belligerency five times.' Kissinger was very embarrassed to be caught offering a formula which ran so contrary to Egypt's crucial interests. He also realised that this trick had given us an inkling of his rather insidious and devious style.

He hastened to disassociate himself from the proposal, saying that this was simply a formula the Israelis had given him. To be sure, he had not told us this at the beginning. Kissinger added that the formula had been drafted by Mordechai Gazit, the director general of the Israeli prime minister's office. 'No way,' I replied. 'It was Rosen's draft.' (Meir Rosen was legal advisor in the Israeli Foreign Ministry.) Kissinger repeated that it was Gazit's, but I insisted that he was wrong because no one in Israel could weave such attractive but deceptive phraseology except Rosen. On his next visit to Aswan, Kissinger confirmed that the formula had indeed been drafted by Rosen.

This incident was quite revealing in a number of ways. First, it showed how Sadat was inclined to give his consent automatically without analysing or even reading carefully what he was offered. Secondly, it demonstrated that Kissinger was not the honest broker he always claimed. Thirdly, it reflected the inherently devious Israeli style which sought to extract political gain from any occasion. (However, it also suggested that the Israelis had underestimated Egyptian cunning.) Rabin tells the story in his autobiography, but it is interesting that he does not explain the subject matter of the Israeli proposal.[1] He simply refers to the incident, without admitting Israel's deception in attempting to make Egypt end belligerency unwittingly.

This was not the only incident indicating Kissinger's espousal of Israel's point of view. He always tried to hide his bias by cursing the Israelis and constantly making funny and unflattering remarks about the Israeli leaders, to convince us that he was on our side.

Unfortunately, his rather obvious ruses were fairly effective with Sadat, who tended to take decisions on impulse, without consulting other members of the Egyptian delegation. This combination of Kissinger's manipulations and Sadat's impulsiveness was very damaging for Egypt. One episode illustrates the point: during the final stages of the negotiations for the first disengagement, Kissinger had a separate meeting with Sadat. After the meeting Kissinger and I were riding together in a limousine when he boastfully and triumphantly tapped his chest, saying: 'Ismail, it's here. Nobody can wreck it now.' My reaction was cool: 'There is only one man who can wreck it completely.' Kissinger was taken aback and inquired, 'Who is he?' 'It's me, I can wreck all this with one line announcing my resignation.' He was so upset that he practicallly jumped from his seat in the car, pleading: 'Please, Ismail, please don't.' He then intimated that Sadat attached great importance to that agreement, and wanted the two of us to have a ceremonial meeting with the press, and then return to him. I arranged instead for a formal meeting of the two delegations at the New Cataract Hotel at Aswan. On the American side, Kissinger, Bunker, Eilts, Saunders, Atherton, Quandt and the State Department legal advisor were present. I, General Gamasy, Mohamed Riad, Ahmad Osman, Omar Sirry and others represented the Egyptian side. The reporters and photographers were allowed in for a few minutes to record this so-called ceremonial meeting, but we then settled down to serious negotiations for two hours behind closed doors. Kissinger relayed to the participants the terms of the agreement he had reached with Sadat on military issues. President Sadat had suddenly agreed that the Egyptian military presence on the east side of the Canal would be limited to 7,000 men and 30 tanks. By so doing, he had astonished everybody, including Kissinger and the Israelis. In fact, Kissinger had argued all along that Sadat could not possibly settle for less than 250 tanks.[2]

General Gamasy, who had not been consulted, was very upset, feeling that he and the Egyptian army had been humiliated. His eyes filled with tears, he rose quickly from his seat, retiring to a far corner of the hall and started to weep. Everybody watched General Gamasy uneasily. The Egyptian delegation was affected and emotionally moved, sharing Gamasy's humiliation. From the look on the faces of the American delegation, one could easily see they too were upset by the injustice inflicted upon Egypt. But Kissinger, typically only thinking in personal terms, turned pale and kept on muttering 'What did I say wrong?' When General Gamasy returned to the table, silent and downcast, Kissinger started showering him with extravagant praise. Hoping to rectify the damage he had caused, Kissinger kept saying that the Israeli military fully appreciated General Gamasy's capabilities, and even admitted fearing him above all other Arab generals. General Gamasy, who is a very modest man, listened in silence. The dishonour was not to be expunged by a few words of personal praise. Sadat had single-handedly given away all that the Egyptian army had won with great effort and sacrifice. Without consulting anybody, he had caved in to the Israeli request that the Egyptian military presence east of the Canal be reduced to nothing. The Israelis could then claim that they had almost restored the situation to the position before military operations started on 6 October 1973. According to Kissinger Sadat was apparently quite taken aback by the attitude of his senior officers and was to comment: 'My army! First I had trouble convincing them to go to war. Now I have trouble convincing them to make peace.'

During that same meeting, Kissinger also tried to extract important political concessions, but he failed. The issue, once again, was the end of belligerency between Israel and Egypt. The Israelis were not openly asking for the end of belligerency at this point, and certainly they had not made it a precondition for military disengagement. Instead, they were hoping we would sign papers implying the end of belligerency without fully understanding what we were doing. On this occasion, Kissinger submitted a few proposals typed on yellow paper. I read them and rejected them all, because each dealt with an issue related in one form or another to ending belligerency between Egypt and Israel. These proposals required Egypt to stop voting against Israel in the UN and international organisations, to stop the anti-Israeli campaign in the Egyptian media, to close the Palestinian Broadcasting Station in Cairo, to agree that the Israeli airline be given the same treatment as all other foreign airlines, and to stop its economic boycott of Israel and of foreign companies dealing with Israel. When Kissinger saw that I had rejected all these proposals, he did not defend them, but rather tried to disclaim American responsibility; they were Israeli proposals, he said, and he had only been asked to convey them to us. Kissinger did not tell the Egyptian delegation whether Sadat had seen or approved these proposals. I understood, however, why Kissinger was anxious to have a ceremonial meeting, rather than a working session: he might then claim that these proposals, too, had been accepted by Egypt. Kissinger's efforts to make Egypt declare an end to belligerency continued to the very end. I was checking a final time the American proposals which both Sadat and Golda Meir were supposed to accept and sign, fearing that some change might have been introduced. My suspicion was well founded: going through the neatly typed document, I came across three words added in ink, 'ending of belligerency'. I cross them out. Kissiner, who was watching me closely, shouted 'What are you doing?' 'Deleting three words,' I answered. Kissinger raised his voice, 'But this is the hand-writing of President Sadat.' I told him, 'I am aware of the fact that this is the hand-writing of President Sadat. You can go back to him and tell him that I have deleted what he has added to the typed text.' Members of both delegations were watching tensely. Kissinger was embarrassed and kept silent. I finished checking the document, the meeting came to an end and we went back to President Sadat. I expected that Kissinger would complain about my deleting the words or at least that Sadat would notice that his own words were missing. To my surprise, neither happened. Kissinger apparently knew that it was easy to manipulate Sadat but he also understood that there was no point in insisting once I and the rest of the Egyptian delegation had been alerted. Sadat, for his part, was too oblivious to details to notice that he was being manipulated or that the result of the manipulation had been undone.

In the course of these negotiations, Kissinger did all the talking; he was very strict with his subordinates and did not authorise them to utter a word. This caused problems in the American delegation. From his very first trip to Aswan, Kissinger almost completely ignored the American ambassador to Egypt, Hermann Eilts. In fact, I learned that the ambassador was instructed not to take part in the meetings and was not even fully informed. Eilts was not prepared to accept such behaviour from anybody, not even Henry Kissinger. Eilts' general irritation was obvious and when I asked why he admitted that it was because of Kissinger's attitude. I tried to convince Eilts to avoid a showdown with Kissinger, and even tried to bring about a reconciliation. During a moment of relaxation on a trip to Luxor to visit the Valley of the Kings, I brought up the issue with Kissinger. I suggested that he rely more on Eilt's judgement and give him the respect he deserved as ambassador of the United

States. I insisted that Kissinger should ask Eilts to join us in his private cabin on the presidential aeroplane to discuss the problem. Kissinger agreed and Hermann Eilts was summoned. Kissinger opened by apologising for any misunderstanding. Eilts in turn was very outspoken, asking that a minimum of mutual respect should exist in their dealings.

I was very pleased about the reconciliation, but problems between Kissinger and Eilts continued to arise periodically. During the unsuccessful discussions on the second disengagement in Aswan Kissinger and Eilts had a major showdown. I learned about it from Joe Sisco, who rushed to me breathlessly announcing that Hermann Eilts had submitted his resignation. During an American staff meeting discussing the Egyptian–American relationship and the role of the United States in the negotiations between Israel and Egypt, Eilts had forcefully made his opinion known. Kissinger had commented: 'The American ambassador to Egypt has gone native.' Eilts lost his temper and submitted his resignation on the spot, using harsh language. When I heard the story, I asked Joe Sisco to send Hermann Eilts to meet me. Eilts was still very angry, feeling that Kissinger's words were not only humiliating, but unjustified as well. The truth, Eilts argued, was that Kissinger was leaning too much against Egypt in favour of Israel, and this did not serve the best interests of the United States. I worked hard to pacify Eilts and arranged for a meeting between him and the Secretary of State during which Kissinger apologised and retracted his accusation. Eilts withdrew his resignation.

The first disengagement negotiations led to complications in the relationship between Egypt and Syria. President Hafez Assad wanted a simultaneous disengagement on the Syrian–Israeli front, but he had refused to agree to an exchange of prisoners of war, which the Israeli government considered a precondition for any negotiation. When Kissinger started his first shuttle between Jerusalem and Aswan, Assad and his colleagues started both an open and a covert campaign to discredit Sadat and Egypt. The Syrian media claimed Sadat was getting ready to sign a peace treaty with Israel and to end belligerency, thus betraying the Arab cause. Assad despatched messages containing the same charge to many Arab heads of state and asked them to intervene and stop Sadat from signing an agreement. A veritable procession of Arab foreign ministers started to arrive in Aswan. We clarified the Egyptian position and explained that the Syrians' problem stemmed from their refusal to exchange prisoners of war. But Assad persisted, and at one stage he even despatched a top Syrian official, who was the Prime Minister of the so-called federal government of Egypt, Libya and Syria, to convince Sadat not to finalise an agreement with Kissinger.

When it became clear that the negotiations would end with the signing of a disengagement agreement, Assad changed his tactics and cabled Sadat, authorising him, in his capacity as the High Commander of the Egyptian and Syrian front, to negotiate a similar disengagement on behalf of Syria. However, Assad did not authorise Sadat to negotiate an exchange of Syrian and Egyptian prisoners, or at least an exchange of names. Therefore any effort on the part of Sadat was bound to be a non-starter. On the day the agreement was to be signed, Assad personally telephoned Sadat pleading with him in the strongest terms to postpone the signing for a few days. Relaying the conversation, Sadat told me that he answered that it was too late for a postponement and that Kissinger would be arriving from Jerusalem on the same day to finalise the agreement.

The deterioration of relations between Egypt and Syria had many causes and, while Syria carried most of the blame, some responsibility also rested with Sadat. Assad was under pressure at home to achieve some progress on disengagement in the Golan Heights but also to maintain a militant posture. Caught between these conflicting pressures, he accused Sadat of abandoning the Arab cause to demonstrate that disengagement could only be achieved by selling out to Israel. It is also probable that the Soviet Union also encouraged Assad to take a stand against Sadat. For his part, Sadat did little to improve relations with Syria. When Syria had dropped out of the fighting early in the war, Sadat had delivered a barrage of accusations and counter-accusations and never tried to restore the direct line of communications with Assad which had existed previously.

The Syrians were not sincere about a disengagement at this stage, but they were upset when they realised Sadat was stealing the show. Had they been sincere, they would have compromised on the exchange of prisoners. Furthermore, Assad could have flown to Aswan and either achieved a simultaneous disengagement on the Syrian front or at least stalled the Egyptian initiative. Only a few months later, Assad was to agree to a disengagement on the Golan Heights, following the Egyptian procedure, but by this time

President Nixon and his colleagues insisted on the lifting of the oil embargo as the price for putting pressure on Israel.

The other Arab countries were not directly involved in negotiations at this time. However, in the course of his shuttling Kissinger did visit Jordan and Saudi Arabia. Ostensibly, he was trying to improve American bilateral relationships with these two countries. Less openly, he wanted to establish a personal relationship with King Faisal and to neutralise King Hussein at least for a time, so he would stay out of the picture. Behind the scenes, Kissinger was also seeking to sow jealousy and discord among Arab leaders and in particular between each of them and Sadat. To achieve this, he used to tell stories about Sadat's intentions to his Arab colleagues and he also referred to the Egyptian president as the leader of the Arab world. Kissinger stressed this point above all in his talks with King Faisal, and by doing so he succeeded in earning Faisal's hatred and contempt. In fact, King Faisal sent a very strong message to President Nixon, protesting about the attitude of his Secretary of State. Faisal complained mainly because Kissinger had given him the impression that the United States was shifting its attention from Saudi Arabia, the traditional American friend in the area, to Egypt and Sadat. This was confirmed to me by Nixon personally when I saw him in Washington after the first disengagement. He related this incident adding that he was shocked by Kissinger's methods, which he had never authorised. He then added, 'I was embarrassed and I simply instructed my staff to send a copy of King Faisal's message to my Jew boy.'

Kissinger did not confine his disruptive activities to the Arab world and Egypt. He also wanted to aggravate the tension between the Soviet Union and Sadat, trying to convince Moscow that Egypt had already moved from the Soviet to the American camp. For example, he once suggested to me that it would be in the best interests of our two countries to keep Moscow completely in the dark about the negotiations at Aswan for the Egyptian–Israeli disengagement; the Russians would learn the results through the news media. By then I knew Kissinger well enough to be sure that he had a different plan in mind: Egypt would stop communicating with the Soviets, but Kissinger would continue to inform them. By doing so, Kissinger would kill two birds with one stone. Moscow would be outraged by Egypt's behaviour and conclude that Egypt had shifted completely to the American camp, and Kissinger would appear to Moscow as the only channel through which it could get serious information. Fully aware of Kissinger's intentions, I continued from time to time to put the Soviets in the picture on the progress in the negotiations. I knew I had done the right thing when I arrived in Moscow in January 1974 after the conclusion of the first disengagement. While thanking me for my efforts to keep the Soviets informed, Gromyko added that Kissinger, too, had communicated with them almost daily. I explained to Gromyko what Kissinger had tried to do, adding he was a deceptive man and liked to fish in muddy waters. I added that I had tried to keep our friends in Moscow informed without involving them in unnecessary details. Gromyko accepted my explanation and said that he was fully aware of Kissinger's character. I will add here that in his memoirs Kissinger admitted that he kept the Soviets informed about these negotiations.[4] Needless to say, he did not admit that he had tried to keep me from informing the Soviets.

The disengagement agreement between Israel and Egypt, it should be stressed, was a purely military document, and as such it did not differ in any way from the armistice agreement signed by the same parties in 1948. The military character of the document was reflected in the fact that it was signed by Egypt's and Israel's chiefs of staff in a ceremony at Kilometer 101, witnessed by General Ensio Silasvuo. The agreement provided for the withdrawal of all Israeli forces to a line several miles east of the Suez Canal. Egyptian troops were permitted to remain east of the Canal, but only in a very narrow strip in which the number of men, tanks and artillery pieces would be severely limited. United Nation forces would be deployed between the Israeli and the Egyptian lines.

We had been quite successful in keeping any clause with political implications out of the disengagement agreement. From the military point of view, however, President Sadat had made major and unnecessary concessions. I had not been involved in the military aspect of the negotiations, but the magnitude of the concessions forced me to intervene once, in an effort to change the location of the Egyptian missile sites, bringing them closer to the Canal. My efforts were unsuccessful because Sadat forcefully instructed me not to insist on this point.

The scale of the military concessions in such a disengagement agreement should normally reflect the deployment of the opposing armies. Our concessions would only have been justified if our troops had not been in a position to stand up to Israel. However, in the end the concessions reflected not our military capability but

Sadat's aversion to any further fighting. He was not prepared to reopen the military confrontation with Israel. His repeated statements to the contrary were just pretence. As a consequence he accepted a virtual return to the pre-war situation.

It has been claimed by Henry Kissinger that the signing of the first disengagement agreement was accompanied by an exchange of letters between Sadat and Golda Meir.[5] Apparently in his message Sadat asked Meir to take seriously his statements about peace, and to take advantage of Kissinger's services in pursuing a peace dialogue. To this, claims Kissinger, Meir answered warmly, expressing the conviction that both countries should devote their efforts to achieving permanent peace. Kissinger even presents direct quotations from both letters, but in my opinion it is extremely doubtful whether these letters ever existed. I certainly never saw them or heard any mention of them, either from Sadat personally or from any of those around him. Considering how close I was to Sadat in this period, I cannot believe that I would not have heard of such an exchange.

It is a fact, on the other hand, that there was an exchange of letters between Sadat and Nixon on the one side and Nixon and Golda Meir on the other, clarifying further the modalities of the military disengagement and also containing assurances about other steps which could be taken to consolidate peace. In one of these letters Sadat, prompted by his concern over renewed fighting, agreed with the USA to two additional Israeli demands not contained in the agreement proper: the reopening of the Suez Canal and the reconstruction of the cities and devastated areas west of the Canal. These measures represented added guarantees for the Israelis. If Egypt invested a great deal of money in reopening the Canal and rebuilding the cities, it would hesitate before resuming military operations and incurring new damage. Its international prestige would be adversely affected by a renewed closure of the Canal. It was also better for Israel if Suez and Ismailia went back to normal civilian life rather than remaining armed camps: they would have more warning before a new military operation.

Reopening the Suez Canal

The reopening of the Canal did not take place until 5 June 1975, but I will discuss it here because it provides additional insight into

Sadat's state of mind. It also reflects Sadat's concern for his own personal image and grandeur. Two issues related to the reopening of the Canal are of particular interest in this respect: the choice of the reopening date and the decision to include an American warship in the first ceremonial convoy.

Sadat informed me that he wanted to reopen the Canal formally on 5 June 1975. He wanted to have an impressive ceremony and to lead a big convoy of ships through the waterway in person. I objected that the date was wrong and I urged Sadat instead to postpone the reopening until the second disengagement agreement on the Israeli–Egyptian front had been signed. Attempts to finalise the second disengagement had failed in March 1975, and I thought the reopening of the Canal would be an additional card in our hands to bring pressure on both the Americans and the Israelis when negotiations resumed in September. Sadat appeared receptive to the suggestion, but later he went back to his previous idea, insisting that the reopening of the Suez Canal should take place on 5 June 1975. The date had a symbolic value. On 5 June 1967, under the Nasser régime, the Egyptian army had suffered a devastating defeat as the result of a preemptive Israeli strike, which led to the closing of the Canal. By choosing to reopen the waterway on the anniversary of the defeat, Sadat wanted to demonstrate that he was the hero who had brought Egypt back from the humiliation it suffered under Nasser's leadership. Paradoxically, the idea of choosing that symbolic date was not Sadat's, but that of Mohammed Heikal, the editor-in-chief of *Al-Ahram* under Nasser. Heikal told me himself he had suggested the date. I was surprised and dismayed to hear that the suggestion for a move which would enhance Sadat's prestige at the cost of weakening Egypt's negotiating position had come from a devout Nasserite. When I explained my objection to the date, Heikal said he had not considered that angle. But by then the damage had been done. I made one more effort to convince Sadat to postpone the reopening in the presence of Mamdouh Salem, the Prime Minister. Salem agreed completely with me, but Sadat could not be swayed and ordered us to implement his decision.

About two weeks before the ceremony took place, a new development occurred. One afternoon Sadat called me on the phone, shouting emphatically. 'What's wrong, Mr President?' I inquired. He demanded that I contact the Americans and request them to send two US battleships to take part in the ceremonial convoy which would follow the Egyptian destroyer carrying Sadat. I told Sadat in all frankness that it was a bad idea: the presence of American warships was not only completely unnecessary but could be adversely interpreted in many ways. Sadat was unconvinced and explained his fears: 'No, impossible. Without the American ships, I cannot cross. The Israelis would fire at me.' I laughed and told him that this was not only impossible, but unimaginable. Sadat was very angry and kept repeating, 'No, they will fire at me. You don't know the Israelis, Ismail.' Realising that Sadat was genuinely worried about the Israelis, I tried to minimise the damage: 'O.K. But why two American ships? One is enough. It will serve the same purpose.' Sadat agreed and I called the US ambassador to convey Sadat's wish. Hermann Eilts also started laughing, but naturally sent Sadat's request to Washington. The US government consented and the cruiser *Little Rock*, flagship of the Sixth fleet, took part in the convoy which crossed the Suez Canal on 5 June 1975.

This is the real story behind the appearance of the *Little Rock*; it was not a gesture of recognition for the American Navy's help in clearing the Suez Canal, as some writers argued. The participation of the *Little Rock* did not escape the sharp eyes of the foreign reporters covering the ceremony. While the convoy was going through the Canal, I suddenly found myself surrounded by a large group of correspondents who bombarded me with questions about the presence of the *Little Rock* in a convoy composed solely of commercial ships. I was forced to limit myself to some evasive answers which left everybody unconvinced. The reporters' imagination took off from there.

Notes

1. *The Rabin Memoirs* (Boston: Little, Brown and Company, 1979), p. 259.
2. See Abba Eban, *An Autobiography* (New York: Random House, 1977), p. 561.
3. Quoted in Henry Kissinger, *Years of Upheaval* (Boston: Little Brown and Co., 1982), p. 836.
4. Henry Kissinger, *Years of Upheaval* (Boston: Little, Brown, and Company, 1982), pp. 818, 843–4.
5. *Years of Upheaval*, pp. 836, 844.

5   THE END OF THE OIL EMBARGO AND THE SYRIAN–ISRAELI DISENGAGEMENT

Immediately after the signing of the first disengagement agreement between Israel and Egypt on 18 January 1974, Damascus started an abusive campaign against Egypt. This not unexpected campaign was carried out through the media and through diplomatic channels, and was directed above all at the Arab world. President Assad personally took part in this campaign, but the major role was played by his Foreign Minister, Abd El-Halim Khaddam. Assad and Khaddam accused Egypt of betraying the Arab cause in general and its only partner in the October War in particular. In Egypt, we were following closely the Syrian campaign of defamation and receiving envoys from throughout the Arab world conveying the Syrian viewpoint. I was not very worried, however, because I was sure that the Syrian campaign would not last and that ultimately everybody, including Syria, would realise that the facts did not support the charges.

I limited myself to denouncing the campaign from time to time. At the same time we sent envoys to the heads of many Arab states to explain exactly what happened in Aswan, and to show the weakness of the Syrian position. When the Syrian leadership at last realised that they were engaged in a futile exercise Cairo began to receive signals, directly from Damascus and indirectly from other Arab countries, that it was time for Egypt to try and get a similar first disengagement on the Syrian front. We were prepared to help, but there were two major obstacles: Washington's insistence that the Arab countries lift the oil embargo before the USA intervened again; and the prisoners of war.

The Arab Summit at Algiers

These obstacles had to be removed before Egypt could take steps to influence Washington to put pressure on the Israelis. Assad finally realised this and sent out discreet signals that he would not be opposed to the lifting of the oil embargo. This initiative led to the small Arab summit meeting in Algiers on 13 February 1974.

83

President Boumedienne of Algeria, King Faisal of Saudi Arabia, President Assad of Syria and President Sadat attended. The formal meetings were predominantly ceremonial, while the real discussions took place and agreement was reached behind closed doors. Some of these unofficial meetings were friendly, such as one between Sadat and Assad: there was no heated discussion and the Syrian President was smiling and forthcoming. Others were tense. On one occasion, for example, Faisal openly provoked Assad, asking him very loudly in front of many witnesses whether it was true that the Syrians had accepted the ceasefire on the Golan Heights in 1967 prematurely, allowing Quneitra to fall into Israeli hands without firing a single shot. He also stated that the Syrian commander in Quneitra had received the equivalent of US $300 million from the Israelis for his cooperation. The commander was Assad himself. Fortunately, he did not hear Faisal well because Sadat outshouted Faisal, trying to convince him that it was not the time to bring up this very embarrassing rumour. King Faisal desisted and from then on things went on smoothly.

After many informal meetings, the four heads of state summoned the Saudi Minister of State for Foreign Affairs, Omar Al-Saqqaf, and myself. At the beginning of the meeting, Sadat looked at Assad, pointed at me and said: 'My brother Assad, Fahmy is the only man who can get you a first disengagement on the Syrian front.' Addressing me, he added, 'You go to Washington and bring Kissinger to Damascus to start a shuttle in order to negotiate a disengagement on the Syrian front.' I replied that it was not necessary for me to go personally to Washington, but I could very easily ask Kissinger to go to Damascus through diplomatic channels. 'I understand why Fahmy does not want to go. He has previous engagements with Pompidou and Tito,' explained Sadat, adding: 'Don't worry, Ismail, I will contact them and ask them to postpone your appointments.' Sadat then explained: 'We have agreed that both Saqqaf and Fahmy should go from Algiers to Washington to meet with President Nixon and ask him to instruct Kissinger to come back to the area in order to get a disengagement on the Syrian front. Moreover, you are authorised to inform President Nixon that the Heads of State agreed to lift formally the oil embargo within two weeks.' President Assad had also agreed to give Washington a list containing the names of the Israeli prisoners of war in Syria. Assad added smiling, 'Fahmy, I will send you the original list to be delivered to Nixon and a copy for your personal use.' I must add in this connection that earlier, during the anti-Egyptian campaign carried out by Damascus, President Assad had become so desperate to unblock the situation that he had told Boumedienne that he would give the list of prisoners to the Soviets so they would relay it to Washington. President Boumedienne was appalled and insisted that the list should be passed on to Washington by an Arab intermediary.

This is what happened in Algiers. Contrary to other reports, the formal decision to lift the oil embargo was reached in Algiers during this summit. The Americans had exerted colossal pressure on King Faisal to lift the oil embargo, but he could not give in to the American request without some face-saving excuse. The solution devised was that of establishing a link between the lifting of the oil embargo, the exchange of prisoners and disengagement on the Syrian front. This was the real purpose of the Algiers meeting.

Saqqaf and I immediately left Algiers for Washington. We had to spend the night in Paris on the way, and while there I informed Washington that we would arrive the next day. I asked the American Chargé-d'Affaires in Paris to come to my hotel and requested that he inform Washington that Saqqaf and I were on our way and wanted to confer with President Nixon on behalf of the four Arab Heads of State who had met in Algiers.

Pique at the Quai d'Orsay

I had not planned to meet with French officials in Paris, because I was simply stopping off on my way to a different mission. However, the French press announced Saqqaf's and my presence, with much speculation about the Algiers summit and the nature of our visit. When the French Foreign Minister, Michel Jobert, learned I was in Paris, he decided to interpret my failure to contact him as an insult to himself and France. Jobert's attitude, which almost led to a major diplomatic crisis between Egypt and France, can only be explained by his personality. The French Foreign Minister was a very capable and ambitious man, but he took offence easily and had difficulty in communicating, often appearing cold and arrogant even when he did not mean to do so. On this occasion, Jobert asked his Chef de Cabinet to contact the Egyptian ambassador in Paris and to inquire why I had not seen fit to get in touch with him. The Chef de Cabinet also hinted that unless I requested a meeting there would be serious repercussions on Egyptian–French relations.

I was furious and instructed our ambassador to call back Jobert's Chef de Cabinet and tell him that I was not on an official visit to Paris. However, it would have been in keeping with the French tradition of courtesy for the Foreign Minister to contact me and suggest a meeting. Since the French had not lived up to their tradition, I saw no point in taking the initiative and asking for a meeting. Any negative repercussions on French–Egyptian relations would be the responsibility of the French side. I also told our ambassador to add that, if Jobert asked to see me, I would accept. The Egyptian ambassador carried out my instructions and five minutes later the French Chef de Cabinet called back, extending Jobert's invitation. I went to the Quai d'Orsay but I found that Jobert, while very courteous, was formalistic, non-responsive and in fact unwilling to discuss anything of substance. I tried to initiate a discussion on various topics, but the only answers which I received from him were 'mais oui', 'mais non'. After almost half an hour of this, I realised that I was wasting my time and took my leave. Being annoyed at Jobert, I could not resist teasing him and on my way out I mentioned that I was going to Washington to meet his worst enemy, Henry Kissinger, and sarcastically inquired whether he wanted me to carry any message. As I expected, Jobert exploded, shouting he had nothing whatsoever to tell Kissinger. This episode is quite revealing of Jobert's peculiar temperament. Not surprisingly, shortly thereafter he lost his post at the Quai d'Orsay.

Protocol in Washington

On our way to Washington on 16 February, Saqqaf and I, together with our aides, had to change planes in New York. As we were approaching Dulles Airport, the plane was shaken by a tremendous explosion, which spread panic among the passengers and sent the US Secret Service men, charged with our safety, leaping on top of us to protect us in case this was a terrorist attack. It turned out later that the mishap was due to a short-circuit which had caused a boiler to explode in the galley and a window to break, depressurising the cabin. The plane landed a few minutes later and was surrounded by security officials who held the passengers for hours while they carried out an investigation. Fortunately, Saqqaf and I were immediately whisked away and found Henry Kissinger waiting for us with his son and his assistants.

Normally Kissinger did not wait for or see off foreign ministers, but knowing that he demanded a pompous reception for himself I had warned him before his first trip to Egypt that I was a firm believer in reciprocity. I followed diplomatic convention to the letter: if a foreign minister received me at the airport, I did the same for him; conversely, if I had not been received by the foreign minister personally, I sent the head of the Protocol Department to meet him. Henry Kissinger got the message but was also very disturbed, and argued that he simply could not treat me differently from the other foreign ministers. He added that he never went to the airport even for the foreign ministers of the NATO countries. I just answered: 'It's up to you to decide.' Fearing that I might not accord him the fanfare which he liked to get on his arrival in Egypt, from then on Kissinger waited for me and saw me off in Washington. This treatment was noted by all observers.

Upon our arrival at Dulles Airport, we said a few words to the press and then were escorted to our hotel. Later on, Kissinger called on me to find out the purpose of our sudden visit before our meeting with Nixon. I made it a point not to tell him anything before the formal meeting with the President. Kissinger was also trying to stir up trouble between Egypt and Saudi Arabia. Apologising for being late, he made a point of telling me that he had met with Saqqaf for a few minutes and had intended to go directly from Saqqaf's suite to mine, on the same floor of the hotel. He said he had not told Saqqaf that he was on his way to see me, but Saqqaf was suspicious and wanted to be sure that Henry did not come to me. According to Kissinger, Saqqaf felt that the so-called traditional relationship between the United States and Saudi Arabia required that the Secretary of State see him but not me. Kissinger was very embarrassed when Saqqaf insisted on accompanying him not only to the elevator, but down to his car. Kissinger claimed that he had to drive off and go around the block waiting for Saqqaf to get back upstairs. Only then could he come and see me. I smiled, but to Kissinger's disappointment I did not comment. It was far too obvious that Kissinger wanted to create tension between Saqqaf and me; it was a standard ploy of his.

In his memoirs, Kissinger presented a different version of the incident, apparently forgetting what he had told me.[1] There, he claims that he had come to see me first, and that I was the one who escorted him to the car to make sure he would not go and see Saqqaf. The point at issue is not which Arab Foreign Minister was being petty but the fact that Kissinger chose to interpret Saqqaf's courtesy in escorting him to the car as a demonstration of inter-Arab jealousy, and did not miss the opportunity to tell me about it in an effort to cause some problems.

On the next day I saw Kissinger at the State Department. During that meeting I informed him that President Assad had agreed to send to Washington the original list of the Israeli prisoners of war. Kissinger was very pleased and we agreed that, when the Syrian representative arrived in Washington with the list, Kissinger would receive him and accept the document. The Syrian representative arrived that afternoon and was received by Kissinger at the State Department on the following day. To my astonishment, he rushed to see me immediately after the meeting, informing me that Kissinger had refused to accept the list of prisoners. I was furious because both the Israelis and the Americans had insisted for months that the problem of the prisoners of war had to be solved before negotiations for a disengagement on the Syrian front could begin. After the Syrian envoy left, I called Henry, expressing my surprise and my anger at his behaviour. My surprise was doubled when Kissinger explained that he had refused to receive the list because he could not guarantee that it would not be leaked to the Israelis. I told him: 'But this is impossible. We convinced Assad to send the original list to Washington and now Washington cannot receive it!' Kissinger was very embarrassed, especially when I added, 'Henry, it is beyond belief that the American Secretary of State cannot keep a confidential paper in secrecy.' I insisted that he receive the Syrian representative on the following day and he reluctantly consented.[2]

As I said, I was amazed by Kissinger's behaviour. However, he may have been correct when he said that 'in the State Department, there is no guarantee that a secret will be kept for twenty-four hours'. He was probably right in assuming that the secret would be leaked to the Israelis, because there were many Israeli sympathisers in the State Department and the White House. If the list of prisoners was leaked, Kissinger would lose a major card in his expected negotiations with the Israelis. In the evening, I asked the Syrian representative to meet me and I told him why Kissinger had refused to receive the list of prisoners, adding that after my talk with him the Secretary of State had changed his mind and would accept the list.

To my renewed surprise, the Syrian envoy then told me a fantastic story. After seeing me, he had returned to his hotel and, nervous because of the presence of so many Zionists around him, he had sent the original list and the copy back to Damascus. I was very disappointed. I told him that, if he felt insecure, he could have taken the room next to my suite and that in any case he had made a major mistake when he sent the list back to Damascus. The man was trembling and said: 'Mr Minister, even you refused to receive your own copy.' I did not comment, but insisted that he request Damascus to send him the documents again so that things could move ahead. It is true that I had refused to receive the copy President Assad had sent for me. Once Kissinger had refused to receive the original, I could not accept my copy, fearing that the Syrians would imagine I was in collusion with Kissinger: the Secretary of State, it could be said, had refused to receive the original copy, but I had discreetly passed my copy to him. Kissinger could then show it to the Israelis while feigning innocence. However, I did not explain my reasoning to the Syrian representative.

At any rate, both the original list and copy arrived again from Damascus and the Syrian representative gave it to Kissinger. To complete the story, I should add that later on President Assad personally informed me that his representative had not in fact sent the lists back to Damascus, but had burned them in his bathtub.

President Nixon received Saqqaf and myself in the Oval Room on 19 February 1974. Henry Kissinger was also present. We conveyed to President Nixon the formal message given to us by the four heads of state in Algiers: first, they had decided to lift the oil embargo within two weeks; second, they expected that President Nixon in return would instruct his Secretary of State to establish active contacts with both Syria and Israel with a view to reaching an agreement on the disengagement between their forces in the Golan Heights. Third, in order to assist the Americans in their endeavour, President Assad had agreed to give them the list of the Israeli prisoners of war as a proof of his good faith. President Nixon was very pleased and instructed Kissinger to contact all parties and start action to achieve a disengagement. As usual Kissinger wanted to delay. While expressing his satisfaction, he once again argued that the United States as a superpower could not act under threat or pressure of what he termed 'blackmail'. Therefore, the lifting of the embargo could not be conditional on the resumption of negotiations. I was very angry and I told Nixon: 'I do not believe that it is advisable to interpret the decision of the four heads of state as a threat or blackmail. On the contrary, I believe the decision to lift the oil embargo shows that they were flexible and indeed very generous when they made this offer.' I reminded him that the oil embargo had had serious repercussions for the United States and concluded: 'I hope that the step taken by the Arab heads of state will be appreciated.' President Nixon hastened to make clear his gratitude at the lifting of the embargo.

After the meeting, Nixon accompanied us to the Rose Garden where he insisted that we say a few words to the press. He spoke first, indicating that his meeting with us had been very constructive and that he had instructed the Secretary of State to go to the Middle East in order to help Syria and Israel negotiate the disengagement between their forces. At Nixon's request, I then told the press about our mission and our appreciation for the American role, but without referring to the decision to lift the oil embargo. Then President Nixon accompanied me to my car, an action which I appreciated as an indication of his esteem for the Egyptian role in the Middle East and as a significant signal about the evolution of American–Egyptian bilateral relations.

Lifting the Oil Embargo

While Kissinger resumed his efforts in the Middle East, the oil ministers of the Arab states were scheduled to meet in Tripoli, Libya, to establish the procedure for lifting the embargo. But suddenly on 10 March, President Muammar Qaddafi of Libya reneged on his previous agreement to host the meeting, although the oil ministers had already arrived in Tripoli. After this, Ahmed Hilal, the Egyptian Oil Minister, was instructed to inform his colleagues that Cairo would be pleased to host the meeting. So the Arab Oil Ministers flew to Cairo, but Qaddafi had a second surprise in store: he cabled that, after reconsidering the situation, he would be glad to let the meeting of the Arab Oil Ministers take place in Tripoli on 12 March. The Arab Oil Ministers agreed to go back to Tripoli, but a series of bilateral contacts among the foreign ministers of the participating countries revealed that Qaddafi was still trying to prevent the lifting of the embargo. He had agreed to host the meeting, but he would not allow a decision to lift the embargo to be taken on Libyan soil. In addition, the Libyan Oil Minister threatened that Libya would vehemently denounce any participating country ready to allow oil to flow once again to the United States and Holland. At this point, the Kuwaiti Oil Minister, Abdel Rahman Attiki made it known that he had reliable information that Libya had already violated the embargo, signing a deal to provide the United States with almost 60,000 barrels of Libyan oil daily through Brazil. It was clear that the conference would not reach any constructive decision, but just become an arena for inflammatory rhetoric. The Egyptian Oil Minister contacted me to convey his misgivings. It was then agreed that the conference should have a recess and be moved from Tripoli to a neutral city, where the atmosphere would hopefully be more auspicious to formulating constructive recommendations. The meeting finally took place in Vienna on 18 March. Agreement was reached on the following:

(1) that the oil embargo against the United States should be lifted unconditionally and that the decision would be reviewed when the OPEC conference reconvened on 1 July in Cairo.
(2) that Italy and Federal Republic of Germany would be treated as friendly countries and thus that their needs would be met.
(3) that the embargo on Holland would continue.

After this constructive meeting in Vienna, General Gamasy and I accompanied President Sadat on 18 March on a formal visit to President Tito. We spent two days in Brioni, on a very successful trip which cemented further the existing bilateral relations with Yugoslavia, particularly in the military field. A week later Kissinger went to Moscow, in order to prepare the third Summit Meeting between Chairman Brezhnev and President Nixon. But he also talked with both Brezhnev and Gromyko about the Middle East, and they agreed that the USA and the USSR should coordinate their efforts in order to achieve a first disengagement on the Syrian front. There were also contacts between Cairo and Moscow with a view to bringing joint pressure on the United States to push for a disengagement on the Syrian front.

In the meantime, the Watergate scandal was reaching its climax, and it appeared increasingly doubtful that Nixon would be able to weather the storm. It was only natural that other countries should be concerned. For us in the Arab world, the main question was what effect Watergate would have on the willingness and the capacity of President Nixon and his administration to be involved in further moves to settle the Middle East crisis. During the extraordinary session of the UN General Assembly devoted to the energy problem, virtually all foreign ministers had direct contacts with the Nixon administration in order to assess the likely impact of Watergate. On 11 April, two days after my arrival in New York, I went to Washington to meet with Kissinger. A week later I went back to see President Nixon.

During that meeting, the American President made it clear to me that he would fight to the end. While acknowledging the gravity of the situation, he declared that he would not give in to the pressures to relinquish the presidency. I never saw President Nixon so determined to fight and to overcome the consequences of Watergate, while at the same time carrying on with his policies. In particular, he assured me of his continuing commitment to promote a peaceful solution in the Middle East. I also inquired on this occasion whether President Nixon would proceed with his planned official visit to Egypt irrespective of what was happening internally in the United States. He confirmed that he would come to Egypt as agreed, and added that he also expected that by the time of his visit Kissinger would have succeeded in concluding a disengagement on the Syrian front. He also informed me that Washington had reached an agreement with Moscow to the effect that, when Kissinger started his shuttle diplomacy again, Gromyko would be travelling close to the area, and would meet Kissinger in Geneva and Cyprus. His own visit to Egypt, Nixon specified, should take place toward the end of May, as soon as Kissinger achieved positive results in the disengagement. In fact, Nixon added, he hoped to be able to visit Syria too after coming to Egypt. As soon as I arrived back in Cairo on 20 April, President Sadat despatched Ahmad Ismail, the Minister of War, to Syria in order to inform Assad of what I learned in Washington, including Nixon's wish to visit Syria too.

Negotiating the Syrian Disengagement

By late April, the negotiations over the Syrian–Israeli disengagement were under way in earnest. While Kissinger stole the limelight, Egypt was more quietly but very deeply involved in the process, too. Much progress was made, but there were numerous setbacks as well. One helpful step was a meeting between Gromyko and Kissinger in Geneva, which led to the issuing of a joint communiqué on 29 April. In this document, the United States and the Soviet Union committed themselves to work together for a solution of the Middle East crisis and stated that they both favored the early reconvening of the Geneva Conference. Next day, Kissinger arrived in Egypt with his new bride Nancy and met with Sadat at Maamoura near Alexandria. He wanted to inform President Sadat of the latest developments in Geneva and, by visiting Cairo before any other country, to demonstrate the political importance of Egypt in the eyes of Washington. On 1 May Kissinger arrived in Damascus and started his shuttle between the Syrian capital and Israel. He put a lot of effort and energy into this endeavour, but it took him almost a month to achieve anything, because the Israelis and the Syrians both proved very intransigent. During this month, Kissinger paid visits to Saudi Arabia and Jordan, both to give Syria and Israel time to mend their fences and to put the Saudi and Jordanian monarchs in the picture, and ask them to use their good offices with Damascus.

The setbacks were numerous. First, there was a delay at the beginning of the negotiations, because of the sudden resignation of Golda Meir on 11 April and the formation of a new cabinet headed by Yitzhak Rabin. A much more serious problem arose when three Palestinian guerrillas seized a school in the Israeli town of Ma'alot, demanding the release of 23 Palestinian prisoners. When the Israeli army stormed the school, 16 teenagers were killed and 70 wounded. The fedayeen were also killed. As a reprisal, the Israelis initiated a week-long series of raids in southern Lebanon. Planes and gunboats hit Palestinian camps, killing at least 61 persons. This made Kissinger's job extremely difficult. He encountered almost unsurmountable obstacles which led him periodically to the point of quitting and returning to Washington.

In fact, Kissinger almost gave up at the very end. Very late one night, I received a message through Ambassador Hermann Eilts, in which Kissinger intimated that he was discouraged by the lack of progress and would go back to Washington. When I received this message, I remembered what Kissinger had told me about his experience in negotiating between the Israelis and the Syrians: the two were so alike in their intransigence, reversals of position, arguing on every comma, that when he was in Tel Aviv he thought he was still in Damascus, and vice versa. On other occasions, when he was angry he had used all sorts of uncomplimentary epithets about both the Syrians and Israelis. This did not mean that Kissinger did not have great respect for some of the leaders on both sides. He praised Dayan often and repeatedly told me that Assad was a real statesman, and a leader of great coherence and capacity for lucid arguments. The problem was that neither side was willing to be flexible.

On receiving this message I immediately answered advising Kissinger not to quit. Instead he should go back to Damascus within twenty-four hours and try to speak to President Assad in a more conciliatory way. I even outlined such conciliatory arguments. In the meantime, I told Kissinger, I would despatch the Egyptian chief of staff, General Gamasy, to meet with President Assad and his aides in an attempt to smooth their ruffled feathers and to convince them to sign the disengagement agreement. When I informed President Sadat of Kissinger's message and of my intention to send General Gamasy, he agreed. General Ismail, the Minister of War, was very sceptical of the possibility of success and was not in favour of sending General Gamasy, but he was overruled.

In Damascus, Gamasy met President Assad. After a preliminary exchange of views, Assad summoned his military colleagues and some advisers and Gamasy explained to them with the help of maps the intracacies of the disengagement agreement, arguing that it would serve a useful purpose as a first step to bolster the precarious ceasefire on the Syrian front. Knowing Gamasy, and his professional military background and his honesty, the Syrians listened to his arguments. Noticing the change of mood among his colleagues, Assad suddenly inquired whether they now understood the proposals and were ready to accept them. When the Syrian officers nodded approvingly, Assad adjourned the meeting and authorised Gamasy to report that Syria was ready to accept the agreement. Gamasy came back and told me of his success. I informed President Sadat and sent a message to Kissinger telling him that he could now safely proceed to Damascus because the way was finally paved for the conclusion of the disengagement agreement on the Golan Heights. Kissinger was very appreciative of our efforts and proceeded to Syria. The disengagement agreement on the Syrian front was concluded on 31 May 1974; Israel and Syria accepted a separation of forces, the creation of a UN-policed buffer zone between them and a gradual thinning out of forces.[3]

On 6 June, Israel returned 382 Syrian prisoners of war and Syria sent back 56 Israeli prisoners. Once this was accomplished, the way seemed clear for the formal ratification of the agreement in Geneva, but further difficulties arose. To my surprise, I received information from Kissinger that Assad and his colleagues insisted that Egypt should sign the agreement on behalf of Syria. For political reasons President Assad did not want to affix his signature and fully commit Syria. Instead, he wanted Egypt to sign under the pretext that Syria and Egypt had formed a unified military command under Egyptian leadership. As long as this unified military command was in existence, argued the Syrians, it was natural that the Egyptian military representative in Geneva should sign on behalf of Syria. I knew the Syrians well enough to understand their manoeuvre – in fact, I had expected it. They wanted to be able to claim later that it was Egypt which negotiated and later signed the agreement with Israel, and that Syria was not bound by it. I therefore rejected the Syrian request. In fact, I instructed the members of the Egyptian delegation to the military subcommittee in Geneva to absent themselves from the final negotiations and the signing ceremony. The Syrians and the Israelis finally came face to face in Geneva, in a meeting chaired by General Siilasvuo as representative of the UN and attended by one representative each from the USA and USSR, the co-chairmen of the conference. The final touches did not take a long time and the disengagement agreement between Syria and Israel was finally signed.

As expected, the Syrian propaganda machine immediately went into high gear, glorifying the Syrian policy and President Assad's leadership of the Arab world. The Syrians boasted about the 'major differences' between the Egyptian and Syrian disengagements agreements, and repeated this slogan often enough that they probably convinced themselves that there were fundamental differences. For example, Damascus claimed that one major difference was that Egypt accepted that the United Nations troops remain in the buffer zone between the Israeli and Egyptian armies, while in Syria they had only accepted the presence of UN observers. It is certainly true tht during the negotiations the Syrians had rejected the presence of the UN forces and this had threatened to halt the negotiations because Israel had insisted that UN forces be stationed in the buffer zone. When Kissinger cabled me that he had reached a deadlock on this problem, I advised him to suggest to the Syrians that the buffer zone be policed by UN observers, but that their numbers be increased greatly. The Syrians were glad to accept this face-saving device and the Israelis went along with the proposal. This little episode illustrates how the Syrians distort for propaganda purposes and how they waste everybody's time to maintain a facade of militancy. Despite Syria's rhetoric, after the signing of the Syrian–Israeli disengagement agreement the political ties between Damascus and Cairo were restored. The usual huggings of brotherhood were exchanged once again whenever the two heads of state or their ministers met.

Official Recognition for the PLO

In the months following the October War, and while the disengagement agreements were being negotiated, the first steps were also being taken to reach a 'disengagement' between Israel and Jordan. 'Disengagement' was of course a misnomer, because there had been no fighting between Israel and Jordan during the October War. In fact, Jordan's refusal to become involved had exposed Syria to an enormous amount of Israeli pressure. The issue of disengagement on the Jordanian front was thus not a military but a deeply political one. What was at stake was not a consolidation of the ceasefire and an effort to decrease the likelihood of a renewal of hostilities, but the final political solution of the Middle East crisis. It was Jordan's and America's intention to bury the political issues under the guise of disengagement. It was the intention of most Arab countries, and Egypt in particular, to make sure that this did not happen.

Any settlement between Israel and Jordan touched directly on the rights of the Palestinians and the role of the PLO. The position of King Hussein at this juncture was very clear: there was no separate Palestinian entity but only the United Hashemite Kingdom. He, therefore, spoke for the Palestinians. The King had even gone to the extent of issuing legislation to implement this notion declaring the existence of the United Hashemite Kingdom and extending Jordanian laws and citizenship to the Palestinians on the West Bank.

After the October War, King Hussein's authority to speak for the Palestinians was being questioned. His own prestige had reached its lowest ebb, because he had sat on the sidelines while Egypt and Syria fought. Conversely, the PLO was beginning to gain political recognition and widespread acceptance. A confrontation started taking shape in December 1973 when King Hussein agreed to participate in the Geneva Conference despite the fact that the Palestinians were not represented. The fact that he had included some individual Palestinians in the Jordanian delegation satisfied nobody except the King himself and Henry Kissinger who was determined to liquidate the Palestinian problem through its 'jordanisation'.

After the first brief meeting of the Geneva Conference King Hussein and Prime Minister and Foreign Minister Zaid Al-Rifai worked hard to push Kissinger to negotiate an Israeli–Jordanian 'disengagement'. Kissinger was all too willing. But it was clear to me that the Arabs should prevent this attempt to sweep the Palestinian issue under the carpet. In order to do this, we should establish two clear rules to guide our dealings with Jordan. The first was that we should not recognise the legality of any step the King took on his own initiative or with US support. The second was that we should maintain very close contacts with King Hussein in order to understand his plans. Our goal was to implement a general strategy in four stages. In stage one we should put an end to the Jordanians' claim that they spoke for the Palestinians. In stage two we should give official recognition to the legitimacy of the PLO and its political role. In stage three we should prepare a framework for the recognition of the Palestinian rights to statehood. In stage four we should help negotiate and formalise the relationship between the Jordanian and Palestinian state, if they so desired.

As part of the process of implementing stage one, I had made a point of avoiding all official contacts with the Jordanian delegation at Geneva but I left the channels of communication open. When a member of the Jordanian delegation, my friend Abdel Moneim Al Farah, called me, urging me to meet with Zaid Al-Rifai, their chairman, I refused an official meeting but added that if Rifai had anything to discuss he could come and see me informally. Later, when I was in New York in April for the extraordinary meeting of the UN General Assembly and shuttling back and forth to Washington, I made a point of leaving the capital during King Hussein's visit. Apparently, both the King and Rifai got the message. The Jordanian Prime Minister called me to express his and the King's astonishment that I had deliberately left Washington before their arrival. I justified my absence by saying that I had a previous engagement with Kurt Waldheim, an excuse nobody believed.

However the most important step I took to implement stage one of our general strategy, was to warn Kissinger that Egypt would veto any disengagement agreement between Israel and Jordan. I also made it clear that any move on the Jordanian front made without the agreement of legitimate Palestinian representatives would adversely affect Egyptian–American relations. I was later informed that when Kissinger was once pressed by the Jordanians to achieve a disengagement on their front, he answered that he could not do so because of 'Fahmy's veto'. For a period of time subsequent to these events, the Jordanians, particularly Zaid Al-Rifai, were very suspicious of me. Here I should make it clear that I had and still have very high regard for the King of Jordan, his brother Prince Hassan and his army, and the passing of time has helped once again to restore my friendly relations with Zaid Al-Rifai. I remain however resolutely opposed to the 'Jordanian option' as a solution to the Palestinian issue. The Palestinians must exercise their right to self-determination, both inside and outside the occupied territories, thus deciding their own future. Then they can make their own choice on what kind of linkage, if any, should exist between the Palestinian state and Jordan.

Stage two of the strategy required the enhancement of the political stature of the PLO and its recognition as the representative of the Palestinian people. Again I devoted much effort to achieving this goal. The crowning success came at a historical meeting of the Arab Heads of State in Rabat on 28 October 1974. The summit was preceded by a meeting of the Council of the Arab Foreign Ministers during which Rifai, as head of the Jordanian delegation, left no stone unturned to prevent recognition of the PLO. He resorted to pleading and threats, attacks and counterattacks. I have to admit that he was very effective in his lobbying, concentrating on Egypt's role and arguing that it was the Egyptians and particularly myself who were pushing the Palestinians and the PLO towards rigidity. I did not react, although I was fully aware of the Jordanian accusations and those of some Arab representatives who have the habit of saying one thing in public and another in private. I never indulged in this double talk. Egypt's position was clear: the PLO, and not Jordan, spoke for the Palestinians.

At one point, Al-Rifai formally proposed that the Arab Foreign Ministers leave all decisions to the Arab summit. There was complete silence in the meeting. After repeated calls, the chairman was on the verge of adjourning the meeting to enable the participants to attend a formal dinner being given by the Moroccan Prime Minister on that night. At that particular moment, I decided to intervene as I wanted to make it clear that Egypt was at the forefront of the Arab struggle and that, once Egypt took a decision, others had no choice but to follow. I asked for the floor. Looking at the faces of my colleagues, specially that of Zaid Al-Rifai, I felt that all of them expected a major statement. I did not disappoint them: 'Egypt fully co-sponsors and supports the PLO request that it be recognised by the Arab countries as the sole legitimate representative of the Palestinian people. Consequently, no other country is entitled to speak for or represent the Palestinian people.' The Palestinian representatives present at the table enthusiastically applauded. On the Jordanian side, there was complete silence and Rifai was so pale he looked frozen. Nobody knew how to reply and the chairman's invitation for comments was met again with complete silence. All delegations needed time to reformulate their own position. The meeting was adjourned and Egypt's call for the recognition of the PLO as the sole representative of the Palestinian people was carried widely by the news media.

The PLO representatives decided to forgo the Moroccan dinner and instead held a major press conference praising the Egyptian position and explaining its implications. At the same time, they vehemently criticised the other Arab countries. After the press conference, the Palestinian representatives divided themselves into several groups in order to contact all Arab Foreign Ministers after the dinner, pressing them to support the Egyptian position.

As soon as the meeting resumed the next day, the Arab Foreign Ministers started to compete with each other to show their country's support for the Egyptian proposal. The motion was adopted almost unanimously, the only opposing vote being that of Jordan, whose Prime Minister wanted to be on record as reserving his country's position on this major new political development. He added that his monarch would make a major speech on this and other problems at the opening of the Arab summit meeting. Despite his efforts, Zaid Al-Rifai had been totally defeated.

When the Arab summit was convened, King Hussein of Jordan immediately asked for the floor. He spoke for two hours, retracing the role of his family since his grandfather took the reins of Jordan, and pleading very strongly and impressively that this role be preserved. However, when he finished, there was a long silence, finally broken by President Boumedienne of Algeria. With his usual candour, he simply announced: 'Algeria does not recognise anybody to speak for the Palestinians except the PLO.' The next speaker was King Faisal of Saudi Arabia, who expressed total support for Boumedienne's stand. In the end, agreement was unanimous. Yasser Arafat then made a very moving speech. In the light of all this, King Hussein of Jordan had no choice but to intervene once again and declare that Jordan would accept the unanimous decision of the Arab summit. He assured his brothers that his régime would cooperate fully to implement this decision, adding that he would take the necessary legislative measures to erase the laws extending Jordanian citizenship to the Palestinian residents of the West Bank. Hussein was sincere and kept his word. When the meeting adjourned, the King of Jordan and Yasser Arafat hugged each other. It was a real and unprecedented victory for the Palestinians.

There is no better proof of Egypt's position on the Palestinian issue and of the closeness of its relations with the PLO than the role it played in gaining recognition for the PLO at Rabat. Neither was this an isolated incident. All through the meetings of the Arab Foreign Ministers, in the period we are discussing, cooperation between the Egyptian delegation and the PLO remained extremely close. Egypt repeatedly helped the PLO but it never interfered in its internal affairs. I recall with particular fondness my contacts with two PLO personalities, Farouk Kaddoumi, the organisation's 'foreign minister', and Said Kamal, its representative in Cairo.

In light of the role Egypt played on behalf of the PLO in this period, Kissinger's allegations that ever since my first meeting with him in Washington Egypt had decided to concentrate on solving its own problems and that 'it would not let the Palestinians stand in the way of a solution' is simply ludicrous.[4] It can only be dismissed as part of Kissinger's constant attempts to divide the Arab countries. He did so when he acted as 'mediator' in the Middle East crisis. He continues to do so in his memoirs.

The new position of the PLO, first recognised at Rabat and reconfirmed internationally in a number of occasions in the following year, introduced a crucially important element in the efforts to solve the Middle East conflict. Once it was clearly recognised that the Palestinians were an entity in their own right, and not part of Jordan, it became inconceivable that the Middle East conflict could be solved through bilateral negotiations between Israel and each Arab country, because such a procedure would have excluded the main party to the conflict. Kissinger's step-by-step diplomacy had played a useful if limited role in strengthening the ceasefire and bringing about a disengagement, but it could never solve the entire conflict, no matter for how long the process was continued. A final settlement could only come from comprehensive negotiations by all parties, including the PLO. We had to think beyond disengagement and reconvene the Geneva Conference, where such comprehensive negotiations would take place. This became Egypt's primary goal; while it took a long time before a serious effort in that direction could be made, and we negotiated a second disengagement with Israel in the meantime, we never lost sight of that goal.

Notes

1. *Years of Upheaval*, pp. 949–50.
2. Once again, Kissinger's account of this episode bears little relation to reality. See *Years of Upheaval*, pp. 950–1.
3. Kissinger in his memoirs greatly plays down the importance of the role played by Gamasy in bringing the negotiations to a successful conclusion. Needless to say, he does not acknowledge that he asked for Egypt's help because he had reached a stalemate. See *Years of Upheaval*, pp. 1075–6.
4. *Years of Upheaval*, p. 618.

6 NEW FRONTIERS FOR EGYPTIAN FOREIGN POLICY

In the year after the October War, significant change took place and much progress was made by Egypt. On the ground, we had at least succeeded in stabilising the ceasefire on both the Egyptian and the Syrian fronts. To be sure, this was still only a ceasefire and we remained a country at war. The issue of peace still had to be tackled, and it was bound to be a difficult one, because we were determined not to accept a separate treaty with Israel but to work for a comprehensive settlement in the entire area. However, we had also made significant progress in putting Egyptian foreign policy on a new track.

Sadat had appointed me Foreign Minister because, I believe, he appreciated my suggestions and my frankness. Thereafter, he gave me virtual carte blanche in deciding on a course of action. He understood and agreed with the basic principles on which that policy was based and never questioned any of my basic ideas. However, he was not a steadfast person, capable of staying on course at all times, but was easily swayed by other opinions and advice. At times I refused to follow his instructions and usually he accepted my point of view. More rarely he acted on his own initiative, taking decisions which I considered to be very ill-advised. However, until he decided to go to Jerusalem, I was able to maintain Egypt's foreign policy on a strategically correct course. At that point, I saw no hope of salvaging anything and I had no choice but to resign.

The Fundamentals of Egyptian Foreign Policy

The principles which guided Egypt's foreign policy were simple and clear cut. Although I have touched upon some of them previously, particularly when discussing the 1972 *Al-Ahram* symposium, I will explain them here again in more detail. The fundamental principle was that Egypt should maintain its complete independence and avoid excessive reliance on any one country. For twenty years, Egypt had been parked in the Soviet garage. We had become totally dependent on the Soviets for arms, we had allowed them to train our troops and develop our industry, we had even permitted them, for a time, to speak to Washington for us. This was wrong, not because the Soviet Union was the Soviet Union, but because it was a foreign country and a superpower. By definition their interests would never coincide completely with ours, and we should not sacrifice our own interests to theirs. In practice, maintaining our independence meant developing strong relations with the United States, but also avoiding a complete shift from one superpower to the other. There was no point in getting out of the Soviet garage just to park in the American one. Apart from the wider issues of superpower dominance, US foreign policy was susceptible to Israeli and Jewish influence.

A corollary of this fundamental principle was that Egypt should not sign treaties with any superpower. The Treaty of Friendship and Cooperation with the Soviet Union was signed before my appointment as Foreign Minister, and I had no say in that decision, but I believed that Egypt should remain non-aligned and therefore not enter into a contractual agreement with either superpower. Such formal relations only increase the dependence of the smaller country on the superpower, legalising it and making it semi-permanent. A contractual relation between non-equals gives the stronger party a special position, and the smaller country is curtailed in its decision-making. Additionally, such treaties inevitably give the superpower the right to interfere in the internal affairs of the smaller country without giving that country much leverage on the superpower. The superpower remains de facto free to respect or violate its obligations at will. To illustrate this point, Article 6 of the Treaty of Friendship and Cooperation required the Soviet Union to strengthen Egypt's defence capability. The Soviet Union never respected this clause, because it did not give us the military equipment we needed and asked for, but only what it felt like sending, and with much quibbling and procrastination at that. There was very little Egypt could do to force the Soviet Union to honour its obligations.

A second principle guiding Egypt's foreign policy was that Egypt should not pursue this new policy toward the great powers from an isolated position, but from the safety and shelter of the Arab compound. All our actions had to be in accord with the basic principles agreed by the Arab countries; we had to secure their support and guide them in a new direction. Egypt I thought, must assume a position of leadership in the Arab world. This was not just a narrow chauvinistic position on my part, but one dictated by the reality of the Middle East. By any objective standard, Egypt is the most powerful country in the Middle East. It has the population base, the educated manpower, and the army. True, by the 1970s the oil-producing countries of the Gulf, and Saudi Arabia in particular, had the wealth Egypt lacked, but that was not enough in the absence of any other asset. Furthermore, Egypt was the country with greatest responsibility for maintaining the unity of the Arab world *vis-à-vis* Israel. The reason was simple: we were the ones who could most easily destroy this unity by concluding a separate peace with Israel, because the problem of Sinai was not serious compared to that of the Golan Heights, the West Bank and Jerusalem. The Israelis, too, were convinced that Egypt was the most important country in the Middle East and the key to Arab unity, and they demonstrated this through their unceasing efforts to isolate us from the rest of the Arab world.

Only if we maintained unity and cohesion in the Arab world could we hope to achieve a truly non-aligned and neutral stance towards the great powers or any other foreign country. It would not be possible for Egypt to do that alone, if the neighbouring countries were open to foreign intervention or manipulation. We had to create a cohesive Arab military alliance based on Egypt east up to the Gulf, south deep into the Sudan, west into Libya and perhaps further. For this reason, we needed close military cooperation with our neighbours, and we had to play the leading role in these relationships.

Again, this was not a dream of Egyptian domination over the rest of the Arab world. Rather, it was a realistic conclusion based on the fact that only Egypt has, and will have for decades to come, the resources of educated manpower needed to build a strong army. The oil-rich countries can buy weapons easily, indeed much more easily than we can, but they will need a long time to train the personnel to man them. And there is no doubt that the Arab world needs military strength not only to resist Israeli expansionism but also to establish its independence from the great powers. In the long run, this will be in the interest of the great powers themselves, because a politically united and militarily strong Middle East will become an area of stability, rather than an arena for superpower confrontation threatening world peace.

A third principle of Egypt's foreign policy, was that Egypt had to pay more attention to its relations with all major countries. This again meant decreasing our reliance on one or other superpower, finding additional sources of military equipment, and possibly bringing into the solution of the Middle East conflict additional voices which would not always speak in unison with Israel.

I summarised these major principles guiding our foreign policy in a speech to the People's Assembly on 11 January 1977. The two crucial issues I covered were Arab unity and Egypt's relations with the great powers. Some excerpts from that speech will illustrate the purpose of Egypt's foreign policy until Sadat's sudden decision to go to Jerusalem. Concerning Arab unity, I stressed that it was 'the normal evolution of our history'. Arab unity, furthermore, was 'unity of the people and not unity of the régimes or ruling establishments. In other words, it cannot be imposed from above.' But I also made it clear that such unity could not be achieved overnight:

> The process of unity is a dynamic and long movement which needs frequent experiments with a view to give each people enough time and experience before they reach the desired goal. In order for unity to be successful, the prevailing socio-economic conditions should be taken into consideration, in addition to the philosophical trends existing in both countries. This is a must, otherwise any movement toward unity will be futile because it would start from a vacuum.

Concerning Egypt's relations with the United States and the Soviet Union, I reminded the People's Assembly that they 'constitute a special part of our foreign policy, because the superpowers have special weight in our daily lives. Moreover, they command extraordinary potentialities to influence the evolution of events.' Our relations with Moscow and Washington should not be affected by past experience, but look to the future. We should expand our cooperation in all fields, while accepting that there would always be points of disagreement as well as of agreement.

Egypt's relations with the United States were getting strong:

> It is noticeable that our bilateral relations grow daily in a positive way within the necessary limits, so that the growth of this relationship will not adversely affect our capacity to act freely in the best possible way. The US has already offered major

financial help in order to bolster the Egyptian economy. American aid to Egypt reached US $1 billion in 1976. It exceeds the amount the United States gives to any other country except Israel.

Despite these close relations with the United States, Egypt had not lost its freedom of action, and certainly it did not agree entirely with Washington's policies. In particular, Egypt did not concur with the American policy of blindly supporting Israel. Israeli intransigence made such support unjustified and could only undermine the America's position in the Arab world.

Our relations with the Soviet Union were not as good at this time. Nevertheless:

> We are ready to circumvent past and present obstacles which hindered a healthy evolution of Soviet–Egyptian relations. We cannot forget the positive achievements resulting from Soviet–Egyptian relations during the past twenty years, and we are ready to forget the negative aspects.

In this respect, I reminded the members of the People's Assembly that President Sadat had declared a short time earlier that he was ready to meet with Brezhnev to iron out all differences and solve all problems in Soviet–Egyptian relations.

I was well aware that implementing a foreign policy based on these principles would not be easy. Maintaining balanced relations with both superpowers would please neither of them, and Egypt's central role in the Arab world could easily raise fears of Egyptian domination among our neighbours. While there was bound to be opposition to our new policy, I decided from the beginning, we could at least minimise it if we established a high degree of credibility at home and abroad, so that there would be no doubts about our goals. At home, I made a point of establishing a dialogue with the People's Assembly and the press, and I was very proud that both institutions came to trust me. So much so that the People's Assembly, in its annual review of government policy, chose to identify me personally in expressing its support for the policies my colleagues and I were pursuing. I may say that this was not normally the style of the People's Assembly's appreciation of ministers. However, I made an effort to establish credibility with the Assembly and they responded.

The Importance of Political Credibility

In essence, credibility is the passe-partout of a politician. Political leaders cannot make public statements which run completely at variance with their real position, nor make promises which they cannot possibly fulfill and at the same time maintain credibility. In the end a credible politician is an effective politician because he is in a unique position to receive solid information from his colleagues all over the world, who trust him.

An episode involving Bruno Kreisky, the Austrian Chancellor, illustrates this point. A few days before the October War I was asked by President Sadat to go and meet Kreisky in Vienna. The Chancellor was at that time deeply entangled in the Schönau incident. Schönau was a camp for Jewish emigrants from the Soviet Union in Austria, and Israel had started playing too dominant a role there, trying to run the camp and exert pressure on the refugees to migrate to Israel rather than to other countries of their choice. In fact, the Israeli attempts to take over the camp threatened Austrian sovereignty and Kreisky decided to close down Schönau. He was immediately accused by Israel, Golda Meir personally, and Zionist organisations everywhere, of having given in to Arab and Palestinian threats. The purpose of my visit was to show Kreisky our support, in an attempt to counterbalance the pro-Israeli pressures on him.

Kreisky, himself a Jew, was deeply hurt and very angry at the campaign mounted against him by Israel with the cooperation of the United States. Trying to encourage him, I told him in passing that he should not worry too much, because the Schönau incident would make big headlines for one or two days, but would quickly be forgotten as other events captured the limelight. The situation in the Middle East was very tense, I added, and soon world attention would be focused there.

This conversation took place on 5 October, the day before the crossing of the Suez Canal by Egyptian troops. In fact, I had problems returning to Egypt after my visit. In Rome, I missed my connecting flight to Cairo because of a strike, and on the following day all flights to Cairo were cancelled, forcing me to fly to Libya and drive for sixteen exhausting hours before I reached Cairo. At any rate, Kreisky took my words seriously. Immediately after I left he went on a speaking tour to support his candidates in the forthcoming elections, and in his speeches he underlined the imminent danger of a blow-up in the Middle East. When his colleagues tried to minimise the possibility, dismissing what I had told him as standard diplomatic talk, Chancellor Kreisky said: 'No, Fahmy is a very serious man. He does not say such things without having something in mind.' On 6 October, when the news spread all over the world about the Egyptian preemptive strike, Kreisky pointed out to his colleagues that he had been right in taking my words seriously.

A few years later, in one of the Socialist International meetings, Kreisky relayed the same story in the presence of Golda Meir. Meir became furious and accused him of being a traitor. As a Jew, she argued, Kreisky should have relayed my words to the Israeli leaders, enabling them to take precautionary measures immediately. This episode strikes me as a perfect example of the importance of political credibility. To Kreisky, my credibility meant that he could take my words seriously, and thus have advance warning that something momentous was about to happen in the Middle East. To me, his credibility meant that I could suggest to him that big events were about to take place, with absolute confidence that he would not use the information to harm Egypt.

I will not attempt to give a detailed account of all the steps I undertook, with or without Sadat's explicit approval, to implement Egypt's new foreign policy in my four years as Foreign Minister. I will only single out here a few of the most significant exchanges concerning Egypt's policy in the Arab world and our efforts to secure closer relations with some European, Asian and African countries. I will discuss in much greater detail in separate chapters our relations with the superpowers.

Egyptian Relations with the Arab World

With regard to the Arab world we reached a stage where we could discuss problems candidly with our brothers at every level. President Sadat and I visited every Arab country many times, and wherever we went we found open hearts and complete recognition of Egypt's contribution to the Arab cause.

This recognition stemmed above all from the October War. In this respect, it should be mentioned that while Egypt had made the greatest contribution, a number of Arab countries had done their best to support Egypt. The oil-producing countries made a significant contribution by imposing an oil embargo. The role of King Faisal of Saudi Arabia and Sheikh Zayed of the United Arab Emirates can only be remembered with gratitude by Egypt. President Boumedienne of Algeria personally went to Moscow and offered the Soviet Union US $200 million in cash in an effort to convince them to send Egypt and Syria the military assistance they needed. His generosity was all the more remarkable because he had had to borrow that money. Many other countries also helped by sending troops to the front.

Our policy in the Middle East, as I have already stated, had two main goals: to build a network of alliances and thus a safety belt around Egypt, and to maintain Arab unity, both to safeguard our true independence and to force Israel to negotiate a permanent and comprehensive settlement to the Middle East conflict. Arab unity also had to involve people as well as governments, in particular, the Palestinians, in order to help them achieve self-determination and statehood.

The task of creating a safety-net around Egypt was bound to be long-term but we were able to achieve encouraging steps with the Sudan, Syria and Libya. This was particularly true about our relations with the Sudan, a country to which we are closely connected by our joint economic dependence on the Nile and by historical links of long standing. Despite traditional Sudanese fears of Egyptian domination during this period, President Numeri came to realise that the stability of his régime depended on Egypt.

In February 1974 we signed an agreement on economic and cultural cooperation, but we did not push Numeri any further, sensing that he was not ready for it. Later, however, several episodes convinced the Sudanese President that he needed Egypt's help. First, he felt threatened by Palestinian groups, due to a crisis arising from the killing of two American diplomats. In March 1973, American Ambassador Cleo Noel and his deputy George Moore were killed in Khartoum; the two men who were apprehended were suspected of ties with a Palestinian organisation. Under American pressure, Numeri was forced to bring the culprits to trial. In June 1974 just before the trial ended Numeri telephoned me, saying that the verdict would be passed the next day, that the accused would be declared guilty and that he feared further terrorist attacks when this became public. Knowing how precarious the political situation was in the Sudan, I told Numeri that we would send a military plane to take the two men off his hands, as long as they were not sentenced to death. He agreed and we took the men to Cairo.

In the following months, there was another attempted coup in the Sudan and more plots were uncovered. By July 1975, Numeri was beginning to consider the possibility of signing a mutual defence treaty with Egypt to improve his position. He told Sadat that he was ready to sign one immediately when we stopped in Khartoum on our way to Kampala for a summmit conference of the Organisation of African Unity. By the next morning, however, Numeri had changed his mind and did not even mention the issue. For our part, we did not try to press him.

Supporting Numeri in the Sudan

The decisive factor leading to the signing of the mutual defence treaty between Egypt and the Sudan was a very serious coup attempt in July 1976. Numeri, returning from a trip abroad ahead of schedule, managed to escape assassination, but fierce fighting broke out and was only put down with the help of Egyptian troops which we quickly airlifted to the Sudan. As soon as the situation had calmed down, Numeri flew to Alexandria. I knew the time was ripe for the signing of a defence agreement, but was also aware that Numeri, ever fearful of Egyptian domination, would prefer to bring in a third party. For this reason, I had in my briefcase two draft treaties, one for a trilateral agreement among Egypt, Saudi Arabia and the Sudan, and one for a bilateral treaty between Egypt and the Sudan. I knew full well that the Saudis would never sign such a trilateral agreement. Having ambitions themselves to play a central role in the Arab world, they regarded Egypt as a dangerous rival, 'too big, too powerful and too pushy' in the words of a political analyst.[1] Even if the Saudis had agreed to sign, the United States would never have allowed them to do so, fearful that such a close alliance of Egyptian power and Saudi wealth would greatly diminish its own role in the Middle East. Thus, I never thought the tripartite agreement would be signed, but I needed to show Numeri that it was impossible to bring in a third party so that he would agree to sign a bilateral treaty.

On 16 July we flew to Riyadh and submitted the trilateral agreement to the Saudis. They immediately called together a family gathering to discuss the issue and, as expected, came back with the answer that they would not sign. Furthermore, they put a lot of pressure on Numeri not to enter into an agreement with Egypt either. This was what we needed. Numeri, angered at the Saudis' attempt to tell him what to do, asked for an urgent meeting with us. We let him complain at length about the Saudis' behaviour, and when he had finished I took the draft of the bilateral defence agreement from my briefcase. He was happy with it and signed it immediately, in Riyadh. The document itself, however, was dated Alexandria, 15 July 1976. The agreement, valid for twenty-five years, became the basis for very close and significant cooperation between Egypt and the Sudan, continuing unaltered to this day. Our southern flank was secured.

Reestablishing Good Relations with Syria

The efforts to secure our eastern and western flanks were not as successful, but we made significant progress. As we will see later, by late 1977 we managed at least to reestablish diplomatic relations with Libya. As for Syria, we had many ups and downs, but by the end of 1976 our relations were on an even keel again. Our problems with the Syrians stemmed above all from their fear that Egypt would sign a separate peace with Israel, obtaining the return of Sinai and leaving Syria helpless to secure the return of the Golan Heights. Thus, every Egyptian initiative was initially interpreted by the Syrians as a sign that Egypt was making peace with Israel, and they regularly overreacted. I have already described the Syrian campaign against Egypt after the signing of the first disengagement agreement with Israel. They started another campaign, equally derogatory, when we signed a second disengagement agreement in September 1975. Once again, we gave them time to let off steam, knowing that eventually they would see that their fears were unjustified. In fact by the time a six-power Arab summit was held in Riyadh in October 1976 Syria was ready for a reconciliation with Egypt. An enlarged summit held in Cairo only a few days later, on 25 and 26 October, confirmed the reconciliation. One episode is quite revealing of the change of Syrian heart.

During the meeting, which was convened to discuss the crisis in Lebanon, I decided to bring up the issue of the reappointment of Mahmoud Riad, an Egyptian, as Secretary-General of the Arab League. Riad's term was not due to expire for another six months, but I was disturbed by rumours that some Arab countries, prompted by Syria and Jordan, were determined to elect a non-Egyptian as the next Secretary-General. I wanted to put an end to this campaign, demonstrating at the same time that Egypt was still the centre of the Arab world and that the leadership of the Arab League was Egypt's by right. Without informing either Sadat or Mahmoud Riad, I went straight to Assad, and asked him to put the reelection of Riad on the summit's agenda. I also informed King Hussein of my request. Assad agreed and kept his word, formally introducing a motion proposing Riad's reelection. King Hussein seconded the motion. Faced with the support for Riad's reelection by the two Heads of State who were supposedly most against it, the other participants went along with it and Riad was unanimously reelected. Egypt had demonstrated its prestige, and it was also clear we had made peace with Assad.

As a further show of good will, on 27 October Assad also agreed to the appointment of General Gamasy as head of the Joint Syrian–Egyptian Military Command. This command had been formed before the October War, but had been dormant ever since the ceasefire. Its existence had been made even more tenuous by the death of the first commander, General Ismail, and by Assad's refusal for over a year to recognise Sadat's appointment of Gamasy to replace Ismail.

A few weeks later, Syrian–Egyptian relations took another step forward. Assad came to Cairo on a state visit and on 21 December 1976 he and Sadat signed an agreement creating a joint political command between the two countries, as well as six committees to coordinate defence, foreign policy, finances, information, education and legislation. In February 1977, the Sudan joined this political command. To be sure, this did not mean that we had succeeded in forming the safety belt around Egypt, but certainly things were moving in the right direction.

In addition to concluding the accords, I took some other steps towards creating a strong network of alliances around Egypt. Specifically, I asked General Gamasy, then Deputy Prime Minister and Minister of Defence, to prepare detailed plans for the concept to be implemented militarily. These plans hinged on the formation of special Egyptian military units, ready to intervene to maintain security in the countries comprising the belt. I also sounded out the United States on my concept of security belts, discussing it with Kissinger and later with his successor, Cyrus Vance. Neither argued against the idea, somewhat to my surprise, but it was also clear that they were not prepared to take it seriously. It is paradoxical that a very similar concept was later set forth by the United States, with its attempt to build a string of 'facilities' in the areas and with the creation of an American Rapid Deployment Force to maintain security in the Middle East. Their objectives were different, however. The American scheme has been ill-received by the Arab countries, because from the American point of view security means protection from Soviet intervention, while to the Arabs security means protection from Israeli aggression. Also the American presence is an infringement of Arab sovereignty. It would indeed be much better for the Arab world if we could develop our own security belts and mobile forces to protect sovereignty.

Strengthening the PLO

The other major component of our policy in the Arab world during that period was our effort to strengthen the position of the PLO, helping it to obtain international recognition. The first step in enhancing PLO status had been the formal recognition of the organisation as the sole legitimate representative of the Palestinian people at the summit meeting in Rabat in October 1974. From that time on, the PLO made immense progress in obtaining worldwide recognition.

The Palestinian voice was heard for the first time from the rostrum of the United Nations when Yasser Arafat delivered his famous speech on 13 November 1974. A few days later, the General Assembly adopted Resolution 3236, recognising the right of the Palestinian people to self-determination. The Assembly also recognised that the Palestinian people are a principal party in the Middle East peace process and invited the UN Secretary-General to establish the necessary contacts with the PLO on all matters related to the Palestinian problem. On the same day, the General Assembly also adopted Resolution 3237, granting the PLO observer status at the UN, with full privileges to attend the Assembly's sessions and meetings in that capacity. Following the example of the General Assembly, all UN specialised agencies granted the PLO observer status. Egypt actively lobbied for all these decisions, giving the PLO its full support.

In December 1975, when the Israelis raided the Palestinian camps in Lebanon, Egypt played a key role in securing PLO participation in the deliberations of the Security Council on that problem. At our suggestion, the Security Council adopted Resolution 383, inviting the PLO to participate in the deliberations on Israeli aggression. It is worthwhile recalling here that when the resolution was adopted the Israeli delegate withdrew in protest for two days, only to come back in a hurry when he realised that his absence was only helping the PLO to dominate the meetings.

Egypt was also responsible for changing the PLO status in the Arab League from observer to fully-fledged member in 1976. I personally addressed a letter on this point to the Arab League and the proposal was accepted by all other foreign ministers. The PLO in this period also made great progress in obtaining the recognition of a large number of countries. I was responsible for some of these steps. In March 1974 I had obtained from Gromyko a statement that the Palestinians should be represented at the Geneva conference, and in October 1974 I convinced the Soviets to recognise the PLO as the sole representative of the Palestinians. I also arranged a meeting between Yasser Arafat and French Foreign Minister Jean Victor Sauvagnargues, in Beirut on 21 October 1974, and another meeting between Yasser Arafat and Gerhard Schroder, chairman of the foreign relations committee in the Bundestag of the Federal Republic of Germany, in December 1974. The German Minister of State for Foreign Affairs and the official spokesman of the PLO in Beirut then met in September 1975 in the Lebanese capital. When Mexican President Luis Echeverria formally visited Egypt in August 1975, I persuaded him to receive Yasser Arafat personally.

As a final step, when President Sadat addressed the UN General Assembly on 29 October 1975, I suggested that he introduce a resolution establishing that the PLO would be invited to attend the Geneva Peace Conference on an equal footing with all other parties. This draft was adopted as Resolution 3375 on 10 November 1975. It requested that the PLO as the representative of the Palestinian people be invited to participate in all the efforts, talks or conferences dealing with the Middle East, and it asked the UN Secretary-General to instruct the two co-chairmen of the Geneva Conference to take the appropriate steps to invite PLO representatives to any new session of the conference.

It was, of course, impossible to get the United States to recognise the PLO at this time, or to agree publicly to its participation in the Geneva Conference, but we did try at least to soften American public opinion. One of the major attempts was the speech given by President Sadat to a joint session of Congress on 5 November 1975. I had personally worked hard on the speech, painstakingly redrafting it numerous times to develop an argument in favour of the PLO which would appeal to the Americans, reminding them of their own struggle for self-determination in the past and of the statements in defence of human rights made by many American presidents. Before Sadat delivered the speech, I showed the text to Eilts and Sisco, asking for their comments as Americans, for their opinion about how such a speech would be received by Congress, and for additional suggestions. I was happy to see that they were both impressed. As for their suggestions, I rejected Sisco's but incorporated Eilts'. Sadat was the first Arab leader to address a joint session of Congress, and it was appropriate that he should put the main emphasis on Palestine.

These episodes comprise only a small part of the steps taken by Egypt in the Arab world and on behalf of the Palestinians in this period. However, they demonstrate how much the Arab world changed and progressed toward unity in this period and above all how much the status of the PLO was enhanced. By 1977 the PLO had become a fully-fledged participant in the Middle East conflict, and it was no longer possible to talk of a comprehensive peace in the area without the agreement of the PLO and the creation of a Palestinian state.

The progress made by the PLO and the recognition it received completely belie the Israeli claim that it is only a terrorist rather than a political organisation and that it lacks support among the Palestinians. In reality, the PLO is in every sense a liberation movement responsible for the future of a people, their land and their rights. The Palestinians have amply proven that they see the PLO in these terms during the elections for the mayors of the West Bank and Gaza which took place under the Israeli military occupation. As a result, the Israelis have been trying ever since to remove those mayors. Most foreign countries and international organisations, too, have shown that they consider the PLO to be a legitimate liberation movement and have extended it official recognition. It is only the Israelis who insist that the PLO is simply a terrorist group.

In my experience, all the PLO representatives I have met and worked with have been well-educated and astute politicians dedicated to their cause.

Yasser Arafat (Abou Amar) has assumed his responsibility as head of the El-Fatah group with efficiency and effectiveness and without interruption since 1968. Arafat is a very humane man, and he is a real politician in every sense. This is why he survived in a long uphill struggle against all the currents and undercurrents in the movement and against all physical and political risks. Arafat is not the only remarkable man in the PLO. Among those who impressed me very much are Salah Khalef or 'Abou Ayad', Farouk Kadoumi or 'Abou Lotf', Mahmoud Abbas or 'Abou Mazan', Khaled El Hassan or 'Abou Saīd', Ali Hassan Salameh or 'Abou Hassan', who was murdered by Israel in a commando raid on Beirut, Said Kamal and Gamal El Sorani.

Bringing in the Europeans

Another major achievement of Egyptian foreign policy in the mid-1970s was the establishment of much closer relations with the major Western European countries. My intention was to convince Western Europe to take a much more active role in the Middle East peace process. I thought that the European countries should set forth their own proposals, rather than just sit back and give the United States carte blanche in the Middle East. In fact, such an active role by Western Europe would be very helpful even for the United States, which is hampered in dealing with the Middle East by Jewish influence and by extensive commitments to Israel. All our contacts with European leaders thus were directed at convincing them that they should become more involved. While their reluctance to play an active role did not end overnight, we did make some progress.

We scored a real breakthrough in our relations with France, starting with a tête-à-tête meeting between President Valery Giscard d'Estaing and myself in August 1974. I was very impressed by him. Not only was he open and straightforward, but he had a thorough knowledge of the details of French–Egyptian relations. In this respect he was unique: I have never dealt with any other head of state who was so well informed about the issue under discussion. My first impression of Giscard was only reconfirmed in later meetings. The purpose of the first meeting was to convince him to lift the arms embargo against Egypt, which was part of an overall measure imposed by General Charles De Gaulle on all parties to the Middle East dispute. He did agree to lift the embargo and this opened the way for an important sale of Mirage planes and other military equipment to Egypt.

To build on this promising start, I arranged an official three-day visit to Paris by President Sadat starting 27 January 1975. During that visit, Sadat unexpectedly asked me to try to convince the French President to issue a declaration stating that France was ready to replace the military equipment Egypt had lost during the October War. I was rather surprised that Sadat did not want to raise the issue personally, but I promised to do my best. I passed the request to French Foreign Minister Sauvagnargues, asking him to convey the message to Giscard.

The French President gave us his answer during a discussion of the text of the French–Egyptian communiqué to be issued at the end of the visit. He declared that he was willing to incorporate into the draft a statement to the effect that France was ready to replace partially the arms Egypt had lost during the war, as well as any other formula we suggested. I had not expected this, and I had no formulae ready. In any case, the draft of the communiqué prepared by the French was already very comprehensive. It referred to the new direction taken by French–Egyptian relations since my visit to Paris in August 1974, and it also spelled out clearly the conditions for a just peace in the Middle East. These included the evacuation by Israel of all territories occupied since 1967, recognition of the rights of the Palestinians to a nation of their own, and the right of all states in the region to live in peace within secure boundaries. With the addition of the statement on France's readiness to rearm Egypt the communiqué contained everything we had sought and Sadat was very pleased. This visit was followed by more arms sales, French participation in the development of an all-Arab arms industry based in Egypt and financed mainly by the Gulf countries, and by increased economic cooperation between France and Egypt.

One further episode illustrates the importance of our new relations with France and of that country's willingness to play a role in the Middle East. In early 1976, when the crisis in Lebanon threatened to get completely out of control, I went to Paris and met with Giscard d'Estaing, asking that France intervene physically in Lebanon. French intervention would have been much more acceptable to all parties involved than the intervention of any other foreign power, because of the long-standing relationship between France and Lebanon. However Giscard was reluctant to commit France to physical intervention in Lebanon. I did not press him, but decided to go back to Egypt forthwith, specially since the French President had told me that he had other engagements outside Paris. The next morning I went to the airport and was about to board the plane where I received a message from the Elysée, saying that Giscard had cancelled his trip and wanted me to return to Paris to meet with him. I complied and found that he had given the issue a lot of thought and revised his decision: without wasting any time, he stated that France was ready to intervene in Lebanon. He then explained to me in detail the magnitude of this military intervention, including naval operations, but added that the plan would only be carried out if the right political atmosphere was created. I was very pleased, not only because French intervention would have had a positive impact on the crisis in Lebanon itself, but also because it was very important for us to end the monopoly of the superpowers in the Middle East. In the end, French intervention did not materialise because Giscard, faced with Syrian and United States opposition, decided not to antagonise them. Still, France was becoming more actively involved in the Middle East, and this was for the best.

Another country with which we established very good relations in this period was the Federal Republic of Germany, a country to which I felt a special link, ever since I had been appointed ambassador there. Although I had not been able to take up my post, since I had suddenly been appointed Minister of Tourism and then Foreign Minister, I still felt that the task of reestablishing relations with West Germany should be accorded top priority. In fact, we did much more than just reestablish diplomatic relations. We also established a joint commission, presided over by the foreign ministers of the two countries, and comprising other competent ministers. This commission met once a year to reevaluate the relations between Cairo and Bonn and to remove obstacles to cooperation in all areas. The meetings of the commission effectively complemented the other lower-level discussions which took place constantly to deal with specific issues. They provided overall coordination, strengthened the relationship between Bonn and Cairo, and opened new avenues for further cooperation on every level. This experiment was very highly appreciated in Bonn and in Cairo and proved very successful. This is why I later insisted that the same system be applied between Egypt and other countries like France, the United Kingdom, Italy, the USA and others. Since my first visit to Bonn, I had found a genuine readiness to assist Egypt. It was also clear that Bonn appreciated Egypt's role in the Middle East and considered it was in the best interests of the Federal Republic to develop good relations with Egypt. At this time West Germany was just emerging from a long period of stalemate during which it had been completely absorbed by its conflict with East Germany and with the Soviet Union. Now that these difficult problems were at least temporarily settled, West Germany was eager to open its doors to wider and diversified cooperation. The German leadership at this time was extremely impressive. Chancellor Helmut Schmidt also made a lasting impression on me because of his perceptive and acute analysis of international economic issues but he did not show much interest in political matters. As for Foreign Minister Hans-Dietrich Genscher, we became friends from the first time we met. There was no formality whatsoever between us. He is an honest man, who says what he has in mind. His friendship, I found, is genuine and long-standing. In his political orientation he was noticeably anti-Soviet and a firm believer in the German–American alliance. I also enjoyed tremendously the contacts with Franz Josef Strauss. He is a very learned man and is thoroughly familiar with the currents and undercurrents of the economic and financial situation in Europe. In this regard, I still vividly remember a day at my beach cabin in Alexandria when he lectured me for almost three hours on the energy problems of Europe and of the entire world. Strauss, I concluded that day, is a leading authority on energy problems.

Egypt's relations with the United Kingdom also evolved satisfactorily, and we established cooperation in many areas, particularly the military field. I visited London numerous times, meeting Prime Minister Harold Wilson and James Callaghan, at that time Foreign Secretary. I found in Callaghan all the qualities which make a reliable and sincere friend. I still remember many heated and amicable discussions I had with him in 1975, when I wanted to convince him that the UK, as a permanent member of the UN Security Council, should become one of the guarantors of a peaceful solution to the Middle East problem. Callaghan, much to my disappointment, argued that his government was simply not ready to make such a commitment at that time. Faced with my insistence, Callaghan finally gave me a frank explanation: Britain was still shaken by the crisis in Cyprus, where it had not been able to intervene and maintain peace despite the fact that it had a commitment to do so and also was in a unique position because it had a military base there. As a result, the British government was not willing to make any new commitments unless it was sure of being able to honour them.

I could see the logic of Callaghan's argument, and thus could have accepted the British refusal not to become a guarantor of peace in the Middle East. Much to my pleasure, however, the British government revised that decision. On the very evening following our conversation, Callaghan gave a dinner in my honour and seized that opportunity to announce that his government had reconsidered its decision and would respond favourably to my request. The relationship between Britain and Egypt continued to grow stronger than that. I made a point of meeting all important personalities, including the leaders of the opposition. In particular, I paid a visit to Margaret Thatcher in her office in the House of Commons, and she struck me as a very impressive person, shrewd, and extremely quick to grasp the point in discussion. Already at that stage she gave the impression of being firmly in control of her colleagues and radiating an inherent ability to lead. I extended her, as leader of the opposition, an invitation to come to Cairo and she accepted it.

Asia and America

The new Egyptian foreign policy was not only directed toward Europe, but to other parts of the world. New channels for cooperation with the People's Republic of China developed fast and I was very happy to find that the Chinese leaders were ready to help us by sending some spare parts we needed for the Soviet military equipment. Since then, there have been many high-level visits, and cooperation in the military field has increased and become more diversified. Economic cooperation with the Far East also expanded into many new domains. We strengthened our ties with Japan, and they extended major aid to us and played a crucial role in the enlargement of the Suez Canal.

Another Asian country of particular significance to Egypt is North Korea. We have maintained very good relations despite the efforts of the United States and the Soviet Union to weaken our ties. North Korea started to help us in the military field in various forms before the October War and continued irrespective of the Soviet position. In fact, when the USSR was reluctant to respond to our demands for military equipment, North Korea extended a generous helping hand. Chairman Kim Il Sung had developed a special relationship with Sadat when he had visited North Korea as an emissary of President Nasser. Later, when Sadat was President, Kim Il Sung once sent him a message stating his readiness to enter into serious negotiations with the South Korean government so long as Egypt, as a neutral and non-aligned country, acted as a mediator. He also asked Sadat to inform the USA that North Korea wanted to negotiate. I promptly summoned the American ambassador to convey Kim Il Sung's message. However, as I expected, no negative or positive answer came from Washington. Kissinger wanted to leave the situation in Korea as it was, fearing that serious negotiations through an impartial mediator would ultimately smooth the relationship in favour of the North.

As for Africa, Egypt had long had good relations with the countries of that continent, and it had done its best to help them in their long struggle against colonial domination. Almost all African liberation movements had offices in Cairo or at least were in constant contact with us. I energetically pursued this policy of cooperation with African countries in order to further cement our relations, and also tried to strengthen Arab–African relations in general. The first Arab–African summit was held in Cairo on 7 March 1977. It succeeded in erasing most of the barriers between Arab and African countries and in particular, it helped overcome the resentment of many African countries, whose economies had been badly shaken by the increases in the price of oil. The Saudi Foreign Minister announced that his country pledged over US $1 billion in aid to Africa, and the other Arab oil-producing countries followed suit.

On the whole our policy toward the Arab world and Africa as well as toward the major countries in Europe and Asia was quite successful. The unity of the Arab world was strengthened, and the status of the PLO enhanced to the point where it became impossible to conceive of achieving a comprehensive and permanent peace in the Middle East without Palestinian participation. The European countries were more willing to play a role in the Middle East and this in part counterbalanced the importance of the superpowers. These were all promising trends which, pursued over time, would strengthen the autonomy of the Arab world and remove it from the unhappy condition of being a theatre for superpower confrontation. However we certainly had not come to that point yet. Whether we liked it or not, the superpowers remained the dominant presence in the area and the key to both the peace process and the military balance between Israel and the Arab countries. The most important part of Egypt's foreign policy thus remained the relations with the United States and the Soviet Union.

Note

1. William Quandt, quoted in *Newsweek*, 15 February 1982, p. 22.

BEHIND THE KREMLIN'S WALLS

After the signing of the first disengagement agreement between Egypt and Israel, I decided that it was high time to reactivate contacts with the Soviet Union, in order to show them that we had not moved into the American camp, did not intend to rely solely on the good offices of the United States in our search for peace, and still considered Egypt's relations with the Soviet Union of crucial importance.

I have already mentioned that during the first disengagement negotiations at Aswan I had kept the Soviet Union informed about all major developments, circumventing Kissinger's attempt to prevent us from communicating with Moscow. Immediately after the signing of the agreement, I went to the Soviet Union in January 1974. This was my first trip to that country and it was taken at our initiative, while all subsequent contacts took place upon written request from the Soviet leaders. It was from the beginning a tough mission. I had never dealt directly with Brezhnev and his colleagues, and the matters to be discussed were highly sensitive, since we had challenged our long-standing relationship with the Soviet Union by establishing much closer ties to Washington. The Soviets, in fact, were prone to see our steps as symptoms of an imminent radical shift from Moscow to Washington. Moreover, there were tensions in our relationship stemming from the October War itself. Egypt felt Soviet aid had been insufficient, particularly in light of the American airlift of weapons to Israel. And there had been a serious misunderstanding between Sadat and Brezhnev in the early days of the war, when Sadat refused to believe Brezhnev's claim that Syria had requested him to arrange a ceasefire as early as 6 October. My task was made more difficult, finally, by the fact that the Soviets held me personally responsible for the change in Egyptian foreign policy.

My first problem was to learn to deal with the Soviets. They routinely put up a tough, impressive and impenetrable facade, projecting themselves as a human Kremlin wall to foreign diplomats. But in the end it is a façade, because they are as human as everybody else and extremely hospitable in their own bureaucratic way. However, their convictions and negotiating positions are not artificial, but based on firmly-held principles. I concluded after a little while that the best way of tackling this human wall was to be equally tough and above all very candid, even at the expense of protocol and diplomatic niceties. Once a certain credibility is established, the Soviets are willing to listen and even to show respect for opinions differing from theirs. They are well informed, but have a surprisingly limited experience in dealing with foreign systems, cultures and traditions, let alone understanding of the importance of religion in some countries.

It takes time to learn to deal with the Soviets and understand their tactics. For example, the Russian negotiator never answers 'da' (yes) at the outset. The answer is always 'niet'. Often the first 'niet' means 'da', but at other times 'niet' is 'niet'. The problem is to learn to tell the difference. Once I learned, I enjoyed tremendously negotiating with the Soviets. It was always tough, but they could be outmanoeuvered once their tactics were understood. The important thing is to take them as they are and not as one would like them to be. The Russian bear is not as fearsome as it is made out to be and has many limitations which must be understood by anyone dealing with it.

The first limitation stems from the unshakeable memory of the horrors of the Second World War. The overwhelming majority of Russians I spoke to made the point of telling me that during those dreadful years the Soviet Union lost twenty-five million men in the prime of life. The result is that the Soviet leaders are not ready to take drastic decisions which would lead to war and another colossal loss in human lives. Least of all would they take steps leading to a nuclear confrontation with the United States. The top priority of Soviet policy-makers is to improve relations with the United States and to find an accommodation with them concerning major international problems. We in the Middle East therefore cannot expect the Soviet Union to grant top priority to our problems and to rattle their sabres at the United States on our behalf. The second limitation is that the Soviet Union has limited resources, particularly by comparison to the United States, and cannot be expected to grant unlimited economic assistance to any country. A third limitation is the cumbersome nature of the Soviet system. The decision-making process is slow and policies cannot be expected to change quickly to keep pace with rapidly unfolding international events.

On my first trip to the Soviet Union, I had a meeting with Minister of Foreign Affairs Andrei Gromyko on the same day I arrived. The meeting was very formal, with Gromyko at his most sphynx-like. Choosing his words carefully, he concentrated on three major points: (1) the Soviet Union wanted a comprehensive peace in the Middle East, to be negotiated through the Geneva Conference. It would not accept any solution unless all Arab countries agreed to it; by implication, this meant that the USSR was fearful of, and would not accept, a separate peace between Israel and Egypt. (2) Moscow was closely watching the new trends in Egyptian foreign policy and particularly the rapprochement with Washington. (3) The Soviet Union still considered the Treaty of Friendship and Cooperation to be the core of Soviet–Egyptian relations. It was clear from Gromyko's points that he was very worried about the deterioration of Soviet–Egyptian relations.

On Wednesday 23 January 1974, at 10 a.m., I was received by Leonid Brezhnev in his office. To my surprise, I found that Brezhnev had an exceptionally warm way of greeting his guests, which conveyed many things at the same time. In spite of the tension in our relations, he was not formalistic in any way and struck me as being a true gentleman. This, however, did not conceal the prestige he enjoyed among his colleagues and the fact that he was the only master of the house.

In addition to Brezhnev, Podgorny, Gromyko, other members of the Central Committee, and some aides were present at the meeting. Brezhnev sat in the centre, with Podgorny on his right and Gromyko on his left. As expected, Brezhnev inaugurated the meeting by welcoming me and the Egyptian delegation. Then, quite suddenly and without any warning, he exploded like a volcano. I was taken aback by this fury, and hoped that it would subside soon. However, Brezhnev continued for almost three hours with the same vigour, repeatedly pounding on the table. For three hours nobody talked in the big room but Brezhnev and the interpreter, who had some trouble in transmitting to the Egyptian delegation the full flavour of Brezhnev's anger and ferocious attacks. After three hours of this tirade, I was getting rather angry myself, but despite Brezhnev's provocation I was forced to continue listening patiently and to appear as composed as possible. I have to admit that Brezhnev had reasons to be angry on some of the points he raised. But there was also a lot of rhetoric in his speech, and in his anger he kept jumping from one problem to another. I also had the distinct impression that he had been poorly briefed on some issues, possibly deliberately.

I thought of interrupting Brezhnev, but decided instead to choose a more subtle way of signalling to him that he was going too far. I picked up one of my large cigars and lit it, pulling my chair back from the negotiating table. Puffing on my cigar, I asked the interpreter to enquire of Brezhnev whether I could smoke. Brezhnev responded that surely I could smoke cigars and should have done so from the very beginning. I answered that I had noticed that he was very nervous and had already finished almost two packets of cigarettes and that I was not sure whether the smell of the cigar would bother him. Apparently, Brezhnev got the message that I had had enough of his reprimand, and suddenly stopped, saying: 'I have finished.'

During his three-hour tirade, Brezhnev had lectured us on the lofty principles guiding the Soviet Union's policy toward the Arab countries. He specifically said that Soviet assistance was motivated by the sincere desire of the Soviet Union to help small countries free themselves from colonialism and neo-colonialism. He preached that the Soviet goal was to help the Arab countries liberate their lands from the hands of the Israeli aggressors. He stressed that Soviet assistance was given in order to improve the economic conditions and the standard of living of the Arab people, serving the masses and not individual leaders. He insisted that the Soviet Union was only assisting progressive regimes and he made it clear that the Soviet Union was not so wealthy that it could give large amounts of financial aid without achieving anything. Pounding on the table, he stated that the Soviet Union during the previous eighteen years had extended almost $21 billion worth of aid to the Arab countries alone.

He then turned to Egypt and launched into an extensive discussion of what the Soviet–Egyptian relationship was and should have been. The Soviet leaders and the Soviet people had extended a generous helping hand to Egypt because under Nasser the country was pursuing progressive policies. He described in detail Soviet military aid to Egypt from the early 1950s to the October War of 1973, proudly concluding that all the successes the Egyptian army scored in that war were due to the fact that the Soviets had built up, trained, and equipped it with massive amounts of sophisticated weaponry.

Brezhnev also declared that after the first ten days of fighting in

October 1973 an extraordinary catastrophe was threatening the Egyptian army. He did not elaborate on this point but he intentionally said: 'We took serious decisions which made everybody know our intentions. These decisions were extraordinary in nature, and had major consequences. We also made our position very clear to the United States through the appropriate channels.' After the war, the Soviet Union had given Egypt further help by appointing a very select commission to determine exactly what happened before, during, and after the ceasefire, ascertaining what lessons could be derived from the military operations and from the performance of all the participants in the 1973 War.

Brezhnev then launched with unusual bitterness into the story of the ceasefire requested by President Assad at the very beginning of the October War. He shouted: 'Can you offer any justification as to why President Sadat had no confidence in me? Why did he not believe me when I sent him a message stating that President Assad had asked us formally to request a ceasefire on 6 October 1973?' Brezhnev added, 'We are not a small power. We are a big power. We have our records. Our records show that President Assad asked us for a ceasefire three times and still President Sadat did not believe us. Can you explain to us why President Sadat is taking such a position?' Brezhnev informed us that even Tito knew of this request, because the Soviets had contacted him to enlist his help in convincing Sadat that the Syrians had requested a ceasefire.

Then Brezhnev reverted to the Soviet–Egyptian relationship after Nasser's death. He specifically pointed out that there had been a real change in Egypt and he wanted to know whether we were still friends, whether Egypt continued to pursue a socialist path and to fight colonialism and imperialism as Nasser did. Brezhnev added: 'I have no quarrel with you because you want good relations with the United States. I deal with the Americans, too, and I would like to enjoy better relations with them. But I am against Zionism, the Zionists are all around us, they attack us behind our backs, and we shall resist them till the Arab lands are completely liberated and the rights of the Palestinians are restored.'

Finally, Brezhnev turned his attention to Kissinger and to the first disengagement between Egypt and Israel. He declared that Kissinger wanted to split the Arab world and that he never uttered a word of truth. Then Brezhnev said that he could not understand the first disengagement and the procedure followed to achieve it.

Once again, Brezhnev brought up the question of confidence between Sadat and the Soviets. I noticed that he was repeating the same points but from a different angle, reminding us of all the USSR had done to help Egypt. He referred in particular to the industrial complex which the Soviets had helped Egypt to erect, arguing that it had no parallel in other countries of the Third World. After this reminder of Soviet generosity, Brezhnev talked about the necessity of having continuous consultations between Moscow and Cairo, so we could understand one another better. He repeatedly stressed that Moscow must be directly informed of our intentions and not learn about them through the news media.

When my turn to speak came, I decided to comment thoroughly on all points raised by Brezhnev, starting with an extensive *tour d'horizon* concerning the Soviet–Egyptian relationship under Nasser and Sadat. But I also invited Brezhnev to let bygones be bygones. The misunderstandings which had occurred before and after the conclusion of the Treaty of Friendship and Cooperation was due, I told Brezhnev, to the absence of confidence between Moscow and Cairo. Both sides were responsible for this lack of confidence, because in our diplomatic exchanges we had not come to grips with existing problems, but had chosen to ignore them. I would now speak with all candour about these problems, hoping that Brezhnev and his colleagues would not be offended, but would understand the reasons for my frankness: friendship could not flourish unless we openly discussed the existing problems, as they were in reality and not as we wanted to view them.

At this point Brezhnev interrupted by saying 'I welcome that approach. We want our relationship to be built on that basis. This is how it should be among friends.' Encouraged by Brezhnev's comment, I pointed out that the Soviet leadership did not grasp the true significance of Moscow's relationship with Egypt. The Soviet leadership should have understood from the very beginning that Egypt was not just another small power: strategic, political, cultural, and historical factors made Egypt a country with a special role, unmatched in the Middle East or Africa. As a result, when Nasser turned toward the Soviet Union in 1954, concluding the famous Czechoslovakian arms deal, he had granted the Soviet Union an entry visa valid not only for Egypt but for the entire Middle East and for other Third World countries, in Africa and in Asia. If the Soviet leadership continued piling one misunderstanding on top of another, and did not grasp the real significance of its relationship with Egypt, it would be granted an exit visa by Sadat – the same man who had signed the Treaty of Friendship and Cooperation between Moscow and Cairo.

I described at length the ups and downs in the Soviet–Egyptian relationship during Nasser's era and later under Sadat. Any objective evaluation of this relationship, which extended over a period of more than 20 years, would lead to the simple conclusion that the Soviet leadership had taken a very cautious and conservative attitude towards Egypt, while it should have followed the opposite policy. Instead of taking advantage of the extraordinary opportunities offered by two decades during which the United States had virtually no presence in Egypt, the Soviets had quibbled on every point, creating tensions. A smooth Soviet–Egyptian relationship could have been a model encouraging other countries to build bridges with Moscow. To make it clear what I meant, I made a comparison between the military, political and economic aid which Washington permanently and almost automatically extended to Israel, and Soviet aid to Egypt. Israel had received from the USA enough military assistance to surpass not only Egypt, but all the Arab countries. It had received economic assistance in the form of grants and not loans, and also the latest industrial technology. This military and economic aid, coupled with the political guarantees given by the USA, had allowed Israel to attain a point where it could challenge the whole Arab world, continuing its aggressive and intransigent policies at the expense of its neighbours, including Egypt. After twenty years of Soviet cooperation Egypt was not able to cope with Israeli aggression, let alone liberate the occupied Arab territories, despite its much greater potential and human resources.

This was the situation, in spite of the fact that the Soviets were present everywhere in Egypt – in the army, in industry – and that the USSR was granted exceptional facilities no other foreign power had received. Soviet advisors served with the Egyptian army even at the battalion level, there used to be more than 20,000 military experts and technicians and the U.S.S.R. had unlimited access to naval and air facilities. If we added to this that the Soviet Union participated extensively with Egypt in building the new industrial complex, it was difficult to understand why the Soviet–Egyptian relation had not been smoother.

I then proceeded to take up every single point Brezhnev had raised and to analyse it. I told him that I was astonished to hear that he was personally responsible for blocking the shipments of Soviet arms to Egypt. I was also puzzled, and wondered why he should take a decision which went clearly against the interests of Egypt, a friendly country. Sarcastically, I asked Brezhnev: 'Whom was the Soviet leadership afraid of? Could it have been the United States, the only country which might have discovered the arms shipments to Egypt? Comrade Brezhnev and his colleagues know for sure that the United States has continued furnishing Israel with enormous quantities of arms, of superior quality, both during and after the ceasefire.' I added that the Soviet embargo was not confined to new arms, but it even covered spare parts for Soviet equipment already given to Egypt. 'How would President Sadat and especially the Egyptian people judge the Soviet leadership when they become aware of this shocking and unfriendly decision?' I inquired.

Brezhnev had not expected such open criticism, and interrupted me to justify his decision: 'What would the world say if the Soviet Union continued sending arms to Egypt after the ceasefire?' I retorted vehemently: 'You mean, what would the United States do once it discovered that you are continuing to supply arms to Egypt? But the United States never stopped sending arms to Israel, as you well know, Comrade Brezhnev.' I also embarrassed him by adding: 'Most probably there was an agreement between Washington and you not to send arms to the parties, but the United States did not adhere to it and you did, putting Egypt in an intolerable situation.'

I made it clear to Brezhnev and his colleagues that we could not accept such a decision from the superpower which persistently claimed to be our best friend, determined to extend all forms of assistance to help Egypt repel the aggressor. In this connection, I read out to Brezhnev and his colleagues the text of Article 8 of the Treaty of Friendship and Cooperation, according to which Moscow is duty-bound to help Egypt build its defence forces to repel all forms of aggression. Brezhnev's decision to discontinue arms shipments to Egypt was a clear-cut violation of the Soviet commitment. Concluding on this point, I said that I could only advise Brezhnev and his colleagues to reconsider their unacceptable decision.

I then commented on Brezhnev's statement that the Soviet Union had given $21 billion worth of aid to the Arab countries, and questioned the accuracy of the figure, pointing out that Iraq and Algeria paid in full for everything they received and that assistance provided to Egypt and Syria did not even come close to that amount. At any rate this assistance was being repaid and would be fully reimbursed in the future. I added that the Soviet attitude to our debt could only be interpreted as provocative and drew Brezhnev's attention to a message which had been sent to Sadat during the October War, even before the ceasefire became effective, demanding the payment of interest on the Soviet debt. I asked Brezhnev whether he thought that it was conceivable that Egypt could repay anybody anything at such a critical moment. The Soviets knew perfectly well that Egypt was in no financial position to make any payments. Brezhnev was visibly embarrassed.

Seizing this opportunity, I pointed out that the tension existing at the moment between Moscow and Cairo was nothing new. There had always been tension between President Nasser and the Soviet Union about arms supplies and the solution of the Middle East problem. This had eventually forced Nasser to accept the so-called Rogers plan while sitting in the Kremlin with Brezhnev. I then started discussing President Sadat's problems with the Soviets, mentioning his four trips to Moscow. At this point President Podgorny interrupted me and embarked on a diatribe against Egypt. To my surprise and satisfaction he was cut short by a simple wave of Brezhnev's hand. On another occasion, Brezhnev cut off Gromyko in the same way. Brezhnev's interventions proved to me and my colleagues that there was no collective leadership in the Soviet Union, but only one leader – Comrade Brezhnev.

I touched upon the so-called process of communications and consultations between Brezhnev and Sadat, saying that any objective appraisal of the messages exchanged by them would have led to the same conclusion, namely that they showed no friendship, no confidence, not even appreciation of the other's credibility. I had noticed that Moscow's replies were always evasive and Brezhnev was consistently avoiding the main issues. He repeatedly reminded us that confidence should reign between the two countries, but never gave specific answers. As an example, I mentioned the long message which Sadat had sent to Brezhnev in October 1973, after the ceasefire. President Sadat had requested a long list of arms and ammunition to replace what Egypt had lost during the war. Brezhnev's reply to the message had been vague and ambiguous, and in fact he ignored Sadat's request. He had referred again to the need for mutual confidence and informed President Sadat that Kissinger had told the Soviet leadership that he intended to negotiate a disengagement between Egypt and Israel in January

1974. I commented that what Brezhnev had really meant was that he would not provide Egypt with more arms, and that he had tried to justify his decision by suggesting that a disengagement would remove the need for arms. Here I told Brezhnev bluntly that we had not known of Kissinger's intentions until we had received Brezhnev's message, and that upon receiving the information we had contacted the Americans in order to work with them toward disengagement.

I proceeded to explain exactly what had happened in the first disengagement. I said that the disengagement followed what was almost a standard formula for a ceasefire agreement between combating forces, with no political strings attached. It was neither a treaty nor a political agreement, but just a military formula aimed at separating the forces. I reminded Brezhnev and his colleagues that they were quite aware that a new war would have world-wide implications. That is why the Soviet Union and the United States had co-sponsored the ceasefire resolution, Resolution 338, which confirmed the ceasefire and proposed the Geneva Peace Conference.

I pointed out:

> You, Mr Brezhnev, took the decision to stop sending arms after the Americans and the Russians had co-sponsored the ceasefire resolution. You did not want us to resume the fighting, although the Israelis violated the ceasefire and were strengthening and reinforcing their position on the West Bank of the Suez Canal. Faced with the Israeli advance Egypt had two options, to fight again or to work for a disengagement. You foreclosed the possibility of fighting by refusing to send arms, thus you forced us to work for a disengagement.

I argued further that the Soviet Union, too, should be realistic about the alternatives open to it. There were only three. It could help the Arab countries and the Palestinians fight for their own land by force. If it chose this alternative, the Soviet Union had to close the military gap between Israel and the Arab countries. If it rejected this alternative, it had two other choices; it could cooperate with the United States to impose a solution in the Middle East; or it could cooperate with the United States to convene an international conference in which all parties would negotiate a just solution to their conflicts. There were no other alternatives. The Soviet Union should make a clear choice and Egypt would abide by it. The present indecisiveness of the Soviet leadership kept Egypt from following a coherent policy. Under the circumstances, the disengagement had appeared as the best solution: it did not preclude any option in the future, but it decreased the probability that fighting would erupt accidentally. Furthermore, the disengagement had awakened international public opinion to the necessity of reaching a solution. I concluded by saying that I did not see how the disengagement could be contrary to the interests of the Soviet Union.

Brezhnev followed my explanation very attentively, and finally stated: 'Now I fully understand your position!' Then, indulging in a bit of theatre to save face, he looked reproachfully at his colleagues, declaring: 'No one has previously explained to me what you have just stated, Comrade Fahmy.' I proceeded to draw a very simple sketch on a piece of paper, explaining to Brezhnev the lines of the first disengagement. He suddenly went over to his desk, brought back a Russian map of the Suez Canal area, and asked: 'Please, draw the lines of the first disengagement on my own Russian map.' I did so and he repeated: 'Now I understand and approve of what you have achieved.' Naturally, I was pleased by his statement and took advantage of his sudden change in attitude to ask: 'I hope you will express your opinion in a written message to President Sadat. I would like to take this message back with me.' Brezhnev complied and I had the pleasure of giving Sadat this message during the wedding celebration for his eldest daughter Lobna. Later, the Soviets witnessed together with the Americans the formal ratification of the disengagement by the Egyptian–Israeli subcommittee at Geneva.

The atmosphere in Brezhnev's office suddenly thawed out and we went on to an amicable exchange of views. Brezhnev was now relaxed and sought my opinion about various Arab leaders and about the situation prevailing in certain Arab countries. To begin with, he startled everybody with the following question: 'Comrade Fahmy, what do you think of Qaddafi?' Without giving me a chance, Brezhnev himself promptly answered the question by saying, 'That young man is crazy. He is always attacking the Soviet Union vehemently, without any justification whatsoever. Until now I have refused to meet him, although Nasser told me that he was a nice boy.' Brezhnev concluded: 'He is an unbalanced fanatic.' Then to my surprise he asked: 'What do you think of Jalloud? We believe that he is more balanced.'

From Libya, Brezhnev shifted to Iraq. The Soviet Union sincerely wanted good relations with Iraq, but there were serious problems. The Iraqi government had closed the Soviet cultural centre in Baghdad and taken repressive measures against Communist Party Members. Brezhnev then analysed the unstable situation in Syria and the Sudan, and finally discussed Algeria.

At the end, we reverted to Egypt. Brezhnev expressed the hope that consultations between our countries would become frequent, 'as they were during the old days', and expressed his concern about the new rapprochement between Cairo and Washington. He commented about my frequent visits to Washington and about Kissinger's shuttle in the Middle East. My reaction was simple but to the point. I reminded Brezhnev that Gromyko had never visited Syria despite the close relations between the two countries for almost 18 years. I added that Boumedienne had complained to me that no high Soviet official had ever visited Algiers. The Soviets should not expect to sit behind the Kremlin walls waiting for everyone to come to Moscow. Brezhnev replied: 'You are right and I have already instructed Gromyko to go to Damascus and Algiers.'

In conclusion, I believe that my first encounter with the Soviets was a complete success, despite Brezhnev's opening volcanic eruption. The Soviets accepted the first disengagement and Egypt thus could pursue its policy of maintaining strong relations with both superpowers.

8 BREZHNEV FALLS SICK

In dealing with the Soviets Egypt had overcome the first hurdle in its game of nations, but there were more to come, because the root problems in the relationship with the Soviet Union had not been solved. One of these issues was the Soviet decision not to send Egypt the remaining two-thirds of the arms negotiated for in 1973. A second problem was the repayment of the Egyptian debt. The third was Sadat's personal feelings toward the Soviets. My meeting with Brezhnev in January 1974 had led to a heated exchange about the Soviet refusal to honour the arms deal, but despite our accusations the Soviets would not relent. In the following months, there were frequent exchanges between Moscow and Cairo, and we repeatedly brought up the subject, but to no avail. To make matters worse, the Soviet kept pressing us on the repayment of our debt. By late 1974, Moscow was insisting that Egypt should pay back $500 million a year, a sum which Egypt simply could not raise given the prevailing economic conditions. We offered to pay back $10 million a year for the time being, and to increase our exports of commodities to the Soviet Union to help repay our civil debt. Our positions were so far apart that compromise was not possible.

As for President Sadat, his hostility towards the Soviets remained as great as ever. The root cause was his appreciation that before Nasser's death the USSR had never looked upon him as an acceptable successor. In this connection, Sadat personally told me of a revealing incident. In 1970, when his health was rapidly failing, Nasser had gone to the Soviet Union for a complete medical check-up. During a luncheon in honour of the Egyptian delegation, of which Sadat was a member, Kosygin undiplomatically asked Nasser: 'Who comes next in the line of succession in Egypt?' Nasser was appalled by this tactless reminder that the Soviets did not think he had long to live and hesitated before answering 'Vice-president Mohamed Anwar al Sadat.' But Kosygin pressed further: 'Who comes after Sadat?' President Nasser knew what Kosygin was driving at, but just answered 'Ali Sabry.' Kosygin was then satisfied and dropped the matter, but Sadat got the message and never forgot it.

The problem, from Egypt's point of view, was that Sadat was

never able to set aside his personal resentment and cultivate good relations with the Soviet Union to counterbalance the new ties developing between Egypt and the United States. Even Washington's refusal to provide military assistance to Egypt was not enough to convince Sadat that we badly needed Soviet aid. Instead, he seized on every occasion to vent his spleen at the Soviet Union, in public and in private. His frequent anti-Soviet utterances were dutifully picked up and prominently displayed by our Egyptian newspapers, greatly complicating my task of convincing the Soviet leaders that Egypt was not moving into the American camp, but merely wanted relations with both superpowers.

Gromyko in Cairo

All exchanges between Egypt and the Soviet Union in 1974 took place against the background of these unsolved problems. After my trip to Moscow in January, there was an interval of a few weeks, before Gromyko visited Cairo on 1 March. It was his first visit to Egypt for five years. Upon his arrival, I asked Gromyko why he had changed his schedule and stopped in Syria first. He simply shrugged and smiled, saying 'I don't know. I received a cable from Damascus urging me to stop there first to discuss urgent questions which needed special attention. I was surprised when I found nothing urgent to discuss. My feeling is that the Syrians just wanted to prove that I visited them first.'

The first formal meeting during this visit took place at the Foreign Ministry. We exchanged views about the progress in the Middle East and in particular about the active negotiations taking place to achieve the first Syrian–Israeli disengagement. We also discussed the possibility of resuming the Geneva Peace Conference.

On 4 March President Sadat received Gromyko, who then embarked on an overview of the evolution of Egyptian–Soviet relations, stressing that his statements represented the views of the Central Committee. The memorandum from which he was reading covered all international and bilateral aspects of the relation; it was a clear, straightforward paper, without ambiguities: the gist of the message was simply that the Soviet leaders wanted to know where Egyptian–Soviet relations stood.

The atmosphere was tense: President Sadat was very angry

because the USSR was still not responding to his previous requests for arms and spare parts; the Soviets were beginning to worry about the evolution of Egyptian–American relations. At one point, President Sadat interrupted Gromyko, protesting against what he called 'interference in the internal affairs of Egypt'. Egypt was an independent country, he declared, and he would not accept any interference in its affairs. Gromyko appeared very surprised, because he had in fact not said anything which constituted interference in Egypt's internal affairs. He pointed out that he was reading from a written policy paper and that there was nothing in it that could be considered as interference in any way. He added that there might have been something wrong with the interpreting and, if that was the case, it had to be corrected immediately. To avoid unnecessary complications, I whispered to President Sadat in Arabic that Gromyko had not said anything wrong. President Sadat said: 'In that case, we can resume the talks.'

This incident illustrates Sadat's attitude toward the Soviets. He was insecure and oversensitive whenever he dealt with them. With the Americans, it was always 'my good friend Henry' and total willingness to accept any suggestion. With the Soviets, Sadat's attitude was one of great suspicion and of readiness to interpret every statement as an attack against Egypt and an insult to himself.

Gromyko continued delivering the message which concentrated on the Soviet leadership's desire to develop and strengthen friendly relations with Egypt. The Soviets reaffirmed their support of all steps taken to terminate Israeli aggression and stressed the necessity of negotiating a comprehensive peace agreement through the Geneva Peace Conference. They also indicated the Soviet desire to participate in the clearing of the Suez Canal. Sadat responded favourably to this request, telling Gromyko: 'Fahmy has already informed the Soviet ambassador in Cairo of our approval.'

On crucial issues, however, the Soviets were not forthcoming. Gromyko did not mention anything about the delivery of new arms or spare parts, nor did he refer to our other specific requests in other fields. President Sadat chose to comment on Moscow's silence about his request for new arms and ammunition. But he also tried to explain Egypt's foreign policy to Gromyko, and particularly the new developments in Egyptian–American relations. He then explained his efforts regarding a disengagement on the Syrian front. Finally he expressed his admiration for Brezhnev and asked Gromyko to convey his warm feelings to the entire Soviet leadership, emphasising that it would be highly desirable to have a summit meeting between Brezhnev and himself in Cairo. Gromyko seemed happy with the outcome of the meeting and on our way out he gave the press some very positive statements, singling out the participation of the Soviet fleet in the clearing of the Suez Canal.

Gromyko and I resumed our discussions that same day at the Foreign Ministry. It was agreed, among other things, that contacts between us would continue. Much of the discussion, however, centred on the wording of the final communiqué to be issued at the end of the visit. We finally agreed on a friendly statement in which both parties advocated the immediate convening of the Geneva Peace Conference. That simple word 'immediate' was the outcome of a highly significant discussion. Originally, the Soviets had insisted that the communiqué should incorporate the same language which appeared in the Syrian–Russian communiqué issued a few days previously. Namely, it would state that the two parties had agreed that the Geneva Peace Conference should be convened no later than the beginning of April 1974.

I objected strongly to this date because it left no time for preparations. But my objections raised serious doubts within the Russian delegation as to whether Egypt had changed its position regarding Geneva and wanted instead to pursue bilateral negotiations with Israel through United States mediation. As the Russians are very suspicious people, I explained clearly to Gromyko that my objections were merely that the date was unrealistically close. I also stressed that the reason why the Geneva Conference had not been reconvened yet was simply that there was no basic agreement on the participation of the Palestinians, and specifically the PLO. I added that the Soviet Union, as co-chairman of the conference, could pursue direct contacts with the United States to overcome that difficulty. Only after we settled the issue of Palestinian representation would the road to Geneva be open.

I added that once the problem of Palestinian representation was solved Egypt would be ready to go to Geneva immediately. I also proposed that instead of mentioning a specific date, the communiqué should call for the immediate convocation of the Geneva Conference on the understanding that once the Russians informed me that the problem of Palestinian representation had been solved, the conference would be convened forthwith.

The Soviets saw my point, but still objected, claiming that they would not be able to explain the discrepancy between the communiqués issued in Damascus and Cairo. I pointed out that I was not responsible for the mistakes the Soviets had made in Damascus, especially since they had not consulted me when they agreed on that date, although they knew beforehand that their next stop was Cairo. In the face of my strong objections and in light of my explanation, Gromyko accepted my formula.

Gromyko left Cairo on 5 March, and Kissinger left Damascus on the same day, on his way back to Washington after the completion of the first Syrian–Israeli disengagement. This coincidence was highly symbolic. It showed that both superpowers were still playing a role in the Middle East and had to be a part of any solution there. Unfortunately, Gromyko's visit to Cairo, while successful in keeping the lines of communication open between Cairo and Moscow, had not gone any further. None of the problems in Soviet–Egyptian relations was solved as a result of his visit: arms shipments were not resumed; no agreement was reached on the repayment of our debt to the Soviet Union; and Sadat's attitude towards Moscow remained as hostile as ever.

The Trip to Moscow

Communications between Cairo and Moscow remained frequent, however. On Tuesday 23 April the Soviet chargé d'affaires in Cairo came to see me with a message from Brezhnev and the Central Committee requesting new consultations and asking President Sadat to agree to my departure for Moscow. Three days later Sadat sent Brezhnev a favourable reply. Almost a whole month elapsed and suddenly on 19 May the Soviets answered, reiterating their sincere desire for further contacts, but informing us they had other commitments, especially in relation to President Nixon's visit to Moscow in June 1974. President Sadat replied on Thursday 6 June, expressing his hope that these consultations would take place as soon as possible. Apparently, the Soviets were very eager to have consultations and only Nixon's visit caused a postponement: during a formal dinner the Soviet chargé d'affaires in Cairo gave in honour of the newly- appointed Egyptian ambassador to Moscow, Hafez Ismail, the chargé enquired when I intended to go to Moscow.

At the end of June, I announced that I would be going to Moscow in July 1974. In the meantime, I accompanied President Sadat on an official visit to Bulgaria, starting 30 June. Upon our return to Cairo, I agreed to the date proposed by Moscow – 15 July, about two weeks after the end of President Nixon's visit. I took all the necessary steps to prepare for the trip. I wanted the visit to be a turning point and I intended to cover all aspects of the bilateral relations between Egypt and the Soviet Union. For this reason I chose a strong delegation at ministerial level, representing all fields of co-operation between our two countries.

However, on 10 July, while I was on the beach in Alexandria, I received an unexpected telephone call from the Soviet Ambassador, Vladimir Poliakov, who had arrived in Alexandria with a very important message from Moscow. I received him on the same day and he informed me that the Soviet leaders wanted to know whether I was arriving by special plane or on a scheduled flight, and that they would like to have the names of the members of the Egyptian delegation, as well as to be informed in advance of any special requirements or demands I might have. It was quite clear that the Soviets wanted the visit to take place and to be a success.

To my surprise, two hours later Ambassador Poliakov came back to my beach cabin with a new coded message from Moscow which he had not even had time to tranlslate yet. He did so in my presence and I was shocked to find that the Soviet leadership expressed their regret that they could not receive the Egyptian delegation. The message offered no explanation.

What could possibly have happened in two or three hours to make the Soviet government change its mind completely? Had we in Egypt done something wrong, without being aware of it? Or had the Soviets suddenly received some important information about major events in the Middle East or in another part of the world which had forced them to change their minds about the visit? The message was very dry; it neither apologised nor proposed that the meeting would be held at a later date. Such a message came very close to being provocative and it was certainly humiliating. The Soviet ambassador was in a most delicate position and very embarrassed, especially as he had not been informed of the motives behind the sudden change, either. I passed on this incredible message to President Sadat, and for a while we had no more communications with Moscow.

The abrupt cancellation of the visit caused a lot of speculation in Egypt. One hypothesis at the time was that the decision was due to Brezhnev's sudden illness. This interpretation was substantiated by the fact that the visits of President Bhutto of Pakistan and of Adam Malek, Deputy Prime Minister and Foreign Minister of Indonesia, were also cancelled. Similarly, French Foreign Minister Jean Sauvagnargues, who visited Moscow in August, was not received by Brezhnev. Another speculation was that all the cancellations were due to serious disputes within the Soviet Politburo itself. Both explanations left many Egyptian officials unconvinced, however. They pointed out that President Nixon's visit had taken place as scheduled and concluded that my visit had been cancelled because the Soviets were angered by the frequent visits to Cairo of senior American officials, including President Nixon. In the end, no one could be sure of the real reasons behind the sudden cancellation of my visit because the Soviets never offered an explanation.

During the months of July, August and September I was busy with other problems. I had official engagements in Paris and Washington to promote Egyptian–French and Egyptian–American relations through the newly established joint committees. These committees were entrusted with the task of discussing and developing programmes with a view to promoting bilateral relations. In Washington, where I went shortly after Nixon's resignation, I had very extensive talks with the new president, Gerald Ford, as well as with Kissinger, Secretary of the Treasury William Simon, and other senior US officials. These extensive contacts including two meetings with President Ford drew the attention of diplomatic circles and the media.

Among those who followed my talks in Washington very closely was Anatoli Dobrynin, the Soviet ambassador to Washington. After I had a breakfast meeting with President Ford, Dobrynin requested an urgent appointment with me. We met in my suite at the Madison Hotel for more than two hours, covering the bilateral relations between our two countries and the Middle East question. I took the opportunity to complain forcefully about the Soviet attitute towards Egypt, citing many concrete incidents. I asked Dobrynin to explain his country's behaviour, but he could not do so and was very uncomfortable. The meeting was useful, however, because it enabled us to deal with a wide range of subjects and to exchange views frankly.

Among the topics we discussed was the sudden cancellation of my planned visit. He could not provide an explanation, but he stated that the consultations between our two countries had to be resumed in the near future. At the end of our meeting, on his way to the lift, he was asked by the press when the Soviet–Egyptian talks would be resumed. He answered, 'Minister Fahmy can go to Moscow any time.' When I was asked to comment on Dobrynin's statement, I only said that I was not sure whether anything would come of it and whether Dobrynin had the authority to issue invitations before he consulted his own government. From Washington, I flew to New York to attend the UN General Assembly, and then returned to Cairo. As soon as I arrived, I received an urgent message from Brezhnev and his colleagues, referring to Dobrynin's meeting with me. The Soviet leaders proposed that my long-overdue visit should take place in October 1974.

I arrived in Moscow on 14 October, accompanied by an important delegation which included the Ministers of Planning and Foreign Trade, Chief of Staff General Gamasy, Deputy Minister for Aviation General El Sessy, Under-Secretary for Foreign Affairs Mohamed Riad and other experts. We were received very warmly and I was informed that Brezhnev would receive me the next day. This was unusual, because meetings with Brezhnev do not normally take place until the end of the visit.

On 15 October, I met Brezhnev at the Kremlin. On the way to the conference room, Egyptian Ambassador, Hafez Ismail, reminded me that Brezhnev was celebrating his tenth anniversary as First Secretary of the Communist Party and suggested that I seize the opportunity to congratulate him. Brezhnev received me with a huge hug. He also started to complain jokingly about the many trips which I made to Washington and the various visits of Kissinger to the Middle East. When the official meeting started, Brezhnev delivered the welcoming speech which normally sets the tone of the meeting. It was cordial. When my turn came, before embarking on the substantive issues I congratulated Brezhnev on his 10th anniversary as First Secretary of the Party. He was surprised and pleased, thanking me warmly. Apparently my congratulations touched his sensitive and human side. In my experience Brezhnev's human qualities could be felt and counted upon in his handling of decisions, and this meeting proved it. He would relax completely once he got the measure of the person he was dealing with and felt he was straightforward. In many ways he was a shy man who warmed to human contact. He was very conscious of his achievements and proud of them and took great pleasure in others appreciating them. When he chose to act he did so and decisively on the spur of the moment, alone without reference to his colleagues. After thanking me, Brezhnev added a few words about his experience in office and its heavy load. I took advantage of this unique occasion to corner him by saying: 'A moment ago I congratulated you, Mr Secretary. Now I withdraw my congratulations.' The interpreter translated and Brezhnev, taken aback, wanted to know: 'How come you congratulate me one minute and withdraw your congratulations the next?' I explained that I had congratulated him because it was his 10th anniversary as First Secretary of the Community Party, but that I did not see how a world statesman like Brezhnev had not thought of visiting Cairo for ten years, either in Nasser's or Sadat's time. I pointedly added: 'Nixon came to Egypt only a few months after the resumption of diplomatic ties between Washington and Cairo.'

While the interpreter translated, I noticed very significant signs on Brezhnev's face, reflecting his approval of what he had just heard. But to tell the truth, I never expected his reaction. Leaving his chair, Brezhnev went to his desk, opened a drawer, brought out his appointments calendar and sat back in his chair. Without reference to the Central Committee, he opened the calendar and said: 'When do you want me in Cairo? January or February?' This was the real Brezhnev, Brezhnev in action, Brezhnev full of vigour and authority, Brezhnev in full command.

There was spontaneous applause from both sides to this historical decision. I welcomed his unprecedented step and added: 'January would fit in well with President Sadat's schedule.' Brezhnev agreed upon the date and started to draft a communiqué related to his decision. This communiqué, which was released right after the meeting stated:

> On October 15th, 1974, Comrade Leonid Brezhnev, General Secretary of the Central Committee of the Socialist Party, received the Egyptian Foreign Minister and it was agreed that a meeting between the Soviet and Egyptian leadership would constitute the most important step in the evolution of relations between the two countries . . . During the talks, there was full agreement on the salient problems which would serve as a basis for future agreements to be concluded during that meeting. Furthermore, it was agreed that the summit meeting between Leonid Brezhnev, General Secretary of the Central Committee of the Soviet Socialist Party, and President Anwar al Sadat,

President of the Arab Republic of Egypt, will take place in Cairo in January 1975.

I felt that I had obtained a major victory. I was convinced that only a face-to-face meeting between Brezhnev and Sadat in Cairo could solve the existing serious problems. My theory was that Brezhnev and Sadat would not like the summit to fail. Consequently, I expected that a Brezhnev–Sadat meeting would set the Egyptian–Soviet relationship on a completely new path. Brezhnev, too, was optimistic and happy. 'I always feel at ease when I negotiate with Comrade Fahmy,' he declared at the end of the meeting.

During the remaining days of my visit, I had several meetings with Gromyko and his colleagues. The talks took place in a congenial atmosphere, because Brezhnev's decision to come to Cairo had set a new tone for Egyptian–Soviet relations. During the talks, Gromyko kept repeating that Moscow regarded Cairo as its main friend in the Middle East. However, he stubbornly kept on bringing up the problem of our debt to the Soviet Union. I tried to explain to him what he already knew, that the effects of repeated wars and our overall economic situation made it almost impossible to raise this issue again. Gromyko insisted that we must repay the debt, in annual instalments of $500 million.

I conveyed President Sadat's message to the effect that we could not afford to pay more than $10 million per year for the time being. Gromyko became angry and insisted that we should pay $500 million annually. I repeated that we could not possibly pay that much, but that we were ready to increase a little our exports to the Soviet Union, as a way of stepping up our payments. I tried to give Gromyko many examples in which countries facing difficulties similar to those of Egypt had been either totally or partially exempted from paying their debts. I also reminded him that we had never said that we did not recognise our debts, adding that Moscow's uncompromising approach at this time was becoming a serious obstacle to further development of friendly relations between Egypt and the Soviet Union. I finally asked Gromyko to stop using this disagreement on the payment of debts as an excuse for not providing the additional weapons or spare parts needed by the Egyptian army.

Unfortunately, the Soviets did not relent on the debt issue, neither in these talks nor later. When a high-ranking Egyptian delegation visited Moscow on Gromyko's request, it failed to achieve any results concerning commercial and industrial relations. The delegation returned to Cairo empty-handed because the relevant Soviet ministers refused to discuss any problem until the question of the debt was solved.

Another problem I encountered during my talks with Gromyko was that he refused to include the results of the talks in a communiqué. When I pressed him to explain the reason for this refusal, I was told that, once a communiqué was issued after talks between Brezhnev and a foreign visitor, there could not be another communiqué related to lower-level talks. Officially, the visit of the foreign delegation comes to an end with the issuing of a communiqué at Brezhnev's level.

I was neither pleased nor convinced by this explanation, but the Russian rules had to be respected. However, after laborious efforts I managed to convince Gromyko that we should at least issue a statement on that part of the talks which dealt with the PLO. After consulting Brezhnev, Gromyko approved the release of a very short communiqué stating that the government of the Soviet Union recognised the rights of the Palestinians to self-determination and the PLO as the sole representative of the Palestinian people. This was the first time that the PLO was recognised in such a capacity by the Soviet Union, and I was very pleased. The PLO leaders and the Palestinians hailed the decision. Full Soviet recognition of the PLO was a turning-point in the Soviet–Palestinian relations. From then on, Yasser Arafat and his colleagues were received by Gromyko and other official members of the Soviet government, and not by the 'Afro–Asian Association' in Moscow, as had been the case earlier. This was a major accomplishment as far as the PLO was concerned, and it was first implemented when Gromyko later visited Cairo and met Yasser Arafat for the first time at a reception in my honour at the Soviet embassy.

Plans for Brezhnev to Visit Cairo

The declaration that Brezhnev would visit Egypt in January 1975 got front page headlines throughout the world. Both the Soviets and the Egyptians started preparing for that summit. My main objective was to secure adequate supplies of weapons for the Egyptian army on a permanent basis and at the same time to promote the Egyptian–Soviet relationship. Planning for the summit, I counted on Brezhnev's decisions because my experience suggested that his power could not be directly challenged by the Central Committee. Furthermore, with his formidable ability for direct discussions, Brezhnev could overcome all obstacles. I suggested to Sadat that he should talk to Brezhnev candidly, making it clear the Soviets could not take Egypt for granted.

Egypt, as a non-aligned country, should deal with both the Soviet Union and the United States. The degree of closeness to one or the other was not really that important: what counted was our ability to generate competition which serves our interests. President Sadat did not resist the idea of a meeting with Brezhnev. On several occasions, he welcomed publicly the forthcoming meeting, stressing his special respect and sympathy for Brezhnev.

Recall to Moscow: Brezhnev's Visit Postponed

Everything was set, committees and delegations from each country were formed and had started the preparations. Every major paper gave the meeting big headlines. But suddenly, President Sadat received a message from the Central Committee and Brezhnev, stating in their standard terminology that it was time for further consultations on the highest level, and proposing that Foreign Minister Fahmy and Minister of Defense Gamasy proceed to Moscow in late December 1974.

I was surprised because there was no justification for this trip, just two months after the first one and so close to Brezhnev's visit. I even expressed my surprise to the Soviet chargé d'affaires, but he could not offer an explanation, either.

In any case, I thought it best to accept the invitation. Upon my arrival at the airport in Moscow, I naturally asked Gromyko the reason why I had been recalled to Moscow. To my surprise, I did not get any explanation. This is the Soviet system – you ask a question and you do not get an answer.

The Egyptian and Soviet delegations met that evening. At the opening of the meeting, Gromyko read a written statement of a political nature, emphasising the long duration of the Soviet–Egyptian friendship and the assistance rendered to Egypt by the Soviet Union. Choosing his words carefully, Gromyko concluded:

Fahmy presents the Arab case at the United Nations

Fahmy with three American Presidents (Richard Nixon [top left],
Gerald Ford [bottom left] and Jimmy Carter [top right])

Fahmy and Brezhnev squaring off. Fahmy congratulates Brezhnev on his ten years as
First Secretary and then witdraws it (see pp 142-3)

Sadat and Fahmy separated by Kurt Waldheim, Secretary-General of the United Nations

The moods of Henry Kissinger

Soviet moods: Fahmy with Gromyko (above) and Brezhnev (below)

Fahmy with British Prime Minister, Harold Wilson (right) and Foreign Secretary James Callaghan

'The Soviet Union always honours its contractual commitments.' The atmosphere was unusually solemn. Defence Minister Marshal Andrei Grechko and a number of high-ranking military officers were present, looking extremely serious. As soon as he had finished, Gromyko gave the floor to Marshal Grechko, who also read a long written statement. 'In implementation of a decision taken by the Soviet Central Committee, the Soviet government has decided to send to Egypt the following airplanes and arms,' he declared. He then read out a long list of military equipment, including the MiG–23 planes we had never received before. He added that the decision had been made in accordance with the obligation of the Soviet Union, emanating from the Soviet–Egyptian Treaty of Friendship and Cooperation. Like Gromyko, Marshal Grechko concluded his speech by saying, 'With this decision, the Soviet Union will have honoured all its contractual commitments to Egypt.'

While Grechko spoke, the military members of the Egyptian delegation had been taking notes. When the Soviet minister read out the list of equipment to be delivered, Gamasy and I knew that this was the undelivered part of the arms agreement negotiated in 1973. We were very pleased, not only because the shipment included the MiG–23s, other sophisticated equipment and the spare parts we badly needed, but also because the decision to release these weapons was a major political step. The fact that the Soviets had decided to release this shipment prior to Brezhnev's visit to Cairo, rather than at the time of the visit, furthermore suggested that a new agreement would be reached at that time.

I was encouraged by this new turn of events, but did not want to give the Soviets the impression that we were completely satisfied. So I told Gromyko that it was time the Soviet authorities should establish a military bridge between the USSR and Egypt. I had never seen Gromyko as upset as when I mentioned a military bridge; he argued vehemently that such a move was unthinkable because it would have very negative repercussions internationally. Knowing he was afraid of the American reaction, I hastened to explain that I was not referring to a massive airlift of military equipment, which would undoubtedly be detected by US electronic surveillance. What I meant was simply that the USSR should respond positively and on a continuous basis to our future requests, without quibbling, with as little bureaucratic delay as possible, and with greater respect for delivery dates. Specifically, I asked the

Soviet Union to respond favourably to a request submitted by President Sadat after the October War to make up for the losses of equipment we had incurred in the conflict. General Gamasy and I then argued that certain changes should be introduced in the list of items to be delivered at this time, in view of our changed needs in the aftermath of the war. Here, however, it became clear that Soviet bureaucracy had not changed, and that the Soviet delegation was not empowered to add a single bullet to the list without a new high-level decision, involving Brezhnev himself.

When the meeting was adjourned, I was still very puzzled about the reason why we had been recalled to Moscow so urgently. Clearly the announcement that the military deliveries would resume could have been transmitted to us by the Soviet military attaché in Cairo or incorporated into the new Soviet–Egyptian deal which we expected would be agreed upon during Brezhnev's visit to Cairo the following month. There had to be a political reason for this urgent summons, but when I questioned Gromyko, again I received no answer, only a brief reminder that he would pick me up next morning at 11.15. Further efforts on my part to get at least some clue from our embassy about the reason for these meetings led nowhere.

The next morning, Gromyko arrived punctually and escorted me to a car. The motorcade started off, and passed by the Kremlin without going in. When I asked Gromyko where we were heading, he simply replied that he was taking me outside Moscow. Twenty-five minutes later, we pulled up in front of a large yellow building in the suburb of Kolsova. I commented that it looked like a hospital and Gromyko finally gave me a clear answer. 'It is a hospital, and you will meet Brezhnev here.' Gromyko, Grechko, Gamasy and I were made to don white hospital coats and we were taken into a large room where Brezhnev was lying in bed. Nobody else was present.

Brezhnev was exceptionally cordial. He embraced me in a powerful bear hug, explaining 'See, I am fine and feeling strong. Tell my brother and friend Sadat that I will come to Cairo when these people let me go.' This was the first clue that he would not come to Cairo in January. Brezhnev was determined to convince us that he was not seriously ill. He kept on joking, and at one point asked Grechko: 'How secure is this place?' Grechko, who was not in a jocular mood, stood stiffly to attention as if about to issue an important order, answering: 'This area is so secure that no rocket in the world could hit it without being destroyed first.' Brezhnev seemed proud of the answer.

Despite Brezhnev's rather healthy appearance and his attempt to minimise his illness, it was clear that there must be something seriously wrong with him and that he was under strict doctors' orders to stay in bed, or he would not have received us in the hospital at a time when his illness was a closely- guarded secret. At any rate, he finally explained to us why we had been called to Moscow. He wanted us to see for ourselves he was in the hospital, he explained, so that there would be no doubt in our minds that his trip was not being postponed for political reasons. The problem, he added, was how to make a public announcement that his trip to Egypt, Syria and Iraq was being postponed without giving rise to far-reaching speculations. Naively, I suggested that the simplest way would be to announce the truth, namely that the trip was being postponed due to Brezhnev's ill health. That, Brezhnev replied, would indeed be the simplest way, but it could not be done under the Soviet system. I insisted that everybody knew leaders were human beings and could fall ill. It was normal practice in all countries to announce the postponement of events because of the ill health of leaders. Brezhnev was adamant that the Soviet system did not allow such a practice.

It was apparent to me from his comments that not only the Soviet people, but most probably the majority of the Central Committee, were unaware of his illness. I am certain that I was one of the first foreigners at that time to know that Brezhnev had been hospitalised. Accordingly, I did not insist that the communiqué on the postponement of the visit should mention Brezhnev's health, and simply said that I was sure we could agree on a formula without any problems. Brezhnev was satisfied and added, 'I asked you to come in order to assure you of our good will and I will be pleased if you stay till you and Gromyko reach agreement on the draft of a communiqué on the postponement; then we can dispatch it to Damascus and Baghdad in order to get their approval.'

I agreed and expressed my thanks to Brezhnev for his effort to avoid unnecessary misunderstandings in our relations. Knowing that he should rest, I decided not to discuss any new topics with him, so I took my leave, expressing my sincere wish that he should regain his health quickly and visit Egypt in the near future. Brezhnev again asked me to convey his best wishes to President Sadat and to tell him that he would certainly come to Egypt and visit his 'brother and friend Sadat' soon. Brezhnev added that Gromyko had informed him about my previous discussions with him and Grechko, commenting 'I realise that both men are giving you a hard time. I advise you to keep on whipping both Gromyko and Grechko till you get what you want from them.' During the ride back, Brezhnev's last remark kept ringing in my ears. It was not only a clear invitation for me to insist on what I wanted to get, but also an explanation of how a foreign negotiator might reach his aims with the Soviets: 'Use the whip', Brezhnev had said. The best and surest way to get something from the Soviets is indeed to be tough, to take a hard line, and persistently insist on one's point of view. In my negotiations with the Russians, I never forgot Brezhnev's advice.

Arriving at the guest house, Gromyko and I drafted a communiqué on the postponement to be sent to Damascus and Baghdad for approval. Without any difficulty, we reached agreement on a very simple formula which did not include any reference to Brezhnev's hospitalisation. While we waited for Syrian and Iraqi approval to the formula General Gamasy and his colleagues held various meetings with their Soviet military counterparts. Gamasy again tried to introduce some changes into the list of arms which General Grechko had read out, but he only succeeded in changing a few delivery dates. For my part, I had several meetings with Gromyko and our discussions covered various bilateral and international issues. On the bilateral level, I complained about the difficulties we were encountering in our commercial and industrial exchanges with the Soviet Union. Gromyko promised that he would speak to his colleagues in each field and would remedy the situation.

After the approval of both Damascus and Baghdad reached Moscow, the following communiqué was issued:

> In accordance with the agreement reached between the leaders of the Soviet Union and the leaders of the A.R.E., the Syrian Republic and the Iraqi Republic, it was agreed to postpone the visit of Leonid Brezhnev, Secretary General of the Central Committee of the Communist Party of the Soviet Union, to these countries to a later date. This visit was due to take place in January 1975 and the time of the new visit which will be convenient to all the parties will be fixed at a later date.

Inevitably, the communiqué gave rise to all sorts of speculations, all of them unfounded. This was the consequence of the Soviets' insistence on concealing Brezhnev's illness. I must stress again here that, had Brezhnev not suddenly fallen ill, Egyptian–Soviet relations would have taken a very different course. The visit would undoubtedly have led to an increase in Soviet military aid to Egypt, helping narrow the gap between Israel and the Arab countries in this respect, and thus imposing a restraint on Israeli aggression. The remaining part of the 1973 arms deal, which started arriving very promptly after my trip to Moscow, was not sufficient. A visit by Brezhnev would also have implied full recognition of Sadat himself, forcing him to abandon his hostility to the Soviet Union. Indeed, Brezhnev's visit would have changed the politics of the Middle East. The US was very aware of this, reacting with dismay to the announcement that the visit would take place and with delight when it was postponed. Brezhnev's illness had indeed far-reaching historical consequences. He took a long time to recover and then the hot season started in Egypt, and Brezhnev, for health reasons, never travels in hot weather. In the intervening months Kissinger succeeded in negotiating the second disengagement agreement on the Egyptian–Israeli front, and from then on there was no way of convincing Sadat that he still needed the USSR.

FORD AND KISSINGER: THE END OF AN ERA

The Egyptian contacts and exchanges with the Soviet Union during 1974 were all the more important because relations with the United States remained rather delicate throughout the year. To be sure, there had been an enormous improvement in US–Egyptian relations ever since the October War. Diplomatic ties had been reestablished. Nixon had visited Egypt in mid–1974 and extensive cooperation agreements between Egypt and the US were signed at that time. But I remained somewhat sceptical. The US was still committed, first and foremost, to Israel. It was not prepared to give Egypt any arms. To complicate matters, by August 1974 Nixon had been forced to resign and we had to find out whether the new Ford administration would pursue the same policy toward Egypt.

Nixon in the Middle East

President Nixon's visit to Cairo in May 1974 was, from our point of view, part of the process of removing Egypt from the Soviet garage and helping us regain our complete independence, showing that we would deal with both superpowers. For Nixon, the visit was both a message to the Arab countries that US policy in the Middle East had changed, and an attempt to distract domestic attention from the Watergate scandal.

This was the first visit to Egypt by an American President, but Nixon had already come to our country as Vice-President. In fact, he told me that he had never forgotten that trip, and particularly his visit to the Aswan High Dam built by the Soviets. He was very sober about that experience: 'I was standing on the High Dam, looking at that enormous Russian monument. I remembered the fatal mistake that President Eisenhower and [Secretary of State] Dulles made when they refused to help Nasser finance the project, leading Nasser to nationalise the Suez Canal. Because of this one big American mistake, the course of history has changed and the Russians have come to Egypt in full force. It was a turning point which shattered all hopes of reconciliation between Nasser and Washington.' It was thus only natural that President Nixon should be the one to take the initiative and demonstrate ostentatiously, with his own visit, the American come-back to Egypt. He wanted to emphasise that he had brought about Egypt's shift from the Soviet Union to the United States, and he insisted on coming to Egypt personally.

En route to Egypt, Nixon stopped in Salzburg, when he started having fairly serious health problems with phlebitis. Against his physician's advice, he stubbornly insisted on continuing his trip. He had a very demanding schedule in Egypt, but he refused to make any changes in it. He rode into town from the airport standing in an open car, to receive an overwhelmingly friendly reception from the crowds lining the road. Periodically he would order the car to stop and would mingle with the people, with the security officers frantically running after or around him while he shook hands, smiling and chatting with the crowd. He had many formal and informal meetings with President Sadat and high Egyptian officials, attended formal luncheons and dinners and, with his usual stamina, did not want to miss the famous ride on the antique royal train from Koubba Palace to Alexandria. Apparently, the euphoria of the visit was good for him, because he left Egypt almost completely cured. Then he proceeded to Israel and I believe he kept to an equally gruelling schedule there. All this reflects the personality of the man and his determination to score political points and gains.

During the talks which took place in Cairo and Alexandria, President Nixon was candid and precise. He did not need to put on a show to impress people. His authority was strongly felt by everybody and it was clear that he ran the show single-handedly on behalf of the United States. Kissinger was there, and so were Alexander Haig and others, but they were simply an entourage, a backdrop for the President. In all the talks, he was open and straightforward. One meeting at Abdeen Palace in Cairo stands out in my memory. It took place in President Sadat's office, which had been King Faruk's. President Nixon and Kissinger attended on the American side, while President Sadat and I represented Egypt. At the end of the discussion of various points related to the future Egyptian–American relationship, I decided this was a unique opportunity to hear from the President of the United States himself, what the US position was regarding the ultimate solution of the Middle East crisis. I told President Sadat in Arabic of my intentions and he agreed. I then conveyed my question to Nixon. Without a moment's hesitation, he answered 'Achieving complete Israeli withdrawal from Sinai is no problem. Withdrawal from the Golan Heights is also possible, but with some effort. As for Jerusalem and the West Bank, this will be the real problem, but we shall find a solution for it.' This unambiguous answer accurately reflects Nixon's character and determination. Had he stayed in office, he would undoubtedly have used all his power and influence as President of the United States to obtain the Israeli withdrawal from the occupied territories, defying the Jewish lobby and other pressure groups. I must add that I have never heard any such definite statement from Nixon's successors. Neither Ford nor Carter, with whom I discussed the same issues on more than one occasion, had the political courage to take a firm stand.

Nixon's visit was crowned by the issuing of a joint declaration outlining the steps which would be taken to strengthen US–Egyptian relations. This rather lengthy document carried the title 'Principles of Relationship and Cooperation between Egypt and the United States'. The declaration was composed of a preamble and five parts. The first part dealt with the problem of peace in the Middle East. It stressed the two parties' commitment to 'a just and permanent peace' in the Middle East, in accordance with Security Council Resolution 242 and taking into consideration 'the legitimate interests of all people in the Middle East, including those of the Palestinian people, and the right of all states in the area to exist.' Peace negotiations would take place within the framework of the Geneva Peace Conference, and Egypt and the United States would engage in a process of consultation at all levels to facilitate the peace process.

The rest of the document dealt more specifically with Egyptian–American relations and was very detailed indeed. It foresaw the creation of a Joint Cooperation Committee under the chairmanship of the two foreign ministers; and an agreement on cooperation in the nuclear field, to enable Egypt to meet its growing energy needs through nuclear energy. The two parties also agreed to set up a number of joint working groups to submit recommendations to the Joint Cooperation Committee on a variety of problems, ranging from the clearing of the Suez Canal to the opening up of Egypt to American private investment, the rebuilding of the Opera House in Cairo and the shipping of the Tut Ankh Ammon treasure to the United States to be exhibited around the country. The last item in the document was an announcement that President Nixon had extended a formal invitation to President Sadat to visit the United

States in 1974 and that President Sadat has accepted the invitation. This gives the gist of how the new relationship between the United States and Egypt was envisaged. The declaration of principles was ambitious and comprehensive, covering a wide range of issues and expected avenues of cooperation. New high level institutions had been created to help implement the new progress. The close cooperation envisaged by this agreement was unprecedented in Egyptian history; Egypt had never had such close relations with any country, not even with the Soviet Union whose presence in Egypt was dominant for twenty years. It is true that many Soviet–Egyptian committees had been created, but none of them was officially legalized and openly announced. The other remarkable aspect of the declaration is that it referred to long term programmes, which would need a long and stable uninterrupted relationship to be implemented, rather than to one shot deals which could go quickly into effect and just as quickly be forgotten. All these programmes started being implemented immediately, in stages, with the exception of the restoration of the Opera House.

While the declaration was very comprehensive concerning economic and cultural relations, it was totally silent about a point of crucial importance to Egypt, namely military aid. In fact, military cooperation between the US and Egypt was not even formally discussed until a later date, and even then with considerable lack of success. This was a situation which Egypt could not tolerate. We were still in state of war with Israel. The United States, for all its new friendship for us, was still much more committed to Israel than it would ever be to Egypt, and American weapons kept on pouring into Israel. The result was that the gap in military capability between Israel and Egypt was continuing to grow. The conclusions to be drawn from this state of affairs were very clear. On the one hand, we should continue knocking on the door of the American arsenal, making it clear to the United States that a country in Egypt's situation simply could not be satisfied with economic aid alone. On the other hand, we should do everything possible to maintain and strengthen our relationship with the Soviet Union, the country that had provided us with arms for twenty years, and at much more favourable prices than the United States ever gives.

The second half of 1974 introduced a new complication in Egypt's relations with the United States. Nixon's tour of the Middle East might have boosted his morale, but it did nothing to make Watergate go away and in August he was forced to resign. This had significant and negative repercussions for us. Nixon, it is worth repeating, was blunt and decisive, and not afraid to stand up to Israel and the Jewish lobby in the United States. He was also extremely well-informed about all aspects of the Middle East situation. For all of Kissinger's reputation, there was never any doubt in my mind that Nixon and not Kissinger was making the crucial decisions.

The Ford Administration

President Ford was an altogether different person. As president, he was an accident of history. He had not chosen to play the crucial role in world affairs the American President has to play and was not prepared for it. His knowledge was scant, although it improved somewhat with time, and he lacked the courage to make decisions. This meant that Kissinger came into his own in this period, establishing policies and making major decisions. This was very clear in all meetings I had with Kissinger and Ford. The President did not talk much simply because he did not know much. Every time I saw him, I found him a little more informed, but never quite enough. Kissinger would do almost all the talking during the meetings and if President Ford said anything, it was usually, 'What do you think, Henry?' Then Henry would start to lecture us, injecting the President's name into whatever he said: 'I believe that President Ford thinks . . .', 'I am sure that President Ford does not mean . . .', 'I am sure that President Ford would prefer that this is done in such a manner . . .' or 'I cannot speak in the President's name, but I believe that the president would like to say . . .' All this, Kissinger used to utter in the presence of President Ford, who simply kept nodding his head.

I was very worried after Nixon's resignation, because I did not know what the change portended for US–Egyptian relations. In September 1974, when I was in New York for the meeting of the UN General Assembly, I met with Kissinger and I expressed to him my profound worry. How could I be sure that US–Egyptian relations would serve the best interests of my country, in view of the character of the American system, with its continuous changes in administration, the occasional high level scandals, the pressure groups, the currents and countercurrents and the personal interests and ambitions of each high US government official? We could not develop a solid relationship with the United States if the cast of characters in Washington was forever changing, I told him, unless I received an assurance that the decisions reached would be binding on future presidents or administrations.

Kissinger was very upset. He became very pale and described my words as serious and dangerous criticisms, adding that President Ford should hear them for himself. He hurried over to the telephone, which rested on a grand piano, and called Ford on a direct line, insisting that he should receive me the following morning for breakfast. While he was on the phone, I kept on protesting, 'What the hell are you doing? I'm not used to getting up early and talking politics before 10 o'clock.' But President Ford agreed to see me for breakfast, and I had to set aside my reservations about the uncivilised hour. I must admit I was curious to see what a Presidential breakfast was like.

The following day, the breakfast took place in President Ford's dining- room. Only President Ford, Kissinger and myself were present. It really was a Presidential breakfast, very well prepared and served. I repeated exactly what I had said to Kissinger and expressed myself bluntly, because I felt that if we did not have clear assurances of continuity we would be running a great risk. Ford gave me his assurance that US policy would not change.

There was in fact no reversal in the US policy towards Egypt under the Ford administration. This meant that we did not suffer great set-backs but we did not make much progress either. It was still clear that while the United States wanted to have closer ties with Egypt to pull us out of the Soviet orbit, it was not prepared to make substantive concessions to achieve this aim. Least of all was it prepared to give us arms. I am convinced that things would have been different if Nixon had stayed in power. It is true that the cooperation agreement signed during his visit to Cairo did not have a military dimension, but I think that he was realistic enough to know that he could not continue to have good relations with us if he refused us military aid but continued to arm our enemies. But Kissinger was different. First of all, he was too pro-Israeli. Secondly, he was overconfident in his ability to manipulate people: rather than tackle the admittedly delicate problem of convincing the US Congress that there were sound reasons for giving Egypt some military equipment, he preferred to try and pull the wool over our eyes by false promises and vague talk.

In fact, we had already had a sample of Kissinger's approach to the issue of military aid before Nixon's visit. At the end of April 1974, the Secretary of State had come briefly to Egypt, prior to undertaking the shuttle between Damascus and Tel Aviv which led to the disengagement on the Syrian front. Officially, he had come to discuss the forthcoming negotiations, but he was also worried about our exchanges with the Soviet Union, which had been intensifying in the preceding months. He knew that we desperately needed military assistance and was afraid we might mend our fences with Moscow in order to get it. We met with Kissinger and his team at Maamoura, Sadat's summer residence near Alexandria, and during the talks Kissinger suddenly brought up the issue of arms. 'Mr President,' Kissinger said, 'I think it is high time that we embark on a new strategy of cooperation in the military field. I believe that it is high time that Washington should provide Egypt with all its military needs, but there will be major difficulties at home and a very negative reaction by the Israelis. So we propose, Mr President, that military coopertion between our two countries should go through three phases, to give everybody time to get used to the idea. The first phase will be completely commercial, with Egypt paying for whatever military hardware it gets. The second phase would be 50/ 50: Egypt will pay for 50 percent of what it gets and the remaining 50 percent will be in the form of a grant-in-aid. By the time we reach the third phase, Mr President, Congress and the Israelis will be accustomed to this new relationship, and we will be able to supply all military equipment in grant form.'

I had never expected to hear such a statement from Kissinger and certainly did not believe a word he said. I watched the expressions on the faces of his American colleagues; they were shocked and unbelieving. There was no policy decision whatsoever in Washington at that time which came even remotely close to what Kissinger had proposed. One senior American official told me later that Kissinger was 'nuts' and that he had no basis for his statement. But Sadat, as usual, was naively optimistic. 'I am ready, Henry. I am ready,' he said. It was clear to me that Kissinger simply wanted to hypnotise us in Egypt and to sabotage our attempts to strengthen relations with Moscow. He never admitted this, of course, but he did admit it was only a manoeuvre. A few months later I asked him why he had made such a statement, and he tried to justify himself by saying that he wanted to reassure us because he felt that Egypt was very worried about the status of relations between Washington and

Cairo, especially after the Watergate scandal. Such behaviour did nothing to increase our confidence in the US.

Despite the fundamental problems which marred our relations with the United States, we had to recognize that there was little hope of making progress toward peace in the Middle East at this time other than by relying on Kissinger and his step-by-step approach. The United States was the only country with enough clout in the Middle East. The Soviet Union had isolated itself through its shortsighted policy of denying Egypt arms, and the European countries were sitting on the sidelines. The Arab states were making some progress toward unity, but certainly were not a united block yet; in any case, they needed an intermediary to deal with Israel and only the United States could play that role. As long as Kissinger remained at the helm of US foreign policy, there could be nothing but step-by-step negotiations in the Middle East. To be sure, Egypt at this point favoured a comprehensive peace in the entire area, including the settlement of the Palestinian problem. But as long as the situation did not allow such a comprehensive settlement to be negotiated, we were willing to work toward a second disengagement agreement, so long as it remained a purely military agreement and did not involve political concessions to Israel. A further disengagement along the lines of those negotiated in 1974 on the Egypt and Syrian fronts was acceptable to us, and could be useful in maintaining the momentum of negotiation. In fact, we even hoped that it could be followed by a similar second disengagement between Syria and Israel. We were adamantly opposed, however, to accepting any clauses which could imply in any way that Egypt was making a separate peace with Israel. Peace, we made clear to all, could only be negotiated in unity by the Arab countries and the PLO, never by Egypt alone.

The Second Disengagement Agreement

After many preliminary contacts, Kissinger decided that a second disengagement would be possible and in March 1975 initiated a second shuttle between Egypt and Israel. The situation, however, was not propitious. The Israelis of course showed their usual intransigence, insisting that Egypt agree to end belligerency as the price for even a minor withdrawal. Furthermore, tensions in the Middle East during 1975 were greater than ever, because the political situation in Lebanon had exploded. This had very important consequences, particularly for Syria. The civil war in Lebanon strengthened the hard-liners in Syria, and changed Assad's stance. Here was a chance for Syria to play an important role, perhaps even to revive its old claims on Lebanon. Assad, relieved by the new Lebanese situation of some of the internal pressure, became less receptive to the idea of a second disengagement agreement. It is indeed paradoxical that the explosion in Lebanon, which worked against what Kissinger was trying to accomplish at this time, was precipitated and supported by a CIA operation in cooperation with a special Israeli CIA branch.[1]

The first meeting with Kissinger on the second disengagement took place at Sadat's rest house at the Barrage and it was rather desultory. We exchanged points of view and when the meeting was over, but still in front of Kissinger, Sadat asked me to prepare in writing a formula for a second disengagement on the Egyptian–Israeli front. My reaction was that this formula should be prepared by the Americans in their capacity as mediators and that Kissinger was the man to perform this important task. To my amazement, Sadat told me that he wanted me to do it because Kissinger had no idea where to start and in which direction to go and that Kissinger himself had told Sadat that I should be in charge of this task. I don't know whether it is true that Kissinger had told Sadat he had no idea where to start, but if he did, it was just a tactic on his part to find out the Egyptian position from the outset. In any case I told Sadat: 'I will do it, but not today, because I am giving an official dinner in Kissinger's honour at my home, to provide him with the opportunity of meeting the Vice-President, the members of the government and some newspaper editors.' However, Sadat insisted that I prepare the formula immediately, adding that he would come and have dinner at my place on the same evening with Henry Kissinger and myself alone, and that I should cancel all other invitations. I answered reluctantly, 'It's all right with me if you come and have dinner with us, but when I cancel my previous invitations I have to say this is your specific desire, Mr. President.' He agreed entirely and consequently I instructed the head of protocol in the Foreign Ministry to cancel the invitations and to mention specifically that it was President Sadat's wish.

Later that day, I dictated to my chef de cabinet, Ambassador Omar Sirry, two formulas for the second disengagement, one more comprehensive than the other. The first called for disengagement along a line from Al-Arish to the oil fields at Ras Muhammad. The second more limited formula would lead to the complete withdrawal of the Israeli forces beyond the strategic Mitla and Giddi passes in the middle of Sinai to the east, and beyond the oil fields at Abu Rodeis and Ras Sudr to the south. As to the other components of the disengagement, I added some articles, deliberately modelled on those of the 1949 Armistice Agreement between Egypt and Israel.

Before we started dinner that night my chef de cabinet arrived and gave copies of the two versions to Kissinger and me. Sadat got upset, shouting: 'Where is my copy? I want to read it too.' Kissinger was satisfied with the proposals, and commented favourably on them. He pointed out, however, that the Israelis would refuse to withdraw to the Al Arish-Ras Muhammed line or would impose major political concessions, amounting to a de facto peace treaty. Kissinger knew we would certainly refuse to make such concessions. As I expected, he liked the less ambitious line and said he would concentrate on convincing the Israelis to accept it.

After Kissinger left for Jerusalem, Sadat and I flew to Aswan to wait for him. This was Sadat's idea, because he felt that Aswan, where the first disengagement had been agreed upon, had some mystic atmosphere or influence, and that he soon would be able to reach a second disengagement there. However, the reports we received from Kissinger on every return trip showed that the Rabin government was not ready to reach an agreement for a variety of reasons. First, the Rabin government was not in full control of the Israeli internal situation and it needed time in order to be able to take serious decisions. Second, the Israelis were watching anxiously the new developments between Moscow and Cairo, especially after President Brezhnev had announced his intention to visit Egypt, Syria and Iraq for the first time. The postponement of the visit had not assuaged their fears. Third, the Israeli government apparently thought that the Arab countries were so divided that there was no danger of a renewal of fighting. Israel could thus be intransigent and dictate conditions it knew beforehand Egypt would never accept. Fourth, as it appeared later, the Rabin government was being deliberately intransigent in the hope that the United States, desperate for some progress, would offer Israel major commitments in return for its cooperation.

In order to stall negotiations, the Israelis declared that they would never withdraw completely from the Sinai passes but only to the middle of them. They also insisted that any agreement should incorporate a clause ending belligerency between Egypt and Israel. Kissinger had real problems this time, because he knew that we would never accept anything less than an Israeli withdrawal to the east of the passes and that we would never adhere to the Israeli request to end belligerency. As time went on, Sadat and I became convinced that this time Kissinger would not succeed. Thus, we suddenly asked him to bring back from his next trip to Jerusalem not new political proposals but a map showing exactly the line to which the Israelis were prepared to withdraw. He did this, but when we looked at the map and asked him to show us exactly where the Israeli line would be, he was vague and evasive in his answers, saying that the Israelis could not establish where the eastern part of the passes started. This was a typical Israeli ruse, because it is very clear where the passes start and where they end. The Israelis simply wanted to maintain control of the passes and to put pressure on Egypt.

Realising that Kissinger was not really in command of the situation and that at this point his leverage on Israel was almost nil, President Sadat told him, 'Henry, next time you go to Israel, you get them to agree to our proposal, or you put an end to this shuttling and return from there directly to Washington.' Kissinger was upset and tried to convince Sadat to allow him to come back to Aswan one more time before he went back to Washington. We refused, because we wanted to put the blame for the failure of the talks squarely on the Israeli side and thus wanted the shuttle to end in Jerusalem. I will not elaborate on what happened between Kissinger and the Israeli cabinet or on the atmosphere in which he was received because this has been amply covered in other books. It will suffice to say that Kissinger did not succeed in swaying the Israelis and returned to Wasington empty-handed. As soon as we were informed that Kissinger had left for Washington, I went to the old Cataract Hotel in Aswan and gave an international press conference, explaining why Kissinger's efforts had failed and putting the blame completely on the Israelis. Kissinger too thought the responsibility lay with Israel and convinced President Ford to send Rabin a strongly worded letter. He then started a period of reappraisal of the situation.

For our part, we also re-examined the situation and decided to take measures to bring more pressure to bear on Israel. As a first step, when the mandate of the UN security forces in Sinai expired we announced that we would not renew it for the normal six months, but only for three. We also held military manoeuvres on the West Bank of the Suez Canal. Finally, we decided to make our position public and announced that Egypt would not accept anything less than total Israeli withdrawal from the Sinai passes and the return of the oilfields to Egypt, and that we would not make any political concessions whatsoever.

In the early summer of 1975 the effort to negotiate the second disengagement resumed. In this connection, I should mention a meeting between Ford and Sadat which took place in Salzburg on 1–2 June. This was the first meeting between the two presidents and it was important in solving the delicate issue of the manning of the early-warning stations in Sinai. By this time, the Israelis had decided to be more forthcoming. An American military team had been sent to survey the passes to establish where they start and end, and the Israelis were ready to withdraw to the eastern slopes. However, they insisted on retaining control of the early-warning station they had built there with US help. Needless to say, we could not accept this and we intended to discuss this issue with Ford and Kissinger in Salzburg.

On our way to the meeting, Sadat, Vice-president Hosni Mubarak and I were riding in the same car and discussing the problem of the early-warning station. It was agreed that Sadat should tell Ford and Kissinger that Egypt would allow the monitoring station to remain, on condition that it was manned by American civilians. In addition, the US must build another station for us, also manned by American civilians. In a rare spontaneous response, Ford immediately reacted 'I believe that this is a saleable proposal. I can sell it back home. What do you think, Henry?' Kissinger was not ready to commit himself. As he always did on such occasions, he looked at Sisco for help, but Sisco was not ready to say anything either. There was an awkward pause and finally Kissinger cautiously answered 'This is interesting, Mr President, but I must take it up with the Israelis.' The idea was eventually accepted.

It is worth while recalling here that the reopening of the Suez Canal took place around this time, on 5 June, at Sadat's insistence, despite my advice that he should wait in order to put pressure on Israel until specific progress had been made in the negotiations. In any case the Israelis had relented somewhat by this time, so that in September Kissinger had enough hope for a settlement to resume his shuttle. However, the Israelis were not about to sign an agreement without extracting enormous concessions from the United States. Kissinger was confronted with a barrage of requests for economic aid, military equipment and most important of all a political commitment to follow the Israeli dictates in all aspects of the Middle East issue. He gave in to the Israeli requests and signed a series of secret agreements with Israel. In these agreements, the United States pledged increased economic assistance to Israel, and guaranteed to supply it with oil and to provide large new amounts of sophisticated military equipment. More seriously, the United States also signed a memorandum committing itself to coordinating its strategy at Geneva with the Israelis and to support the principle that all negotiations should be bilateral, between Israel and each Arab country, and not multilateral, between Israel on one side and all Arab countries on the other. Furthermore, the US guaranteed that it would not recognise the PLO or negotiate with it without Israeli consent and until the PLO formally recognised Israel's right to exist and accepted Security Council Resolutions 242 and 338.

Kissinger did not inform us that the United States intended to sign such extensive agreements with Israel until he came to Egypt to finalise the second disengagement. Ten minutes before the formal meeting, he and Sisco briefed me on the US–Israeli accords: I was dismayed, and immediately had strong second thoughts about finalising an agreement. The new, large scale military assistance would widen even further the gap between the Israeli and Egyptian military capacity, while the US commitment not to recognise the PLO or take any other initiative without Israeli consent would make American policy in the Middle East even more an extension of Israeli policy than it already was. This was an unnecessarily high price for Egypt to pay for withdrawal east of the passes.

I was even more dismayed during the formal meeting when at the last moment Kissinger pulled another of his tricks out of his inexhaustible bag, suddenly requesting that President Sadat himself sign one of the documents. Sadat as usual welcomed the idea and gave his approval immediately. I was forced to contradict him in public declaring, 'No, President Sadat will not sign the agreement.' Sadat was astonished, 'Why, Ismail, I have already signed the first disengagement.' I reminded him that he had not signed an agreement with Israel, but American proposals. Sadat then changed his mind: 'Yes, Henry, Fahmy is correct. I did not sign any papers with Israel, only American papers.' Kissinger had to agree that this was the case, but still tried to be clever and to manoeuvre us into signing a direct agreement with Israel, with all the political repercussions it entailed. 'O.K., Mr President, I will sign on behalf of the United States, Allon will sign on behalf of Israel and Ismail will sign on behalf of Egypt.' I did not want to interrupt Kissinger, but the minute he finished, I said, 'I am not going to sign any single paper related to the second disengagement,' and I abruptly withdrew from the meeting and walked out to the garden.

Sadat suspended the meeting and hurried after me asking, 'Why are you so angry?' I explained to him that from the very beginning, I had made it clear that we must not give this disengagement agreement undue political significance, and that neither the Minister of War nor I should sign any paper. Instead, the agreement should be signed by the Chiefs of Staff of Egypt and Israel, underlining its military character, and by the respective permanent representatives at Geneva, where it would go for further discussion and ratification by the Egyptian–Israeli military subcommittee of the Geneva Conference. I also seized on this opportunity to convey to President Sadat the information which had come into my possession just before the meeting: in exchange for their modest withdrawal, the Israelis had extracted from the US major political commitments and a colossal amount of military assistance. None of this appeared in the disengagement agreement, but the truth was that this new political and military American commitment would enhance dramatically the Israelis' position in the future and make them more intransigent. This would make a future comprehensive solution of the Middle East conflict almost impossible unless the Arabs simply surrendered to the Israeli dictates. President Sadat understood my position, yet argued 'But the paper which I am going to sign only deals with the American surveillance station.' 'This is true,' I admitted, 'but we have to gain more time with a view to bear more pressure on Israel and the United States, or at least to get some military assistance from the Americans to counterbalance what they gave Israel.' Sadat could see my point but he was afraid that if he followed my advice the second disengagement would again be indefinitely postponed.

Since I would not sign, he would get somebody else to do it. He clapped his hands, the officer in charge came running, and Sadat ordered him to call Mahmoud Salem, the Prime Minister. Salem came and Sadat told him, in front of Kissinger and me, 'Fahmy does not want to sign any paper. You sign instead of Fahmy.' The Prime

Minister stiffened to attention, said 'Yes, sir,' and signed on Egypt's behalf. Sadat was overjoyed and that night, at a lavish banquet celebrating the disengagement, he was in a very festive mood, complimenting me all the time despite the fact I had refused to sign.

It is important here to clarify some points about the second disengagement, because many writers, particularly Israeli ones, have falsely presented it as a major political victory for Israel, or even as a peace treaty under another guise. This is simply not true. The United States made major political concessions to Israel, but Egypt made none. It is a complete distortion to claim that the language of some articles implied the end of belligerency, and this will become evident to anybody who takes the trouble to read the document carefully. Article 1, for example, stated that 'the conflict between them (the parties) and in the Middle East shall not be resolved by the use of force but by peaceful means.' Article 2 declared: 'The Parties hereby undertake not to resort to threat or use of force or military blockade against each other.' Article 3 stipulated: 'The Parties shall continue scrupulously to observe the ceasefire on land, sea and air and to refrain from all military and para-military action against each other.' Article 5 ran: 'The United Nations Emergency Force is essential and shall continue to function and its mandate shall be extended annually.' Finally, Article 6 clearly stated: 'This agreement is regarded by the parties as a significant step toward a just and lasting peace. It is not a final peace agreement.' Certainly, all these articles make it quite clear that the conflict between Egypt and Israel had not come to an end, and that no peace treaty had been signed.

Other commentators, less willing to distort the facts completely, found more subtle arguments to show that the second disengagement was a major political breakthrough for Israel. They argued that this document contained explicit references to the renunciation of force, and that this must surely imply the end of belligerency. My answer to these people is that they should compare the language of the second disengagement agreement with that of the Egyptian–Israeli General Armistice Agreement signed on 24 February 1949 at Rhodes, Greece: they will find identical expressions there. Yet, three major wars between Egypt and Israel had taken place since then, in 1956, 1967 and 1973. The 1949 Armistice Agreement repeatedly committed the parties to renouncing the use of force. Article 1, for example, stated that 'the injunction of the Security Council against resort to military force in the settlement of the Palestinian question shall henceforth be scrupulously respected by both parties.' The same Article again repeated that 'no aggressive action by the Armed Forces – land, sea or air – of either party shall be undertaken, planned or threatened.' The article finally concluded that the establishment of the armistice was 'an indispensable step toward' the liquidation of armed conflict and the restoration of peace in Palestine.'/ Although many similar quotes could be extracted from the 1949 Armistice Agreement, this is sufficient to show that the 1975 disengagement did not introduce any new language or concepts. This is not accidental, I must point out. In dictating the Egyptian proposal for disengagement to a line east of the passes, I had consulted the Armistice Agreement and was most careful to use the same wording.

Henry Kissinger

The negotiating of the second Egyptian–Israeli disengagement was Henry Kissinger's last major appearance on the Middle East scene. In the following months no new initiatives were taken because the American Presidential campaign was underway in earnest, and with Ford's defeat Kissinger passed from the scene. I want to record here my final impressions on this man who played such an important role in the Middle East after the 1973 war. I have already talked about some aspects of his personality which became very evident in the course of our contacts: his tendency to manipulate people, his constant attempts to take advantage of Sadat's trust and impulsiveness to extract major concessions from him, and his tendency to present Israeli papers as American proposals, only to disavow them quickly when we refused to accept them. Another side of Kissinger which was always evident was his overbearing vanity, and his determination to be at centre-stage. It was rather exhausting to see him preening himself in front of the cameras. However, although these weaknesses were annoying at times, they had no real political consequence.

Certainly, there was a personal, human side to Kissinger I liked and enjoyed. The more relaxed social occasions we shared with our wives were always a pleasure. And of course above all Kissinger is a highly intelligent and able person of tremendous stamina.

But the problem for us was that the ideas he conveyed to us on what to do in the Middle East were unacceptable. These ideas can be easily summarised. Kissinger had no policy of his own, no theory about how to proceed toward a settlement. For all the fanfare, Kissinger in the Middle East was basically Israel's envoy. He never brought us a genuine American proposal. He never suggested a compromise solution to break an impasse. If we made new suggestions, he would seldom express his opinion, but would simply say that he would check with Israel.

During Nixon's tenure as President, Kissinger's bias was somewhat kept in check. Nixon was strong and decisive, and had no intention of allowing Israel to make policy for the United States. Unfortunately for us, Kissinger played his hand extremely well during the unfolding of the Watergate scandal, kept his distance from Nixon's entourage – 'that bunch of crooks', as he called them once in my presence – and survived to be Ford's Secretary of State. At this point, there was nobody to control him and he took the Israeli side more blatantly than ever. There is no better proof of this than his willingness to subject American policy in the Middle East to an Israeli veto and to commit the American tax-payers to pouring enormous sums in economic and military aid into Israel, merely to obtain Israeli surrender of a thin strip of Egyptian territory in the second disengagement. I am sure that this would never have happened if Nixon had still been President.

A final question needs to be raised about Kissinger. How was it possible for him to play such an important role? His personal qualities, his ambition, and his ruthlessness do not provide the whole explanation. Nor, as I have already argued, did he impose himself by virtue of a coherent, overall strategy for settlement in the Middle East, because he had none. What helped Kissinger achieve his prominent position in Middle East affairs was above all Sadat's personality and his propensity to agree to all American proposals. Another factor was the complete vacuum which existed in the aftermath of the October War. Although the Arab front had elements of cohesion, under the surface they were caught between the elation of their initial success and the consciousness that the success could have turned into another major disaster. They had used the oil weapon with great effect, and the United States and Western Europe were shaken. Having imposed the embargo, however, the oil producers did not know what to do with it, how to use it for the maximum benefit of the Arab cause. Israel for its part was very deeply shaken by the war due to the large number of Israeli men killed or taken prisoners; and its political leadership was deeply divided by accusations and counteraccusations about who was to blame. The Soviet Union was paralysed by uncertainty, caught between its commitment to Egypt and its fear of provoking the United States, and thus chose to withdraw from the peace process. Europe was dormant as far as the Middle East was concerned, suffering from absence of leadership in all major countries. The United States itself was gripped by the Watergate scandal. It was this unusual set of circumstances which allowed Kissinger to impose himself as the only man who could find a solution, a miracle worker on whom the future of the Middle East depended. It was this unusual set of circumstances in the end which allowed him to play the Israeli hand at the expense of the Arabs.

Notes

1. David Hirst and Irene Beeson, *Sadat*, (London: Faber and Faber, 1981), p. 198.

10 EXIT VISA FOR THE SOVIET UNION

The signing of the second disengagement was inevitably received with extreme suspicion in many quarters. No amount of careful draftsmanship could keep other parties from interpreting the document as they saw fit. As we expected, Syria greeted the agreement with a new, bitter campaign against Egypt, accusing it once again of betraying Arab solidarity and moving towards a separate peace with Israel. This campaign eventually subsided, just as the first one had, and by late 1976 relations between Egypt and Syria had become close and cooperative once again. The PLO, too, initially reacted with hostility to the agreement, but the cooling of relations with Egypt did not last long. One reason was that all our actions after the signing of the agreement made it crystal clear that our policy had not changed at all, that we were not seeking a separate peace, and above all that we were more convinced than ever that the solution of the Middle East conflict hinged on the recognition of Palestinian rights.

Of much greater long-term consequence was the Soviet reaction to the signing of the second disengagement. This time they could not be convinced to accept the step we had taken and even refused to witness the ratification of the agreement by the Israeli–Egyptian military subcommittee at Geneva, as they were supposed to do as co-chairman of the conference. The hardening of the Soviets' position is easily explained. They knew that their role in the Middle East was becoming increasingly marginal, and that the United States was the clear arbiter of the situation. After all it was the United States which had negotiated three successive disengagements between Israel and the Arab countries. Unable to help negotiate settlements or to prevent its allies from signing them, the Soviet Union had no choice but to take a hard-line position.

After the signing of the second disengagement Sadat was even more certain that he did not need the Soviet Union and that the entire solution of the Middle East conflict could only come from the United States. He thus did nothing to bring about a reconciliation with the USSR. Instead, he escalated his campaign of verbal abuse against it, and was answered in kind by the Soviets. Relations steadily deteriorated.

It is important to point out once again that Sadat's attitude was unjustified. We should not have relied totally on the United States, particularly in view of the enormous political, economic and military concessions Kissinger had just made to Israel. Furthermore, our relationship with the United States still lacked a military dimension. Our modest requests for military equipment had been totally ignored. In October 1975, when Sadat went on his first official visit to the United States, we decided to press this point and submitted a request for a small sale of military equipment. It was limited to about twenty C-130 transport planes, some pilotless reconnaissance planes or drones, and some transport vehicles. Deliberately, our request contained no items of major importance and certainly no offensive weapons. Equally deliberately, however, we sought to obtain the planes from the US government and not from commercial sources, because we wanted to establish a precedent. Kissinger had agreed to this procedure. However, when the Israeli lobby in Congress put up a hard fight against the transaction, Kissinger changed his mind. First he cut the number of C-130s from twenty to six, then pressed us to obtain the planes from commercial sources and not through an official transaction with the US government.

Kissinger sent me a message through Ambassador Eilts, explaining that he was being attacked personally over the C-130s issue and that he was afraid of the repercussions on his career. He pleaded with me to help him avoid a fight with Congress by acquiring the planes through commercial channels. I asked Eilts to inform Washington and particularly Kissinger that I rejected the proposal and I formally insisted that either the transaction be completed with Congressional approval, setting a precedent, or not at all. I took this position without consulting Sadat, but later he approved it unhesitatingly. Receiving Ambassador Eilts's report, Kissinger decided to run the risk of going through with the transaction on my conditions. It was approved by Congress in early 1976 after much arguing, but at least a precedent had been set. Although the major obstacles to military cooperation with Egypt and the United States had been Israeli influence in Congress my impression was that Kissinger himself was never in favour of embarking on that road for personal reasons, despite the extravagant picture he had painted for us at Maamoura about the future phases of US military aid to Egypt.

Abrogating the Treaty of Friendship

Despite all these difficulties in US–Egyptian relations Sadat decided to write off the Soviet Union and to put all his eggs in the American basket. In March 1976 he asked me to meet him at his rest house at the Barrage. It was a tête-à-tête meeting and in his rambling fashion Sadat started to tell me how he had had trouble sleeping the previous night. He was very tense, he told me, although he did not know why. Then in the early hours of the morning the idea came to him that it was time to abrogate the Treaty of Friendship and Cooperation with the Soviet Union. After that, he had slept peacefully. He added that he had not informed anybody of his decision and that I should maintain the secret. Why Sadat had reached the decision at this time, I am not sure. Certainly, there were long-standing problems between him and the Soviets. The final straw was probably a letter we had just received from Indian Prime Minister Indira Gandhi, in which she informed us that she could not respond favourably to Egypt's request for arms and spare parts. The reason was that the Soviet Union, which had provided the equipment to India in the first place, had vetoed the transaction.

I want to stress here that before this date Sadat had never discussed the possibility of abrogating the Treaty of Friendship and Cooperation. In his memoirs Kissinger claims otherwise, but I have serious doubts about this version. According to him, Sadat talked of his intention to abrogate the treaty at least twice. The first time was during a meeting between Kissinger and Sadat at the Barrage in December 1973. The second time was during a conversation they had in Aswan about a month later.[1] On this second occasion, Kissinger writes, Sadat expressed his intention to abrogate the treaty by the end of 1975. I have the gravest doubts about the veracity of Kissinger's statement. I believe that he just invented these two episodes in order to convince the reader that he had managed to drive a wedge between Sadat and the Soviets from the very beginning. In reality, Sadat did not decide to abrogate the treaty until March 1976.

I told Sadat that the abrogation of the treaty was a very serious step with multiple consequences and that, irrespective of the Soviet intransigence during the last three years, we should postpone the implementation of his decision for the time being. Instead, I proposed that President Sadat send a strong message to Brezhnev, decrying the deterioration in relations between Moscow and Cairo and protesting the Soviet refusal to allow India to provide us with spare parts. We should end the message with a serious warning to the Soviet leadership that, if they did not alter their behaviour toward Egypt, they would have to bear the consequences of their irresponsible attitude. I added that President Sadat should mention that he, as President of Egypt, could not remain idle in the face of a Soviet position which could not be described as friendly and most important of all which would lead to the weakening of the Egyptian armed forces.

I also suggested another alternative to President Sadat. He could send the Soviet leaders an outright ultimatum: either they reconsidered their position vis à vis Egypt and took concrete steps to improve the Egyptian–Soviet relationship, or Sadat would freeze the Treaty of Friendship, and confine the relationship to the lowest formalistic basis. The second proposal, I thought, would serve our purpose much better. It would give the Soviets a strong signal, but would still provide them with a last opportunity to re-examine their position. I reminded Sadat that when China broke with the Soviet Union, it froze its Treaty of Friendship, but did not abrogate it.

President Sadat listened attentively but he was still in favour of abrogating the Treaty. I tried to convince him that my two proposals served exactly the same goal of making clear to the Soviets that Egypt had had enough; at the same time the proposals would leave the door slightly open, making it possible for the Soviets to readjust their position. He was not convinced, but did not insist on his position. A few days later, however, he reactivated the decision to abrogate the treaty and informed me that the time had come to implement it. He asked me to take the necessary political and legal steps, adding that he still had not discussed the question with any other Egyptian official.

Before complying with Sadat's decision, I prepared a written memo for him, explaining the pros and cons of the abrogation of the treaty and the reasons why I disagreed with the decision. I again explained what steps should be taken instead. I wrote this memo to put my position clearly on record. Sadat personally added some comments on the paper, stating that he had taken the decision personally and against my recommendation. I then took the steps necessary to implement the decision. I called in the Soviet Ambassador and gave him a message for the Soviet leaders. I left immediately afterward to inform the cabinet and finally went to the

People's Assembly, which sanctioned the decision on the same day.

One may wonder why I did not submit my resignation at this time, since I disagreed with Sadat on such a major issue. In fact, I came close to resigning, because all my experience with the Soviets suggested that it was a mistake to consider the coolness of their attitude toward us as final. The Soviets had amply proved to us that they often reverse their decisions. For example, they had refused to send us arms in the early days of the Sadat régime, but after Sadat had expelled the Soviet experts, Brezhnev and his colleagues had agreed to a major arms deal with Egypt. After the October War and the ceasefire, they had suspended the shipment of the outstanding portion of the weapons, but then had again reversed the decision in December 1974. This time too, I was convinced, the Soviets would eventually change their position toward Egypt, if we handled the matter correctly. This meant taking a hard line with them (Brezhnev himself, after all, had told me that you must whip the Soviets if you want something from them), but also making it clear that we wanted better relations. Certainly, we should not take a public stance that would humiliate them internationally. Despite these considerations, I decided not to resign because I had never regarded the Treaty of Friendship and Cooperation as essential. In fact, as I have argued, it did not even fit in with my policy line that Egypt should be non-aligned and in principle should not enter into contractual agreements with the superpowers.

As expected, the abrogation of the Treaty of Friendship and Cooperation between the Soviet Union and Egypt received much attention from foreign governments and the world media. Various interpretations and counter-interpretations were set forth. Some American writers argued that this step was prearranged between Washington and Cairo through the so-called 'back channel'. They argued that Sadat was simply fulfilling the two conditions imposed by the USA as the price of good relations with Washington, namely, 1) the expulsion of the Soviet experts from Egypt, which Sadat had completed in July 1972, and 2) the termination of the Soviet–Egyptian Treaty of Friendship and Cooperation. To support this point of view they spread the rumour that Prince Sultan of Saudi Arabia, on his way back from Washington, had conveyed to President Sadat a message that it was time he got rid of the Soviets. I know of no evidence to support this story. Although it is fair to say that the Soviets apparently had a similar explanation for Sadat's sudden decision. Much later, after I had resigned I was visited in

Alexandria by a senior Soviet strategic analyst who told me that the Soviets were sure that the idea of abrogating the treaty had been suggested to Sadat by a highly-placed Saudi official who had visited him shortly before Sadat made his announcement. It was not Prince Sultan that the Soviets suspected but a Saudi close to King Faisal who was thought to be a regular conduit for American intelligence.

In fact, the abrogation of the treaty fitted only too well with Sadat's own feelings against the Soviet Union and with his previous style. There is no need to look for an external cause for this decision. It was simply the culmination of a trend which had started with the expulsion of the Soviet military experts in 1972, developed into a verbal campaign of abuse by Sadat after the October War, and now came to its logical conclusion. I had personally tried to moderate Sadat's hostility towards the Soviet Union, and to convince him to pursue a balanced policy towards both great powers, but I had known all along that his personal feelings might well prevail in the end. While I opposed his decision to abrogate the treaty, I cannot say that I was surprised by it.

The abrogation of the Treaty of Friendship and Cooperation was followed by the inevitable blast and counterblast in the information media of the two countries. Relations between Egypt and the Soviet Union reached their lowest ebb and were confined to a routine exchange of information concerning the implemention of old agreements on industry and trade which still remained in effect. It is important to stress that for all their anger the Soviets really could do nothing once Egypt had decided to abrogate the treaty unilaterally.

There are two lessons to be learned from this experience. The first is that the 'supermarket diplomacy' of the 1970s serves little purpose: treaties which can be bought ready for use and readily discarded without consequences mean nothing. The second is that for a country like Egypt it is in many ways easier and safer to deal with a superpower than with a small or medium-sized country. A superpower will not bother to go to war over the abrogation of a treaty, but simply write off the loss as a bad investment. Examples of this abound. When Qaddafi asked the British and the Americans to evacuate their bases in Libya, they left without resistance, although binding contracts entitled them to the use of those bases. In Indonesia, President Suharto expelled the Soviets without encountering any resistance on their part. In Iran, the US allowed itself to be forced out and humiliated by the seizing of hostages after a very long period of deep involvement in all aspects of life in that country. In Somalia, Siad Barre expelled the Soviet Union suddenly, again without repercussions. One could cite many examples of the ease with which a small country can free itself from a great power, cancelling binding treaties and putting an end to long-standing relationships.

I argued earlier, that I am against treaties between superpowers and weaker countries because they put the small country at the mercy of the superpower. This is true. The small power has no leverage, and the superpower can dictate its conditions, respecting or violating the clauses of the treaty as it sees fit. But it is also true that in these circumstances the small country has the ultimate weapon of abrogating the treaty itself. The small country can do this with impunity, because the use of force to maintain the relationship entails too great a risk for the superpower; armed intervention would be perceived as a reversion to colonial times and might also lead to confrontation with other countries.

There is in fact very little the superpowers can do to impose compliance on a small ally short of using force. The reason is simple enough: in the small countries of what we know as the Third World, most of what happens depends on the personality in power at a particular time. The relations established by the superpowers in the Third World never bind them to a country, but to a man or a small group of men. If the man goes, so does the relationship. In fact, the relationship can collapse even if the man just changes his mind, as Sadat did.

The only way for a superpower to decrease its dependency on the whims or political stability of individual leaders, is to become a supplier of arms to the country. Any Third World ruler will think long and hard before jeopardising his major source of arms, even if his country is not at war. Third World rulers are all dependent on their armies to stay in power, even if the régime is ostensibly not a military one, Yet, the superpowers forget this very often. The Soviets, for example, forgot this simple fact of Third World politics when dealing with both Nasser and Sadat. Both leaders turned to the Soviet Union because of their dire need for weapons, not for ideological reasons. Both started turning away from it when the flow of military supplies was interrupted or slowed down to a trickle. The difference was that Sadat found a much more forthcoming United States, not as far as arms were concerned but at least in the negotiations over the Middle East crisis.

The abrogation of the Treaty of Friendship and Cooperation

forced the Soviets to reassess the Middle East situation and their influence there, and by late 1976 they clearly concluded that they should start mending their fences with Egypt. I believe that this decision was based on two factors. First, they must have realised that by pursuing a hard line against Egypt, their ally of long-standing, they risked losing influence on other Middle Eastern and African countries, because they would become sceptical about Moscow's reliability. Secondly, the Soviets must have become aware that by accepting a de facto and legal break with Cairo they would be giving free rein to the United States, not only in Egypt, but also concerning the solution of the entire Middle East problem.

Meetings with Gromyko in Sophia

In the fall of 1976 the Soviet ambassador in Cairo requested a meeting with me, and delivered a message from the Soviet leaders to President Sadat. It was a very dry message, requesting a meeting between Gromyko and myself to take place in Sofia, the capital of Bulgaria. Although the message was curt, it nevertheless represented an important and extraordinary initiative on the part of Moscow. It was also significant that it made no reference at all to the abrogation of the Treaty of Friendship and Cooperation. Possibly, by this omission the Soviets wanted to convey the impression that they did not recognise the Egyptian decision as legally valid. At any rate, I immediately informed the Soviet ambassador of Egypt's positive reaction to the initiative. Later, I informed President Sadat of the content of the Soviet message and he agreed that the encounter should take place.

The meetings in Sofia started on 4 November 1976, in a highly charged atmosphere and amidst much international attention and speculation. Most observers seemed convinced that this would be a one-shot operation, not to be followed by further meetings. However, my own conviction was that there was more to it, since this major initiative must have been taken after a serious and comprehensive reappraisal of the Russian–Egyptian relationship. The Soviets would not expose themselves lightly to the danger cf a second public humiliation if the meeting failed to bring about reconciliation. The choice of Sofia also was a conciliatory move, while it was not politically a neutral country, it was outside the boundaries of either country. There was some ground for optimism as to the ultimate outcome of the Sofia meeting, but I had no illusion that it would lead to the final solution of any issue. Rather, I expected protracted and perhaps acrimonious preliminary exchanges, followed by slow progress on substance.

This is exactly what happened. The first formal meeting was devoted to statements and counter-statements from both sides, equally anxious to put on record their respective positions, to justify them, and to show that all blame lay with the other party. Gromyko, for instance, lectured us on past events, defending Soviet behaviour and complaining about the 'persistent and premeditated line' which President Sadat took in 'distorting the position of the Soviet Union'. In his best professorial style, he also recited for us the principles in which the Soviet Union believed and which it practised.

I listened to Gromyko's prepared speech patiently and without undue concern, knowing that it is standard Soviet practice to make harsh statements for the official record. As I expected, just under the official harshness, the message conveyed by Gromyko was rather encouraging. He made four points of special significance: first, the Soviet leadership wanted to restore Egyptian–Soviet relations; second, it was conscious of Egypt's central role and leadership in the Middle East; third, the Soviets had apparently re-examined their past experience and were ready to learn from it, changing their behaviour toward Egypt; and fourth, the Soviets wanted to erase completely the consequences of the abrogation of the treaty; to this end, they wanted to give any new agreement between us the status of a binding document, ratified by the competent political institutions of the two countries. While I was pleased with the first three points, I was not ready to accept the last one.

In my answer, I also summarised the vicissitudes of Egyptian-Soviet relations and the reasons which had led to the final rupture, rebuffing all the accusations which Gromyko had hurled at us, and putting the blame on the Soviets. I reminded Gromyko that during the previous three years I had repeatedly warned the Soviet leaders that their continuous haggling and beating about the bush when discussing major issues would imperil the ties between Cairo and Moscow. As far back as my first trip to Moscow in January 1974, I reminded Gromyko, I had warned Brezhnev that if the Soviets persisted in their old tactics, they would be granted an 'exit visa' by

Sadat, and would lose everything they had gained as a result of the 'entry visa' issued by President Nasser in the early 1950s. This had now happened and they only had themselves to blame, because they had not honoured their commitments, as stipulated in the Treaty of Friendship and Cooperation. In particular, they had not honoured the military obligations of Article 8 which stated: 'The Soviet side is responsible for strengthening the Egyptian defense capabilities to enable Egypt to stand against all forms of aggression.'

I concluded that it was clear to us that the Soviet Union had deliberately not lived up to its commitments and that therefore we seriously doubted whether the Soviet Union was really a friendly country. As a consequence, the Soviet idea that all problems would be solved by reactivating the old treaty or concluding a new one was unacceptable to us. There was no magic in signing a document before we understood each other and became convinced that both of us would change our attitudes. The mere existence of the previous Treaty of Friendship and Cooperation had not solved our problems, and the signing of a new formal paper would not solve our problems either.

Gromyko looked ill at ease while I was talking. He did not reply immediately and we agreed instead to hold a second meeting. He came back armed with legalistic arguments to prove that the USSR had respected the terms of the treaty to the letter. Gromyko's argument was very simple: the Soviet Union had honoured all its commitments under its 'contractual obligations', by which he meant that the Soviet Union had delivered to Egypt all the equipment specifically mentioned in any contract signed between Cairo and Moscow.

While it was true that Moscow had delivered all arms specifically mentioned in a contract, this did not mean that it had discharged all its obligations. Moscow had broad commitments to Egypt under the Treaty of Friendship and Cooperation, most importantly a commitment to strengthen our defense capability. It is normal practice in international relations that these broad commitments are then translated into specific agreements negotiated between the two parties and having the value of 'contractual obligations'. The Soviet Union had negotiated such an agreement concerning the supply of military equipment in 1973, and had fulfilled all its terms in 1975. However, it had refused to negotiate any other arms deal, and thus it had not honoured the spirit of its broader commitment to strengthen our defences under the Treaty of Friendship and Cooperation.

I made it clear to Gromyko that we would not be convinced by his casuistry. The treaty put the Soviet Union under the obligation to build Egypt's defence capabilities so that it would be able to repel 'all forms of aggression'. This meant that the Soviet Union had to build up our armed forces so that they would be equal, if not superior, to those of Israel. The Soviets had failed to do this. Even when a contract was signed, it never contained the items Egypt wanted in order to resist effectively Israeli aggression, but only a selection of weapons clearly inferior to what Israel had. After these contracts were signed, the delivery dates were never respected. The result was that the Egyptian commanders were unable to plan ahead sufficiently and the political leaders were placed in a very awkward situation, since political decisions had to be based on Egypt's military capabilities. The 1973 arms deal was a perfect example of all these problems.

I made all these points clear to Gromyko without mincing my words, and at the end I added sarcastically that while the Soviet Union was not honouring clauses which were in the treaty, it seemed to honour faithfully other clauses which were not in it. I could not find any words in the document that obliged the Soviet Union to provide us with second-rate equipment and then to render this equipment totally useless by withholding spare parts. Yet this is what they had done to our planes, radar and missiles, now largely inoperative because of the lack of spare parts. The Soviets would be totally responsible if Israel took advantage of the situation to carry out another preemptive strike. Furthermore, I added, where was the clause in the treaty that gave the Soviet Union the 'right to confiscate Egyptian property'?

Uncertain whether he had understood correctly, Gromyko asked me to repeat this last question and, after listening to the interpreter a second time, he started pounding the table in a rage, shouting he would not sit quietly and listen to such accusations. This was not an accusation but a fact, I told him. In agreement with our maintenance contract signed by the two sides, Egypt had sent a large number of airplane engines to the USSR to be overhauled. These planes, their engines and the cost of the overhauling had been fully paid for by Egypt. Nevertheless, the Soviet government had refused to send the engines back to Egypt for over a year. Surely this amounted to confiscation of property. The result was that 92 Egyptian planes were grounded, in addition to those paralysed by lack of spare parts. I pointed out to Gromyko that if such an incident had happened between Egypt and any Western government or corporation, we would have brought them to court in their own counry, and got back the engines plus an indemnity. But in the case of the Soviet Union, because of the characteristics of their system and the existence of the Treaty of Friendship and Cooperation, Egypt was in no position to do anything but to keep reminding the Soviet government of its obligations – but to no avail.

It was obvious that Gromyko was cornered and could find no excuse for the Russian behaviour. I insisted on receiving an answer, and he vaguely said that there must have been some sort of misunderstanding, or a snag in the Soviet bureaucracy. Finally, without even consulting Moscow, he said that the problem was not very serious and that I could consider it already solved; the 92 engines would be delivered to us immediately after his return to Moscow. Gromyko kept his word and the engines which had been in Soviet hands for over a year were finally returned to us.

Having solved the problem of the airplane engines, Gromyko requested a short recess, to be followed by a private meeting. In the closed session, and as I expected, Gromyko's tone changed drastically, becoming much more conciliatory. Nevertheless, he stubbornly re-opened the question of concluding a new formal treaty between Egypt and the USSR. I made it clear that Egypt would not draw up a new treaty or revive the old one, because it would solve nothing and would be an admission that the abrogation had been a mistake. I would not agree to anything more than the issuing of a joint communiqué sanctioning the reconciliation which might take place between Moscow and Cairo. I then surprised Gromyko by asking him to collaborate with me in reviving the summit meeting between President Sadat and Comrade Brezhnev which had been cancelled when Brezhnev fell ill at the end of 1974. I told Gromyko that we should make every effort to revive the summit, because it was bound to open the way for an agreement on all other pending questions, and thus for the restoration of good relations between Egypt and the USSR. But I also made it clear that the Soviet leadership should re-examine carefully the lessons of the recent past, and change their policy accordingly. I insisted again that the Soviet Union was duty-bound to equip Egypt on a permanent basis with sophisticated arms and spare parts. To my surprise and satisfaction, Gromyko announced that the Soviet leadership would furnish Egypt with whatever arms it requested, with no limitation on quantity or quality. I have to confess that I did not believe what I heard, and I asked ¹ Gromyko to repeat his statement. He did this, adding for emphasis, 'Everything, without exception'.

Another encouraging sign was that neither in the private meeting nor in the full encounters of the two delegations did the Soviets mention the Egyptian debt. In fact, this was the first time in any negotiation that the debt was not mentioned. All these signals were very promising, and I concluded my talks with Gromyko by pledging that a joint communiqué would be issued at the end of the summit between Brezhnev and Sadat, tentatively scheduled for September 1977. The communiqué or declaration would be comprehensive and provide adequate guidelines for the future relations between the two countries. Gromyko did not accept the idea that the summit should only be followed by the issuing of a communiqué rather than the signing of a treaty, but did not reject it either. It was evident that he was not authorised to make a decision and, feeling that he needed time to consult with Brezhnev, I proposed to adjourn the meeting.

During our second tête-à-tête meeting, Gromyko again tried to convince me that a new treaty should be signed and ratified, but I continued to reject the proposal. He pointed out that any paper signed by the two countries, whether in the form of a treaty or of a declaration would have to be submitted to the Soviet legislature for ratification. I only said that the Soviets were entitled to follow their own procedures, but that, in Egypt's case, political declarations or communiqués are not subject to ratification by the Assembly. Rather, we only inform the Assembly of the contents of the document. Gromyko was very insistent that any document issued at the summit should be formally ratified by the parliaments, but I held my ground and he finally accepted the point.

Arms Purchases

This meeting in Sofia appeared to be a turning point in our relations with the Soviets. We had hit them hard, and once again they had come back in a more conciliatory mood and prepared to supply us with arms. The problem of the payment for arms from the Soviet Union, however, raised some controversy in Egypt and initially even revived Sadat's hostility. This issue had not even been discussed between Gromyko and myself. We both knew that Egypt would now have to pay cash for all military equipment, since there no longer existed a special relationship between the two countries. This did not create a problem because Saudi Arabia and other Gulf states were ready to finance our purchases. In fact, Saudi Arabia had just paid for the six American C-130s we had bought from the USA after so much controversy.

When it became clear in Egypt that the Soviet Union was ready to sell arms to Egypt but not to provide them on special terms, many voices were raised, arguing that if this was the case we should turn elsewhere for our purchases. The idea that it was necessary to diversify our sources of arms was suggested by many, while others argued that the Soviet equipment was not worth purchasing, because it was inferior to what could be obtained in the West. These criticisms were ill-founded, in my opinion, and disregarded some basic facts. First, the Egyptian army had been trained and equipped by the Soviet Union for twenty years. Certainly, it was much easier to build it up fast if we continued to provide the equipment with which our men were familiar, rather than having to retrain them to handle different weapons. Second, the Soviet weapons were not inferior. In all arms market there are good and bad weapons, sophisticated and unsophisticated equipment. The problem was simply that of choosing the Soviet equipment most appropriate for our needs. In any case, our experience in the October War had shown clearly that Soviet equipment was certainly not grossly inferior to the American. Third, the Soviet Union is capable of providing large quantities of equipment quickly, while in the Western countries production capacity is limited and waiting periods are long. Furthermore, in the United States arms sales are subject to complex political checks. They must be approved by the President and the Congress, which are quite open to the influence of the Jewish and Zionist lobby. Fourth, it is against the national interest of Egypt to depend on the United States for arms. The

United States is Israel's arms supplier and the United States will always aim at maintaining Israel's military superiority. As for the theory that Egypt should get its weapons from a wide variety of sources, eliminating its dependency on any one country, while I support the principle, I can only caution that this would cause enormous training and logistic problems, and could possibly weaken our armed forces, rather than strengthen them.

Meetings in Moscow

After this first meeting in Sofia, the Soviets continued to move with their usual ponderous slowness. Probably, this was due to their own internal problems in this period, with Brezhnev's failing health and the unfolding of the conflict which led to Podgorny's ousting and to other changes in the Soviet leadership. A second meeting between Gromyko and myself was not scheduled to take place until early June 1977, in Geneva. At the last moment Gromyko informed me that he could not leave Moscow, and asked me to see him there. I answered that I would go to Moscow with the proviso that Gromyko should then come to Cairo the following August. He agreed to this solution and on 8 June I arrived in Moscow.

I had a first meeting with Gromyko, dedicated almost entirely to the discussion of the draft of the communiqué to be issued when Brezhnev visited Cairo for the summit meeting with Sadat. I did not like the draft at all: it was heavy and pompous and replete with irrelevant general statements on disarmament, colonialism, neo-colonialism and imperialism. As for the part dealing specifically with Egyptian–Soviet relations, it contained no clause spelling out Soviet responsibility for strengthening Egypt's defence capability. I think this omission was due to my insistence that this document should be issued as a declaration and not as a treaty. It did not imply that the Soviets were going back on their promise to equip the Egyptian army. More serious was the fact that the Soviets had included a statement about the necessity of 'harmonizing the political line' of the two countries. I could not accept such a statement because it could be interpreted to mean that cooperation with the Soviet Union was conditional on the political line chosen by Egypt in its foreign or even domestic policy. Thus the Soviet Union would later feel free to go back on any cooperation agreement on the grounds that our political choices did not conform to Soviet principles. At any rate, I decided not to get into a detailed discussion of the draft with Gromyko, but simply said I would study it and then send him an Egyptian counterproposal.

The meeting with Brezhnev followed, and it was extraordinarily cordial, considering the circumstances. There was no doubt in my mind that the Soviet Union had decided that Egypt was far too important a country in the Middle East for the Soviet Union to have bad relations with it. Brezhnev was extremely forthcoming, and when I reminded him that we urgently needed spare parts because most of our planes were grounded he waved his arms high in the air, promising that 'all your planes will fly again'. Another positive sign was that he too did not raise the issue of the Egyptian debt.

I left Moscow after these two encounters quite optimistic about the future. The Soviet Union had decided Egypt was important to them, and certainly the Americans had reached the same conclusion since the time of the October War. This was the best situation for Egypt, creating the conditions for us to maintain good relations with both superpowers without becoming dependent on either. The Soviets had agreed to sell us arms, and as long as we had the hard currency to pay for our purchases there was little likelihood that they would go back on their decision. Saudi Arabia and other Gulf countries were ready to provide the necessary funds.

Unfortunately, events did not live up to these optimistic expectations. Neither Gromyko's visit to Cairo in August, nor the Brezhnev–Sadat summit in September materialised because the Soviet Union had once again plunged into a dialogue with the United States, both on the general issue of détente and more specifically concerning the Middle East conflict. Whenever the Soviet Union is negotiating with the United States, it drops all its other contacts, and above all refrains from taking steps which might cause negative reaction in Washington. In this particular case, once the dialogue with the United States was open, the Soviet Union decided to wait before it started selling arms to Egypt and before Brezhnev came to Cairo. But they never had a second chance to pick up the threads of their policy toward Egypt. Sadat saw the Soviet silence as a new rebuff and turned once again to the United States. The Soviet Union was again relegated to a very secondary role in the Middle East.

The Soviet Leadership and Egypt

It is opportune here to reflect on this period in Soviet–Egyptian policy because of the divisions among the Soviet leaders and their total lack of understanding of the Egyptian system or that of any other Third World country. The Soviet leadership in this period was deeply divided about Egypt. One group, undoubtedly headed by Brezhnev, understood the importance of Egypt in the Arab world; this group was also aware that Egypt needed an ally more than ever and that it would turn to the United States if the Soviet Union drew back. The other group was also probably convinced of the importance of Egypt, but distrusted Sadat, worried about his anti-Soviet attitude and probably was very disturbed by the new assertion of Egyptian independence. Egypt had gone to war without consulting the Soviets and had had a noticeable rapprochement with the United States since then. This group was apparently convinced that if the Soviet Union exercised enough pressure by withholding military supplies Egypt would eventually return to the Soviet fold. Repeatedly, this group was proved wrong. Sadat's decision to expel the Soviet experts, his acceptance of the American role in the disengagement negotiations, the abrogation of the Treaty of Friendship and Cooperation, were all signs that Egypt was not caving in, but fashioning a new policy. Every time, Brezhnev's group was able to impose its views for a while, signing an arms deal, resuming arms shipments, and finally taking the first steps toward reconciliation after the abrogation of the Treaty. But these steps never went far enough and fast enough to have a decisive impact on Sadat and allay his suspicions of the Soviet Union.

The policy of the hard-line group was based on a complete misunderstanding of Egypt. They thought that by withholding arms they would create enormous domestic pressure on Sadat and that his people, and above all his army, might revolt. But that is not the way things work in Egypt. Once a leader is in power, people continue to support him without much bickering or questioning. They take it for granted that their ruler is a committed nationalist and knows best what is good for the country. The result is that the leader in Egypt, as in many countries, can take major decisions without worrying about public opinion. It takes much more than external pressures to turn the people against their leader. In fact, in most developing countries it is domestic problems which turn the people against a ruler, not foreign policy issues. On the contrary, in countries that have been subjected to colonial domination people react strongly against foreign pressures and rally blindly behind their governments. This is why the Soviet game not only failed but backfired. The Soviet attacks on Sadat, reported in the local media, rallied public opinion behind the President. He began to appear as a bastion of Egyptian independence against the Soviet Union, which had an enormous appetite for intervention in Egyptian affairs. It was the Soviet Union's lack of understanding of the Egyptian system which led in the end to the deterioration of Soviet–Egyptian relations and to the failure of their policy in Egypt.

Notes

1. *Years of Upheaval* (Boston: Little, Brown, and Company), pp. 768, 829.

11 CARTER SEEKS A COMPREHENSIVE SETTLEMENT

With the inauguration of the new Carter administration in January 1977, things started moving again in the Middle East. The long period of stagnation which followed the second Egyptian–Israeli disengagement came to an end. The new administration brought in new personalities and a fresh outlook and a real determination to score some success in the peace-making endeavour. As a relatively unknown personality, both in the United States and abroad, Jimmy Carter needed to do something to build up his image. The major domestic problems — unemployment, inflation, and the energy crisis — were too intractable to serve this purpose. International issues appeared to offer the greatest hope.

This link between internal politics and foreign policy was, from our point of view, both a strength and a weakness of the Carter administration. On the one hand, it suggested to us that the new President would keep the Middle East high on his agenda. On the other hand, it also indicated that his moves in the Middle East would be highly susceptible to domestic pressure: he would be keeping a close eye on the Jewish lobby.

We studied Carter's early moves in foreign policy, and we found the signals to be very mixed. The prominence given to human rights was not altogether reassuring. True, this was a lofty principle but it was also a pompous and empty slogan which no government was prepared to implement fully at home and certainly not the United States. In fact, the human rights slogan was only really used to put pressure on the Soviet Union, and even there mainly where Jewish dissidents were concerned. If Carter had been an angel from heaven, as his associates portrayed him, he would have landed in Palestine, where a whole people was deprived of its human rights. It did not take us long to conclude that we could not expect a solution to the Middle East problem to emerge from Carter's commitment to human rights.

Another issue high on Carter's agenda was that of Soviet–American relations and détente. It was clear that he did not want confrontation, reacting cautiously to the Soviet Union's new dynamic strategy in Africa, Afghanistan and Cambodia. Rather, he followed his own active counterstrategy, strengthening the ties with Peking but also continuing the SALT II negotiations. All these moves on the international chessboard were fairly positive from our point of view because we thought détente would assist the full participation of both superpowers in an international solution to the Middle East conflict.

Carter's handling of the Panama Canal issue was also rather encouraging. It was by mere chance that the issue had reached the final stages at this point, but it was to Carter's credit that he saw it through to the end, pushing the final agreement through a reluctant Congress despite strong opposition. The Panama Canal Treaty was a test of Carter's ability to cope with and manipulate domestic opposition, and he passed it.

Carter's new team was also fairly reassuring. We had no reservations about his Secretary of State, Cyrus Vance, whom we knew to be a man of integrity and extensive diplomatic experience. A lawyer by profession, he viewed things as being right or wrong, not of various shades in between and he was a straightforward person, easy and pleasant to deal with. The new team in the National Security Council was well staffed with Middle East experts. The National Security Adviser Zbigniew Brzezinski, was one of the authors of the Brookings Institution Report on the Middle East, which provided a solution of the problem on the basis of a return to the pre-1967 borders and the creation of a Palestinian entity. Unfortunatey, we soon discovered that Brzezinski was difficult to deal with and more inclined to lecture experienced diplomats as if they had been undergraduates than to discuss issues with them. More seriously, he turned out to be untrustworthy, reneging on his position concerning the Palestinian right to statehood while in office, only to embrace that position again when he returned, later on, to the academic world.

The New US Strategy

The Carter team started working on the voluminous Middle East file as soon as it came to office. The President, Vance and Brzezinski wasted no time in devising a new strategy radically different from Kissinger's. Abandoning the Republican administration's step-by-step procedure, they started looking for a way to negotiate a comprehensive peace. It was apparent from the very beginning that President Carter himself had decided to take an active role in the Middle East issue and he became the first American President willing to make numerous public statements on the Middle East and particularly the Palestinian problem, the most delicate part of it. In the Middle East it was clear that the new American President was seriously committed to doing something, personally.

President Sadat and myself started to establish our contacts with President Carter, Vance and Brzezinski, but Carter acted more swiftly. On 22 January 1977, I received through Ambassador Eilts a brief oral message from Vance. The gist of it was that President Carter attached the highest importance to making significant progress that year toward a just and lasting peace in the Middle East. He had thus asked Vance to visit certain key Middle East capitals so that the USA would have the benefit of the views of the major leaders in the area when it developed its own thinking about how progress toward peace could best be achieved. Vance especially wanted to visit Egypt and have the opportunity to meet President Sadat and myself before going to any other Arab country. He intended to visit Israel, come to Egypt, on 17 and 18 February, and then proceed to Syria and Saudi Arabia.

We were pleased with the message, because it revealed not only that Carter wanted to move quickly, but also that he recognised Egypt's key role in negotiating any solution. Carter personally reiterated the same point in a message to Sadat brought by Vance in February: 'I count heavily on your advice as we begin to find ways to make significant progress this year towards a just and lasting peace in the Middle East. This is why I considered it important that you be the first head of state in the Arab world with whom Secretary Vance will meet . . .'

Vance's visit in February was only the first step in a series of contacts, in person and in writing, between Washington and all parties to the Middle East conflict which came to be known as 'the proximity talks'. Having decided to seek a comprehensive settlement in the Middle East, the Carter administration focused its efforts on reconvening the Geneva Conference. The purpose of the proximity talks was to work out a formula for convening the Geneva Conference acceptable to all and to reconcile as much as possible the position of the various parties prior to the opening of the Geneva Conference. I may add here that the proximity talks also helped to cement a special relation between Washington and Cairo.

Carter and Vance kept us fully informed about their contacts with other parties to the Middle East conflict and we had far-reaching exchanges not only on the immediate issues but also about problems concerning the Horn of Africa and the Arabian peninsula. However, I want to stress that in this period Egypt did not seek to take advantage of this special relation with the United States to further its own interests to the detriment of other Arab countries.

The central obstacle to the convening of the Geneva Conference was the problem of PLO representation. Israel obviously was opposed to it but the Arab countries would not accept a conference without Palestinian representation. The PLO had been recognised at Rabat as the sole representative of the Palestinian people, and therefore the PLO had to be in Geneva and participate fully in the proceedings.

It may be worth summarising at this point the position of the main parties as it emerged during the constant exchanges in 1977. The Arab countries were united on main principles in dealing with Israel, although disagreement on procedure and details still existed. This unity had been achieved in the meetings of the Arab League and the summits of the heads of state. The fundamental Arab principle was that no country should take unilateral decisions which would split the Arabs and undermine the roots of their solidarity. Any breach of this principle, it was understood, would have serious repercussions on the Arab cause, which had acquired unusual strength from the October War. The war had cemented Arab relations under Egyptian leadership in a fashion unprecedented in Arab history.

In addition to this overriding principle, the Arab states were also committed to the following points:

1) Israel forces must be completely withdrawn from the territories occupied in 1967.
2) The right of the Palestinian people to exercise freely their right to self-determination must be recognised, leading to the establishment of an independent Palestinian state.
3) The PLO is the sole legitimate representative of the Palestinian people.

It was also clear amongst Arab official circles that within the framework of a comprehensive peace settlement, the Arab governments would be ready to sign peace agreements with Israel, ending the state of belligerency. That did not necessarily mean that the Arab countries, including Egypt, would be ready to normalise relations with Israel before the lapse of a long transitional period during which Israeli behaviour should be kept under close scrutiny and observation. Sadat himself was very outspoken on this point. In early 1977, reacting to a question addressed to him at a press conference as to when normalisation would take place between Israel and Egypt, Sadat answered forthwith, 'Not in my generation'. Five months later Sadat was asked the same question, and this time his more optimistic answer was that 'normalisation could take place within five years of the signing of a peace agreement with Israel'.

From this, one summarises the Arab peace conditions as follows:

1) The Arab countries would only conclude a comprehensive peace agreement with Israel, refusing separate peace.
2) By doing so, they would recognise the existence of Israel as a Middle Eastern country.
3) The Palestinian question should not be treated as a humanitarian problem, but principally as a political problem. The Palestinian people were entitled to statehood, not charity.
4) Normalisation with Israel should be postponed till Israel proved that it was worthy of trust.

Despite this basic unity on the main principles, there were some divisions in the Arab camp, prompted above all by fears that each country would in the end only think of safeguarding its own interests. The country which could most easily pursue this course was Egypt. A settlement between Israel and Egypt could have been reached without too many problems, if Egypt had wanted. President Nixon had already told us that Sinai was no problem, whereas Israel was not readily prepared to return the Golan Heights to Syria and less so the West Bank and Jerusalem to the Palestinians. Progress here could be made only if Egypt held fast, accepting peace with Israel only if the demands of the Syrians and the Palestinians were met. Understandably, Assad and the PLO were very suspicious of Sadat, fearing he would make a separate peace. For this reason, Assad insisted that the Arab countries should be represented by a unified delegation at Geneva, with one voice speaking for all. Egypt agreed to this request, because it had no intention of betraying the other Arab countries. As for the PLO, there was a real danger at this point that it would take too uncompromising a position, thus totally defeating the possibility of success at Geneva. We stayed in close touch with Syria and the PLO, to reassure them about our intentions and at the same time to convince them to remain flexible.

The real obstacle to Geneva was not the divisions and suspicions in the Arab camp, but the position of Israel. Israel did not want multi-national negotiations and the convening of the Geneva Conference. In fact, there was never any public statement by Israeli leaders supporting the conference, even after they had privately informed the United States that they would attend. The Israelis believed that they could not dictate their will on a united Arab front, but if they could negotiate with each country separately, and above all isolate Egypt from the other countries, they might obtain what they wanted. While insisting on separate negotiations, the Israelis summed up their position as follows:–

1) Israel would not withdraw to the frontiers which existed prior to 1967.
2) Israel would not accept the establishment of an independent Palestinian state, and specifically rejected any discussion about what it called 'foreign sovereignty' in 'Judea and Samaria' (the West Bank), and Gaza.
3) Israel would never yield on the status of Jerusalem: the city would remain united and be the eternal capital of Israel.
4) Normalisation should take place immediately upon the signature of peace treaties, with open frontiers and everything else this concept entailed.

The position of the United States was the most ambiguous. Carter wanted a settlement in the Middle East, but he knew that there could be no comprehensive peace until the Palestinian problem was solved. This meant that the United States should at least establish direct contacts with the PLO and eventually recognize it. However, the pressure from Israel and the Jewish lobby against contacts with the PLO was enormous. Furthermore, Washington was bound by the formal guarantees Kissinger had given to Israel as part of the agreement on the second disengagement on the Egyptian front: the United States had pledged not to negotiate with or recognise the PLO until it in turn recognised Israel's right to exist and accepted Security Council Resolutions 242 and 338. In addition the United States had given Israel a guarantee that it would consult with it on every new move in the UN or at the Geneva Conference. Much of the future of the peace negotiations thus depended on the US handling of the PLO issue. It was clear to us that Carter had no real policy of his own here, but would follow Israel's unless the pressure of the Arab states made it impossible for him to do so.

The meetings, exchanges, messages and countermessages among the parties during the summer and autumn of 1977 were innumerable and very complex. Rather than present a chronological account which would only confuse the reader, I will analyse the major issues under discussion and the progress made on each. The Carter administration had three main goals:

1) Finding a formula for the convening of the Geneva Conference acceptable to all parties in the conflict. This implied solving the problem of Palestinian representation.
2) Reaching an agreement between the United States and the Soviet Union concerning the basic framework for a Middle East settlement.
3) Paving the way for the signing of peace treaties between Israel and each Arab country in a state of war with it by asking each party to submit in writing a draft treaty to the United States. The Americans would then prepare a compromise draft.

It has been stated by some writers that the efforts to convene the Geneva Conference were bound to fail because there was no agreement on a formula. In fact there was agreement that the conference would be convened in December 1977 according to the following formula:

1. The Arab parties would be represented by a unified Arab delegation for the opening sessions at Geneva. Within the delegation there would be Palestinians, possibly including not well-known members of the PLO.
2. Separate working groups or subcommittees for the negotiation of peace treaties would be formed as follows:
   (a) Egypt–Israel
   (b) Syria–Israel
   (c) Jordan–Israel

(d) Lcbanon–Israel
(e) The West Bank, Gaza, the Palestinian question and the question of refugees would be discussed among Israel, Jordan, Egypt, the Palestinians and perhaps others as determined at the opening session of the Geneva Conference.
3. The working groups or subcommittees would report to the plenary.

This formula, represented a compromise between the Arab, and particularly Syrian, insistence that the Arab side be represented by a unified delegation, and the Israeli insistence that it would accept only bilateral negotiations with each country. What was still unsolved in September 1977 was the question of how the Palestinians would be represented both in the united Arab delegation and in the subcommittees charged with negotiating the future of the West Bank and Gaza.

Meetings with the Americans

This was the major topic of discussion during two high level meetings between the Egyptians and the Americans in Washington on 21 September 1977. I will discuss these meetings extensively, because they were very significant. While they revealed serious unresolved problems, they also made it clear that there were good possibilities of success, as long as the Arab countries stuck consistently to their strategy. Against this background, it will be easier for the reader to assess Sadat's extraordinary move in going to Jerusalem.

The first meeting was a brief tête-à-tête between President Carter and myself; it was followed immediately by a full meeting of the Egyptian delegation and the American Middle East team in the Oval Room. President Carter welcomed me and explained why he wanted to see me alone. He was extraordinarily candid and honest. He confided to me that it was essential for him to clarify some points which, in his opinion, might complicate the solution of the Middle East crisis and create serious difficulties on the long road of mutual understanding and collaboration between Egypt and the United States. He wanted to make his position as clear as possible on two issues which President Sadat had repeatedly taken up with him. The first was Sadat's assertion that Carter could put pressure on Israel.

Commenting on this first point, President Carter said: 'President Sadat repeatedly asks me to exercise major pressure on Israel, but I want you to know that I simply cannot do it because it would be a personal political suicide for me.'

The second issue concerned Soviet–American relations:

> President Sadat frequently urges me to be tough with the Soviet Union. On this too, I want you to understand that since I became President of the United States, the Soviet leadership has spared no effort to criticise my administration's position on détente. Brezhnev himself has stated during the last six months that I was personally responsible for what he called a drastic change in the United States's policy in this regard. Mr Deputy Prime Minister, I want you to understand that I can neither provoke the Soviet Union nor bear pressure on them. I have to do something to prove to the Soviet leadership that they were wrong in their assertion that I am responsible for what they called a change in the United States policy. I simply can not bear pressure on Moscow because this would be a second political suicide for me.

Having made his position as clear as possible on these two major issues, President Carter discussed with me the latest developments regarding the Middle East crisis and particularly the Palestinian question. We also compared notes on ways and means of fostering the bilateral cooperation between the United States and Egypt.

While I was very impressed by President Carter's honesty I was also disappointed and particularly I was not at all convinced that he did not have any leverage on Israel. His unwillingness to be tough with the Soviets did not worry me as much, because I was already convinced that the USSR should be involved in the peace process and not kept out as a dangerous meddler. In fact, Carter's fear of the Soviet Union had positive results from our point of view, leading the American President to negotiate with the Soviets a joint statement establishing a common superpower framework for negotiations at Geneva, as we shall see later. However, I was really dismayed to find President Carter so hesitant and so ready to put his personal future above the major issues of war and peace in such a sensitive and strategic area as the Middle East. A weak President is bad enough, but a frightened President is terrifying.

Here I should add that later I conveyed to Sadat what Carter had told me, expecting him to grasp immediately the significance of those statements and that we could not rely solely on the United States. Sadat should have re-evaluated America's role in the peace process and particularly his firmly held and frequently repeated belief that 99.9 per cent of the final settlement lay in the hands of the United States. After Carter had personally admitted his limitations, President Sadat should never have continued to depend entirely on the United States as his major partner.

The larger meeting which followed the tête-à-tête encounter only deepened my dismay. President Carter was accompanied by Vice-President Walter Mondale, Cyrus Vance, Zbigniew Brzezinski, Robert Lichwoods, David Aron, Alfred Atherton, Hermann Eilts, William Quandt and Jeremy Shakhter. On the other side of the table were myself, Ambassador Ghorbal, Ambassador Osama El Baz, Minister Plenipotentiary Mohamed Shaker and Dr Mohamed El Baradei. President Carter opened the meeting with a general comment to the effect that his previous talks with me were comprehensive, good, candid and friendly. Then he proposed we should first take up the question of the PLO, stressing his conviction that Egypt should continue to encourage the Palestinians to accept Security Council Resolution 242 as the basis for any solution. He had already sent this request to President Sadat and again repeated it to me in our private meeting, he added.

Carter conceded that the PLO had the right to express reservations on that paragraph of Resolution 242 which deals with the Palestinians as refugees, but added that he firmly believed that the PLO would probably accept this formula if Egypt made a major effort to convince them and Syria exercised a similar, but more limited, effort. If the PLO accepted Resolution 242 as a basis of the settlement, Carter added, he would then appoint a personal representative to establish formal contacts with the PLO and its chairman Yasser Arafat. He said:

This step [the PLO accepting Resolution 242] is not only essential, but a principal one and I want to be very clear that unless this step is implemented, I would not be in a position to directly talk to the PLO, because we cannot violate the agreement concluded between the Israeli and American governments during the second disengagement agreement between Israel and Egypt. I firmly believe that Israel does not want any contacts at all between Washington and the PLO, under any conditions. However, if the PLO accept Resolution

242 we go around the opposition of Israel. I hope that we can come to an agreement on this point. In view of the fact that Yasser Arafat has already established indirect contacts with us through the intermediary of the Saudi, Syrian and Egyptian governments, I hope that an acceptable formula for direct contacts will materialise.

Also in relation to the PLO problem, President Carter assured me that the United States would be actively involved:

I hope that you will have complete confidence in us. I promise that I will exert every effort and I will not be discouraged, but rather will continue to use all our capabilities and potentialities in order to reach a common agreement.

The third point which President Carter took up was the difference between the United States and Egypt as to the amount of substantive progress which should be accomplished before going to the Geneva Peace Conference.

While Egypt believes that a substantial part should be agreed upon before Geneva formally starts, the US does not believe that this can be achieved because of the hard line taken by the Israelis on many major aspects of the negotiations.

To the dismay of the Egyptian delegation, President Carter in clear and simple words then again admitted his impotence in dealing with the Israelis:

It is important that you do not forget that my influence on Israel is proportionally related to the scope of support which I get from American public opinion, Congress and the Jewish circles in this country. I want to be abundantly clear that in the absence of such a triangular support my ability to influence Israel is minimal.

Listening to President Carter the Egyptian delegation was shocked in spite of the fact that we had long been aware of Carter's weakness. The very fact that the President of the United States chose to make such a statement in a formal meeting had a negative effect on the Egyptian side. If President Carter was not ready to have a showdown with the Israelis Egypt simply could not count on the United States. Rather, Egypt should try to broaden the peace process as much as possible, introducing additional actors and new pressures on the United States. In order to do this, we had to ensure that the Arab governments and Arab public opinion were mobilised behind Egypt. Egypt must take steps to attract public opinion in the Arab world, while President Sadat should approach the Arab leaders, healing rifts and strengthening unity. We could not confront Israel in negotiations without united Arab support. Washington must understand that Egypt could never be separated from the Arab world and that Egypt could mobilise Arab support at will.

Secondly, Carter's candid confession of US impotence made it imperative that Egypt exert all efforts to encourage the Soviet Union and other Western powers to play an important part in the global solution of the Middle East crisis. If Egypt negotiated alone, it might get its territory back – but it would get that in any case. However, by negotiating a separate settlement it would undermine the chances for overall peace and above all for a solution of the Palestinian question. We would betray the Arab cause and achieve nothing.

Despite Carter's candid confession, I found some reason for reassurance and hope in his position. We shared the view that the best chance for peace rested in the early convening of the Geneva Conference with the full participation of the Soviet Union. Here, I must emphasise that Carter was personally involved, devoting much time and a lot of effort to ensure the success of the conference. There was not the slightest hint that Carter was encouraging direct contacts and negotiations between Cairo and Tel Aviv. In fact, his own perception of his weakness and of the political costs to himself of a confrontation with Israel ruled out that possibility: direct negotiations between Egypt and Israel would force Carter to be at the centre of the action, exactly where he did not want to be. It has been alleged that the Americans were actively involved in establishing direct contacts between Begin and Sadat, paving the way for Sadat's trip to Jerusalem. This is not true. Not only was Carter not behind these contacts, but he was not even aware that they were taking place. By the time our meeting in the Oval Room took place an envoy of Sadat had met with Israeli Foreign Minister Moshe Dayan in Rabat, as we shall see later, but Carter knew nothing about it.

Many other important issues were discussed in the Oval Room

that day. One was that of Arab representation at the Geneva conference. Carter took the position that

> In my opinion one united Arab delegation is the best formula to overcome the Arab differences. That delegation should incorporate representatives of the Palestinians or the PLO provided they are not leading, very well-known personalities of that organization.

After the plenary session, where the Arabs would be represented by one delegation, the conference should be divided into various negotiating subcommittees, added Carter. The task of these groups was to negotiate peace treaties between individual Arab countries and Israel. There were few problems concerning the procedure for negotiating peace between Israel and established Arab governments. The knotty issue was how to negotiate a solution about the West Bank and Gaza. President Carter's view was that Jordan and Israel could negotiate about these areas, provided that Palestinian representatives were included in the Jordanian delegation. As for Egypt and Syria, according to President Carter, they could approve or abstain from approving whatever agreement was reached between Israel and Jordan.

The problem of the refugees, President Carter argued, should be the object of separate negotiations by a multi-national group in which Israel, Egypt, Jordan, Syria, Lebanon, Kuwait, Iraq and possibly other states would participate. This group should deal with the issue of compensation for the refugees as a separate item, completely independent from the negotiations related to the peace settlement. President Carter did not give too much importance to the site where this multinational group should meet, whether in Geneva, Cairo or somewhere else.

As to the Soviet Union's role, President Carter argued:

> The Soviet Union is a co-chairman of the Geneva Conference. This automatically means that we should put them into the picture concerning the understandings we have reached with you [the Arabs] and Israel. We should get their approval on all these agreements or at least some of them.

Stressing again the importance of full Soviet participation, Carter added a very revealing comment about himself: 'It is simply not feasible for me to satisfy the multitude of wishes of the various parties. Similarly it is simply not correct to assume that the United States alone bears the responsibility of success or failure.'

Summing up his idea, President Carter set forth this view:

The best course to follow is in my opinion to convene the Geneva Conference and to prevent it from adjourning immediately as happened at the end of 1973. On the contrary, the Geneva Conference should continue its work until it carries out, within a reasonable period, the mandate with which it was entrusted. We will exert all our effort to guarantee that the conference reaches an agreement regarding all substantive problems, without exception. I hope that I can obtain your agreement.

In Carter's opinion, Israel and Syria would be the parties most reluctant to adhere to the aforementioned procedure. For that reason, he intended to meet in the coming week with Abd El-Halim Khaddam, the Syrian Foreign Minister and with Israeli representatives.

President Carter concluded his intervention with a plea for Egypt's support:

While I realise that my suggestion does not correspond with your own preference, I hope to get your approval and the assistance of President Sadat. Frankly, I don't see any other alternative and believe that my suggestions can be crowned with success.

After listening to Carter, I had the impression that although he was quite familiar with the various issues he was unsure of himself and he did not feel he could make events unfold according to his plans. This is why I stressed from the outset that Egypt was ready to cooperate with the United States as much as possible, but that Washington must be ready to play an important and effective role. At the proper time the Americans must be prepared to present their own proposals to bridge the gaps between the parties. I made it clear that unless the President of the United States was ready to assume this responsibility, some parties would succeed either in blocking the convening of Geneva Conference or in preventing it from achieving concrete results. The peace conference would bog down in procedural technicalities and no substantive agreement would be reached. Egypt was certainly ready to go to Geneva. In fact, we had gone there in 1973 although both Israel and Syria opposed the conference, with Assad boycotting it completely and Israel sending a delegation only after tremendous pressure from Washington. However, we believed that for the Geneva Conference to succeed, prior agreement on the major substantive problems was necessary. The mere convening of the conference was not an end in itself and we did not want to see the conference meet and fail because of poor preparations.

One of the major stumbling blocks, I continued, was the question of the participation of the PLO and it should be given adequate preparation. I fully agreed with President Carter's suggestion that the PLO should accept Security Council Resolution 242 prior to the conference, with reservations about the term 'refugees', thus enabling the United States to establish formal contacts with it. But this was not enough. Israel should be asked to simultaneously recognize the PLO.

> With all candour, Mr President, I do not see how or on which ground we have the right to pick and choose between the members of the PLO, between those who are famous and well-known and those who are not famous. All members of the PLO are active, committed to its policies, and bound by its decisions. It is my fervent hope that we do not let ourselves become entangled in the hypothesis that there are serious differences among the members of the PLO. Mr President, you want us to put pressure on the PLO to accept Resolution 242. We, in turn, believe that it is fair and equitable to ask you to bear pressure on Israel to recognise the PLO.

I added that Egypt would never go to Geneva without the PLO: 'Mr President, there is only one circumstance under which Egypt would go to Geneva without the participation of the PLO, namely if the two chairmen addressed an invitation to the PLO to attend and the latter chose to formally decline the invitation.' But I also tried to reassure President Carter:

> I would like to emphasise that we in Egypt continue to bear pressure on the PLO to accept Resolution 242. We told its leaders that they should not waste more time or effort on semantics. The most important thing is that they find a formula to accept Resolution 242 with certain reservations, and then sit

down formally with the representatives of the United States. Once the PLO obtains recognition by the United States, the problem is half solved.

I then informed President Carter that I had already communicated our position on this crucial point to Brezhnev and Gromyko, and I had found that their position was identical to ours. Some Arab countries, however, were anxious to prevent the PLO from accepting Resolution 242. In light of these attempts, Carter should immediately contact the PLO informally, thus strengthening the hand of moderate PLO members by making it clear that American recognition would follow the acceptance of Resolution 242. In this connection I reminded Carter that in fact this was going to happen under President Nixon's and President Ford's presidencies, but unfortunately did not materialise.

Direct informal contacts between the US and the PLO were crucial at this stage. If they were successful, they should be followed by official contacts on the basis of a formula worked out between the PLO and the United States representatives. In fact, I had already passed on to Cyrus Vance a formula I had personally discussed with him. But the United States had to realise that the PLO could not accept Resolution 242 unless the US made a move in its direction. My discussions with Yasser Arafat had made it clear that a major obstacle to the PLO's acceptance of the resolution was the clause referring to 'the right of every state to live in peace'. Arafat rightly feared that if the PLO accepted that clause it would in practice unilaterally recognise the state of Israel and its right to live in peace, but would receive no guarantee for or recognition of the right of the Palestinians to live in peace within an independent national entity. It was imperative that the Palestinians be given a guarantee that the United States recognised the Palestinians' right to statehood. The Palestinians had also made it clear to me that for them going to Geneva without mutual recognition constituted a great risk. President Carter must understand the Palestinian dilemma and find a formula for establishing indirect and discreet contacts with the Palestinians.

The only alternative to such direct US–PLO contacts would be to submit a new resolution to the Security Council. The preamble of this new document should refer to Resolutions 242 and 338 as the basis for a peaceful settlement in the Middle East. However, the operative part of the new draft should recognise the Palestinian problem as a political rather than a refugee problem. I made it clear that Egypt was ready to push such a resolution in the Security Council, adding that I hoped that the United States would not try to obstruct the unanimous adoption of such a move by the Council. All I asked of President Carter was his tacit approval so that the Council would adopt the motion. I added: 'I believe that my proposal does not run counter to the United States's position, since President Carter himself has made it clear on many occasions that the Palestinian problem is a political and not simply a humanitarian one.' Here President Carter abruptly interrupted me: 'As I understand your proposal, Mr Deputy Prime Minister, you are talking of submitting a new draft and not an amendment to Security Council Resolution 242.' I replied in the affirmative, adding that the new draft would go further than simply affirming resolutions 242 and 338. This upset Carter. 'I want to be very clear that, if your proposal is to amend 242, the United States will veto it. On the other hand, I am ready to look into the formula on which you and Cyrus Vance agreed.' Fearful of the negative effect of his statement on the Egyptian delegation, President Carter hastened to add,

I want it to be clear for the record that as President of the United States I have already gone further than my predecessors. Let me sum up what I am ready to accept.
1) Israel must withdraw to the pre-1967 borders, except for minor rectifications.
2) The Palestinians must have a homeland. It is clear that these two elements are positive for the Arabs, but negative for the Israelis.
3) I am speaking of a genuine peace and not merely the ending of the state of belligerency.
4) I am ready to contact the PLO. You and the Saudis have demonstrated your readiness to assist.

At this point I said: 'I believe that the Syrians would help, too, if they were assured that they would regain full control of the Golan Heights.' 'But I cannot guarantee that the Syrians will get back the Golan Heights,' Carter answered immediately, revealing once again his unwillingness to put pressure on Israel.

After this very clear, interesting, and revealing exchange of views President Carter returned to the Geneva Conference, trying to summarise the difference between the American and Egyptian positions:

It is abundantly clear that the disagreement between us is centred on the extent to which the preparations for Geneva should go; we believe that the conference should be convened and work should start there, but the Egyptian side espouses the position that everything should be almost finished before Geneva's gates are opened. I firmly believe that the two positions are not irreconcilable and we can work out a compromise. I propose that we set a date for the conference and at the same time we Americans send a team to shuttle between Cairo, Tel Aviv and other Arab capitals trying to reach through these direct contacts as much agreement as possble. Everybody would go to Geneva on this basis. I guarantee to you, Mr Fahmy, that we will be active partners in the process of negotiations irrespective of the time it consumes. The advantage of this new procedure is that once everybody is in Geneva, a world public opinion would be created and the momentum would push everybody towards ultimate success. For example the Europeans until now are still reluctant to make their views known lest their declared position impair the delicate balance essential for the process of negotiations. This is exactly the attitude of American public opinion. However, if we all go to Geneva, the party proven to be intransigent or uncooperative would be internationally condemned by public opinion, even if it was Israel with whom we have the closest of relations.

Carter went back to the issue of Palestinian representation, and in the course of the following exchange made some statements with far-reaching implications. He started out on an optimistic note, arguing that the problem could be solved if the United States started a dialogue with the PLO immediately. He minimised the issue of who should represent the PLO, whether Arafat himself or unknown personalities. Only the Israelis considered the difference important. He argued further that it was preferable to separate the refugee problem from that of the West Bank and the homeland. The refugee problem would be the object of multinational discussions, not necessarily at Geneva. The future of the West Bank and Gaza and the issue of a Palestinian homeland would be discussed at the conference by Israel and Jordan, with Palestinian representatives joining the Jordanian delegation. Carter added that Assad agreed that the refugee problem must be dealt with on a multinational basis. I replied that this did not imply that Assad agreed that the PLO should be part of the Jordanian delegation, and even less that the PLO agreed to let Jordan speak for the Palestinians. Carter's reply was surprising: 'Mr Fahmy, I would like to know the Egyptian position; you should not worry about the Syrian or Palestinian positions, let me handle this myself.'

This was a stunning statement. It could imply that Carter had already had serious contacts with the PLO and that these contacts were fruitful or at least promising. Secondly, it meant that President Carter and his American colleagues were aware of something about the Palestinian position which we in Egypt did not know. Lastly, it meant that Carter and his colleagues were hiding important information from Egypt. Concerning Syria, Carter's statement implied that he was in constant contact with President Assad, and that these contacts revealed Syria to be ready to give in on the issue of Palestinian representation. If Carter had good reasons to say 'leave the Syrians and the Palestinians to us', I was in a sense delighted, because the greater flexibility of these two intransigent parties enhanced the probability that the Geneva Conference would be successful. On the other hand, I was also worried, because the implication was that Egypt was not fully aware of the latest position of the Palestinians, Syrians and other parties to the dispute. If this was really true, Egypt was no longer the leader in the peace process. For these reasons, I was perturbed when I heard President Carter making this unusual declaration, but also had serious doubts that his optimistic statement was based on solid ground. In fact, I was almost sure this was just bravado. However, I could not leave such a statement unchecked, because if it was well founded Egypt had to reassess the situation.

My inquiries after the meeting revealed that Carter's colleagues were as surprised as I was by his casual 'leave the Syrians and the Palestinians to us'. Eilts, the former ambassador to Cairo, assured me that there was absolutely nothing in the US files to justify the statement. Still unsatisfied, I also checked with both the PLO representatives and Abd El-Halim Khaddam, the Syrian Foreign Minister, who were at that time in New York. They all categorically denied that there was any change whatsoever in their stance as we knew it in Cairo. They assured me that they had always informed me fully of their position and would continue to do so in the future.

Even President Carter eventually admitted that his bravado had no basis, and asked for Sadat's help in convincing Syria and the PLO to be more flexible. I will discuss that episode later on, because strangely and paradoxically it was to play a role in strengthening Sadat's determination to go to Jerusalem.

Going back to the Oval Room meeting, while the various hypotheses about Carter's statements raced through my mind I also had to answer the President's direct question about Egypt's position on Palestinian representation and the future relationship between a Palestinian homeland and Jordan. I told him that Egypt did not exclude that some kind of special relationship might ultimately develop between Jordan and the West Bank, and would even accept that a declaration to this effect be agreed upon prior to the Geneva Conference. But the main point to be kept in mind was that the Arab countries had recognised the PLO as the sole legitimate representative of the Palestinians and that even King Hussein of Jordan had supported this decision. I added that I was sure that President Carter and his colleagues would agree with me that a lot of support and prestige had been gained by the PLO since that time, and that Arafat could not agree now to a vague formula for Geneva that left open to doubt whether the PLO in fact spoke for the Palestinians. There was a real risk, I added, that if we did not solve the problem of Palestinian representation quickly, a new Arab summit would be convened. This would make everybody more intransigent and complicate further an already complex situation.

Carter and his colleagues were listening attentively and I could see they understood and appreciated my points. The one exception was Zbigniew Brzezinski. In my opinion, Brzezinski was essentially an amateur, a professor at heart and insecure enough of his position to feel the need to show off all the time. The academic bent influenced everything he said. When he analysed a situation, he was inclined to indulge in hypotheses, counterhypotheses and theories, and seldom tried to reach a realistic and practical conclusion, taking into account the hard facts of political life. He talked to impress his students, not to make concrete suggestions. It was also very clear that Brzezinski felt dwarfed by Kissinger's legacy, and that he was both very frustrated and very determined to prove himself his predecessor's equal. But he only managed to confuse things. I believe that the hesitancy and confusion in Carter's foreign policy was due in large part to Brzezinski's advice and the influence which he exerted on the President. In this particular meeting Brzezinski was at his worst. Rather nervously, he started to lecture all of us about the real position of the Palestinians, minimising their plight. He seemed to think the rest of us knew nothing of the situation. A deep silence reigned all over the room and everybody appeared quite bored with this pointless lecture. But Brzezinski, having overcome the initial nervousness, was apparently enjoying himself and basking in what he must have interpreted as the rapt attention of the undergraduates in the Oval Room. For my part, I was shocked, not only because of Brzezinski's arrogance in lecturing us all, but also because of the real hostility and bitterness he expressed toward the Palestinians and their problems. The issue of Palestine was presented by him as merely a humanitarian one, and thus of marginal importance to the hard-core political problems. It was also clear that he thought nobody else understood the issue and that we should automatically accept his opinion.

I decided to be patient and to refrain from entering into a hollow debate with Brzezinski out of respect for President Carter and his colleagues. I simply said:

> I have listened with due care to what Mr Brzezinski has said. I can only tell him that it is very clear that sitting here in Washington, almost 6,000 miles away from our area, he can enjoy the luxury of saying what we have just heard from him. But I am sure that if he put his feet in our shoes in the Middle East, he would come back to earth.

President Carter understood exactly what I meant and cut Brzezinski short, summarising once more the American position in the following clear and precise way:

> 1) The United States must safeguard its interests in the Middle East. These interests are genuine and wide in scope, going well beyond the Arab–Israeli conflict. This is why we are not watching from the sidelines, but are actively involved in negotiating a comprehensive settlement acceptable to all concerned.
> 2) We are encouraging negotiations between Israel and the Arab countries, and at the same time exerting every effort to narrow the differences among the positions of the Arab countries.
> 3) We are ready to give the Soviet Union a role in the peace

process so they will not disrupt the Geneva Conference.

4) What I want from you, Mr Fahmy, is confidence in me and enough flexibility to allow the negotiations to start. In return, I give you my word that the United States will be fair to everyone in the negotiations. We will be honest, talking to all parties in the same manner.

5) The US will always try to single out the points of agreement in the various positions, and work for a fair compromise where differences exist.

6) The Arab side overestimates the United States's capacity to influence Israel. As I told you before, my ability to bear pressure on Israel is limited by the role of the Congress, the influence of Jewish groups and by American public opinion.

7) President Sadat has confidence in my capacity to bring about agreement on the major problems. I hope he will also have confidence in my evaluation of which is the best way to start the negotiations. This is a problem of secondary importance. I can assure you that the procedure we follow will be fair to everybody. I will exert every effort to establish contacts with the PLO. I have also been informed that Dayan is trying to convince Begin to be more flexible about the choice of individuals acceptable to Israel as Palestinian representatives. I will follow closely any change in the Israeli position.

My answer to Carter touched on three major points. First, while I admired the honesty which had led him to admit the limits of his influence on Israel, I had to stress that the Arabs were not asking him to perform miracles, but only to play an active and constructive role in the peace process. Second, I stressed that he should not misconstrue Egypt's insistence that the Geneva Conference be adequately prepared for. Egypt had been the first country to negotiate with the Israelis, at Kilometer 101 and during the step-by-step process. The problem was that Israel was doing its best not to be pushed to negotiate collectively with the Arab countries at Geneva. Without adequate preparation, we would only convene the conference to listen to the same Israeli rhetoric we had heard from Eban at the first meeting in December 1974. Eban's speech had not addressed any issue, but was pure propaganda for home consumption. Carter interrupted, inquiring whether we had not done the same thing, but I denied this had been the case and stressed again that we wanted a real conference, in which the problems could be tackled seriously, and insisted on thorough preparations for this reason. Third, I pointed out that Egypt's insistence on this point should not be understood to mean that we wanted the conference merely to rubber-stamp agreements already reached. We only wanted to settle some details which needed protracted discussions and negotiations with the Israelis, to save time at Geneva, and also to make sure we would not get bogged down on procedure, but would address the real issues.

When I finished, Carter asked:

Where do you propose the pre-Geneva discussions should take place? I personally believe that it is simply not practical for an American mediator to shuttle back and forth between Cairo, Tel Aviv, Damascus and other capitals. It would be much easier if representatives of all the parties were gathered in one hotel. My question is simply whether you agree that everybody could stay in one place. Could the negotiations, for instance, take place in Jerusalem?

I knew Carter was challenging us and simply answered, 'Mr President, Jerusalem is not a neutral place at this time. However I am ready to go there if Jerusalem is declared an international city.' President Carter hurriedly dropped the suggestion, asking instead if we would accept a neutral place like Geneva or New York. I inquiried in turn whether he saw this meeting as a substitute for the Geneva Conference and added that when we talked of contacts in preparation for the conference, we envisaged that they would take place through diplomatic channels with the United States. I was personally ready to meet with Cyrus Vance anywhere in Europe or I could come back to Washington to confer with him or President Carter.

Then Carter inquired whether I had any objection to his seven points. I just answered that I hoped that President Carter agreed with me that we should concentrate our efforts on solving the problem of PLO representation and participation in Geneva, adding that I was sure that a lot of good would come of the long-awaited contacts between the United States and the PLO.

At this point, President Carter sought my opinion on a hypothetical question. Would Egypt agree to represent the Palestinians at Geneva, if Yasser Arafat requested it, and the PLO accepted Resolution 242, recognising the right of all states in the

Middle East to live in peace? I gave President Carter an affirmative answer because if we recognised the right of the PLO to represent the Palestinians we should also recognise its right to delegate that task to another party. The problem with Jordan representing the Palestinians was that the PLO had never asked it to do so. I reassured Carter that the PLO in any case appeared ready to be reasonable in its requests; in fact Yasser Arafat had personally informed me, during the negotiations for the second Egyptian–Israeli disengagement, that all he wanted at this stage was a piece of land wide enough to raise the Palestinian flag, even if it was not more than 5 kilometres wide. I added that President Carter could be sure that the Palestinians were determined to reach an agreement, 'but the problem is that you in the United States must contact the PLO'. President Carter repeated again his belief that a formula could be found if the PLO accepted Resolution 242, and repeated that Egypt could play a major role in convincing the P.L.O. Here Cyrus Vance intervened for the first time to emphasise once again that it was a must for the PLO to recognise the right of Israel to exist, erasing all doubts that the Palestinians' goal was to destroy Israel. Vance insisted that the PLO had to change its image if it wanted to play a positive role. I replied that we needed a fair and comprehensive formula which recognised the right to exist of all states, including the Palestinian state.

To my surprise, Brzezinski intervened again, arguing that the United States could not prejudge the outcome of the negotiations by agreeing in advance to the establishment of a Palestinian state. In Brzezinski's imagination this would open the United States to accusations of having already entered into an alliance with the PLO and of espousing its point of view. There was no need to mention a Palestinian state, in any case, for a formula recognizing the right of all states to exist would inherently cover the issue of the Palestinians without spelling it out. I pointed out that as long as the PLO was not given a specific guarantee, it would be most reluctant to make concessions. Then I proposed that President Carter could provide this guarantee by writing to President Sadat assuring him that a national homeland for the Palestinians would be established in the West Bank and Gaza. President Carter replied: 'I cannot give you this assurance.' 'I am fully aware that you cannot give the guarantee directly to the PLO; but does this mean that we will not be able to give the P.L.O. that assurance on your behalf?' I asked. Secretary Vance replied, 'You can inform the PLO that the United States will exert every effort to put the Palestinian problem on the provisional agenda of the Geneva Conference.'

Not being able to solve the problem, President Carter again inquired whether I was not in a position to accept his seven points. Without entering into specifics, I reiterated that the problem was the PLO and added that anything which the PLO accepted, Egypt would accept, and anything which the PLO rejected, Egypt and all other Arab countries would reject. Feeling that we had reached a dead-end, Carter suggested he meet with me another time after talking to the other Arab Foreign Ministers, but then pleaded with me again to accept the American plan for convening the conference, which he outlined yet another time. I refrained from commenting on President Carter's summation, but reiterated that Egypt was ready to go to Geneva on the following day if the PLO was also invited. President Carter repeated, 'I must speak to them first and in the absence of direct contacts, there is no way to make them participate in the conference in an independent capacity.'

Incredibly, we repeated the same exchange once more. Carter asked me again to agree to the seven points. I told him again that the crucial issue was the participation of the PLO. Vance repeated that Israel, and thus the United States, would not agree to the presence in any form of well-known PLO leaders or of famous personalities with an 'affinity' for the PLO. At this point I could no longer put up with this desultory going round in circles and inquired whether we should subject the Palestinian representatives to a lie detector test to ascertain their 'affinity'. Carter once again asked us to trust that he would do his best to overcome his difficulty. I answered that we had confidence in him and that is why we wanted the United States to work out a compromise proposal for a final settlement in the Middle East. President Carter replied that the time would come when he would show that our confidence in him was justified by submitting a comprehensive proposal. On that note, the meeting came to an end after a brief exchange on the deteriorating situation in Southern Lebanon.

I have talked so extensively of this meeting because it portrays very clearly where things stood in late 1977. From the Egyptian point of view, there were both positive and negative elements in the situation. On the negative side, President Carter's weakness loomed large. His frank statement linking exerting pressure on Israel to political suicide was the most negative element. It meant he would not exert much pressure on Israel and would hesitate in establishing contacts with the PLO. He would on the other hand abide by the guarantees Kissinger had given Israel that the United States would not recognise the PLO or support any resolution or move in the UN without Israeli approval, thus allowing US policy to be dictated by Israel. If the United States did not establish contacts with the PLO and did not recognise the right of a Palestinian state to exist, the PLO would remain inflexible, making it more difficult to find an acceptable formula for Palestinian representation. The United States was also unwilling to guarantee to Syria the return of the Golan Heights. This would make Assad more rigid and, understandably, unwilling to come to Geneva.

On the positive side was Carter's determination to convene the Geneva Conference, providing a truly international arena for the negotiations. This would bring other forces into play, and forces, moreover, which Israel could not manipulate as easily as it manipulates the US. Carter's intention to get the Soviet Union actively involved in the Geneva Conference was very important to us. We had resisted in the past Kissinger's efforts to shunt the USSR aside. The fact that the Carter administration had abandoned the step-by-step approach, in which the United States remained the biased arbiter, was an enormous step forward for the Arab side. In addition, for all his timidity on crucial moves, Carter was playing an active and very positive role in reconciling the points of view of the various parties. He differed from Egypt concerning the amount of preparation necessary before the conference started, but was certainly not trying to lead everybody to Geneva without previous negotiations and contacts. In fact, his efforts had already led to some agreement on a formula for the conference which was viable as long as we solved the difficult problem of Palestinian representation.

It is not my intention to minimise the problems which existed at this time, but one should not overestimate them either, as many analysts have done. Disagreement was to be expected. In fact, if everybody had been able to agree on an ideal basis for convening the conference, there would have been no necessity for a conference at all. Carter's formula was not perfect and would not make everybody happy, but there has never been and there will never be a solution in the Middle East that can make everybody happy. I always felt that we would be very successful if we found the means to make everybody equally dissatisfied, sharing fairly the burden of the compromises necessary for peace.

While there were good reasons for optimism, it was also clear that we had to choose our strategy carefully and follow it closely. Our goal had to be to go to Geneva, thus fully internationalising the peace process. We should do nothing to upset the apple-cart and interrupt the process. The situation did not call for dramatic new moves, but for painstaking efforts to remove one by one the obstacles to the conference. Above all, it was a time for the Arabs to reconcile their differences and stick together. If we did that, the chances of success were great.

12 A JUST AND FINAL PEACE IS ON THE HORIZON

I discussed in the previous chapter the international efforts to reconvene the Geneva Conference, stressing in particular the role of the United States and the Soviet Union. Enormous progress had been made, due in large part to the US insistence that all parties to the conflict go beyond rhetoric and put down concrete proposals for peace. Among these proposals were the two draft peace treaties submitted by Egypt and Israel. It is now time to examine in some detail these two documents, as well as the draft later submitted by the US as a compromise proposal.

The very existence of these two draft treaties was a significant development. Never before in the thirty years of conflict had Israel and Egypt managed to get beyond rhetorical statements and put on paper their own ideas concerning the format and nature of the peace to be concluded between them. But from the point of view of Egypt there was a further important element: the American compromise proposal was very close to, and in fact almost entirely espoused, the Egyptian position.

This point needs to be stressed in view of statements which have been made about the situation prevailing before Sadat's trip to Jerusalem. It has been asserted that the international situation was so bleak and desperate and the prospects for peace so remote that President Sadat had no alternative but to take it upon himself to act alone and, with his courageous trip to Jerusalem, break the stalemate. Nothing could be farther from the truth. The Carter administration had rejected the Israeli view of peace, as outlined in their draft treaty. This document went far away from any attempt at peace. It demonstrated that the Israelis did not just want to end belligerency, to achieve secure permanent boundaries, and gain Arab recognition. It was an attempt to manipulate the peace process to achieve total domination of Egypt's destiny, and restrict its role in the Middle East. In fact, as will appear later, some of the clauses the Israelis proposed had no parallel in any previous treaty regulating peace between countries.

The Egyptian Draft Treaty

In early August 1977, Secretary of State Cyrus Vance had come to the Middle East to solicit written peace proposals from all parties. The Carter administration intended to examine these proposals and then prepare compromise draft peace treaties. Vance met with Sadat and myself at Gianaclis near Alexandria and explained Carter's plan. We welcomed the new American approach and told Vance that, if he returned to Egypt after his tour of the Middle East, our draft would be ready. The Secretary of State was very pleased. We then exchanged views on various topics, covering extensively the bilateral relationship between Egypt and the United States. In the course of the exchange, a completely different subject was suddenly brought up. Secretary Vance intimated to President Sadat that American intelligence would like to get from Egypt, if possible, a specific piece of Soviet military equipment in order to examine it thoroughly. To my amazement and dismay and that of General Gamasy, the Defence Minister, President Sadat enthusiastically responded to the American request. Cyrus Vance was delighted.

Sadat was very pleased with the new American move and asked me to prepare the Egyptian draft treaty before Vance's return. I dictated the document and sent it to the President who took it with him to Ras El-Tin Palace in Alexandria, where he was going to receive the credentials of several new foreign ambassadors. After the formal ceremony was over, President Sadat examined the draft almost word by word, an unusual step for him. From the expression on his face, I knew he was satisfied. Indeed, when he finished going through the papers, he congratulated me on 'that perfect draft'.

Cyrus Vance visited Saudi Arabia, Jordan, Syria, Lebanon and Israel, and came back to Egypt. He was received by Sadat at his summer residence at Maamoura near Alexandria. This meeting stands out vividly in my memory because of an incident very revealing of Sadat's attitude and personality. Discussing the outcome of his tour, Vance informed us in particular of the Israelis' interpretation of Security Council Resolution 242. In their view, Vance explained, the resolution did not require total Israeli withdrawal from the territories occupied in the 1967 War; it did require, on the other hand, not only the end of belligerency between Israel and the Arab states, but also full normalisation of relations. It was a very biased interpretation, diametrically opposite to the Egyptian one. To my complete surprise, when Vance finished, President Sadat said in no uncertain terms that he was in full agreement with that interpretation. I had no option but to intervene, and disagree most firmly. I sensed immediately that Sadat was going to insist on his position and in fact he did so. Either he had not listened carefully when Vance had described the Israeli position or he had not grasped what it meant. This was typical of Sadat. He often failed to follow arguments closely, read documents carefully and weigh all arguments. Moreover, once he had taken a paticular position he stuck to it stubbornly, as he did in this case. I felt that it was important not to give President Sadat further opportunity to elaborate on that particular point, lest it appear that there was serious disagreement between him and myself. I therefore cut the meeting short. I whispered in Sadat's ear that to avoid a heated and useless argument he should end that meeting and instead sit alone with Secretary Vance in order to give him the Egyptian draft treaty I had prepared. The President fortunately agreed and the meeting came to an end. Sadat remained alone with Vance and handed him the Egyptian draft treaty. The American Secretary of State read it very carefully and declared he was very encouraged by the Egyptian approach and specifically by the contents of the document.

Here it is opportune to summarise the Egyptian draft. The document was composed of two parts. The first part consisted of our points enumerating the fundamental requirements for a permanent and just peace. The first requirement was the complete and total withdrawal of the Israeli forces from all Arab territories occupied since June 1967. The second requirement was the recognition of the inalienable right of the Arab people of Palestine to establish their own state. The third one was recognition of the rights of every state in the area to live in peace within secure and internationally guaranteed boundaries. The fourth was a commitment by all states in the area to conduct their relations in accordance with the provisions of the United Nations Charter and in particular without resort to the use of force and by resolving differences by peaceful means. After enumerating these four essentials for peace, the document stated: 'Egypt is ready to sign the following agreement with Israel simultaneously with other Arab countries concerned.'

The second part of the Egyptian draft was the peace agreement between Egypt and Israel, consisting of five preamble clauses and nine Articles.

Article 1 declared that the agreement and its annexes would constitute the final peace agreement between the parties, in accordance with the purposes and principles of the United Nations Charter and in conformity with Security Council Resolution 242.

Article 2 ran as follows: 'The Israeli government solemnly undertakes to: (a) withdraw its forces from the Egyptian territory occupied since 5 June 1967 to the international boundaries of Egypt; (b) withdraw its forces in accordance with an agreed time-table, to be implemented within three months of the signing of this agreement. The arrangements of the time-table are outlined in the annex.'

Article 3 spelled out the Egyptian obligations: (a) Egypt undertook to ensure the freedom of navigation in the Suez Canal in accordance with the 1888 Constantinople Convention; (b) Egypt undertook to ensure freedom of navigation in the straits of Tiran in accordance with the principles of international law.

Article 4 required the two parties to (a) establish demilitarised zones astride and along the borders between them, the width of which was not to exceed 5 kms on each side; (b) accept the stationing of United Nations peace keeping forces on their territories along the borders; (c) accept the installation of electronic devices and an early-warning system in their territories close to the borders.

Article 5 dealt with the obligation of the parties to: (a) undertake to respect and acknowledge each other's sovereignty, territorial integrity and political independence; (b) respect and acknowledge each other's right to live in peace within secured and recognised boundaries; (c) ensure that acts of belligerency or hostility did not originate from or were committed from within their respective territories against the population, citizens or property of the other party; (d) refrain from any interference in each other's domestic affairs; and (e) refrain from the use of force during the implementation of the agreement.

Article 6 had special importance: the parties declared that the conflict between them had ended and they undertook to terminate all claims and states of belligerency.

Article 7 established that after a period of five years the parties would examine ways and means to promote the consolidation of peace between them.

Article 8 stipulated that the parties agreed to establish a joint commission to consider any problem arising in the execution of the agreement.

Article 9 declared that 'this agreement shall be guaranteed by the United States of America and the Union of Soviet Socialist Republics. It shall be submitted for the approval of the Security Council.' Moreover, the parties agreed that other states could become parties to the above mentioned guarantees.

Cyrus Vance, as I mentioned, was extremely pleased with the text. He appreciated our efforts to present a balanced draft and promised us that he would submit this paper to President Carter. His only comment was that he hoped that when the parties negotiated the final agreement, Egypt would be ready to change the word 'agreement' appearing in the heading and other parts of the text to 'treaty'. We told him that this depended on the Israeli response to the substantive points, and that we would consider his proposition with an open mind. Later when President Carter received me in Washington, he repeatedly referred to the Egyptian text, expressing admiration for the equanimity of the underlying philosophy and the precision of the drafting. He added that he had been told I was 'an internationally reputed draftsman' and thought I deserved the reputation.

A final observation about the Egyptian draft treaty is in order here. It represented the official Egyptian position approved by President Sadat, who personally handed it to Secretary of State Vance. Furthermore, while it was given to the American side in complete secrecy, it contained nothing which violated the collective position taken by the Arab leaders.

However, it was shortly after these successful exchanges with the United States that Sadat responded to Begin's invitation to establish direct contacts with Israel in Morocco. In early September, as usual, I left Cairo to attend the regular session of the United Nations General Assembly. I spent a couple of days in Paris and then flew straight to Washington. Almost at the same time, Dayan was on his way to New York and Washington. He flew from Israel to Belgium, then mysteriously disappeared. Rumours and speculations started circulating, suggesting that Dayan and I had met in secret. This was certainly not true and I issued a public statement denying it. The truth was that Dayan had gone to Rabat to meet for the first time Hassan Tuhami, Sadat's envoy. He then returned to Jerusalem to report to Begin. I knew that the meeting between Tuhami and Dayan was taking place, although Sadat personally had not informed me. However, I had dismissed the move as having no particular significance and representing no threat to the peace process. Sadat was simply responding to an invitation from King Hassan and in any case such direct Egyptian–Israeli contacts had taken place before.

At the United Nations

I proceeded as scheduled to Washington, where I had the various meetings with President Carter and Secretary Vance described in the previous chapter. The latter gave me a copy of the Israeli draft treaty. I then went on to New York, where I addressed the UN General Assembly on 28 September. My speech had a precise purpose: I wanted to spell out our position in detail to prove to everybody, especially the USA and Israel, that Egypt only had one philosophy and one position, whether it was proclaimed in public or embodied in confidential documents. The entire speech constituted a genuine challenge for Israel. I made it clear from the outset that Egypt and the Arab countries were ready for real peace. I described the situation in the Middle East during the last thirty years as unique, with a state of 'no war, no peace' prevailing throughout that period. The area was like a volcano which erupts at regular intervals, with all that that entailed in human suffering, danger and misery. I added that this state of affairs was even worse than the global wars that had erupted in certain parts of the world for limited periods. Then I clearly said:

A state of war such as that prevailing in the Middle East creates a material and psychological climate that is detrimental to stability and an obstacle to progress and prosperity: everything depends upon the unknown. The Middle East has accordingly been destined to continuous sapping of its human and material resources and to a regrettable waste of energy and potential.

Furthermore, I made it as clear as possible that the Arab countries recognised the dangers inherent in such a situation, and that they endeavoured to replace the conflict and particularly the state of 'no war, no peace' in the Middle East with peace based on justice. But Israel made progress toward peace impossible:

A glance at the events in the Middle East since 1947 and even earlier makes it evident that one party has taken it upon itself to launch aggressive war at regular intervals and to prepare for such war under a heavy smokescreen of duplicity and hollow propaganda, deluding itself that it has succeeded in fooling the world. In this false belief, it claims that its aggression is actually self-defence, that its expansionism is motivated by the need to ensure its continued existence, and that occupation and the uprooting of a whole people is essential to the coexistence of peoples and nations. We are entitled to ask whether the aggressor has learned anything from the lessons of history and from the experience of other countries which have been exposed to similar storms. How can the aggressor make coherent its contradictory claims — for instance, the claim that it desires to live in peace and its insistence upon occupation and expansion? Is it admissible that Israel claims that we should acquiesce in its 'right to live in peace', while Israel is still occupying our territory and refusing in a manner unprecedented in history to agree to the granting of a whole people (the Palestinians) its legitimate and inalienable rights? What kind of coexistence can be envisaged as a result of occupation and domination? Are we expected to recognise those who do not even recognise the basic principles of law and human rights?

I also made it clear that the worst aspect of the Israeli behaviour was that it insulted human intelligence as well as our ability to distinguish between right and wrong. I then addressed the following challenge to the Foreign Minister of Israel:

If Israel truly advocates peace, I challenge its Foreign Minister to stand here before the representatives of the peoples and nations of the world and declare from this very rostrum Israel's willingness to withdraw completely from Arab territories and to recognise the right of the Palestinian people to establish an independent state on the land it cultivated and on which it built its civilisation for thousands of years.

I clearly said that no matter how long Israel procrastinated and persisted in its oppression, it would be unable to prevent the establishment of an independent Palestinian state.

Referring to the Israeli regulations imposed on the Arab

population in the territories occupied since 5 June 1967 or even before, I indicated that everybody knew Israel treated Arabs as second class citizens. These measures exposed the Israeli policy of annexation and territorial expansion. I then added that there could be no stronger proof of these expansionist ambitions than the statement from the official Israeli spokesman, 'You cannot annex to Israel territory that belongs to the Israeli people, because this territory was originally theirs. You do not annex your own territory.' Commenting on this, I addressed the following question to the Assembly: 'What further proof of Israel expansionist intentions is needed?'

Concluding my statement to the General Assembly, I summarised Egypt's view of the requirements for an overall peace as follows:

1) The withdrawal of Israeli forces from all Arab territories occupied since 5 June 1967.

2) The establishment of an independent Palestinian state on Palestine territory, and the recognition of the right of the Palestinian people to return.

3) The recognition of the right of every state in the area to live in peace.

4) The provision of the necessary guarantees for all peoples of the area to live in security on their own land and to enjoy their own property. We did not object to any collective or bilateral guarantees, including any guarantees provided by the United States for Israel, on condition that they did not constitute a threat to Arab national security. Instead, we were willing to examine all forms of guarantees, whether in the form of buffer zones, demilitarised zones, the establishment of United Nations forces, the reduction of forces or arms in areas adjacent to the border, or even the use of modern early-warning systems for the detection of any developments that would endanger peace. The guarantees could also include political commitments provided by members of the United Nations.

5) Agreement on the following: the establishment of a nuclear-free zone in the Middle East; regulation of conventional armaments, since a race in this field would increase tension and thus the possibility of a future conflict; an end to the present Israeli immigration policy. The continuation of such a policy of open-door immigration from all parts of the world could only trigger further

aggression and expansion at the expense of the Arab countries.
6) The return of Arab Jerusalem to those who had a right to it territorially, historically and culturally, namely the Palestinians.

It should by now be clear that the Egyptian official position was recorded both in the draft treaty we gave to Washington and in my statement to the General Assembly. Egypt was ready to sign a peace treaty with Israel simultaneously with the other Arab countries the moment agreement was reached on the Palestinian problem. We wanted peace and our position was in complete conformity with the rules of international law: our draft did not seek extraordinary concessions from, or impose unusual conditions on, Israel. The Israeli draft treaty was couched in rather different terms.

The Israeli Draft Treaty

The Israeli draft was handed by Dayan to Vance on 19 September 1977. I received a copy from Vance two days later. This voluminous document was not a peace treaty, but an effort by the Israelis to dictate their will on Egypt. I did not discuss the draft with Vance, because we both knew that the crucial document would be the American compromise proposal.

The Israeli treaty was composed of a preamble and 42 Articles. It was accompanied by two other documents marked 'top secret'. The most important, dated 7 July 1977, stated that Israel was ready to participate in a resumed session of the Geneva Conference after 10 October 1977. It is important to stress here that the Israelis had never declared in public that they would participate in the Conference. The document further stated that at the conclusion of the public session of the reconvened Geneva Peace Conference three mixed commissions would be established, namely: Egyptian–Israeli, Syrian–Israeli, Jordanian–Israeli. Moreover, the Israelis proposed that, if the Geneva Conference could not be convened due to the Arab countries' insistence that the PLO be represented, one of two alternatives should be followed: 1) the establishment through the good offices of the United States of the three aforementioned mixed commissions in keeping with the precedent followed in Rhodes in 1949; or 2) the establishment of the same commissions in agreement with the principle of proximity talks.

The preamble of the Israeli draft not only dealt with ending the state of belligerency between Egypt and Israel, but embodied phrases touching upon measures to prevent threat of war in future; to establish a just and lasting peace in which every state in the area could live in security; to recognise each other's sovereignty and independence within secure and recognised boundaries; to resolve to live in friendship, cooperation and good neighbourly relations and, most significant of all, to remove the barriers which denied to both peoples the free exchange of information, ideas, goods and services. Israel, in other words, wanted not only peace, but the fettering of Egypt in a web of special, close and binding relationships. Subsequent Articles made this even clearer.

Article 1 of the Israeli draft treaty declared the immediate termination of the state of war between the two countries.

Article 2 was composed of two items. The first was a reciprocal commitment by Egypt and Israel to recognise and respect each other's sovereignty and political independence. The second item stipulated that, 'Neither party shall support claims against the sovereignty or political independence of the other, if such claims are made in future by any state, group or organisation.'

Article 3 stipulated that the parties would not use force against each other.

Article 4 dealt with boundaries. However, it did not spell out the commitment of Israel to withdraw completely from Sinai to Egypt's recognised international borders. Instead, it stated that the boundaries between Egypt and Israel would be agreed upon between the parties in accordance with a protocol and a map to be annexed to the treaty. The parties would respect unreservedly each other's territorial integrity within the new boundaries, renouncing any future territorial demands against the other. These new boundaries should be considered inviolable.

Article 5 stated that diplomatic relations would be established within a month after the treaty entered into force, with the exchange of diplomatic representatives at the level of ambassador.

Article 6 committed the parties to concluding a bilateral agreement for the purpose of normalising commercial relations within a yet unspecified number of years from the entry into force of this treaty.

Article 7 dealt with the establishment of cultural relations. A cultural agreement would be drawn up between the parties within a unspecified number of years from the date the treaty came into force.

Article 8 was very revealing. It simply stated: 'Israel undertakes to evacuate its armed forces from all territory on the Egyptian side of the boundary established by this Treaty, in accordance with the attached timetable.' However, its title was not 'Withdrawal of Israeli Forces', as it could logically be expected, but 'Deployment of Forces'. Furthermore, it again made it crystal clear that Israel envisaged new boundaries and not the international boundaries which existed between Egypt and Palestine under the British Mandate. The wording of the clause was also extremely biased: it did not refer to the land occupied by Israeli forces as Egyptian territory, but it invented a new phraseology, calling it 'all territory on the Egyptian side of the boundary'. The Article could not have been more revealing of the Israeli claim that historically even Sinai was not a purely Egyptian territory, but that there were some Jewish claims to it.

Article 9 stated that all areas evacuated by the Israeli armed forces would be demilitarised and that all existing limitations of armament and forces would remain in effect; Sinai, in other words, would remain under the restrictions imposed on Egypt as a result of the second disengagement between Egypt and Israel concluded in 1975. It is worthwhile pointing out that the Egyptian draft treaty, too, called for the establishment of a demilitarised zone along the borders, but stipulated that both countries should draw their forces back from the border. In the Israeli concept, the burden fell entirely on Egypt.

Article 10 dealt with the restrictions of military activities which might emanate from each side.

Article 11 addressed the question of prevention of terrorism coming from either side.

Article 12 was, in my opinion, the only constructive proposal coming from the Israeli side: it sought to limit the arms race, regarding it a waste of resources and a source of tension. The details of such arms limitation were to be spelled out in a separate document to be concluded within a still unspecified number of years after the conclusion of the treaty.

Article 13 dealt with the settlement of financial claims.

Article 14 stated that 'Egypt agrees not to invoke against Israel the provisions of Article X of the Constantinople Convention'. This Article gave Egypt sole responsibility for the security of the Canal.

The Israelis, thus, were asking Egypt to renounce its rights and never to close the Canal to Israeli ships for security reasons. Article X was respected by all countries and until this day Egypt has never accepted any limitations whatsoever on its right to be the sole guarantor of the security of the Suez Canal.

Articles 15 and 16 touched upon free navigation and overflight in the Straits, the Gulf of Suez and the Gulf of Agaba.

Article 17 prohibited the two parties from engaging in economic warfare against each other, and specifically required Egypt not to boycott third-country firms doing business with Israel.

Article 18 similarly prohibited hostile propaganda and incitement.

Article 19 was a standard clause committing each party not to intervene in the domestic affairs of the other.

Article 20 was certainly tailored to suit Israel. It asked each to refrain from acts harmful to the other party's diplomatic or other relations with third states or with international organisations. Moreover, it specifically required Egypt to support Israel's membership in regional organisations.

Article 21, entitled 'Hostile Organisations' was unique and unprecedented: 'Neither party shall accord any international or diplomatic status whatsoever to any organisation whose object is the destruction or subversion of the other party. The parties shall oppose the grant of such status to any such organisation by any other state or international organisation.' It obviously meant that Egypt should stop recognising the PLO, close down its offices in the country, and oppose all Arab countries which did not follow suit.

Article 22 sought to eliminate 'Prejudice in teaching', even requiring the two countries to introduce 'courses of study aimed at bringing about a positive appreciation of each other's history, values and traditions'.

Article 23 required the parties to withdraw all their reservations and declarations to multilateral conventions relating to the recognition of the other or affecting the applicability of the convention to the other party, and to refrain from making such reservations or declarations in the future. Specifically, this meant that Israel expected Egypt, which in the past had signed multilateral conventions with the reservation that it would not apply their terms to Israel, to rescind such reservations. Israel also requested Egypt to amend all internal legislative and administrative acts designed to give effect to such reservations and declarations.

Article 24 dealt with the freedom of movement between the two countries including accessibility to places of religious and historical significance. These issues were also discussed in Article 29.

Articles 25, 26, 27 and 28 dealt with communications between the two countries. Air, road, and railroad links were to be opened and improved, postal and telecommunications services established, and ports open to each other's ships.

Article 30 touched upon the human rights of the citizens of the two parties.

Article 31 dealt with freedom of movement, with Article 32 specifically concentrating on the rights of Jews to emigrate at any time from Egypt to Israel or to any other country of their own choice, without impediment of any kind whatsoever.

Article 33 was in practice addressed solely to Egypt, which was requested to support any draft resolution submitted to any organ of the United Nations or other international organisations aimed at revoking existing resolutions directed against the other (namely Israel). In particular, Egypt was asked to undertake to support the revocation of General Assembly Resolution No. 3379 which declared 'that Zionism is a form of racism and racial discrimination'. Moreover, the same Article requested each party to oppose any draft resolution hostile to the other party that might be introduced in the future.

Article 34 again clearly indicated that Israel planned to etablish special relations between Egypt and Israel in all aspects of life. It read: 'The Parties recognise that history and geography have created an objective affinity of interests between their countries, and that their economic and human interests are closely related. The Parties agree to promote this natural association for their mutual benefit.'

Article 35 dealt with the problem of the refugees who were living in each party's territory.

Article 36 touched upon a humane problem, namely the 'Respect for Graves and Right of Reburial' of nationals of each party.

Article 37 was the most curious and perhaps the most telling of all. It consisted of a blank page with only the title word 'Nationality' on it. Apparently, the Israelis had not dared to spell out their ideas in writing, and had forgotten to detach this page when they submitted the draft to the United States. What did the Israelis have in mind? Did they intend that the Egyptians should lose their own nationality? Or perhaps they were being a little more modest and only wanted the Israelis and the Egyptians to share some kind of newly-invented 'co-nationality'? This would not have been the first Israeli invention, but I have to admit that it would have been the most daring.

Article 38 envisaged mutual cooperation for development in various fields. The Israelis, as usual, were careful not to forget one single activity, as though they wanted to share the air we breath in Egypt.

Article 39 foresaw the granting of a general amnesty to the nationals of the other party imprisoned for criminal offences.

Article 40 dealt with the creation of a Joint Committee to supervise the implementation of the Treaty.

Article 41 specified that, in a conflict between the obligations of the parties under the present treaty and their obligations under any international agreement, the Israeli–Egyptian treaty would always prevail. It further prohibited the parties from adhering to any treaty or agreement, arrangement or understanding with any third party which would be incompatible with the provisions of this treaty. The real aim of Article 41 was to nullify Egypt's commitments and obligations as stipulated in the Joint Arab Defence Treaty; Egypt would have to renounce all obligation to its Arab sister states.

The remaining Articles dealt with the mechanisms for settling the disputes which might arise and provided for the transmission of the treaty to the Secretary General of the United Nations for registration in accordance with the provisions of the United Nations Charter. The last page of the Israeli draft provided the space for the signatures. It carried the dateline 'Geneva', with the date left blank. Clearly, the Israelis intended to submit their draft to the Geneva Peace Conference. In fact publication in this book is the first time that the Israeli draft has been released. The Israelis never published it for fear of exposing their far-reaching scheme to control the area.

The American Draft Treaty

With the submission of the Egyptian and Israeli draft treaties, the hard work done by President Carter and Cyrus Vance was coming to fruition. The parties had now submitted their own views and the 'proximity talks' promoted by Carter meant that de facto negotiations between the Arab countries and Israel had already started through the mediation of the United States. The extensive Soviet–American negotiations on a framework for peace in the Middle East were ultimately crowned by the issuing of the Joint American–Soviet Declaration of 1 October, 1977, in which the two co-chairmen of the Geneva Conference agreed on the essentials of peace and fixed the opening date. There was a general mobilisation to bring the parties to the negotiating table and the United States clearly considered Egypt's role as crucial, as was demonstrated to me in Washington and New York.

In September and October 1977, as I have said before, I met with President Carter, Secretary Vance and his colleagues many times. Moreover, in Washington I seized the opportunity to receive many American politicians to explain our point of view. I was even invited to address the Senate Foreign Relations Committee on 23 September 1977 and I was invited by the Foreign Relations Committee of the House of Representatives for a discussion on the same day.

The most important meeting I had with Vance took place on 25 September, when he handed to me a secret American proposal with the title 'Outline of Possible Peace Treaty between Egypt and Israel'. At first glance, I had certain objections to some parts. Cyrus Vance accepted my comments and promised to correct the text as I proposed. He intimated to me that this first draft was the result of an attempt by his subordinates to build a bridge between the Egyptian and Israeli drafts by simply picking and choosing from one draft or the other just to prove that they were not biased in favour of Israel or Egypt. The second draft was delivered to me later on the same day by Ambassadors Roy Atherton and Hermann Eilts. Cyrus Vance later told me that he also transmitted a copy of that text to Dayan. The second official American draft differed from the first on several important points but the gist of the draft can be swiftly stated.

It comprised five preamble paragraphs and an operative part composed of 11 Articles. It was clear from the preamble that relations between Egypt and Israel would be based on the provisions of the United Nations Charter and on accepted norms of international law, governing international relations in time of peace. Similarly, it referred to the desire of the two parties to develop the normal relations of states at peace with one another. It did not try to establish extraordinary links between Egypt and

Israel. The treaty also specified that peace should be in accordance with the principles of Security Council Resolution 242.

Coming to the operative part, Article 1 committed the parties to respect and acknowledge each other's sovereignty and political independence, as well as each other's right to live in peace within secure and recognised boundaries. The same Article also specified that the parties should not resort to the use of force, should settle disputes by peaceful means and do all in their power to ensure that acts of belligerency, violence or hostility did not originate from and were not committed from within their respective territories.

Article 2 spelled out clearly that 'the permanent border between Egypt and Israel is the international border between Egypt and the former mandated territory of Palestine'.

Article 3 stipulated that the Israeli withdrawal to the permanent borders would take place in stages, beginning with the coming into force of the treaty and synchronised with the implementation of its other provisions.

Article 4 dealt with the free passage of Israeli ships and cargoes through the Suez Canal and through the Straits of Tiran, according also the right of overflight to civilian aircraft.

Article 5 stipulated that, in order to develop normal relations, the two parties should draw up a special protocol outlining the process. Normalisation would be achieved in stages, beginning with the coming into force of the treaty, parallel to and synchronised with the implementation of all other provisions.

Article 6 dealt with the security arrangements.

Article 7 stated that once all the provisions of the treaty were implemented, the two parties would terminate all claims and states of belligerency between them. This was a logical sequence.

Article 8 was of paramount importance because it touched upon two very sensitive and dangerous issues. It ran as follows: 'In order to eliminate the arms race which is wasteful and a source of tension, the Parties agree: (a) to sign and ratify the Nuclear Non-Proliferation Treaty; (b) to regulate the size of their armed forces and the type of their armaments and weapons systems.' I welcomed this particular Article not only because I had made the same points, in my speech before the United Nations General Assembly on 28 September 1977, but because I am certain that the instability of the Middle East is mainly the result of the imbalance in the military systems of Israel and the Arabs which is due to the flow of sophisticated arms into Israel from the United States. I was indeed pleased to see that the United States itself, the guarantor of Israel, was keen to have a certain balance of armaments in the area.

Article 9 spoke about the creation of a joint commission consisting of representatives of the parties under the United Nations chairmanship, to operate until the treaty was fully implemented in order to resolve problems arising in the execution.

Article 10 bound the parties to seek and accept guarantees for the provisions of the treaty by the United States, the Soviet Union and the United Nations Security Council.

Lastly, Article 11 referred to the fact that the treaty would enter into force upon signature and ratification according to the constitutional processes of each party.

The American draft was a simple one. It was couched in unambiguous terms and it arranged the sequences of events in the most normal and logical way, starting with the withdrawal of Israeli forces to the international boundary of Egypt and ending with the termination of the state of belligerency between the parties upon completion of withdrawal and implementation of all other clauses. It was also a draft in full agreement with the principles of Resolution 242 that Israel should withdraw completely from the occupied territories. The American draft treaty explicitly stated that the border between Egypt and Israel was the border between Egypt and the mandated territory of Palestine, without modifications. This is important, because the United States had originally taken this position in 1967, but had then abandoned it, introducing instead the concept that 'minor rectifications' of the borders were acceptable. In other words, America's position since 1967 had steadily deteriorated and moved closer to Israel's, but the draft treaty indicated a return to the original position, in conformity with Resolution 242.

It should be clear by now that there is a great similarity between the Egyptian draft and the American draft, not because of connivance, but simply because the two countries respected the normal, accepted rules of international law and of logic. They did not try, as the Israelis did in their draft proposal, to invent new norms of international law or a new logic to enable them to dictate their own views. In their draft the Israelis did not plan to withdraw to the international boundaries of Egypt; furthermore, they wanted to start with the immediate termination of belligerency, while they requested that their troops continue to occupy Sinai till everything was normalised and agreement reached on the so-called new borders between Egypt and Israel. I personally did not regard the Israeli draft as a bargaining document but simply as a statement of the Israeli philosophy and aims.

13 MORE PROGRESS TOWARDS GENEVA

The US–USSR Joint Declaration

Shortly after the meeting in the Oval Room at the White House on 21 September an important new development took place in the preparation for the Geneva Conference. The United States and the Soviet Union issued the Joint Declaration of 1 October 1977, in which they outlined the conditions for peace in the Middle East acceptable to the two superpowers.

The salient points contained in the Joint American–Soviet Declaration were the following:

1) Both governments are convinced that vital interests of the peoples of this area as well as the interests of strengthening peace and international security in general urgently dictate the necessity of achieving as soon as possible a just and lasting settlement of the Arab–Israeli conflict. This settlement should be comprehensive, incorporating all parties concerned and all questions.

The United States and the Soviet Union believe that, within the framework of a comprehensive settlement of the Middle East problem, all specific questions of the settlement should be resolved, including such key issues as withdrawal of Israeli armed forces from territories occupied in the 1967 conflict; the resolution of the Palestinian question, including ensuring the legitimate rights of the Palestinian people; termination of the state of war and establishment of normal peaceful relations on a basis of mutual recognition of the principles of sovereignty, territorial integrity and political independence.

The two governments believe that, in addition to such measures for ensuring the security of the borders between Israel and the neighbouring Arab states as the establishment of demilitarised zones and the agreed stationing in them of United Nations troops or observers, international guarantees of such borders as well as of the observance of the terms of the settlement can also be established, should the contracting parties so desire. The United States and the Soviet Union are ready to participate in these guarantees, subject to their constitutional processes.

2) The United States and the Soviet Union believe that the only right and effective way of achieving a fundamental solution to all aspects of the Middle East problem in its entirety is negotiation within the framework of the Geneva Peace Conference, specifically convened for this purpose, with participation in its work of the representatives of all the parties involved in the conflict, including those of the Palestinian people, and legal and contractual formalisation of the decisions reached at the conference.

In their capacity as co-chairmen of the Geneva Conference, the US and the USSR affirm their intention through joint efforts and in their contacts with the parties concerned to facilitate in every way the resumption of the work of the conference not later than December 1977. The co-chairmen note that there still exist several questions of a procedural and organisational nature which remain to be agreed upon by the participants to the conference.

3) Guided by the goal of achieving a just political settlement in the Middle East and of eliminating the explosive situation in this area of the world, the US and the USSR appeal to all the parties in the conflict to understand the necessity for careful consideration of each other's legitimate rights and interests and to demonstrate mutual readiness to act accordingly.

An attentive reader may have noticed that the American–Soviet statement of 1 October 1977 did not mention any UN resolutions, not even the Security Council Resolution 242. The reason for this omission was explained to me by American Under-Secretary for Political Affairs, Philip Habib, who represented the American side in the most difficult negotiations with the Soviets. Habib told me that the original Soviet draft mentioned practically every resolution on the Palestinian question adopted by the General Assembly and the Security Council. Since all the UN resolutions sided against Israel, the Soviet draft had a pronounced pro-Arab and pro-Palestinian slant. As a counter move, Habib stated, the Americans had suggested references to only a few resolutions, with emphasis on Resolution 242. After long and arduous negotiations, with each side insisting on the incorporation of different resolutions, a compromise was reached whereby the Declaration would not refer to any UN resolutions at all. Instead, it was agreed that the Declaration should only outline basic principles which could serve as the basis for a comprehensive solution and guidelines to the concerned parties in their deliberations at Geneva.

Despite the remaining procedural difficulties, the US and the USSR took it upon themselves to contact their own clients to bring them to the peace conference and embark on serious negotiations at Geneva. For example, I know that the Soviet delegation in New York immediately dispatched one of its counsellors to meet with the PLO representatives at the Plaza Hotel, requesting them to make public their support for the American–Soviet statement and after a long discussion he convinced them to do so. The PLO delegation later came to meet me at the Waldorf, to explain why they had accepted the Soviet–American statement and inquiring why I did not support it. I explained that I basically accepted the Declaration, but had reservations on some specific parts and therefore would not welcome it in a public statement.

My position concerning the Declaration was rather complex and it is worthwhile discussing it here. I had been aware since early September that the US and the USSR had already started negotiations on a common framework for a comprehensive settlement of the Middle East crisis, having been informed by Cyrus Vance. Vance had not elaborated on the negotiations because I had not asked him to do so. At this stage, I did not want to be involved in the details or to let myself be dragged into a process initiated by the two superpowers without consulting Egypt. I was satisfied that if the two superpowers reached an agreement, the parties to the conflict would have, for the first time, a general outline from the Soviets and the Americans showing how far they would go. Additionally, agreement between Washington and Moscow on a framework would eliminate a lot of bickering among those who still claimed that there was a basic difference between the superpowers as to the ultimate solution of the conflict. Despite this positive appraisal of the Joint Declaration, I did not think Egypt should support it officially after it was released. To begin with, Egypt's support would have automatically hardened Israel's position. In addition, such support might also lead the Palestinians and the Syrians to think that Egypt had been involved in the preparation of the Declaration. Finally, I wanted to keep the Egyptian options as open as possible, in case new political developments took place, making it ncessary to change our position.

As I had expected, the Israeli reaction to the Joint Declaration was negative in the extreme and Foreign Minister Dayan was simply furious. They wanted the last word and they naturally could not achieve this if their major ally negotiated behind their back with the Soviets and reached even a general agreement pertaining to the final settlement of the Middle East question. The Israelis wanted to control all American decisions. In particular they were anxious to prevent any unilateral move which the Americans might take regarding the PLO or any other aspect of the Middle East problem. Indeed, they had achieved this when they had forced Kissinger to guarantee that the US would neither recognise the PLO nor take any step in the United Nations without consulting Israel.

The Israelis' rejection of the Joint Declaration was exceptionally harsh because Israel had not even been informed about it, let alone consulted. Israel concentrated its attack on President Carter personally, claiming that he was responsible for what had happened because of his eagerness to mend his fences with Moscow. Accordingly Dayan, who was then in New York, requested an urgent meeting with President Carter. On 4 October, they argued for many hours until Dayan was able to extract from Carter a new statement reassuring Israel that Washington would not depart from its previous commitments.

Meetings with the Americans

After meeting with Dayan, President Carter received me on 5 October. Walter Mondale, Cyrus Vance and Zbigniew Brzezinski were present. In the light of Dayan's denunciation of the Joint Declaration, I asked President Carter and his colleagues about their commitment to the document particularly after the assurance which Dayan had successfully extracted. President Carter confirmed that 'the United States, on the highest level, will continue to be fully bound by whatever it has agreed with the Russians in that declaration'.

Despite this positive beginning, Carter then made a new suggestion which revealed the extent of Israeli machinations to avoid collective negotiations with the Arabs at Geneva, as well as President Carter's occasional impulsiveness. 'Mr Deputy Prime Minister,' he stated, 'it would be my dream if I could arrange a meeting between you and Dayan. This would represent the climax of my career.' I have to admit that I was completely taken by surprise. Needless to say, President Carter's proposal, if implemented, would have destroyed the American effort to reconvene the Geneva Conference because of the extreme negative Arab reaction to a private meeting between me and Dayan. Such a meeting would have confirmed the worst suspicions of Syria and the PLO that Egypt intended to solve its own problems at their expense. A meeting between me and Dayan would have driven a wedge in the Arab camp, isolated Egypt and destroyed the solidarity which was vital for a comprehensive solution at Geneva. Of course this is exactly what the Israelis wanted.

Listening to Carter, I had no doubt that the idea for the meeting had been suggested by the Israelis, probably by Dayan himself whom he had seen the previous day. I did not think, however, that Carter was consciously playing the Israeli game, laying a trap on their behalf as Kissinger had so often done in the past. Carter was too committed to the convening of the Geneva Conference to do that. Rather, he was so anxious to assure the success of the Conference that he thought a direct talk between the Israeli and Egyptian foreign ministers would help pave the way, just as the proximity talks were doing. What he failed to appreciate was that a direct encounter had very different political implications than the indirect contacts through American mediators. My conviction that Carter's suggestion was not part of an American plot but an impulsive, off-the-cuff statement, was strengthened by the look on the faces of other members of the American delegation, who appeared as bewildered as I was by their President's brainchild.

Confronted with Carter's sudden proposal, I had to throw the ball back quickly into his court. 'Mr President, I am ready,' I answered. 'I have no problem.' It was Carter's turn to be surprised. He grinned, looked at his colleagues and asked in disbelief, 'Are you serious? This would really be fantastic.' I repeated 'I am serious. I have no problem. I am ready at any time.' President Carter could not hide his excitement. 'Are you serious? Do you think we could do this next weekend?' He then turned to Mondale, Vance and Brzezinski and quickly started discussing with them what should be done to arrange the meeting. President Carter then turned to me, saying that the meeting would take place at Camp David and that nobody would know of it. I objected, arguing that while the meeting should certainly be a closed one, a press release should be issued at the end to the effect that, on the initiative of President Carter, Foreign Minister Dayan and myself had met at Camp David to discuss the peace process. I insisted on this procedure, explaining to Carter that with the Israelis secrecy is impossible and that they invent stories to suit their own purposes. For instance, the Israeli media had first invented the story that I had had a secret meeting with Dayan on my way to Washington. Carter talked some more about arrangements and other details, and I agreed to everything he said, but at the end I added: 'When I come to Camp David, Mr President, I shall bring with me Yasser Arafat.' He was really upset and screamed, 'Oh my God, it's impossible.' I explained my position:

> Mr President, as you know there is no difficult problem between Egypt and Israel, except in the long run the problem of national security with all its complexity. This is one thing. But the Palestinian problem is and will continue to be the most difficult one, and we are determined to give it top priority and solve it. I do not see any point in meeting with Dayan without discussing the Palestinian problem. Similarly, to discuss the Palestinian problem in the absence of Yasser Arafat would be a sterile exercise.

President Carter kept on repeating: 'This is not possible.' 'If it is possible for me to meet with Dayan, I do not see why it is impossible for Dayan to sit with Yasser Arafat,' I retorted. At this point, President Carter realised that his so-called dream would not come true and his elation gave way to a subdued mood. The meeting came to an end.

The Israelis did not give up, however. Two days later, a new proposal that I meet with Dayan was put forward by Henry Kissinger. This happened after an official lunch given in my honour by the NBC board of directors, which Kissinger attended in his capacity as advisor to the board. It was a business lunch during which we discussed various aspects of the international situation and particularly the Middle East. After the lunch, the host was escorting me back to the elevator, when suddenly Kissinger asked in a whisper in my ear whether I would do him a favour. I said I would. Then he suggested we go to a private room and meet behind closed doors 'to give the impression to my colleagues on the NBC board of directors that we are discussing top secret, highly important and sensitive questions'. He added that this would show his colleagues that he was still an important political figure constantly dealing with main representatives of foreign countries. I did not hesitate to accommodate him and he informed his colleagues we were going to have a private meeting.

As soon as we were alone, Kissinger started expounding his theory about the Middle East peace process. He was well informed about Carter's plans, he told me, because he received weekly briefings, and he believed that the course on which Carter and his colleagues were embarking was very dangerous and would lead nowhere. Kissinger wanted to make it clear that he was not working against President Carter, but only wanted to help the peace process, because Carter's approach would backfire. Kissinger himself still believed that a solution would only be found through a step-by-step approach, and that the first move should be a third disengagement between Israel and Egypt. I answered that I was against the step-by-step approach and was convinced that the crisis could only be solved by a comprehensive peace. Kissinger insisted. He was a very close friend of Dayan, he explained, and knew him intimately. He was sure that Dayan was the only Israeli who could bring about a third disengagement between Israel and Egypt. We were against the step-by-step approach, I repeated, and we would not go behind Carter's back. Trying to convince me, Kissinger dangled his bait in front of me: he was sure, he said, that he could convince Dayan to agree to a third disengagement along the El Arish-Ras Muhammad line without any political concessions from the Egyptian side. (This meant that over half the Sinai would return to Egyptian hands.)

To my great surprise Kissinger then offered to arrange a top secret meeting between Dayan and myself during the weekend at the Rockerfeller estate outside New York City. I did not tell Kissinger about Carter's proposal that I meet with Dayan, but I was sure that it could not be a mere coincidence. The Israelis were up to something. I rejected Kissinger's offer without any further discussion, but continued to ponder on these two invitations. Why were the Israelis pushing for a meeting with me? While there was no doubt that a meeting between Dayan and myself would admirably serve their purpose of isolating Egypt, they must also be aware that it was extremely unlikely I would fall for their trap. They must have something else in mind. I concluded that Dayan must also be trying to distract attention from the fact that a meeting had already taken place between himself and an envoy of Sadat in Rabat. Here, it will suffice to say that both Begin and Sadat wanted to hide their direct contacts from the United States, fearing that Carter, committed to the Geneva Conference, would quickly intervene to stop them. Dayan's request for a meeting with me was a cover, because Carter would never then suspect that Israeli and Egyptian representatives had already met. However Israel's main concern was to disrupt the Geneva Conference and isolate Egypt from the rest of the Arab world.

A few words about the Rabat meeting are in order here. In early September, King Hassan of Morocco had suggested to President Sadat he send an envoy to confer with Israeli Foseign Minister Dayan. Alternatively, the king suggested that Sadat personally meet with Begin in Morocco. Sadat had chosen the first alternative, without consulting me, and sent his advisor Hassan Tuhami to meet with Dayan in Rabat.

The Russian Attitude

As I stated earlier, the issuing of the Soviet–American declaration on the Middle East peace was encouraging for Egypt and the Arab side in general. We needed the Soviet Union to be involved in the peace process, so that other pressures could counterbalance Israeli influence on the United States. Unfortunately, the attitude and behaviour of the Soviet Union in this period was not altogether constructive. After my June visit to Moscow, the Soviet leaders had stopped communicating with Egypt, becoming totally absorbed by their contacts with the United States. Gromyko had not come to Cairo in August, as we had previously agreed, and had not seen fit to keep us informed about the ongoing exchanges with the United States regarding the preparation of the Joint Declaration. Cyrus Vance had informed me about these negotiations, but not Gromyko. This was very typical of the Soviet behaviour. They constantly declared that the Soviet Union was the only bastion of the Arab world against Zionism and imperialism, and in their messages to the Arab countries the Soviet leaders always insisted on the necessity for continuous consultations between Moscow and other capitals. But in practice, they often avoided direct contact with their so-called friends, giving top priority to their dealings with the United States. If negotiations with the US failed, Moscow reopened its communication lines with its friends in the Third World. In this particular case, the United States and the Soviet Union were able to agree on a joint declaration and the Soviet Union kept aloof not only from Egypt but from all the Arab countries.

After the June meeting in Moscow, we had not heard from Gromyko at all. As I was getting ready to go to New York for the UN General Assembly session in September, I met with Sadat and during our conversation he insisted that I should contact Gromyko in New York. Knowing there was no love lost between Sadat and the Soviets, I wondered why he had suddenly become so eager that I meet with the Soviet Foreign Minister. In turn, I told him that I did not intend to initiate any meeting with Gromyko, but again Sadat stuck to his view. After a long discussion, Sadat ultimately accepted my position when I reminded him that prior to my last visit to Moscow in June it had been formally agreed that my trip to Moscow would take place only if Gromyko publicly pledged to come to Cairo during the month of August.

Gromyko made a point of avoiding even seeing me and other Arab Foreign Ministers during the General Assembly meeting. The same behaviour was apparently imposed on all the delegations from the East European countries. Once on my way to the General Assembly, I noticed, from far away, that the Czechoslovak delegation was sitting in the delegates' lounge. Some of its members noticed me and prepared themselves to greet me but suddenly their foreign minister gave them instructions not to move, pretending they had not seen me. On my part, I also pretended I had not noticed their reaction. This was a solid proof that even the East Europeans had clear instructions from Moscow to boycott the Arabs. Such behaviour was unusual, especially within the UN circuit.

Gromyko's behaviour was also noticed by my other Arab colleagues, and Abd El-Halim Khaddam, the Syrian Foreign Minister, was particularly suspicious. As he told me later, he took the initiative and requested a meeting with Gromyko but he was not received until the night before the release of the American–Soviet Declaration. According to Khaddam, during that meeting Gromyko was particularly extreme and outspoken against American imperialism and its grand designs against the Arab states. Khaddam was so elated with what he heard, and particularly with Gromyko's assertion that the USSR would stand firm behind Syria and its other Arab friends, that he dispatched a long cable to

President Assad. Khaddam relayed the conversation he had had with Gromyko confirming Moscow's solid support. Then, accompanied by his wife, Khaddam left for Disneyland for a vacation. On the next day, he was shocked when the American ambassador to Damascus, who was accompanying him, gave him a copy of the Joint American–Soviet Declaration; Gromyko had never uttered a single word about it the previous day. Khaddam was particularly worried about the negative reaction of President Assad when he read his cable and then learnt from the media of this new American–Soviet venture. As a result, Khaddam cut short his weekend and immediately came back to New York. He came directly to see me, expressing his personal disgust about Gromyko's behaviour and the Russian double-dealing.

President Sadat and the American Attitude

As for the United States, it is important to emphasise once again that both President Carter and Secretary Vance were not only committed to a comprehensive settlement but also consistently consulted all parties involved. Their commitment went far beyond verbal statements to that effect. They exerted much effort to push the parties to the conflict to the Geneva Peace Conference. The Carter administration abandoned any attempt either to force a separate agreement between Israel and any one Arab state or to resort once more to the partial moves favoured by the Nixon and the Ford administrations, and particularly by Henry Kissinger.

Throughout this period Carter went to great lengths to maintain a continuous dialogue at the highest level with the parties trying to push them towards the negotiating table. He took it upon himself to discuss the various issues with Sadat, Begin, Assad and other leaders in the area, even before the release of the Joint Declaration. Taking advantage of visits to New York and Washington by the foreign ministers of the Arab countries and of Israel, he received almost all of them, discussing with each the various aspects of the conflict in detail. The energy that Carter and Vance invested in these 'proximity talks' was ample evidence of their commitment to the Geneva Conference.

In the summer and early autumn of 1977, things were moving systematically towards Geneva. The conference was being painstakingly prepared, all parties had been consulted and the superpowers had agreed on the basic principles. All this indicated that the conference had a great chance of success. This was the scenario prior to Sadat's unilateral decision to go to Jerusalem. How then does one explain Sadat's decision? If everything was going in the right direction why did Sadat choose to take a step which would automatically destroy the effort that had gone into preparing for the conference? Was Sadat unknowingly with Israel to prevent collective negotiations from taking place? He continuously proclaimed that he was in constant contact with President Carter and in full accord with the policy followed by him and yet he intentionally kept his 'full partner' completely in the dark concerning the direct contacts taking place between Egypt and Israel. Specifically, why did President Sadat instruct the Egyptian representative at the Rabat talks to plead with the Israeli side not to inform Washington of the Israeli–Egyptian contacts?[1] Why too did the Israelis, who normally intimately compare notes with the United States, see to it that their ally in Washington should not hear about their secret dealings with President Sadat? Was there collusion between Begin and Sadat or were they simply afraid that Carter would object to the Israeli–Egyptian separate initiative, fearing that it would sabotage the American efforts to achieve a comprehensive peace settlement at Geneva?

While many of these questions about Sadat's motives must remain unanswered it is clear that the Carter administration had no suspicion that Sadat might not be fully committed to the Geneva Conference. On 19 October 1977 Sadat sent Carter a letter dealing with the preparations of the Geneva Conference. It confirmed Sadat's continuing commitment to overcome all obstacles. Although unanimity had not been reached, progress was being made:

> I have explained thoroughly the working paper which I have received enclosed with your above mentioned letter. Moreover, I have discussed its contents with Yasser Arafat where I have noticed that he is forthcoming.
>
> You may recall however that after convening the National Security Council of Egypt I have conveyed to you my agreement on the original American Working Paper which was handed to Minister Fahmy during his visit to Washington. Furthermore my approval of that paper was conveyed to almost all the Arab heads

of states, and as such I am still committed to the main substantive parts of that paper.

I have in the meantime noticed that in the new working paper which was leaked by Dayan as an Israeli paper in the Knesset — there is a serious departure from the original paper to the extent of amending some of the basic points contained in the original, in addition to some new points of procedural character to which I do not attach great significance.

As you most properly know Minister Fahmy conveyed our views to Secretary Vance through Ambassador Eilts on both the substantive and procedural points. In the light of my far reaching talks with Arafat, I attach herewith a reasonable pragmatic formula which I believe could tremendously enhance the chances of convening the Geneva Conference later this year without prejudice to the position of any of the parties concerned.

Having said that, I would like to emphasize that Arafat is still committed to what he told me concerning the representative of the Palestinians at Geneva, as was conveyed to you through Minister Fahmy.

Enclosed with this letter was the Egyptian redraft of the American Working Paper, which read as follows:

WORKING PAPER ON SUGGESTIONS FOR THE RESUMPTION OF THE GENEVA CONFERENCE

1) The Arab parties will be represented by a unified Arab delegation for the opening sessions at Geneva. Within the delegation there will be Palestinians, who may include not well known members of the PLO.

2) The working groups or subcommittees for the negotiation of peace treaties will be formed as follows:

a. Egypt–Israel.

b. Syria–Israel.

c. Jordan–Israel.

d. Lebanon–Israel.

e. The West Bank, Gaza, the Palestinian question, and the question of refugees will be discussed among Israel, Jordan, Egypt, the Palestinians and perhaps others as determined at the opening sessions of the Geneva Conference.

3) The agreed basis for the negotiations at the Geneva Peace

Conference on the Middle East are UN Security Council Resolution 242 and 333.
4) The working groups or subcommittees will report to the plenary.

Carter's reply of 22 October conveyed orally by Ambassador Eilts also revealed no wavering in Carter's determination and certainly no indication that Carter thought Sadat might be having second thoughts. This communication, however, also revealed that the issue of Palestinian representation still remained knotty, together with Carter's conviction that it could be solved.

We have looked carefully at the reformulation of the Working Paper that Foreign Minister Fahmy has handed us. We must be frank in saying that we do not think it would be fruitful to go back to the Israelis on the basis of this version. Given the political realities that we know the present Israeli Cabinet is operating within, there is no hope it could be brought to accept mention in the Paper of PLO representatives at the Conference. Similarly attempting to spell out a broadening of the function and composition of the working group that is to deal with the West Bank and Gaza would probably be impossible for Begin and his cabinet to accept given the intensity of Israeli feelings about 'the Palestinian question'.

I would first like to make it clear – because both President Sadat in his letter and Foreign Minister Fahmy in his comments to you reveal some misunderstanding on this point – that the Working Paper submitted to them is not 'an Israeli document'. It of course embodies some changes from previous versions we talked to the Egyptians about to accommodate some Israeli views, but as President Sadat and Foreign Minister Fahmy know it was not accepted by the Israelis except after prolonged and acrimonious debate within the cabinet. That version contained two important Israeli concessions that the Israelis were most reluctant to make – that the Arabs should be represented at the plenary by a unified delegation, and that Palestinians could be at the Conference on their own right and not as members of the Jordanian delegation. The Israelis fought very hard with us not to give in on these issues.

On the question of Palestinian representation, I can assure President Sadat that the terminology used in the Working Paper we submitted to him will mean proceeding to choose the Palestinians in the manner which Foreign Minister Fahmy discussed with Secretary Vance and myself in New York. As presently worded the paper speaks only of Palestinians without specifying organizational affiliation. While it does not mention PLO for inclusion, and in our judgment cannot given Israeli sensitivities, neither does it explicitly exclude them. It seems to me that this is a formulation that both sides can live with. As I say, it does not represent any change in the manner in which we previously agreed to proceed.

Finally, I would like to thank Foreign Minister Fahmy for raising in his conversations with Ambassador Eilts a very valid question about how we intend to proceed in getting the parties to Geneva once an agreed basis is found on procedure at the Conference. We agree that it will be best not to furnish invitations to each of the parties since otherwise the question of an invitation to the PLO would obviously arise. The procedure we are inclined to favor is that employed to convene the 1973 Conference; it was agreed upon at that time and presumably remains acceptable. Foreign Minister Fahmy will recall that there were no formal invitations issued to the parties for the 1973 Conference. After consultations with the parties we and the Soviets sent identical letters to the UNSYG (the letters do not name the individual parties) and asked him to circulate the letters to the members of the Security Council for their information. This procedure would not in any way conflict with the proposed method for choosing Palestinian delegates. It has the advantage of having been done before and is presumably a procedure the Soviets, Israelis and the Arab parties would readily agree to.

The next letter from Carter to Sadat, on 28 October, was the most revealing and significant of all. It showed, for a change, a decisive Carter, aware of the problem, conscious of the fears of the Arab side, and most importantly ready to take a concrete step to solve the problem.

The exchanges we have been conducting concerning the working paper on procedures for a Geneva Conference have served a useful purpose. They have achieved agreement among the parties on some key points where before there had been serious disagreements and they have pointed the way to the next steps we should now take in preparing to convene the conference. So far as the text of the working paper is concerned, I do not frankly see any likelihood of reaching agreement on a paper acceptable to all parties nor do I believe that this is necessary. Keeping the concerns and desires of all the parties in mind, I believe there is sufficient flexibility and that we have provided sufficient clarification of our views to meet your basic concerns with the understanding that any remaining problems can be worked out at Geneva where every party will be in a position to protect its interests. I believe we can now move boldly to convene the conference in a way which will safeguard the positions of all.

Concerning the difficult issue of Palestinian representation, Carter wrote, significant progress had been made in reaching agreement that Palestinian representatives can be included in a unified Arab delegation, adding: 'On the basis of what you and Foreign Minister Fahmy and I have already worked out, I believe it will be possible for Palestinian representatives to be chosen by the Arab side who will be acceptable to all and who will faithfully represent Palestinian views.'

He was aware that there was concern in the Arab countries that the United States might not insist that the Palestinian issue be adequately addressed at the conference, Carter added. The concern was understandable but unfounded, because he had long been convinced that there was no solution in the Middle East without a settlement of the Palestinian issue. None the less:

> In order to remove any doubts on this score, I am prepared, if the Arab side agrees to the course of action I am proposing in this letter, to make an unequivocal public statement that the Palestinian question, as well as the question of withdrawal and borders of peace, must be dealt with seriously at the conference with the aim of finding a comprehensive solution to all aspects of the Arab–Israeli conflict . . .

This statement by Carter was extremely important. First, this was the first time an American President had been ready to make a forceful public statement on the Palestinian issue. Second, the statement was particularly significant since it came after the meeting between Dayan and Carter during which the American President had reconfirmed Kissinger's guarantees to Israel. Carter seemed to reverse himself on that point and to be now determined not to allow the Israelis to dictate US policy toward the Palestinians. Third, Carter's words made it absolutely clear that he did not seek a separate peace between Israel and Egypt and that he was not aware that Sadat would settle for a separate peace.

Carter's letter continued:

> Furthermore, we have, with difficulty, achieved Israeli agreement that there will be a unified Arab delegation with Palestinian representatives included and that the West Bank and Gaza, as well as the refugee question, will be dealt with in multilateral or functional groups whose membership will include not only the states concerned but the Palestinian representatives as well.

The United States and the Soviet Union as co-chairmen of the conference would work out the procedure for reconvening it. This could probably be done, as in 1973, through a letter from the co-chairmen notifying the UN Secretary-General.

> With these understandings, I propose that I now proceed to work out with the Soviet Union co-chairman a call for reconvening the Geneva Conference. Specifically, I envisage following the procedure used in 1973 with a letter from the co-chairmen to Secretary Waldheim that the parties have agreed to meet at Geneva. The letter would state that the Arab parties have agreed to form a single delegation including Palestinian representatives; it would state that the conference procedures followed in December 1973 should govern the reconvened conference; and it would describe the working group structure as bilateral except for those issues which it is generally recognized lend themselves to a multilateral approach.

President Carter concluded,

> I am convinced that we are now at a critical moment in the efforts my administration had been making since taking office nine months ago to chart a course that will lead to a just and lasting peace in the Middle East. I want to assure again, with all the weight off my office and the strength of my personal convictions, that I intend to persist in the search for peace in the Middle East,

however long this takes, and to use the influence of the United States to the fullest extent in this effort.

While these letters indicate that everything was set for Geneva the key element was Carter's offer to make public announcements to reassure the Palestinians. His readiness to make such a statement was undoubtedly the result of the collective pressure of the Arab side which wanted to be certain, before going to Geneva, of the intentions of the United States as far as the Palestinian problem was concerned.

A further letter that I received on 9 November from Cyrus Vance proves that only 10 days before Sadat's sudden visit to Jerusalem President Carter had already formally proposed to all Arab states the reconvening of the Geneva Conference. As a consequence, Secretary Vance was very concerned about the meeting of the Arab states' foreign ministers scheduled to take place in Tunis on 12 November. He was worried because the Tunis meeting might disturb the carefully-balanced compromise on Palestinian representation which Washington expected to achieve in preparing the Geneva Conference.

As you know, we are presently awaiting the Arab response to President Carter's recent round of letters proposing that we not allow remaining procedural questions to further delay a reconvening of the Geneva Conference. We are encouraged by the serious effort the Arab parties are currently making to coordinate their positions, and we hope that these discussions will enable the Arab side to adopt a common position of agreeing to proceed on the basis the President recommends.

In the meantime, you and your Arab colleagues will be gathering in a few day's time in Tunis for a foreign ministers' meeting. Our latest proposal will of course not be known to the majority of the governments represented, but no doubt the status of our efforts to get to Geneva will be a primary topic of interest to everybody. I hope you and the ministers of the other Arab states who are parties to the negotiations will be able to convey to the conference the importance of not taking decisions or making public statements that have the effect of limiting the flexibility of the governments which have so much at stake in seeing negotiations begin.

In particular, it would be a real set-back – perhaps one that would be fatal to the prospects of reconvening the Geneva

Conference – if the foreign ministers' conference were to endorse any proposition that only through designation of the PLO can Palestinian representation at Geneva be accomplished. Such action would inevitably tend to freeze Arab positions on the most difficult procedural point that we are attempting to deal with. As President Carter has suggested in his recent letter to your Government, there are better means to secure Palestinian representation in a way that will allow for full discussion of the issues involved, without procedural obstacles.

There has been much confusion about the events of this short period but the following facts seem clear:

1) President Carter and his administration were fully committed to convene the Geneva Conference with a view to achieve a comprehensive settlement.

2) The American side admitted that there remained certain difficulties, but was also sure of the positive results of its endeavour. 'I am confident we can overcome the obtacles if we persist in our efforts,' Cyrus Vance had written to me on 9 November.

3) A working paper embodying the procedural points on the basis of which the Geneva Conference would be convened had been drafted; whether or not every single party to the conflict agreed to every single word in it, a workable framework existed. Agreement on every comma was not necessary.

4) The American administration was very keen to avoid any new or additional developments which would make more difficult an already complicated situation. This was why both President Carter and Secretary Vance were very determined either to discourage or temporarily freeze any new moves, proposals, or suggestions.

5) The American administration was apparently not worried that the Soviet side might try to undermine the convening of the Geneva Conference. Neither President Carter nor Secretary Vance ever mentioned directly or implicitly that they were encountering any problems with the Soviets.

6) Neither President Carter nor Secretary Vance knew of the contacts between the emissaries of Sadat and Begin in Rabat. American officials also did not know of Sadat's plan to visit Jerusalem until Sadat himself publicly announced his intentions only three days before he departed for Jerusalem.

7) Begin and Sadat could not possibly have overlooked the

necessity for informing their American partners of their intentions. Therefore they must have deliberately kept President Carter in the dark because they knew he would oppose their initiative. (While this is a major point, I have only seen it referred to once in a column by William Safire in the *International Herald Tribune* of 18 October 1980: 'A shrewd President Anwar El Sadat – without telling Mr Carter – arranged for his historic trip to Jerusalem,' he wrote. William Safire is a very well informed journalist but it seems curious that he should write of Sadat's deviousness but refrain from mentioning that Begin too ought to have informed his ally, President Carter.)

8) The Carter administration would have opposed Sadat's trip to Jerusalem, because they were fully committed to the Geneva Peace Conference. In fact, it seems clear that Begin saw the meeting with Sadat as a means of sabotaging the conference. Israel was consistently against reconvening the Geneva Peace Conference. The Israelis preferred to negotiate with each Arab state separately, starting with Egypt, on the assumption that in this way Israel could dictate its conditions and get the best concessions from each Arab state individually. At Geneva in the face of a united Arab front and in the presence of the two superpowers Israeli bargaining power would be much reduced. The Israelis were very suspicious of the Carter administration because they knew that Carter, and particularly Brzezinski, were very keen to see that the final comprehensive settlement did not depart significantly from the famous Brookings Report of 1975. Brzezinski had been instrumental in preparing that report with other American specialists. The Israelis were very unhappy with the report, which foresaw a return to the pre-1967 borders and the creation of a Palestinian entity.

I have concentrated in this chapter on the international developments taking place in the summer and autumn of 1977 in order to demonstrate that the situation in the Middle East was not hopelessly stalemated, but moving forward towards a comprehensive peace. It is against this background that Sadat's decision was so extraordinary.

Notes

1. Moshe Dayan, *Breakthrough* (New York: Alfred Knopf, 1981), p. 45.

14 WHY I RESIGNED

I had no reason to suspect, in those months of intensive preparation for the Geneva Conference, that a major divergence from this course was imminent. The behaviour of the Carter administration was completely straightforward. Egypt's commitment was also total, and completely in line with the joint Arab position. Sadat certainly appeared to be sticking absolutely to the course of action we had chosen. His constant praise of the draft treaty I had prepared, his warm approval of the other steps I had taken, all indicated a deep conviction that the Geneva Conference was the proper arena for negotiations.

A major stumbling block was of course the issue of Palestinian representation, since the Israelis would not agree to sit at a negotiating table with PLO members. Yet, even this problem was to be solved, because Yasser Arafat had confided to President Sadat that he would accept that 'Professor Edward Saīd, who is an American professor of Palestinian origin and a very trustworthy man, represents the PLO'.

Plans for Sadat to go to Jerusalem

The position of the Israelis left much to be desired, but was not unexpected. It was clear they would have much preferred bilateral negotiations. Yet, they had committed themselves in writing to participating in the conference. There had been some indications in the late summer that they wanted direct contacts with President Sadat, but there was no reason to believe that they would succeed in preventing the Geneva Conference.

The first hint that the Israelis had something in mind had come in August when I received cables from our embassies in Vienna, Washington and London stating that a number of world Zionist leaders had expressed interest in arranging discreet meetings with President Sadat. It seemed extremely unlikely that it was a pure coincidence that all those requests had been sent simultaneously, yet it was not clear what this meant. Puzzled, I conveyed the requests to President Sadat, adding that in my opinion these individuals should not be allowed to come to Egypt because they were well-known Zionists and all their names appeared on the Arab boycott list. I also indicated to the President that a positive response to the requests would create a very adverse reaction in the Arab world. He agreed and instructions were sent to our three embassies expressing our regret that President Sadat would not agree to receive those personalities. Did Begin inspire these Zionist leaders to seek an audience with Sadat in order to suggest a meeting between him and Sadat? I still do not know. However, shortly after we turned down the requests King Hassan conveyed Begin's desire for a meeting. It is possible that Begin turned to King Hassan after his initial attempt to establish contacts through the Zionists failed.

Sadat's position leaves many questions unanswered. He initially put up no resistance when I advised him not to meet with the Zionists. However, only a few weeks later he accepted Begin's suggestion for direct contacts and sent Tuhami to Rabat. Sadat chose not to inform me of Begin's message and his own response. This was the first time that he had refrained from keeping me informed and probably he decided to do so because he knew I would oppose the move. What is still unclear to me is whether there was a direct link between Tuhami going to Rabat and Sadat's own initiative to go to Jerusalem. Sadat himself denied that the Rabat talks were a preparation for Jerusalem, or even for an encounter between himself and Begin elsewhere. He told Dayan:

> In fact, I sent Tuhami to meet you for quite another reason. At the time, preparations were under way for the Geneva Conference, and it was Tuhami's task to ensure that you and we, Israel and Egypt, would reach some kind of agreement before the conference convened so that it would not end in failure. The purpose of your talk with Tuhami was not to arrange a meeting between me and Begin.[1]

President Sadat and I left Cairo at the end of October on our way to Romania, Iran and Saudi Arabia. We arrived in Bucharest on 28 October and were immediately received by President Nicolae Ceausescu and other Romanian leaders. Then we proceeded to Sinaia, a village about 100 kilometres from the Romanian capital. This Romanian village had a special romantic attraction for

President Sadat because it was named after the Egyptian Sinai and because it is a very beautiful resort, full of greenery. But alas, the drama which disrupted the peace effort started in Sinaia.

The morning after our arrival in Sinaia, Sadat briefed me in detail about his meeting with the Romanian President. Ceausescu, Sadat reported, wanted to act as a mediator between Egypt and Israel. In fact, he had already received Begin and had invited Sadat after his talk with the Israeli leader. According to Ceausescu, Begin was seriously determined to conclude a peace treaty with Egypt. 'Begin is a strong man and serious as far as his desire to act,' claimed Ceausescu. Begin had even shown the Romanian leader a plan for peace in the Middle East, complete with a map where the names of all the cities and areas were in Hebrew.

Apparently Begin had intimated that he was ready to sign peace treaties with the Arab countries on the basis of secure and recognised boundaries, and had asked Ceausescu to seek Sadat's reaction to a solution of the Palestinian problem. Israel was offering to create a mini-Palestinian entity in return for the complete annexation of the West Bank and Gaza to Israel. This Palestinian entity would have exactly the same dimensions as Gaza, but it would start at the Lebanese border and extend southward along the Mediterranean. After listening to this unusual Israeli offer, Sadat had asked President Ceausescu whether he had a ruler, so they could measure on the map how far the so-called Palestinian entity would extend south of the Lebanese border and compare it to the Gaza Strip. President Ceausescu did not have a ruler. President Sadat then told him: 'When we do not have a ruler to measure, in Egypt sometimes we use a piece of string and try to compare the measurement on the map.' Ceausescu found a piece of string and with its help Sadat realised that either Begin was out of his mind or his offer was not serious. The territory was minuscule. When President Sadat conveyed all these details to me, I replied that Begin was not serious and that his only motive was undoubtedly to annex the West Bank and Gaza. I added that I did not need to discuss Begin's proposal with the Palestinians to know they would reject it completely.

It was clear that Begin was not sincere. What he really meant was that he was not in favour of a independent Palestinian state under any conditions, but that he intended to annex Gaza and the West Bank. President Sadat agreed with my evaluation of Begin's true intentions. He saw the flimsiness of Begin's proposal, yet it was precisely at this time that he suddenly announced the completely new idea of going to Jerusalem.

We were in the guest house in Sinaia when President Sadat, in his pyjamas and slippers, started to discuss this idea with me. We were not in the air flying over Turkey en route to Iran or crossing mountains, as Sadat has said on many occasions and wrote in his book *In Search of Identity*. He just wanted to shroud his so-called initiative with a mysterious aura. Sadat told Dayan, for example, that the thought occurred to him in a mystic way while flying through the clouds. 'When did you first get the idea of the Jerusalem visit?' Dayan asked. Sadat replied:

When I was on my way to visit the Shah of Iran. It came to me suddenly as I was flying over Turkey en route to Teheran. I was searching for something that would produce shock waves, positive ones. The first idea that came into my mind was something else. This was to approach the five permanent members of the UN Security Council, the representatives of the big powers who have the right of veto, and suggest that they go to Jerusalem. I tell you frankly, I reckoned that since our 'cousins', the Israelis, are always stressing their security problem, big-power representatives sitting and deliberating for twenty-four hours could surely come up with a solution. After that, we, Egypt and Israel, could carry on ourselves. From Iran, as you know, Moshe, I went on to Saudi Arabia, and from there, on the flight from Riyadh to Cairo, I changed my mind. It occurred to me that the five big powers might not achieve what I expected from them, and their failure would aggravate the situation. I therefore decided that I would go myself to Israel.[2]

All this is simply not true. Sadat did not think of going to Jerusalem while flying through the clouds over Turkey or after leaving Riyadh for Cairo. He thought about it in Sinaia and discussed with me an Israeli offer that showed the full extent of their deviousness and lack of good will. It was equally untrue that on route to Tehran Sadat entertained the possibility of a world conference in East Jerusalem. It was I who suggested that idea in an effort to convince him to abandon his plan to go to Jerusalem.

The episode at the guest house in Sinaia unfolded in the following way. When President Sadat finished briefing me on his talks with President Ceausescu and the so-called Begin plan with its ridiculous map, he suddenly declared, 'I would like to seek your opinion about a trip to Jerusalem to deliver a speech in the Knesset'. I have to confess that I was taken by complete surprise. But knowing President Sadat very well, I simply inquired, 'What is the purpose of this visit?' Sadat replied, 'Just to go to Jerusalem and deliver a speech and we come back'. Despite my probing, he was not able to provide any specific information showing that there was a solid Israeli offer for peace which could justify such initiative.

Not receiving convincing explanation, I responded: 'Mr President, is the purpose of your visit to Jerusalem simply to achieve a major publicity stunt?' I then added, 'If this is so, it is certain that you will get first-rate publicity, especially in Western Europe and above all in the United States where the Israelis have a tremendous influence on the information media'. Sadat was not happy with my response. He kept on muttering 'publicity stunt, publicity stunt, publicity stunt'. He then inquired: 'What do you really mean by 'publicity stunt'?' 'What I specifically mean,' I replied, 'is that this visit will achieve great success only in terms of publicity in the news media, television and cameras'. His reaction was subdued and he repeated more than once, 'No, I have never thought of it that way'. 'Mr President,' I added, 'you have never kept any secrets from me. The proof is that in Washington and other places, you used to tell your foreign counterparts on the highest level that what you know, Fahmy knows. So here, I want to ask a simple question, Mr President. Do you have any information I do not know about which justifies this trip?' Sadat assured me that he was not keeping any secrets from me and that he had not received any specific promises or commitments from Begin to justify the trip.

In the course of the discussion, I tried to keep an open mind about Sadat's proposal and also to impress on him that I desired peace as much as he did. I said:

> I am not against peace. I was instrumental and, from the very beginning, responsible for the success of the first and second disengagement on the Egyptian–Israeli front and even for the Syrian–Israeli disengagement. It should by now be evident, Mr President, that both you and I work for peace. But the point is, what kind of peace, and how and when we achieve it?

I then reminded Sadat that we had only two cards to play – recognising Israel and ending belligerency. Since Israel was militarily superior to Egypt and other Arab countries, we could not aim for a military victory. He agreed with me, so I added:

> If we take the plane and go to Jerusalem, the act implies the automatic recognition of Israel and the termination of the state of belligerency. We play our two major political cards and gain nothing. The gain is all on Israel's side and their bargaining power is doubled. We also make the Arabs and the Palestinians furious. And once we go to Jerusalem we cannot retreat. We have no fall-back position, Mr President. We will be cornered, without room for manoeuvering in order to force Israel toward a comprehensive settlement.

Sadat listened attentively and very patiently, but he was very tense, and when his only son Gamal suddenly came into the room where we were sitting alone, he angrily shouted at him to get out. The President then replied that he agreed with me completely, but that he believed that his idea might expose Israel's real intentions. I reacted by saying:

> But this cannot, in my opinion, constitute a major goal and would not lead to the peace we are all working for. It is true, Mr President, that your visit might embarrass Israel vis-à-vis world public opinion, but only for a limited time. Therefore, the impact of the visit itself will fade out unless you are forced to sign, on Israeli conditions, a separate peace limited only to Sinai.

I then argued that if the aim of the trip to Jerusalem was to secure the return of Sinai, it was unnecessary. Sinai was never and would never be a problem. The Israelis knew that there would be no peace in the area if they did not withdraw completely from that region. Three successive American administrations had also been aware of this fact. The proof was that the American draft for a peace treaty between Israel and Egypt stipulated clearly that the Israeli forces would withdraw from the entire peninsula to the international borders which separated Egypt and Palestine under the British mandate.

So, Mr President, Sinai was not and will never be a problem. Now, if your move to go to Jerusalem was motivated by other reasons, such as the domestic economic situation, this again must be handled in a different way, not through a simple visit to Jerusalem. It takes time and specific concrete measures to improve the economic conditions of a country, Mr President. In this regard, we need measures at home and we need the close cooperation of the Gulf states, the United States and all Western powers.

Sadat did not disagree on any of these points, so I tried to convince him again that it was unwise to go to Jerusalem.

Mr President, just believe me, I am not against your meeting with Begin. I am ready to arrange for a meeting in Washington or Geneva, or even to bring Begin to Cairo, but going to Jerusalem is a different matter. By going to Jerusalem, you will play all your cards for nothing and lose completely the support of the Arab countries. You will get from all of them the most unprecedented and extreme denunciations. The United States will never be able to do anything to help once you go to Jerusalem. They will even force you to make the major concessions of your life. You know this very well and this is why you have not informed President Carter about your new idea.

Again Sadat did not argue with me, but just listened. I then tried to convince him that a meeting with Begin outside Israel would be different. Sadat should challenge him to produce a peace plan, and expose him to world opinion if he failed to do so. Then Sadat could even denounce Begin at an international press conference and brief the Arab heads of state in person.

If you follow this procedure, you will challenge Begin and lose nothing. In fact, you will gain everything by proving your readiness to conclude an honourable peace and showing that it is Begin and his colleagues who are the obstacle to real peace. The onus will rest on the Israelis. If you follow this proposal, Mr President, you will gain the support of international public opinion and still have the last word. Your options will be open, you will have more than one fall-back position. Mr President, you should not take any unilateral step which ultimately and definitely will be in Israel's favour. Don't give them a chance to isolate Egypt completely from the Arab world. Once this is done, Israel will start dictating its terms to you.

There was no hope that the Israelis would make major concessions in response to such a dramatic move by Sadat. They were too intransigent. Israel, I reminded Sadat, had attached to its draft peace proposal a secret memorandum stating that they would stay on the Golan Heights, and would never place the Gaza Strip or 'Judea and Samaria' (the West Bank) under 'foreign rule or sovereignty'. Sadat's trip would not force them to change their views. I also pointed out that a unilateral decision to go alone to Jerusalem would be a violation of his commitments to the Arab countries and of his assurances to the Egyptian people that he would support a comprehensive peace settlement, based on the full restoration of the rights of the Palestinians. Sadat had repeatedly confirmed all these commitments in his peace proposals.

Again, he did not argue with me. I felt encouraged by this and decided to suggest an alternative plan, knowing full well that he did not like outright rejection of any of his ideas. I proposed that instead of going to Jerusalem, he should formally convene an international summit conference attended by: 1) the heads of state of all the five permanent members of the Security Council; 2) the heads of the confrontation states, including Yasser Arafat; 3) the Secretary-General of the UN. They would meet in East Jerusalem for two or three days simply to lay down the basic philosophy of a Middle East peace, in the form of a master plan outlining all the major issues involved and the basic solutions to them. Then, this world summit conference would adjourn, instructing the Geneva Peace Conference to take over. In Geneva, the parties would continue negotiating the details of the peace treaties, settling their disputes on the basis of the master plan adopted and guaranteed by the summit in East Jerusalem.

Such an important gathering, I argued, would force Israel to abide by the rules of international law. It would also automatically provide them and everybody else with the international guarantees of the permanent members of the Security Council. President Sadat listened to my counterproposal very carefully. He liked it very much and agreed to every detail. I then told him that I would draft this proposal in the form of a presidential message from him to the concerned parties and that we would send it simultaneously to all those invited to the summit conference. I made it clear that it was imperative to send these messages to all participants at the same time in order to produce a favourable reaction. President Sadat concurred with my proposal and asked me to prepare a draft. His idea to go to Jerusalem appeared to have been discarded.

The discussions between Sadat and myself continued non-stop for almost eight hours. When I left the President's quarters to go to my rest house, I noticed that the press people were still waiting outside, wondering what had happened. I was bombarded with hundreds of questions, but I was not in the mood to utter one single word.

In the rest house, I found Osama El Baz, my Chef de Cabinet, Dr Mohamed El Baradei, legal counsellor in the Foreign Ministry, waiting anxiously for me. After relaxing a little, we had dinner together and I told them little by little what I heard from President Sadat. The minute I finished, Osama El Baz exploded: 'This is crazy. This man is not balanced. He should be prevented even by force to go to Jerusalem.' Dr El Baradei was as strongly opposed to Sadat's idea as El Baz, but did not express himself in such extreme words. Then, El Baradei suddenly asked Osama El Baz: 'What will you do if Sadat insists on going? Will you go with him?' Osama's reply was clear: 'Over my dead body, I will never go to Jerusalem.' After some time, I told them about my alternative proposal to convene a world summit conference in East Jerusalem, adding that President Sadat was very receptive to it. Both El Baz and Baradei were very relieved, but continued to comment adversely on Sadat's idea and the motives behind them. When things calmed down a little, I dictated to El Baz the draft of a message from President Sadat to the heads of state who were going to be invited to the East Jerusalem summit, so that Sadat could see it the next morning. The President approved it without making any changes.

We left by plane for Iran the next day. There, we discussed with the Shah bilateral relations between our countries. President Sadat did not tell the Shah anything about his original idea to visit Jerusalem or about the alternative I had proposed.

From Iran, we went to Riyadh, where we stayed for two days. We had extensive discussions with King Khaled, Crown Prince Fahd, Prince Abdallah, Prince Sultan and Prince Saud Ibn Al-Faisal, the Saudi Foreign Minister. The meetings were fraternal and the Saudis were as usual very courteous. On the second day of our stay in Riyadh, I said to President Sadat, 'What about having a very exclusive meeting with King Khaled and Prince Fahd? We both sit with them, and you, Mr President, inform them of your idea to go to Jerusalem.' Then, I added, 'You should make it clear to them that you are not asking their support or commitment to whatever you will ultimately do. The purpose of your meeting with them is simply to put them in the picture because of their special relation with you. This way you will be aware of their reaction'. I made this suggestion for two reasons: first, I wanted to find out whether Sadat had completely discarded the idea of going to Jerusalem; second, I was hoping that the Saudis' reaction against this initiative would be so vehement as to force Sadat to abandon it once and for all. Unfortunately, Sadat rejected the idea of meeting with King Khaled and Crown Prince Fahd or any other Saudi and telling them anything about his plans. He was in fact furious about my proposal, and insisted that the Saudis would never understand his ideas: 'They are not of the standard or calibre to digest or understand such moves,' he declared.

I decided at least to inform the Saudis about the idea of a World Summit in East Jerusalem. When Prince Saud Ibn Al-Faisal visited me in my suite in the guest house, I briefed him about our intention to call for a world summit to draw up a framework for peace and security in the Middle East. We discussed the proposal in some detail, and he reacted in a very encouraging manner.

The only concrete achievement of our visit to Riyadh was the result of a second meeting, presided over by Prince Fahd and attended by Prince Sultan, Prince Abdallah and Prince Saud. President Sadat seized the opportunity to request the Saudis to put special pressure on President Assad to stop arguing and raising new artificial obstacles to the resumption of the Geneva Peace Conference. Prince Fahd agreed. 'This is what we intend to do,' he said. I then intervened and proposed to Prince Fahd that he should instruct Prince Saud to proceed forthwith to Damascus to get Assad's final and unconditional support for the Geneva Peace Conference.

On 4 November we returned to Cairo where I gave instructions to El Baz and El Baradei to start reproducing the presidential invitations to the world summit conference in East Jerusalem. All the messages were ready that day. Sadat who had agreed about the need to send all invitations simultaneously, called me up, almost screaming when he saw the message. He said he had to inform his friend President Carter before the others. I argued: 'We both agreed to send all the messages at the same time so that there will be no complications. The key to a favourable response from all heads of state lies in forwarding all these messages simultaneously.' 'No, no, Ismail, I have to inform my friend Carter before the others,' answered Sadat. I reminded him that he had not informed the American President of his idea to go to Jerusalem. I added, 'I am afraid, Mr President, that President Carter may think, and his colleagues may tell him, that you are trying to steal the limelight from him by suggesting a new initiative, and thus reject the proposal'. But Sadat remained adamant that his friend Carter should be informed first.

In spite of my scepticism, I then asked Ambassador Hermann Eilts to come to my home on the same night and I gave him a message from Sadat to Carter about the world summit conference and the proposal which would be sent to all participants. In the message, Sadat argued:

> I have been evaluating the evolution of the peace process since the first meeting of the Geneva Conference up to your efforts since you have assumed the presidency. Now, I am fully convinced that much time and effort were spent on issues of procedural nature, to the extent that the procedural aspects overshadowed the substantive essentials for peace. However, I believe that if this situation is to continue unchecked, it would jeopardise the prospects of peace through endless bickering over procedural issues.
>
> For the aforementioned reasons, I would like to inform you that I felt it imperative to move substantially ahead by proposing a new formula which, I hope, would constitute a breakthrough on the road to peace.

The rest of the letter outlined details of the proposal.

On the following day I received Carter's answer. As expected, he was afraid that Sadat's proposal for a world conference would endanger his personal efforts to convene the Geneva Peace Conference in December. Carter wrote, in part:

> Mr President, my own limited experience and study of history indicate that a summit conference is often a better forum for confirming agreements previously arrived at through quiet diplomacy then for reaching new agreements, and especially when the views of the participants are as divergent as they are with respect to the final terms of a Middle East peace settlement.
>
> I believe that we have made good progress, and an initiative as

bold as this may indicate an abandonment of the tediously evolved and fragile agreements already reached.

After Geneva is convened and progress has begun, your proposal could always be made at a crucial and dramatic moment to avoid failure or to consummate success.

You asked me to comment privately and frankly, Mr President, and I have done so. In the spirit of the close personal relationship between us, I strongly hope that you will not make your proposal at this time.

When Eilts brought Carter's reply, Sadat's first reaction was that I had been correct in predicting that the American President would see Sadat's own proposal as an attempt to steal the limelight from him. But Carter's opposition also dissuaded Sadat from carrying out his plan. As a result, the invitations to the summit conference were never sent and all efforts were once again focused on the convening of the Geneva Conference. In the course of these final preparations there was an incident which raised new doubts in my mind about Carter's conduct of his foreign policy and about the lack of coordination between the White House and the State Department.

Carter's attitude, it will be recalled, had always been that he had the peace process fully under control through his contacts with all parties involved. In particular, he had repeatedly asked Egypt to leave the handling of Syria and the Palestinians to the United States. However, shortly after the exchange of letters concerning the East Jerusalem summit, Sadat received another letter from Carter. This letter was hand-written and sealed with the presidential seal. In his short message, Carter reminded Sadat that he had promised to do everything the American President asked in order to help the peace process. Carter then asked for Sadat's help in convincing the PLO and the Syrians to be more forthcoming about the reconvening of the Geneva Conference. Why Carter had changed his mind and asked for Sadat's help remains a mystery to me, because nothing concrete had happened which justified Carter's sudden fears about the position of President Assad and of the PLO. Furthermore, Carter's fear that the Geneva Conference might not be reconvened was not shared by the State Department. Secretary Vance's letter addressed to all Arab Foreign Ministers at their meeting in Tunis expressed full confidence that everything was proceeding smoothly towards Geneva. Clearly, something was wrong in Washington, and in particular in the communications between the White House and the State Department.

Between 5 November and 9 November, we had received three contradictory messages from Washington: a letter from Carter indicating confidence in the Geneva Conference and asking Sadat not to call for the East Jerusalem summit; a second letter from Carter indicating that there were problems in securing the commitment of Syria and the Palestinians to the Geneva Conference; and a letter from Vance again indicating full confidence that the Geneva Conference would convene.

Carter's handwritten note is important in another respect as well. Sadat used to hint that there was something unusual, or extraordinary in this message, creating the impression that it was somehow related to his decision to go to Jerusalem. He also claimed that nobody had read it except himself. None of this is true. The letter contained nothing but the plea that Sadat use his good offices with Assad and the PLO and Sadat personally handed the letter to me, so that I read it and prepared the answer. Vice-President Hosni Mubarak was also present when this happened.

The problem with President Sadat was his inclination to dramatise things and give them undue importance. In many cases, he imagined things which did not take place at all and made public statements in full conflict to what had really happened. His only aim was to make people believe it happened. President Sadat did not worry much about the authenticity of what he said, forgetting that there is always more than one party to every international political event and that there are foreign official records of all communications and transactions.

Among Sadat's flights of fancy was his claim that his answer to Carter's letter was very special and mysterious. He alone, he said, knew its contents. In fact, I prepared it and Sadat simply copied it in his own hand, in keeping with the diplomatic practice that a handwritten letter is answered by another handwritten letter. The answer I dictated was a simple assurance that Sadat would do everything in his power to ensure the convening of the Geneva Conference. In retrospect I have to admit, however, that my draft may unwittingly have revived Sadat's idea to go Jerusalem. Knowing Sadat's fondness for strong words, I included a sentence stating that he would take a 'bold step' to help Carter's efforts. I never thought that the word 'bold' would strike a nerve in Sadat's system and rekindle his idea to go to Jerusalem, but in fact this may have happened.

Whatever might have been in the back of his mind at this time, Sadat appeared more determined than ever to continue working for a unified Arab position before the Geneva Conference. We discussed these issues at length in preparation for the Tunis meeting of Arab Foreign Ministers scheduled for 12 November. This was the meeting that had worried Vance and prompted his letter urging the foreign ministers not to rock the boat. Throughout our talks about the foreign ministers' meeting, Sadat insisted that it was high time to form an Arab strategic front composed of the confrontation states and supported by the Gulf countries. He repeatedly confirmed to me that Egypt was fully committed to the PLO and that the settlement of the Palestinian problem was the core of a just and comprehensive peace. He wanted the Tunis meeting to be 'a historical one under Egypt's leadership'. 'You must insist on a unified front,' he instructed me, 'and that all decisions be more than verbiage; we need a military and political strategy strengthened by financial and physical support.' For this reason, we agreed that the Arab summit meeting which would be proposed at Tunis should not take place at an early date or without preparation. Committees at the ministerial level should first meet to prepare the groundwork and we would need at least three months of preparation. This delay was also intended to give the two superpowers enough time to reconvene the Geneva Peace Conference at the end of December as stipulated. In order to achieve complete Arab unity, President Sadat also agreed that I should hold a press conference in Tunis to announce the resumption of diplomatic relations with Libya.

To underline and dramatise Egypt's commitment to a unified Arab position I decided, with Sadat's approval, to invite Yasser Arafat to Cairo on 9 November. On that day Sadat was going to deliver a major speech to the People's Assembly and Arafat was invited to attend, for the first time, by Egypt's parliament. He accepted, and we sent an Egyptian military aeroplane to bring him to Cairo. Paradoxically, this is the occasion Sadat chose to announce that he was ready to go to Jerusalem.

Sadat was supposed to follow a prepared text in his speech to the Assembly. But suddenly he departed from it and emotionally declared that he was ready to go anywhere in the world, even to Jerusalem, to deliver a speech and address the Knesset if this would help save the blood of his sons. Yasser Arafat was shocked and demanded, 'What is the meaning of this? Is Sadat saying this intentionally in my presence? Have you invited me to come to Cairo in order to hear such a thing?' I assured him that there was no such plan and this was a slip of the tongue. But I was personally not so sure.

I was very upset that President Sadat had not given me advance warning that he was going to refer in such a casual way to the possibility of a trip to Jerusalem. But the members of the Assembly and the Egyptian people did not think that Sadat's statement should be interpreted literally: the applause greeting the announcement did not mean that the members of the Assembly approved Sadat's idea of going to Jerusalem, or even that they believed he intended to go. They were simply carried away when the President declared his readiness to go anywhere in the world to save the blood of his sons, in keeping with a very popular Egyptian saying: 'an Egyptian is always ready to go very far, even to the end of the world to achieve something.' Very few people suspected that Sadat's statement was not just rhetoric. One was Yasser Arafat. Another was General Gamasy, the Minister of Defense, who whispered in my ear: 'He said it again.'

General Gamasy's comment requires some explanation. When President Sadat and I returned from Bucharest, Tehran and Riyadh, he summoned the National Security Council of Egypt on 5 November for a briefing on the trip. Sadat started with a general account of the visits, then he referred in detail to his talks with President Ceausescu, outlining Begin's proposal about the new Palestinian entity. Finally, in a very casual way, as if he was just referring to the Egyptian saying, he added: 'I am ready to go Jerusalem and to give a speech in the Israeli Knesset if this will save the blood of my sons.'

The statement was followed by complete silence. Apparently, nobody took him seriously. Sadat himself did not elaborate on his idea, perhaps because he had not yet taken a final decision or because, as usual, he did not want to give us a chance to comment on and discuss what he said. The silence was broken only by General Gamasy who suddenly shouted stretching out his hand, 'No Knesset, no Knesset. This is unnecessary.' Gamasy was normally a very disciplined man. He never intervened without asking for Sadat's permission, in fact he did not even light a cigarette without asking. But this time he was very upset, fearing that Sadat might mean what he said. Again, there was complete silence in the meeting. Nobody uttered one single word. President Sadat went on to discuss other issues as if he had not heard Gamasy at all.

It had been claimed by senior Egyptian officials that Sadat submitted his idea of going to Jerusalem to the National Security Council, which discussed and approved it. Specifically, this claim was made by Mustapha Khalil, later Prime Minister and Foreign Minister and was also attributed to Kamal Hassan Ali, later Foreign Minister, although he issued an official denial. But the meeting I have described cannot be interpreted by any stretch of the imagination as a discussion of the plan. Sadat never explained the reasons behind his initiative. The National Security Council did not debate the initiative and did not formally approve it. It should be added that Sadat himself stated on many occasions and wrote in his book *In Search of Identity* that he had not discussed the trip with anybody in Egypt, except Fahmy, the Foreign Minister who was against it from the beginning.[3] I will add that if the NSC had approved Sadat's trip I would have resigned on the spot.

After the speech at the People's Assembly was over President Sadat and the members of the government went into the lounge. There he called me in front of everyone shouting: 'It was a slip of the tongue. Please, Ismail, censor it completely.' I promptly gave instructions to delete from President Sadat's speech the phrase dealing with the trip to Jerusalem and the Knesset. Accordingly, there was no reference to it the next day in our government papers but the foreign correspondents attending the session of the People's Assembly prominently reported the statement.

The Arab Foreign Ministers' Meeting

The Council of Arab Foreign Ministers opened in Tunis as scheduled on 12 November, a few days after Sadat's speech. Ironically, the meeting was a triumph for Egypt and a complete victory for the efforts to strengthen Arab unity. The sessions took place in an atmosphere of tension and suspense. Rumours and news were pouring in and criss-crossing from every direction. For the first time, twenty-one out of twenty-two Arab Foreign Ministers were personally taking part in the meeting. The Arab and international information media were represented by a large number of correspondents. The atmosphere was tense because of many disturbing rumours about the initiative which might be taken by the so-called radical Arab countries. Some of them were expected to disrupt the Tunis meeting by espousing extreme positions against the reconvening of the Geneva Peace Conference and seizing this opportunity to attack their rival régimes in other Arab countries.

As usual, before the official session of the Council there was an informal meeting in the suite of Kuwaiti Foreign Minister Sheikh Al-Sabah. At the opening of that meeting, the Syrian Foreign Minister Abdel Halim Khaddam spoke first, explaining in general terms the position of his government and what Syria expected from the Tunis meeting.

I gave enough time to my colleagues to say whatever they wanted and deliberately chose not to speak until the end. This was a policy I followed at all meetings of the Arab League, because I did not want to give the impression that Egypt, as the most powerful Arab country, wanted to impose its will at the outset. This approach also gave me time to digest what my colleagues were saying, and get the feel of the meeting. While explaining the Egyptian stand at the end, I usually succeeded in reconciling some of my colleagues' divergent views. In Tunisia, I scrupulously followed this approach.

After listening attentively to the various points of view, I summed up the Egyptian position as follows:

We in Egypt believe that we have reached a point where we Arabs should tackle our problems in a more serious way, starting by defining our aim precisely and then agreeing to take the practical steps necessary to implement the strategic decisions we adopt during this session.

I added, 'We believe that it is high time to eliminate much of the rhetoric and avoid taking unrealistic decisions which cannot be implemented.' As I had agreed with Sadat, I made it clear:

It is high time that the Arab countries should draw up a concrete and comprehensive military, political and economic Arab strategy. This major Arab strategy should be thoroughly prepared through the various Arab ministerial councils. The ministerial councils should hold in the immediate future extraordinary sessions to discuss the overall policy needed for the successful implementation of this strategy.

The Arab Ministers of Defence should also meet immediately after we adjourn the Tunisian meeting. The purpose of the defence ministers' meeting is to study the military situation from every point of view; they must examine the military capacities and deficiencies of the Arab military systems and compare them with the Israeli military system, proposing concrete steps to remedy the situation in a very short period. A meeting of the Arab Economic and Finance Ministers is also needed in order to examine ways and means to mobilise our financial resources in the service of the military Arab strategy proposed by our defence ministers. Having accomplished their work, these two organs should submit their findings and recommendations to an extraordinary meeting of the Arab Foreign Ministers who would examine thoroughly the reports and formulate clear-cut recommendations for the summit meeting of the Arab states. Accordingly, Egypt proposes that the summit take place in three months, so that the Arab Heads of State can sanction the recommendations of the foreign ministers. The decisions of the Arab Heads of State will be binding on all of us and will provide us for the first time with a major Arab strategy to be automatically implemented and respected by everyone without further delay.

All my colleagues listened very attentively, but as usual, the Syrian Foreign Minister objected. He was not pleased with what I had proposed and in fact declared that after listening to me he had no choice but to return forthwith to Damascus; he added that his plane was still on the tarmac at Tunis airport. His major problem was that he could not accept the recommendation that the Arab summit meeting should not take place inside three months, because the Syrian leadership wanted to have it within twenty days.

The situation was tense, but everybody had to laugh at this suggestion, knowing that for practical reasons the summit could not take place so soon. The Syrians were pushing for the early date so as to push the Arab summit to adopt extreme and far-reaching decisions, thus destroying any chance for reconvening the Geneva Conference at the end of December.

After Khaddam finished, I spoke again, addressing myself to him and said jokingly: 'The best thing for you to do, Abdel Halim, is really to take your plane and go back home.' Everybody laughed and I added: 'We are now here in a very informal meeting and everybody is entitled to his own point of view. But I hate to see my friend Abdel Halim leaving. So, I advise him that after we disperse, he should have a good siesta and meet me at 6.30 in the formal meeting.' Then again in order to tease Khaddam, I told him, 'I recommend that you wear your beautiful blue French suit, the one you bought from Pierre Cardin'. Everybody laughed and on this light note the meeting was adjourned.

At 6.00 p.m., I was waiting for Abdel Halim Khaddam. He arrived and told me that he had a serious problem. The position he had taken in the informal meeting had been dictated by the entire Syrian leadership including the Supreme Council of the Baath Party. Furthermore, the Syrian leadership had approved the speech he was expected to deliver at the opening of the formal meeting. This speech was 36 pages long. My suggestion was that Khaddam should not deliver his speech at all, but simply distribute it to the newsmen as a press release. At the same time, I promised him that if he did so, I would defend him at the Council meeting whenever anybody criticized or attacked Syria, and particularly if this criticism came from Sadoon Hammadi, the Iraqi Minister of State for Foreign Affairs.

I also had a private talk with Abdul Menaem el-Tireki, the Libyan Foreign Minister, and warned him that if he did not cooperate in the Council and resorted to Libyan rhetoric, I would not resume diplomatic relations with Libya during our stay in Tunis.

The first formal meeting of the Council was inaugurated by a speech from the Tunisian Prime Minister on behalf of President Bourguiba. Tunisian Foreign Minister, Habib El-Chatty, then took over as chairman of the meeting and Mahmoud Riad, Secretary General of the Arab League, followed with an introductory speech. The general debate was then declared open and the chairman asked if anyone wanted the floor. He did not get any response. Complete silence reigned in the conference room. This was quite new because usually several speakers wanted to intervene quickly, and particularly Khaddam of Syria. After the lapse of a few minutes everybody was looking at Khaddam, but to no avail. Almost ten minutes passed, and there was still complete silence. The atmosphere was most unusual and the chairman inquired again whether any foreign minister would like to speak. Again, there was no response.

I interrupted the silence by jokingly saying: 'It has become a custom that if Khaddam does not speak first, then nobody speaks at all, and there will be no vitality in our meetings.' Everybody laughed except Sadoon Hammadi, the Iraqi Minister of State, who felt provoked by my comments, apparently thinking that this silence was part of some tactical move prearranged between Damascus and Cairo. So he immediately asked for the floor and started to criticise almost everybody, but particularly Syria. He then unexpectedly declared that the problems and misgivings which have loomed on the Arab horizon and the inadequate and inefficient decisions of the Arab world were the direct result of the position which 'the most powerful and biggest Arab country had adopted vis-à-vis the Soviet Union'.

Hammadi did not mention Egypt by name, but it was clear that he was referring to Egypt. I did not interrupt him; instead I was closely watching the angry expression on the face of my Syrian colleague. It was clear he intended to speak the minute Hammadi had finished. To avoid this calamity and prevent the usual savage exchange between the Iraqi and Syrian representatives, I asked for the floor immediately after Hammadi ended his venomous speech. I denounced the Iraqi policy and role in the Arab world. I defended Syria and the Palestinians. I praised the Gulf states. They were the real 'consolidation' states because they had helped Egypt and Syria to sustain defeat and prepare for the future. But Iraq, I said, was doing nothing.

Contrary to my normal approach in such meetings, I had no option but to lecture my Iraqi colleague on global power politics and various other questions related to the stability of the Middle East. Lastly, I strongly criticised the Iraqi leaders because they had never really participated in any war with Israel and had done almost nothing until that time. They had not even honoured their own financial pledges to the Palestinians. The Iraqi government simply chose the easiest way, doing nothing concrete but adopting a very extreme and irresponsible position, and rejecting every Arab move. In such a way it tried to hide the truth and convince itself that it had indeed contributed to the Arab cause and particularly to the Palestinian question. This, I pointed out, was tantamount to having no position whatsoever.

During my extempore speech, I was watching all my colleagues around the table and I felt, with some satisfaction, that I gained their complete support by simply turning the tables on the Iraqi delegation. I formally introduced the Egyptian position, repeating the points I had made at the previous informal meeting. Again, I noticed that the reaction of almost all my colleagues around the table was positive: Egypt was serious and it was proposing concrete practical measures leading to agreement on a major Arab strategy.

After I finished, Abdul Menaem el-Tireki, my Libyan colleague wanted to assist his Iraqi counterpart, lest his silence be interpreted in Libya as an indication that he had sided with me and left the Iraqis isolated. He whispered to me that he wanted to speak, but I reminded him that if he did so, I would not resume diplomatic relations with his country. Heeding my warning, he decided to cooperate and did not utter a single word at the meeting. At the end of the session Sadoon Hammadi, who had been brought up and educated in Egypt, came up to me, to apologise and explain the pressure he was under.

The other speakers at the meeting all focused on the Egyptian proposal, expressing full support for it. The only opposition came from Khaddan of Syria who really was in a delicate position because his instructions required him to push for an Arab summit within twenty days. To reach a compromise and to absolve himself with his own leaders in Damascus, Khaddam asked the Sudanese representative to propose that the Arab summit should take place after one month. When I rejected this suggestion, the Sudanese representative proposed as a compromise that the summit should be held within two months. But I stuck to my position, saying, 'No, it cannot be before three months because it needs a lot of preparation if we are really serious'. Both Khaddam and the Sudanese representative finally acquiesced and the Council of the Arab Foreign Ministers adjourned on 15 November 1977 after adopting the Egyptian proposal in its entirety.

It was a complete success for Egypt. It is also a fact that all formal and informal deliberations were very promising. We were all aware that we should unite and approach things in a concrete way. There was unanimous agreement on the need for strict commitment to whatever Arab strategy we agreed upon. Internationally, the meeting attracted much attention. Inevitably, information leaked to the press about the atmosphere of the meeting and the details of the debate, and the newswires carried many articles. The atmosphere was very elated. Habib El-Chatty, was much impressed by the atmosphere and very proud of the meeting he had chaired, and felt that 'great progress had been made because of the objectivity and constructiveness of the proposals made by the Egyptian delegation'. In his closing speech he gave Egypt high credit for the success of this extraordinary session.

The Tunisian meeting was indeed an extraordinary affair and it adopted unprecedented decisions. In many ways it was an historical event for Arab nationalism.

During the Tunis meeting, President Sadat called me twice on the telephone. The first time he wanted to be informed about the atmosphere of the meeting and the decisions the foreign ministers were likely to take. He also inquired when I would go back to Cairo, and I told him that I could not return until the meeting ended. During the second conversation Sadat was very upset and nervous. He ranted against Begin in robust language. His rage was directed above all against the appeal Begin had addressed to the Egyptian people on 11 November, in reply to Sadat's announcement that he was ready to go to Jerusalem. Begin had tried to convince the Egyptians that he wanted peace, but it was clear he meant peace on his own terms. For example, he explicitly declared that 'Judea and Samaria', or the West Bank, were Israeli lands. Sadat asked me to prepare a strong rebuttal. I gladly did this and it was carried by the Egyptian papers as a Ministry of Information release.

There was a lot of talk in the corridors of the conference about Sadat's intentions. It was rumoured that Sadat would indeed go to Jerusalem, and everybody was fearful that Egypt might take a unilateral step. I spared no effort to assure my Arab colleagues in the formal meetings that Egypt was fully committed to whatever I had said during the present sessions. I stated that, if there was no comprehensive peace, Egypt would reject the return of Sinai even if Israel presented it on a golden platter. I stuck to this position throughout the Tunis meeting.

Jerusalem Again

Just before returning to Egypt I made good my promise to the Libyans and I announced in a press conference the formal restoration of diplomatic relations between Egypt and Libya. Then I flew back on a special plane, arriving in Cairo at 3.00 p.m. on 15 November. Upon my arrival I was told that President Sadat wanted to speak to me urgently. He finally contacted me on the direct line between us and enthusiastically inquired about what happened in Tunisia. He barely allowed me to start explaining before he started complimenting me on how I had handled the Syrian Foreign Minister and others. Thanking him, I continued to describe the atmosphere which prevailed in Tunisia and the issues which were discussed, summing up the positions of the various Arab Foreign Ministers. Moreover, I explained to Sadat how I had managed to postpone the Arab summit of Heads of State for three months, so that the Geneva Peace Conference could take place as expected in December. I added that this was a good solution because, if we encountered serious obstacles in Geneva, we could fall back on the Egyptian proposal to convene a world summit in East Jerusalem. The Arab summit could meet before the one in Jerusalem, giving us a chance to elaborate an overall Arab strategy reflecting the latest political events. Sadat was extremely happy and interrupted me more than once saying, 'Bravo Ismail, bravo Ismail, bravo Ismail'.

To my complete surprise, however, the moment I finished talking Sadat suddenly shifted back to his idea to go to Jerusalem and deliver a speech in the Knesset. It was inconceivable to me that he could revert to Jerusalem after talking about Geneva, a new Arab strategy and a new Arab summit, and after all the praise he lavished on me for my achievements in Tunisia. My shock became more profound when Sadat informed me that he had already instructed his press counsellor, Saad Zaglool Nassar, to announce on radio and television at 8.30 p.m. that the President intended to go to Jerusalem and deliver a speech in the Knesset. For a moment I hoped that Sadat might be joking, so incredible did this entire story appear, particularly as he was going to pay a formal visit to Damascus on the next day, 16 November.

I reacted sharply to Sadat's words, and a very heated discussion ensued. We argued on the phone for over an hour. I again strongly objected to his decision to go to the Knesset after all that had been agreed and accomplished in Tunisia. I specifically reminded him of his anger at Begin's address to the Egyptian people and of his own request that I prepare a very strong rebuttal to what Begin had said. Then, I inquired of President Sadat whether, during my stay in Tunisia, he had received any new concrete proposals justifying the revival of the idea to go to Jerusalem. He informed me that there was nothing new whatsoever. Then I inquired of him: 'What new extraordinary development took place which induced you to think once again to go to Jerusalem in spite of the fact that you still have nothing concrete on the basis of which you can justify our trip?' President Sadat had no answer.

I decided to try a different tactic 'Mr President,' I asked, 'is this a dictatorship or a democracy?' 'What do you mean?' he asked in surprise. I merely repeated my question: 'Is this a dictatorship or a democracy?' 'A democracy, of course,' he answered. 'Then I propose that you convene a small group of top officials, tell them of your plan and seek their reaction.' I went on to say: 'I promise that I will not say anything. If they agree with you, or even if half of them agree, I will go along with you irrespective of my personal objection. But if there is massive opposition to your plan, you should reconsider your decision.' Sadat became furious: 'Whom do you want me to consult?' 'Just the top people, the members of the National Security Council,' I answered. He almost lost control of himself, screaming, 'I will not discuss it with anybody, I don't care for anybody's opinion, I will not do it'.

Sadat suddenly became conciliatory: 'OK, Ismail, don't worry and don't get angry. You don't have to go to Jerusalem, you are free to stay in Cairo, but prepare my speech to the Knesset, and after I deliver it, I will come back to you.' My immediate reaction was 'Is this possible, Mr President? Is it possible that the President goes to Jerusalem and his Foreign Minister chooses to stay in Cairo?' I continued, 'Mr President, either we both go to Jerusalem or we both stay in Cairo'.

Realising that the heated argument had lasted for a long time and reached a dead end, President Sadat suddenly told me, 'We can continue our discussions during our trip to Damascus tomorrow'. I reacted to this, 'How are we going to continue the discussion, Mr President, if you have already given instructions to your press counsellor to announce your decision to go to Jerusalem at 8.30 tonight?' He saw the logic of my argument, but was unable to answer. He stubbornly said: 'It was I who gave instructions to the press counsellor to announce this decision.' I answered, 'If you, Mr President, would like to continue the discussion, then the formal announcement must be cancelled'. Apparently, President Sadat was embarrassed, but he only continued to repeat that he was the one who gave the instructions. I again told him, 'I am fully aware of that, but I will contact your press counsellor and instruct him to cancel the announcement. But before doing so, he must contact you, Mr President, to get your final approval since it was you who originally gave him these instructions'. At this point, the discussions between Sadat and myself became very heated indeed. I was very angry and spoke harshly. He finally agreed to call off the announcement.

I called Sadat's press counsellor and instructed him to cancel the announcement of the President's intention to visit Jerusalem. I added that before doing so, he should call Sadat personally. A few minutes later, the press counsellor called me again and reported that Sadat had instructed him to cancel the announcement 'because Fahmy did not want it'.

After making sure the announcement would not be issued and there would be another opportunity to continue the discussions with Sadat, I told my aides and security officers to take an advance plane and proceed to Damascus. Then I spent the entire night re-evaluating the situation, trying to assess whether there were new developments which had pushed President Sadat to revive his idea of going to Jerusalem.

I had initially intended to argue forcefully with Sadat during our visit to Damascus. By the early morning, however, I decided not to join him on this trip but to stay in Cairo. I was almost sure that Sadat would discuss his idea with Assad and, knowing him too well, I also expected him to make the whole thing public specially with the reporters covering his visit to Damascus. My expectation was unfortunately accurate.

On the morning of 16 November I called Vice-President Mubarak, asking him to inform Sadat that I was not feeling well and would not join him on this trip. After the President left for Damascus, Vice-President Mubarak told me that he had conveyed my message to Sadat and that Sadat had replied that he was familiar with my frequent stomach complaints and had then asked Mubarak to remind me to prepare the speech we had talked about. I knew he meant the Knesset speech.

As I had expected, Sadat informed Assad in a closed meeting of his intention to go to Jerusalem. They had an angry discussion during which Sadat once again failed to produce any convincing argument to justify his trip. The Syrian President then completely disassociated himself from Sadat's new adventure. Before returning to Cairo, Sadat told the press about his talks with Assad, revealing that he intended to go to Jerusalem and that the Syrian President opposed the idea. When the media carried the stories from Damascus, I felt I had made the right decision in not accompanying Sadat: by staying in Cairo, I had avoided a public confrontation with the President in a foreign country.

During the press conference in Damascus, Sadat was asked whom he had consulted in Egypt about this new move, and answered he had only spoken to his Foreign Minister, Ismail Fahmy. In his book *In Search of Identity*, President Sadat made the same point, adding that my reaction had been to 'collapse'. This was a favourite expression of his. He often used the term 'collapsed' when his interlocutor disagreed with him or had a different point of view. According to him, former American Secretary of State William Rogers had 'collapsed' during negotiations, meaning he had disagreed with Sadat. He used the same word in reference to two Egyptian ministers whom he dismissed for opposing some decisions. If you disagreed with Sadat, you collapsed.

My Resignation

On 17 November Sadat departed from Damascus for Ismailia. On the same morning Mubarak contacted me on the phone, asking 'What kind of facility do you need to go and wait for President Sadat in Ismailia?' He was very helpful indeed, trying to make things easy and comfortable for me. He proposed that I should take a helicopter. He was even ready to give instructions that the helicopter would take off from a field very close to my residence. But I informed him that I did not intend to wait for Sadat. He was surprised and wanted to know why I did not want to go to Ismailia, and whether I felt all right. I assured him of my good health, and he continued to press me to go with him and wait for Sadat. I answered: 'I have made up my mind and I am not going to wait for President Sadat. Instead I am sending you a sealed envelope which I hope you will hand to him personally.' I did not mention the contents of the envelope to Vice-President Mubarak, but simply sent him the envelope by special messenger.

Upon President Sadat's arrival, Vice-President Mubarak gave him my envelope. Sadat opened it and found my resignation. He immediately informed the Vice-President, other senior Egyptian officials and the American ambassador Hermann Eilts, who had all gone to meet him in Ismailia. General Gamasy asked for Sadat's permission to proceed to Cairo and bring me back with him to Ismailia. Prime Minister Mamdouh Salem also asked permission to join General Gamasy for the same purpose. But President Sadat told them: 'No. You don't know Fahmy. He was all along against the Jerusalem trip and he won't agree to change his decision.' Then Sadat instructed Vice-President Mubarak to release the news of my resignation. The story was carried as a major item by the news media all over the world.

In contrast, it was announced very briefly on our national television and was later completely censored. On the next day, my colleague Mohamed Riad, Minister of State for Foreign Affairs, was called by Vice-President Mubarak and informed that he had been chosen to take over the Ministry of Foreign Affairs for the moment. A very short discussion took place between them, but within six minutes Riad too resigned. He came directly to my place to inform me of his decision.

It should be noted that I chose to submit my resignation in a quiet way without putting pressure on anybody else. My letter of resignation ran as follows:

The President of the Republic.

Because of the present circumstances through which Egypt and the Arab world are going and because of extraordinary and unexpected developments which are going to take place affecting the Arab cause, I hereby submit to your Excellency my resignation fully convinced that I cannot continue in my post and jointly bear the responsibility emanating from new developments.

With my respect and prayers for Egypt and I wish you all success.

I have to admit that I chose to submit my resignation in writing instead of informing Sadat personally because I knew that, had I gone to meet him in Ismailia, either he or the people around him would have put colossal pressure on me to stay. I feared that, because of the good personal relationship which existed between Sadat and myself, at the very end I might give in to the general pressure to stay on and go with the President to Jerusalem. When Hermann Eilts, later discussed this with me, I told him that had I talked to Sadat in person, there would have been a 50 per cent chance of my giving in. Hermann Eilts disagreed: 'No. The chances were 95 per cent that you would have been pressed to go with him.'

My resignation created problems for Sadat, challenging the wisdom of his decision in the eyes of his countrymen and abroad. To counteract this negative impact, he wanted a large number of Egyptian personalities to accompany him to Jerusalem. This was unusual, because he had never taken a large delegation when we both travelled abroad on official visits. He even went to the extent of sending a special plane to get some Egyptian officials and newspapermen who were abroad at the time. Other members of the delegation volunteered their services. For example, Osman Ahmad Osman and Dr Mustapha Khalil, who later became Prime Minister, seized this opportunity and offered to join him in his trip.

Reactions and Explanations

This is the true story of how Sadat decided to go to Jersualem. Throughout our long arguments he never once produced a sound reason to support his decision. During the eight hours of confrontation in Sinaia, Romania, other tête-à-tête meetings, and particularly several more hours of heated debate on the phone I probed in vain for justification. I inquired about evidence, facts, even hints, and got no answers. A perceptive reader may have noticed from my account that the two long conversations we had sounded more like monologues on my part than authentic dialogues. This is not because I am suppressing what Sadat said, but because he said very little. He wanted to go to Jerusalem. He never told me why, but simply tried to appease me. 'Don't be angry, Ismail.' 'You don't have to come with me if you don't want to, Ismail.'

He certainly had not weighed the decision carefully and come to the conclusion that he had no option but to go to Jerusalem. He was not convinced that the Middle East problem would be suddenly resolved by his trip. He could not have believed that as a result of his visit the Israelis would simply withdraw from all occupied Arab territories and agree to the full restoration of the Palestinian rights to statehood.

I am sure that Sadat himself was amazed when he heard the numerous theories which appeared in the press to explain his decision. On the other hand, he was wily enough to appropriate some of them to justify his trip and enhance his prestige as a world leader. Prior to the trip, I never heard anything from Sadat about the so-called theory of the 'psychological barrier'. According to this rather arcane theory, one of the main reasons behind Sadat's trip was his desire to lift the psychological barrier preventing communications between the Arabs and the Israelis. In fact, if anybody needs psychological treatment, it is the Arabs who have suffered defeat after defeat at the hands of the Israelis. Israeli morale has been boosted enough times, it is Arab morale that needs ɔme improvement. If psychological barriers need to be lifted it should be by an Israeli leader, showing that they really want peace.

Another wild notion which has often appeared in the American press is that Sadat decided to go to Jerusalem because he believed in the so-called theory of 'shock treatment'. President Sadat never mentioned this either. He was simply not a man who believed in theories or in decisions reached on the basis of long discussion and thorough appraisal. Jerusalem was no shock to the Israelis, only to the rest of the world. To the Israelis Sadat's decision appeared more as a logical continuation of the direct contacts established in Rabat. That is why, after Sadat declared to the People's Assembly that he was ready to go to Jerusalem, Begin readily extended an official invitation.

However the trip was a shock to the Egyptian people, the Arab world and the Palestinians, not only because it was a surprise, but also because it had serious repercussions for the Arab world and above all for the comprehensive settlement of the Middle East problem. It certainly destroyed Egypt's crucial role in helping the Palestinian people to regain their own land and statehood. Sadat also administered a 'shock treatment' to President Carter and his colleagues, who were taken completely by surprise. Washington did not know how to respond to the initiative. 'In Washington, Carter and the State Department, anticipating at most a resumption of the Geneva Conference, greeted Sadat's statement with a silence less eloquent than confused. Only several days later did the United States government register its belated, and somewhat constipated, approbation,' wrote an observer.[4]

The American media also advanced another explanation, the 'electric shock' theory. President Sadat, some argued, went to Jerusalem because he was a master of extraordinary and unusual decisions, counting on surprise to obtain what he wanted. However, in reality the 'electric shock' notion simply meant that Sadat was an impulsive man who acted without seriously considering the repercussions of his actions. But this is no way to conduct foreign policy.

I should also mention in passing another explanation of Sadat's trip, that he acted as a deeply humanitarian man, determined to prevent suffering and misery. Sadat was simply not that sort of person. An episode which took place shortly before his trip to Jerusalem is revealing in this respect. Sanaa Mahmoud Hassan, the wife of Egyptian Ambassador to Canada Tahsin Beshir, was studying for a PhD in the United States and preparing a thesis or the Middle East question. In the course of her research she visited Israel several times with her professor, collecting information and interviewing some Israeli politicians. When Sadat heard about it, he gave Ambassador Beshir the choice of divorcing his wife or quitting the Egyptian foreign service. Beshir opted for divorce. Still dissatisfied, Sadat then ordered that the woman be stripped of her Egyptian nationality and deprived of her passport. Two months later Sadat visited Israel himself.

Despite all my reservations about the trip to Jerusalem I would have accepted the move even if I did not agree with it, had Sadat set forth a coherent rationale and discussed it with his senior colleagues. It would not have mattered whether his reasoning was based on the 'psychological barrier' theory, or any other theory. The point is simply that he should have had a reason before deciding to go to Israel and he should have submitted it to the approval of the competent political institutions in Egypt.

Sadat did not follow this procedure; he just talked to me, not about any theory but only a sudden idea to which he stubbornly clung. All these theories were simply invented during and after visits by American commentators, particularly Walter Cronkite and Barbara Walters. When commenting on the visit, they tried to give it some philosophical foundation in order to influence public opinion favourably.

After Sadat's visit to Jerusalem the media, fed by Israeli and Zionist propaganda, started to invent stories and anecdotes to build Sadat's prestige. The Israelis were particularly skillful in manipulating Sadat's image with specific concern for peace with Israel so that he should not feel he had committed a serious mistake which might lead to his own demise. Sadat was basically a simple man, proud of being a common villager, and he was easily taken in by the Israeli campaign.

Other explanations of Sadat's sudden decision argue that he was driven to it in desperation at Egypt's plight. It is suggested that the country was in terrible financial straits and it was politically isolated in the Arab world. Sadat had to do something to bolster his position. In fact there is no more substance to these theories than the others we discussed. There was no pressure on Egypt, either internally or externally, which might justify Sadat's trip. While Egypt's economic problems were acute, they could not be solved by empty dramatic steps. Financially there was no problem. The Suez

.anal and oil revenues were increasing fast. The remittances of Egyptians working abroad, particularly in the Arab world, were flowing back in unprecedented amounts. In 1977, the oil-producing Arab countries had agreed to form a consortium in order to boost the Egyptian economy. Moreover, Sadat's new policy to equip his army with the latest and most sophisticated western weapons was fully supported by the Gulf Arab states, especially Saudi Arabia. They paid in cash and in full for these weapons, whether they were American or French. American economic aid to Egypt had already reached high levels before the trip. The major increase had taken place in fiscal 1976, when American economic assistance jumped to US$986.6 million from $371.9 million the previous year. Thereafter, American aid grew only slowly and certainly there was no windfall after Sadat's visit to Jerusalem or the signing of the peace treaty. Politically, there was no internal pressure on Sadat. He was firmly in control and the opposition was negligible.

Relations with the Arab countries could not have been better. The Arab Foreign Ministers' meeting in Tunis had been a triumph for Egypt. Diplomatic relations with Libya had been reestablished. Even Sinai was not a problem. The American draft treaty between Israel and Egypt called for the complete withdrawal of the Israeli forces stationed in Sinai to the international borders of Egypt. Sadat knew this.

The decision to go to Jerusalem was not taken because Egypt was in a desperate position. It was not taken on the basis of a sound asessment of the impact of the gesture. It was not taken to retrieve an otherwise lost Sinai. The only party which benefited from Sadat's initiative was Israel. This is not a conclusion reached with the benefit of hindsight. It was perfectly clear from the very beginning and this is why I refused it.

As a result of Sadat's trip, the collective bargaining and multilateral negotiations leading to the Geneva Conference were first interrupted and then shelved indefinitely. The Soviet role in the peace process practically came to an end, leaving the United States the only great power involved. Without the participation of all Arab countries united on a single position, Israel was left free to manipulate the Palestinian issue as it saw fit. They refused to look at it as a political problem which could only be solved by the creation of a Palestinian state. Rather, they have continued their drive to change the composition of the population and the economic make-up of the West Bank and Gaza until annexation becomes the next logical step. In the meantime they have undertaken the savage slaughter of West Beirut.

Their appetites whetted, the Israelis are now likely to look for new horizons beyond their frontiers. The new theories concerning the strategic importance of Israel and its crucial role as the linchpin of American policy in the Middle East, issued with apparent synchronisation in Washington and Tel-Aviv, encouraged them further.

These new strategic developments could not have taken place at all unless Egypt, the largest and strongest Arab country, was completely isolated from its Arab brothers and forced to accept the Israeli view on the Palestinian question. This is why Begin jumped at the opportunity to slam a wedge in the Arab camp by concluding a separate peace with Egypt.

When Sadat decided to go to Jerusalem, he only made it easier for Begin to achieve his goal. Did he therefore act in collusion with Israel? This would mean that he had further secret contacts with Begin after the Tuhami–Dayan meeting and before he announced his decision to go to Jerusalem. At these meetings, the Israelis would have offered him something to convince him to conclude a separate peace. I do not think this explanation is correct. I have given it serious consideration and found no evidence that there were such contacts. As a result, I believe that Sadat simply allowed himself to be wooed and manipulated by the Israelis until he was forced in a position where he would have either to admit he had made a mistake or sign a separate peace on Israeli conditions.

The Israelis had chosen their man well when they focused on Sadat. He was the President of the most important Arab country. The Israelis studied Sadat's personality thoroughly and understood his huge ambition to be a major actor on the international scene. They must have known his weakness for the *grand geste*, for the unprecedented step and the dramatic move made regardless of risk. The Israelis started to woo him when they contacted him in September 1977 through King Hassan. They did not inform Carter because they feared that cooler heads and more rational minds might keep Sadat on the course leading to Geneva. Sadat responded to their lure because it seemed to offer a possibility of accomplishing something on a personal basis. He, too, kept it a secret from Carter, for fear the American President would oppose the move. But then Sadat went even further, and in his desire to become an international hero he conceived the ill-fated idea to become the heroic peace-maker and go to Jerusalem.

Sadat knew the Israelis would try and use him but he thought he was clever enough to manipulate the whole situation to his own advantage. He thought that he could do it by following a double standard, one when he spoke publicly and the other when he dealt discreetly with the Israelis. This is why Sadat's speech in the Knesset and all other later public statements did not depart from the collective Arab stand. He wanted to prove to Arab public opinion and the Egyptians at home that he was the best advocate of the Arab cause and that he had never departed from what Egypt had agreed with its brethren Arab states. Covertly, however, he continued to make major concessions to Israel; something which he admitted only later.

This is the real story of how and why Sadat became in the end a facilitator of Israeli policies. It is also the story of why I resigned. It was a matter of principle and conscience.

Notes

1. Moshe Dayan, *Breakthrough* (New York: Alfred Knopf, 1981), p. 88.
2. Ibid., p. 87.
3. Anwar El-Sadat, *In Search of Identity* (New York: Harper & Row, 1977).

15 A PRECARIOUS PEACE

I find no satisfaction in recounting what has happened since Sadat's trip to Jerusalem, for while events have shown that I was correct in my assessment of what would result, the consequences for Egypt and the entire Arab world have been too negative to allow me to feel anything but a profound sadness. The events are well known. Sadat's trip to Jerusalem and his speech in the Knesset produced no miracles. These moves did not elicit any concessions from Israel; they were received with a very guarded optimism by the United States and were met with outrage in the Arab world. Sadat made a feeble attempt to convince the world that he was still working for the convening of the Geneva Conference by calling for a preparatory meeting of all parties to be held at the Mena House Hotel in Cairo on 14 December 1977. At the same time, he also started talking about the convening of an Arab summit, during which he would explain the results of his trip and consult the Arab Heads of State about the strategy to be followed in the future. As expected, the Mena House Conference was attended only by the delegations from Israel, the United States, the United Nations as observer, and of course Egypt, while the call for the Arab summit was never formally issued because even Sadat realised that it would be a futile gesture. From that time on Sadat was alone, completely isolated in the Arab world and dealing directly with Israel and the United States. After several months of somewhat desultory exchange, a meeting of Sadat, Begin and Carter at Camp David on 5–17 September 1978 led to an agreement between Israel and Egypt on the framework for a separate peace. A peace treaty was signed on 26 March 1979. It was certainly not the just and comprehensive peace the Geneva Conference could have achieved. In fact it was virtually identical to the draft treaty submitted by the Israelis to the United States in late 1977. Sadat had nothing to show for all his initiatives.

How this situation came about needs to be discussed. Did Sadat go to Jerusalem with the clear intention of making a separate peace with Israel and accepting any Israeli condition as long as Sinai was returned? This is certainly not what he told the Israelis when he

...ressed the Knesset. His speech was harsh and did not depart in ...e least from the position of the united Arab countries that Egypt ...ad been instrumental in shaping during the previous years. Peace, Sadat declared in the Knesset, entailed the following conditions:

> First, termination of the Israeli occupation of the Arab territories occupied in 1967. Second, achievement of the basic rights of the Palestinian people and their right to self-determination, including the right to establish their own State. Third, the right of each State in the area to live in peace within secure borders, guaranteed by agreed-upon procedures that would ensure the proper security of international borders, in addition to appropriate international guarantees. Fourth, all the States of the area should be committed to conducting their relations with one another, according to the aims and principles of the United Nations Charter, particularly, not to resort to the use of force and to resolve any differences among them through peaceful means. Fifth, termination of the present state of belligerency in the area.

Furthermore, Sadat stressed that peace along these lines should be concluded at the Geneva Conference. His trip, thus, was not a substitute for the conference, but part of the process leading up to it, a step taken to overcome the endless discussions on procedure which, Sadat declared, had caused months to be 'frittered away'. Sadat also added a word of warning to the Israelis – and reassurance to the Arab countries: 'I have not and will never adopt a two-faced policy. I have never conferred with anybody except through one language, one policy and one face.' The Israelis, in other words, should have no illusions that Sadat's speech was just meant for Arab consumption, and that he would prove more accommodating in negotiating behind closed doors.

It is interesting to note that nobody believed Sadat. The Arab countries treated his gesture as a betrayal of the Arab cause, and adamantly refused to have anything to do with him. The Soviet Union similarly concluded that Sadat had now moved completely into the American camp and was beyond their reach; it therefore wihdrew completely from the peace process. Similarly, both Israel and the United States refused to take Sadat's militant statements too seriously, because if they had, they would have given up all hope of extracting sufficient concessions to make peace on their own terms possible. Did Sadat expect such adverse reaction? Did he anticipate that even the United States and Israel would express great reservations about the initiative? Did he believe that the Arab world would hail him as a hero, and the Israelis, reassured by his gesture, would simply pack up, move out of the occupied territories, and acknowledge the right of the Palestinians to self-determination? I do not believe that Sadat had any concept of what would happen. The steps he took and the statements he made in the weeks after the trip to Jerusalem confirm that he had no plan. Out of this confusion emerged a tapestry of misrepresentation with which Sadat tried to hide his mistake and his growing embarrassment.

His first step was to call the Mena House pre-Geneva meeting because, as he said, 'Well, for me Cairo is the best place for preparatory arrangements for Geneva.' But the Arab countries' refusal to accept his invitation, left him completely bewildered. We have a good record of Sadat's thinking in this period because his expedition had made him an instant celebrity, and foreign newspapers and television stations were falling over each other to interview him.

On 25 November Walter Cronkite of CBS spoke to him. Cronkite was puzzled by the seemingly contradictory pronouncements Sadat had made in the preceding days: on the one hand, he had repeatedly declared that he would never make a separate peace with Israel; on the other, he kept insisting that, even if all Arab countries boycotted the Mena House conference, he would go to Geneva, alone if necessary. Cronkite was understandably uncertain about Sadat's plan: would he go to Geneva and negotiate on behalf of the Syrians and the Palestinians? Where would his mandate to do this come from? What if the Syrians and the Palestinians rejected what Sadat had agreed upon? Would Sadat then be forced to sign a separate agreement? Sadat had no rational answer to these very legitimate questions, but evaded them by digging in behind the mystical idea of his 'sacred mission':

> If everyone does not agree I shall be proceeding to Geneva, also for the comprehensive settlement, and whenever we reach results I shall be calling an Arab summit here and put what we have already agreed upon before them.

But did Sadat really think the Palestinians or the Syrians would accept any treaty Egypt negotiated for them? Cronkite insisted.

> It is for everyone to decide for himself. I shall be doing my job, what I call a sacred mission, I shall be doing it. This is establishing peace in the area here, because this is the right moment. And as I told you I shall be submitting this to an Arab summit here with all the kings and heads of state and everyone has to decide for himself before this summit.

Did this mean that if the other Arab Heads of State rejected the agreement, Sadat would de facto be signing a separate peace, Cronkite wanted to know. Not really, was Sadat's answer, because he was a 'flexible man' and 'I never cross a bridge before I reach it.' It was no wonder that Cronkite, an old hand at interviewing evasive politicians, should admit to Sadat that 'You have left me in confusion' – Sadat was confused himself.

In an interview with ABC on 27 November 1977 Sadat again set forth the same argument that he would not negotiate a separate peace with Israel, but would continue talking to the Israelis even if all other Arab countries rejected his invitations to participate. Referring to the Cairo conference, the interviewer asked: 'What happens if Jordan says no, Syria says no, the PLO says no. Will there be a Cairo conference?' 'Yes,' answered Sadat. 'Just Egypt and Israel?' the interviewer wanted to make sure. Sadat answered:

> Yes, and I shall be continuing the preparation for a comprehensive settlement. The problem is not an Egyptian problem. It is an Arab problem and the problem between me and Israel is some part of it only. So, and I have declared my intentions, I say I am not going for bilateral agreement or separate settlement or so, not at all. I am working toward a comprehensive settlement so I shall be doing this here in Cairo and I shall be proceeding to Geneva also and whatever results I reach in Geneva I shall be bringing back here for the Arab Summit to decide.

Once again, Sadat failed to explain how he could negotiate alone on behalf of all Arab countries and how he could reach a comprehensive peace settlement when his Arab colleagues totally rejected his initiatives.

I do not know how long Sadat continued to believe that he would not sign a separate peace and that no settlement was acceptable unless it safeguarded the rights of the Palestinians. Certainly by early 1978, Sadat was beginning to be 'double-faced'. While in public he still spoke in support of Palestinian rights, in private he had started to send very different messages to the Israelis. In March 1978, he invited Israeli Defence Minister Ezer Weizman to confer with him in Ismailia. The secret message he had for the Israelis was extraordinary. Sadat, the defender of Palestinian rights, the man whose 'sacred mission' was to work for a comprehensive peace in the Middle East, told Weizman:

I have excluded the PLO from my lexicon. By their own behaviour, they have excluded themselves from the negotiations. But I can say this only to you – not to Begin because the next day Begin would announce: 'Sadat has excluded the PLO!' I have to be able to tell the Arabs: 'The Arabs of the West Bank and Gaza will be able to shape their future, and the Israelis will leave.' I don't care whether Hussein comes in or not. The West Bank and Gaza should be demilitarised. Any solution must guarantee your security. We shall try to find a suitable formula.[1]

The rest of the conversation was equally revealing.

'From your point of view – who is to take charge of Judea, Samaria, and Gaza? Who will rule there?'
'If Jordan enters into the negotiatons – Jordan, the representatives of the local population, and you.'
'From that, I understand there won't be a Palestinian state.'
'Right! But if I say so to Begin, he will proclaim it from the rooftops the following day. But I can tell you: No state! And a small number of military strong points for Israel.'

Ezer Weizman could not believe his ears and comments:

Summarizing my conversation with Sadat put me into a better mood. Like us, the Egyptian president was not interested in a Palestinian state; he was willing to leave our West Bank settlements in place; he would substitute for Hussein should the king refuse to take part in negotiations. I was gratified to have had Aharon Barak listening in on our conversations; without his testimony, no one in Israel would believe me.[2]

For once Sadat meant exactly what he said, and in the final peace treaty the PLO – and the Palestinian people for that matter – were eliminated.

A question which deserves some analysis is why Sadat's position changed so much between November 1977 and the Camp David meeting in September 1978. The explanation lies in two factors: Sadat's own personality, and his isolation in the Arab world.

Sadat went to Jerusalem on a 'publicity stunt', out of desire for personal aggrandizement and fame. He was probably surprised and dismayed when he discovered that the Arab countries ignored his initiative; instead of becoming a hero he had become a pariah in the Arab world. But Sadat was not a man who could admit a mistake and go back to the Arab fold humbled and chastised. He had to save face and show that he had been able to make peace with Israel and get back Sinai.

Unfortunately Sadat and Egypt were left alone to deal with Israel and the United States. To be sure, the Americans claimed they were unbiased mediators, but as Carter had admitted to me in the Oval Office meeting back in September 1977 he did not have the political will to stand up to Israel. He would have done better at the Geneva Conference, because the Soviet–American joint agreement had publicly committed the United States to a certain position and because other international pressures would have forced the Americans to be less biased. But when Sadat destroyed the Geneva Conference, he killed any chance that Carter would stand up to Israel.

Left to their own devices, the Americans merely squeezed Sadat to make further concessions. They forgot all their previous statements concerning the Palestinian question and the rights of the Palestinians and expressed no concern about the future of the West Bank and Gaza. In fact the Americans proved more willing to accept the Israeli viewpoint on the West Bank and Gaza than even the Israelis expected. Dayan, for example, confessed in his memoirs that throughout the negotiations the Israelis were fearful that the US delegation might invoke the clause of Resolution 242 which refers to the inadmissibility of acquiring foreign territory by force. Dayan admitted that had the US invoked that clause the Israeli position would have been greatly weakened: 'We were concerned that . . . we would be told that Israel was obliged to evacuate the whole of the West Bank and Gaza, and that the Palestinians had the right to establish their independent State.'[3] But the United States did not exert any pressure on Israel concerning these crucial issues.

Despite his isolation Sadat could not admit to his own people that he was moving toward a separate peace with Israel. He also could not admit that he had abandoned the Arab cause, and so he set in motion the powerful Egyptian propaganda machine to convince his countrymen that he was following the best course and that it was the other Arab countries which were at fault. His propaganda focused on two major points: the advantange of peace and the treachery of the other Arab countries, which talked in very militant anti-Israeli terms but did nothing and let Egypt do all the fighting.

Peace, Sadat constantly proclaimed, was the key to a better future for Egypt. Peace would be more than the end of warfare, of suffering, and of the death of thousands of Egypt's sons still in their prime. It would also be the beginning of a period of economic renaissance for Egypt, because the country would be able to devote all its resources to development. For thirty years, Sadat told his compatriots, Egypt had sacrificed its sons and its economic resources to help the Palestinians and to further the Arab cause, but it had reaped nothing, certainly not the respect and gratitude of the Arabs. The propaganda hit particularly hard at the oil-producing countries of the Gulf. Egypt had fought the October War with enormous losses and sacrifices but the oil producing countries had sat back and got rich from it, and yet they were refusing to help Egypt solve its economic problems.

By harping on these themes Sadat managed to brainwash Egyptians for a few years. This was made easier by the fact that the President was very careful to hide from his people what peace he had in mind.

Sadat's propaganda machine was efficient, and Egyptians tend to be docile and ready to follow their leaders. Nevertheless, little by little the truth started filtering down to the people through foreign broadcasting stations and more and more questions were raised. The sentiment grew that Egypt should mend its fences with the Arab countries and re-evaluate its relationship with Israel. Tension started to grow in Egypt, and found expression in a variety of ways, particularly the growth of the Moslem fundamentalist groups. The two small official opposition parties took a strong stand against Sadat's flirtation with Israel and the major concessions he had made under the guise of 'normalization'. Sadat took repressive measures gainst these dissident voices, but they continued to multiply and to criticise Sadat personally.

The propaganda machine ground on, but people simply stopped listening. It is not surprising that he was eventually liquidated by a sectarian group. The majority of Egyptians shared the assassins' disillusionment with Sadat and this they expressed by the striking indifference with which they greeted his death. It was more than indifference; it was almost a deliberate attempt to forget that Sadat had ever existed, although he had ruled the country for eleven years and undoubtedly accomplished some very positive things.

What did Sadat obtain in the end? What was the peace that he claimed to have brought to his country? In fact both the peace treaty and 'autonomy' for the Palestinians of the West Bank were a sham. Until now the 'autonomy talks' have not achieved anything, which is not surprising because autonomy was a mock concession offered by the Israelis to soften the impact of their outright rejection of a Palestinian state. In fact, the framework for autonomy accepted by Sadat at Camp David was virtually identical to the plan Begin had submitted to Carter in Washington and then to Sadat in Ismailia in December 1977. It was a thin disguise for Israel's ultimate aim of annexing the West Bank and Gaza.

Just as Sadat obtained nothing for the Palestinians he obtained nothing for Egypt. Although he seemed to have recovered all territories lost during the 1967 War, and he lifted the constant threat of renewed warfare, the true position was not what it appeared. Sadat did not recover the Sinai for Egypt, for the clauses of the peace treaty are such as to prevent Egypt from exercising full sovereignty on the peninsula. To be sure, since April 1982 the area lies within Egypt's borders but there remain major limitations on how Egypt may use that territory. Rather than retrieving the Sinai, Sadat signed away sovereignty over it. He also failed to achieve a lasting solution. The treaty gives all the advantages to Israel while Egypt pays the price. As a result, peace cannot last unless the treaty undergoes radical revision. I am not arguing that a new war between Israel and Egypt is inevitable. Rather, I am suggesting that the task of working out a permanent solution which will remove the threat of war in the Middle East is still ahead of us. The agreement Sadat negotiated impairs Egypt's national security, and therefore the peace is extremely fragile.

The treaty itself is a barely revised version of Begin's original draft. Subsequent changes in the text affected the form but not the substance. For although the number of articles of the treaty prop was greatly reduced from forty-two to nine, the basic text was complemented by voluminous annexes, so that all the clauses contained in the original Israeli draft appeared in the final peace treaty in one form or another. In fact, the treaty signed in March 1979 was even more slanted towards the Israelis than their original draft, because at Camp David Sadat had agreed to make further concessions on the normalisation process and later he had accepted without protest important new political and military commitments by the United States to Israel.

The basic defects of the treaty and the major concessions made by Sadat are the following:

(1) The state of belligerency between Israel and Egypt was terminated and peace established immediately upon the exchange of the instruments of ratification of the treaty, although Israel would continue to occupy the greatest part of Sinai for a period of up to three years (Article 1). The normal order of things should have been total withdrawal followed by the end of belligerency, as both the Egyptian and the American draft treaties envisaged.

(2) The process of normalisation of relations between the two countries started six months after the treaty came into force (Article 3). This meant that Sadat conceived that there could be normal relations between Egypt and a country still occupying Egyptian territory.

(3) All provisions concerning the creation of demilitarised zones and the thinning of forces in the area between the two countries were implemented almost exclusively on Egyptian soil. Thus, the Sinai was divided into three zones. Egypt was not allowed to station any military force in the eastern zone, alongside the border. It could have only up to 4,000 men and strictly limited amounts and types of weapons in the middle zone. The deployment of the Egyptian army was even limited in the zone closest to the Suez Canal. Nowhere in Sinai was Egypt free to exercise its full sovereignty. Some token limitations were also imposed on the stationing of Israeli troops on the Israeli side of the border. But only in an area a few kilometres wide, as contrasted to the entire depth of Sinai. In this paltry strip Israel was entitled to station as many troops as Egypt could have in the entire middle zone of Sinai (Article 4 and Annex 1). In effect the treaty surrendered Sinai's vital strategic value to Egypt and our first

e of defence has been transferred from our frontier to the Suez Canal.

(4) The peace treaty also established that multilateral forces will patrol the demilitarised zone between Israel and Egypt. These troops are stationed at Rafah and Sharm El Sheikh, on the Egyptian side of the border and in the zone where Egypt itself can keep no troops. No forces are stationed on Israeli soil. More importantly there is no justification for the presence of these troops. It made sense to have UN forces between Israel and Egypt after 1956 and 1967, when relations between the two countries were only regulated by the 1949 Armistice Agreement. But it is unjustifiable to have UN forces stationed between two countries which are at peace, have diplomatic relations and are in the process of normalising their relations in all other spheres. A final, very serious problem stemmed from the fact that the UN force was, and will be, predominantly American. The United States is not a neutral party in the Middle East, but deeply involved. In fact, there is no way for Egypt to ask the American troops to leave, because Egypt depends on the United States for military and economic aid. Yet the presence of American forces on Egyptian soil does nothing to further Egypt's interests or to provide it with real security.

(5) The peace treaty, and especially Annex 3, also contains numerous provisions for the establishment of close economic, trade and cultural relations, of freedom of movement and of the improvement of communications between Egypt and Israel. These provisions are apparently innocent but they have far-reaching implications. Such close relations between Israel and Egypt will only isolate Egypt even more completely from the Arab world. Nor, it should be added, was Israel satisfied with the ample provisions of the peace treaty. Under the guise of normalisation, between 1979 and the time of writing they have pushed Egypt into signing forty more agreements.

(6) Annex 3, Article 5, specifies that Egypt and Israel should cooperate closely to maintain peace and security in the area. Such cooperation must be directed against the other Arab countries. It is ludicrous that Israel, which occupies much Arab territory and shows no inclination to give it up, could contribute to security in the area. There are other even more disturbing implications of this Annex. Egypt and Israel agreed not only to reopen road and rail links between them, but also to construct a new road through Sinai linking Jordan, Israel and Egypt near Elat. This road is irrelevant to

peace between them, and such a provision is totally out of place the treaty. When I asked a legal advisor in the Egyptian delegation how such a clause came to be included he told me that it was at the request of the United States not the Israelis. In fact the Israelis, when questioned by this legal advisor, had vehemently denied that this was their idea. Once again Sadat had agreed to do his American friends a favour without actually thinking of the implications. The road is intended for future use by the American Rapid Deployment Force.

(7) Another important concession is contained in the various clauses of Article 6, the most important of which reads as follows: 'The Parties undertake to fulfill in good faith their obligations under this Treaty, without regard to action or inaction of any other party and independently of any other instrument external to this Treaty'; 'The Parties undertake not to enter into any obligations in conflict with this Treaty'; and 'Subject to Article 103 of the United Nations Charter, in the event of a conflict . . . the obligations of the Parties under the present Treaty will be binding and implemented'. This gave the Israelis the perfect device to isolate Egypt from the rest of the Arab world. Israel could now claim that all agreements between Egypt and any Arab country were in conflict with the provisions of the peace treaty and thus void. The Arab security pact that Egypt had signed forty years earlier was therefore no longer binding on Egypt. Yet this pact is the cornerstone of Arab defence policy. The geopolitics of the region make it imperative for the Arab countries to coordinate their policies, to defend themselves against incursions into the area. By persuading Sadat to sign clauses amounting to a repudiation of Arab solidarity, the Israelis had obtained more than just Egypt's isolation. Because Egypt is the key country in the Middle East these clauses struck a savage blow at the entire Arab world.

Egypt therefore bore the burden of the peace treaty. This is not surprising, because Sadat was negotiating from a position of weakness, having yielded the crucial concessions in going to Jerusalem: the trip implied the end of belligerency and the recognition of Israel. The Israelis argued that their proposal for Palestinian autonomy was a major concession to demonstrate their good will after Sadat's trip, but by the time of Camp David Sadat had lost interest in the Palestinians. He continued to make militant public statements and at Camp David he insisted on speaking first

.ting the so-called Egyptian position on record. But in
.egotiation he ignored his own loudly proclaimed principles and
.onditions during the actual negotiations.[4]

The Israelis were aware that Sadat's toughness was a cover.
Dayan himself commented:

> Sadat hurriedly published the 'Egyptian proposal' in the
> Egyptian press so that all the Arab countries would know that he
> had made not the slightest concession to Israel. He had adhered
> meticulously to the extremist Arab line. How, then, would he
> face the later charge that he had not stuck to his words? To that
> he would reply: 'I conceded nothing to the Israelis, not even an
> inch; but I responded to the plea of President Carter, our friend
> and ally, an ally whose help we both need and receive.'[5]

The Israelis understood Sadat was not a man of his word, that he
was fickle and undependable, and they had developed an effective
way of dealing with him. During the negotiations for the second
disengagement Rabin had already come to the conclusion that 'the
way to ensure the success of any agreement with him was to
establish facts on the ground and structure the deal so that it would
pay for him to honor it – or at least hurt him if he did not'.[6]

'Establish facts on the ground' is exactly what the Israelis sought
to do at Camp David and during the negotiations for the peace
treaty. They did not give Sadat anything immediately, because they
were afraid that he would abrogate the agreement once Sinai had
been returned. They therefore insisted that they could not possibly
withdraw from Sinai in less than three years, despite the fact that in
1967 they had succeeded in occupying it in five days. The real reason
was that they wanted to use Sinai as a hostage to ensure that Sadat
would not back on the agreement without forsaking a part of Sinai.
After three years of accepting every humiliation from the Israelis
Sadat would be severely discredited in the Arab world and would be
unable to reverse his policy: new facts would be established on the
ground.

It was not enough for the Israelis to have pushed Sadat into a
situation from which he could not back out. They wanted additional
guarantees that Egypt would not renege, probably knowing that the
peace agreement was only between Israel and Sadat, but not
between Israel and Egypt. They thus insisted that the United States
should guarantee to intervene if Egypt violated the treaty. They

also insisted that the United States should renew all its prev
political commitments to Israel, pledging in particular to expc
any United Nations action or resolution Israel deemed contrary t.
its interests and to the peace treaty.

Israel has long tried to make US policy in the Middle East subject
to its own dictates. What is surprising is that the United States once
again agreed to the Israeli demands. In effect the United States has
given Israel power of veto on its Middle East policy which may
account for the palpable confusion of US policy in the region. The
US guarantees to Israel mean that Washington may not remain
neutral in any conflict between Israel and the Arab countries.

The Memorandum of Agreement signed at Camp David by the
United States and Israel stated among other points:

> The United States will provide support it deems appropriate for
> proper actions taken by Israel in response to such demonstrated
> violations of the Treaty of Peace. In particular, if a violation of
> the Treaty of Peace is deemed to threaten the security of Israel,
> including, inter alia, a blockage of Israel's use of international
> waterways, a violation of the provisions of the Treaty of Peace
> concerning limitation of forces or an armed attack against Israel,
> the United States will be prepared to consider, on an urgent
> basis, such measures as the strengthening of the United States'
> presence in the area, the providing of emergency supplies to
> Israel, and the exercise of maritime rights in order to put an end
> to the violation.

In this agreement the United States accepts the view that
violations of the treaty could only originate from Egypt. Until the
last minute Egypt was not informed that the United States and
Israel were preparing this Memorandum of Agreement: while
Washington proclaimed loudly its friendship for Egypt, it
negotiated in secret an agreement with Israel, making it clear that
Israel was the US ally and Egypt the potential enemy.

The Egyptian delegation saw the danger in the Memorandum of
Agreement. Mustapha Khalil, at that time Egypt's Prime Minister
and Foreign Minister, lodged an immediate protest when he
received a copy of the agreement only twenty-four hours before the
signing ceremony of the peace treaty. On 25 March and again on 26
March 1979 he wrote to Secretary Vance, complaining that the

ιorandum of Agreement was directed against Egypt. In the
.er of 26 March he outlined the reasons as follows:

1. It is contrary to the spirit existing between our two countries
and does not contribute to the strengthening of relations
between them. I wish to put on record that Egypt was never
consulted on the substance of the proposed Memorandum.
2. The contents of the proposed Memorandum are based upon
alleged accusations against Egypt and providing for certain
measures to be taken against her in that hypothetical case of
violations, the determination of which is largely left to Israel.
3. We have been engaged in the final process of negotiating the
Treaty for over a month now, however, we have not been
notified of the intention of the United States to agree on such a
memorandum. Moreover, we learned of it by way of information
and not consultation. Ambassador Eilts gave it to me at 2.00
p.m., March 25, only 24 hours before the scheduled ceremonies
for signature of the Treaty.
4. The United States is supposed to be a partner in a tri-partite
effort to achieve peace and not to support the allegations of one
side against the other.
5. The proposed Memorandum assumes that Egypt is the side
liable to violate its obligations.
6. The proposed Memorandum could be construed as an
eventual alliance between the United States and Israel against
Egypt.
7. It gives the United States certain rights that were never
mentioned or negotiated with us.
8. It gives the United States the power to impose measures, or to
put it bluntly, punitive measures, a matter which raises doubts
about the future relations and could affect the situation in the
whole region.
9. The proposed Memorandum even uses dangerously vague
terms as 'threats of violations' against which certain measures
would be taken. We consider this to be a matter of grave
consequences.
10. It implies that the economic and arms supply are subject to
the sole judgment of the United States Government in
connection with the alleged threats of violations being attributed
to one side.
11. It makes certain aspects of Egyptian–American relations

subject to elements extraneous to those relations and its commitments made to a third party.

12. It implies the United States acquiescence to Israel's embarking on measures, including military measures, against Egypt on the assumption that there are violations or threats of violation of the Treaty.

13. It gives the United States the right to impose a military presence in the region for reasons agreed between Israel and the United States. A matter which we cannot accept.

14. The proposed Memorandum will cast grave doubts about the real intention of the United States, especially in connection with the peace process. It could be accused of collaboration with Israel to create such circumstances that would lead to American military presence in the area, a matter which would certainly have serious implication especially on the stability in the whole region.

15. It will have adverse effects in Egypt towards the United States and would certainly drive other Arab countries to take a harder position against the peace process, and would give added reasons for them not to participate in that process.

16. It would also pave the way for other alliances to be formed in the area to counter the one whose seeds could be found in the proposed Memorandum.

For all these reasons, I hereby inform you that the Government of Egypt will not recognize the legality of the Memorandum and considers it null and void and as having no effect whatsoever as far as Egypt is concerned.

Khalil was so upset about the Memorandum that he wrote the two letters to Vance without even consulting Sadat, as he later told me. Sadat must have been informed about the letters by Vance, but apparently he dismissed them as unimportant, reflecting Khalil's personal views rather than the stand of the Egyptian leadership. The two letters were never answered by Vance and the American delegation made no attempt to refute Khalil's allegations. The peace treaty was signed on 26 March 1979, and so was the Memorandum of Agreement.

This incident is typical of what happened during the negotiations. The rest of the Egyptian delegation were extremely unhappy about Sadat's attitude and his willingness to make conessions to the Israelis as was clear both to the Israeli and the

.nerican delegations. But Sadat simply ignored the opinions of his
olleagues and took decisions single-handedly.

Some readers may object that I have deliberately overlooked
Israel's major concessions to Egypt. After all, Israel gave up the
entire Sinai, and even agreed to dismantle the numerous Jewish
settlements which it had created at great effort and expense. With
regard to Sinai, as I have explained earlier throughout the
negotiations for comprehensive peace, the return of Sinai was never
considered by any of the parties as a problem. It was regarded as a
foregone conclusion, and the efforts of all the parties focused
primarily on methods of dealing with the Palestinian issue and other
elements. As for the settlements, they, like the occupation of Sinai,
were illegal in the first place. There was also no way the Israelis
could have kept them. If the settlements had been maintained
within Egypt's borders, the settlers would have insisted on Israeli
troops to defend them, but there could have been no peace if the
Israeli army remained on Egyptian territory. If the settlements had
been left in Egyptian territory without military protection, the
Egyptians would sooner or later have eliminated them. They
therefore had to go.

In return for this magnanimity, so-called, Israel received much
booty: and from the most important Middle East country.
Specifically, the recognition that Israel is a country with special
characteristics and privileges, to which the normal rules of
international relations do not apply.

It is this special status imparted by the peace treaty and its
attendant American guarantees which are so offensive to the Arab
world. The Arabs would not object to the recognition of Israel as
part of a comprehensive peace settlement. But they do object to the
recognition of Israel as a supercountry different from all others in
the Middle East.

The peace treaty has done much harm to Egypt and the Arab
world. Egypt's national security has been severely impaired
because she cannot defend herself against any Israeli encroachment
without the Israelis screaming that Egypt has violated the peace
treaty, and thus finding an excuse for occupying parts of Sinai again.
The security of the entire Arab world has also been greatly
weakened. Instead of progressing toward a stronger security
system, the Arab countries are more divided than ever. At the same
time the United States is trying to impose its own security system on
the area, on the basis of a strategic agreement with Israel and the

creation of the Rapid Deployment Force. This American–Isr
concept of security is of no help to the Arab world. It prevents t
formation of an Arab security system and makes Egypt and the
Arab countries all the more impotent.

Notes

1. Ezer Weirman, *The Battle for Peace* (New York, Bantam Books, 1981), p.
296.
2. Ibid., p. 299.
3. Moshe Dayan, *Breakthrough* (New York: Alfred Knopf, 1981), p. 166.
4. Dayan, *Breakthrough*, p. 101.
5. Ibid., p. 163.
6. Yitzak Rabin, *The Rabin Memoirs* (London: Weidenfeld and Nicolson,
1979), p. 260.

The Palestinian question is the key to permanent peace in the Middle East. This is not a slogan, but an historical fact. The Middle East problem started when the Zionist movement began sending large numbers of Jews to Palestine, displacing the inhabitants and leading to confrontation between the new Jewish settlers, the Palestinians, and the British Mandate forces. After the British departed, the confrontation between Jew and Palestinian led to the intervention of the Arab countries, and there have been four major wars since the formal establishment of the Jewish state. As I write Israel is trying to scorch the final Palestinian presence from Beirut.

The Arab countries became involved in these wars because they were committed to helping the Palestinian people. Israel has pursued a policy of continuous aggression against the Palestinians forcing the Arab countries to continue their confrontation. This is why the Palestinian problem is the core of the Middle East conflict. It is also why a series of separate peace agreements between Israel and each Arab country cannot bring about a permanent solution in the area.

The Palestinian problem is easily defined: as a result of Israeli action, over a million and a half Palestinians are living as refugees in foreign countries. Those who remained in their former land are now living under the conditions imposed by Israel, conditions which are contrary to justice, equality and decency.

Begin and Sadat knew that the Palestinian problem was so central to the Middle East issue that they could not ignore it. This is why the Camp David accords included a 'Framework for Peace in the Middle East' which paid lip service to the principle of self-government and 'full autonomy' for the Palestinians of the West Bank and Gaza. However, since Camp David conditions for the Palestinians have got worse. The Israelis clearly intend to annex the West Bank and Gaza as they have annexed the Golan Heights and are only waiting for the right moment. In so doing, they hope to eliminate the Palestinian problem, particularly if they succeed in forcing the majority of the West Bank Palestinians to leave their land and go to Jordan or other Arab countries. Despite their obvious intentions the Israelis still claim that they are adhering the letter and the spirit of the agreement on autonomy reached at Camp David. If anybody disagrees with their interpretation of autonomy, the Israelis argue that they know best, because Begin was the original architect of autonomy and thus his interpretation is correct.

The 'Framework for Peace in the Middle East' is a flawed document. It contains contradictions, major omissions, and brief phrases which lend themselves to interpretation with far-reaching consequences. Within a year of signing the framework, Sadat and Begin had completely different interpretations of crucial points in the document. By then Begin had advanced his unique argument that the West Bank was Israeli territory ever since biblical times.

The Preamble of the 'Framework for Peace in the Middle East' and the first paragraph of the Framework proper are sound. Taken by themselves, they set forth the principles which must be the basis for a solution to the Middle East problem. The preamble declares that the agreed basis for peaceful settlement is Resolution 242. It is worth recalling here that this resolution affirms the inadmissibiility of the acquisition of territory by force and calls on Israel to withdraw from all territories occupied during the 1967 War. The preamble also states clearly that the pursuit of peace in the Middle East will be based on the legal norms contained in the UN Charter. The section of the framework dealing with the West Bank and Gaza further reiterates that Resolutions 242 and 338 must be implemented in their entirety. Thus on three counts the Framework requires Israel to withdraw from all the territories occupied during the 1967 War and thus from the West Bank and Gaza.

The Framework also recognises that 'for peace to endure, it must involve all those who have been most deeply affected by the conflict'. This means that the Palestinians must be involved in the peace process, but this principle is not being applied. The Israelis are no more willing to recognise the rights of the Palestinians to choose their own representatives than they are to withdraw from the West Bank and Gaza.

Despite the promising preamble, the rest of the Framework is flawed both by crucial omissions and by the insertion of clauses which contradict the principles set forth at the beginning. I will focus here on the major difference and disagreements between Egypt and Israel.

The Framework does not contain any explicit reference to the

...t of the Palestinians to self-determination, and thus to the ...eation of a Palestinian state. The Israelis have been taking ...dvantage of this omission in that they complain that every mention of the right of the Palestinians to self-determination by Egyptian officials constitutes a breach of the Camp David accords. For example, Begin complained bitterly on this point in a letter he addressed to Sadat on 4 August 1980:

> However, not one word about self-determination (which of course means a state), or about an independent (Palestinian) state appears in any one of the pages, paragraphs, sections or subsections, etc. of the Camp David agreement. Dr Ghali, speaking on behalf of Egypt, committed almost incomprehensible deviations from, and total contradictions to, the Camp David accord [when he talked of the Palestinian right to self-determination] . . .

Another major omission concerns East Jerusalem, which is never mentioned in the Framework. This was apparently the result of a compromise reached at Camp David. Carter had proposed four formulae about Jerusalem; one of them was unacceptable to Sadat, the other three to Begin. The parties thus agreed not to mention Jerusalem in the Framework, with the understanding that the problem would be taken up and solved in the course of the autonomy talks. In a letter dated 2 August 1980, Sadat reminded Begin of the importance of reaching a solution concerning Jerusalem acceptable not only to the 18 million Jews but also the 800 million Moslems around the world. Begin's answer, in his letter of 4 August, was to state that he was aware of the position Sadat and Carter had taken on the issue, but that he could only stand by his own statements and by the decisions of the Israeli Knesset, which had just voted on 30 July that Jerusalem, 'united in its entirety', was the capital of Israel. Since Jersualem was not explicitly mentioned in the Camp David accords, Begin felt free to argue that it was not part of the West Bank and thus not subject to the limitations which applied to that area and to Gaza.

The Framework, moreover, includes a statement that 'all necessary measures will be taken and provisions made to assure the security of Israel and its neighbors during the transitional period and beyond'. The phrase 'and beyond' has given rise to very serious problems. The Israelis insist it means that Israeli troops can remain in the West Bank and Gaza even after the end of the transition period. The Egyptians disagree: 'It is incorrect to claim,' Sadat wrote to Begin on 14 August 1980, 'that the insertion of the phrase "and beyond" in the section related to security measures in the "Framework" meant that any security arrangements which are agreed upon for the transitional period are extended – ipso facto – beyond the transitional period.' The Israelis insist otherwise. The permament stationing of Israeli troops on the West Bank and Gaza effectively precludes the creation of an independent Palestinian state.

Another problem with the Framework is that it allows the continued Israeli occupation of the West Bank and Gaza by Israel during the transitional period. While the idea that the final fate of these areas will be decided only at the end of a transitional period is quite acceptable, the territories should have immediately been removed from Israeli administration and put under the control of an international body, which would prepare the transition to the final status. Instead Israeli settlements have been expanded and multiplied despite Egyptian complaints. In his letter of 18 August 1980 to Sadat, Begin argued that the Camp David accords did not limit Israel's right to create settlements, and that he had never agreed to a moratorium on new settlements except for the few months between the Camp David negotiations and the signing of the peace treaty between Egypt and Israel. Sadat, on the other hand, claimed that Begin had agreed to a moratorium for the entire duration of the autonomy talks.

The Framework for Autonomy is also defective because it deals with the West Bank and Gaza as separate issues, rather than as part of the overall Palestinian problem. Thus, it refers to the 'representatives of the inhabitants of the West Bank and Gaza', rather than to the representatives of the Palestinians. This of course suits the Israelis, who want to exclude the PLO from negotiations. However, the problem of the West Bank and Gaza can only be solved as part of the entire Palestinian issue. In similar vein, the Israelis have insisted that the self-elected council on the West Bank will only have administrative functions which derides the political nature of the problem.

One of the most serious flaws of the Framework is that it does not establish a deadline for opening negotiations on the final status of the West Bank and Gaza. Paragraph A (c) of the Framework simply states that negotiations will start within three years of the beginning

..he transitional period. This transitional period, in turn, will only
.art with the setting up of the self-governing council. Since there is
no deadline for the setting up of this council, and the Israelis are
doing their best to prevent it from ever coming into existence, the
occupation can go on indefinitely, or at least long enough to give the
Israelis time to change the very character of the West Bank. They
apparently hope to delay a decision long enough to be able to
transform the West Bank into a Jewish territory by settlement.

The Framework adopted at Camp David is not sufficient to
protect the rights of the Palestinians and to ensure a just solution.
Yet, the Israelis apparently think that even this vague and
contradictory document is too favourable to the Palestinians. While
continuing to argue that the Camp David accords must be applied to
the West Bank, they are actively seeking to prevent this from
happening by obstructing the Palestinians from choosing their own
representatives. The measures taken against the mayors and other
representatives on the West Bank and Gaza are part of this scheme.

The Israelis have also started arguing that many of the principles
referred to in the Framework, and above all that of withdrawal from
the occupied territories, are not applicable to the West Bank,
because it is not an occcupied territory. The claim is not based on
international law or United Nations resolutions. Begin argues that
'Judea and Samaria' (the West Bank) are part and parcel of the
'land of Israel' since biblical times.

> Our nation was born in Judea and Samaria, not in Jaffa and
> certainly not in Tel Aviv. In Judea and Samaria our prophets
> prophesied, in Judea and Samaria the ancient Jewish culture,
> from which we are nurtured to this very day, was created. Judea
> and Samaria are occupied territory? Judea and Samaria were
> occupied territory by the Jordanians, who conquered the
> Western part of the land of Israel.[1]

Whatever the Bible may say, the West Bank is undoubtedly part of
the territory occupied by Israel during the 1967 War. By signing the
Camp David accords Begin pledged to respect Resolution 242 and
338 as well as the United Nations Charter and thus to withdraw
from those territories. In fact, one wonders why Begin should have
signed any agreement concerning the West Bank if it were already
Israeli territory, as he now claims.

Begin has no intention of respecting the Camp David accords

concerning full autonomy. Not only did he manage to introduce clauses contradicting the basic principles at the time of the signing, but he is now making it clear that from the Israeli point of view the future of the West Bank and Gaza had already been decided. The 'autonomy talks' between Israel and Egypt have achieved nothing, because they were stalemated from the very beginning on the issue of sovereignty over those areas. Negotiations over the future, final status of the territories have thus not even begun. Yet, Israel has already decided that East Jerusalem is forever part of its territory, that the settlements on the West Bank and Gaza cannot be removed, and that self-determination for the Palestinians, leading to the creation of a Palestinian state, is inconceivable.

Since the return of the Sinai to Egypt, Begin has become more and more explicit about Israel's true intentions. He has stated that Israel will never allow the creation of a Palestinian state on the West Bank nor recognise the Palestinians' right to self-determination, because it would amount to the same thing. According to him, it was also 'self-understood that in any future negotiation for the signing of peace treaties between Israel and its neighbors, any suggestion for the dismantlement or removal of any settlement in which Israeli citizens and Jewish people are settled and reside will be rejected'.[2] On 4 May 1982 the Knesset voted a motion of support for his statement ruling out the uprooting of Jewish settlements on the West Bank.

It is paradoxical that the Israelis constantly proclaim that they are ready to negotiate with the Arab countries without preconditions and accuse the Arabs of trying to impose too many preconditions. In reality, Israeli preconditions are the obstacle, in particular the continued Israeli occupation of Arab territory, and the Knesset constitutional amendments imposing legal restrictions on the Israeli side in future negotiations. The decision that Jerusalem must remain united as the eternal capital of Israel is the best example of these amendments. But the annexation of the Golan Heights imposes similar preconditions as it informs the Syrians that the issue is non-negotiable.

The Israeli settlements on the West Bank may very well finish off the Camp David accords on autonomy, particularly if Begin manages to get the Knesset to vote a law forbidding the removal of the Israeli settlements on the West Bank and Gaza. The collapse of the Camp David Framework is not a problem in itself because the Framework cannot provide a just solution for the Palestinian roblem. However, it would be catastrophic if no new alternative solutions were found. Further massive bloodshed would be inevitable and Egypt would have no choice but to join the Arab world in a new confrontation with Israel.

The United States bears major responsibility for putting pressure on Israel to stop following a policy which will lead to confrontation in the Middle East. The solution cannot come from the Camp David accords. It is therefore imperative to convene an international conference to deal exclusively with the Palestinian problem. Israel and the PLO should be invited to attend, together with the five permanent members of the United Nations Security Council, and Lebanon, Syria, Jordan, Saudi Arabia and Egypt. The conference must create an independent Palestinian state with secure boundaries and provide guarantees for both Israel and the new state.

Notes

1. Quoted in *International Herald Tribune*, 29 April 1982.
2. Quoted in *International Herald Tribune*, 4 May 1982.

The political landscape of the Middle East is still undergoing continuous change. The October War, the Camp David accords, the Israeli invasion of Lebanon, have all had far reaching repercussions. The role of the United States and the Soviet Union in this strategic area has been drastically modified, and both powers are presently setting forth new theories about their so-called vital interests and spheres of influence. The map of the Middle East has been changed and will undergo further change. New factors have emerged, new friendships and alliances have been established. The geopolitical situation has shifted greatly. New peace proposals exist – President Reagan's initiative of 1 September 1982, the Arab Summit Conference in Fez, the Brezhnev initiative, and others. It remains to be seen whether further developments will be purely political or also encompass military confrontations between the parties to this chronic crisis.

At the present stage it is still very difficult to predict what will be the future panorama of the Middle East. Sadat's visit to Jerusalem undoubtedly changed the situation in the Middle East, ironically raising high hopes in the Western world for peace in the area while at the same time severely shattering Arab aspirations for a comprehensive peace. The visit changed the norms governing the region from within, as well as in terms of geopolitics. New norms have to be set, new interests and relationships defined, for a solution satisfying all claims to be found. This unfinished process may even lead to a new war, or to the reemergence and entrenchment of the precarious situation of 'no peace, no war' which existed before October 1973.

Clearly no one wants the prolongation of the Middle East crisis. My refusal to support Sadat's Jerusalem initiative was certainly not because I wanted to perpetuate the Middle East conflict. Our endless efforts prior to Sadat's visit to Jerusalem were all directed at achieving peace. I remain fully committed to this goal, but I am convinced that such peace cannot emerge from a settlement which is neither just nor in keeping with the norms of international law. Nor can peace last if it is accepted only by the leader of a country, but not by its people, because they are the ones who will ultimately

`iit or suffer from the nature of the peace agreement. What I
e opposed is 'peace at any price', and above all a peace which
lows the aggressor to continue acquiring land at the expense of the
other party. In my opinion this would be an 'expansionist peace'.

Foremost among the repercussions of these major events that
the Middle East has witnessed is their impact on the states, and
people of the region and the parties directly concerned. In as much
as the October War unified and consolidated the Arab system, the
Camp David accords dealt it a staggering blow particularly by
neutralising Egypt's predominant role and capacity to function
within that system. The Arab system lost its centre of gravity and its
source of guidance. Conversely, whereas the October War shocked
Israelis into the realisation that security cannot be guaranteed by
the force of arms, the Camp David accords and the neutralisation of
the Egyptian military factor seem to have restored the Israeli
illusion that an overemphasis on arms and military action can serve
as the sole basis of security. Both of these results are dangerous and
destabilising.

The Egyptian–Israeli peace does not lay the solid foundation for
a just and durable peace. On the contrary, it was born and remains
a precarious peace which must undergo serious modification if it is
to constitute more than a mere transitional state of affairs between
wars. The best proof of this is the Israeli behaviour and the major
decisions which Begin has taken since his government signed the
Camp David agreement. It should by now be increasingly obvious
that Israel, since it signed the peace treaty with Egypt, is
determined more than ever to make Jerusalem, the West Bank,
Gaza, the Golan Heights, and South Lebanon either de jure or de
facto Israeli territory. This will take place unless Israel is stopped.

Israel obviously planned to profit from the so-called peace
between it and Egypt, and decided to benefit from the new situation
by pursuing an expansionist policy. Israel's policies and practices
after the peace agreement with Egypt lead one to believe that it
perceives the Egyptian–Israeli peace as creating the proper
circumstances for it to continue acquiring more land at the expense
of the Arab side. It was after that peace was concluded that the
Knesset proclaimed Jerusalem as the eternal and indivisible capital
of Israel. It was after that peace that Israel annexed the Golan
Heights and the Knesset voted to support Begin's statement that
the Jewish settlements on the West Bank and Gaza would never be
dismantled. Israel is even setting forth claims to Southern Lebanon

and all Lebanese airspace, on the grounds that both are vital Israeli security. Under the guise of protecting its own security Israel no longer respects the borders of any Arab country as witnessed by the Israeli raid on the Iraqi nuclear reactor in Tamuz in mid-1981. President Hosni Mubarak of Egypt declared on 3 October 1982 that Israel was 'once again beating the drums of war' in the Middle East, a policy which 'will lead to grave consequences from which Israel will not be spared'.[1] All this happened after Sadat made peace with Israel.

Israel's concept of peace in the Middle East is extraordinary. Apparently, it sanctions Israel doing anything it considers necessary to implement its grand schemes, but gives no rights to the Arab countries, not even the right to develop their own resources and satisfy their own energy needs. Security is undoubtedly an important condition for peace, but the concept of security embraced by Israel is unique. The Israeli invasion of Lebanon, including its capital Beirut, and the horrors committed against the Lebanese, Palestinians, and Syrians were atrocious. For the first time, a great part of the world witnessed on the television screen the destruction of a major capital and its civilian population – all in the name of Israeli peace, peace in the Galilee. Perhaps now the Israeli concept of peace with which the Arabs are confronted, is clear for the rest of the world.

Through this so-called peace Israel is seeking a dominant position in the Middle East, similar to that of the former colonial powers and based solely on military superiority. It is only this military superiority which allows the Israelis to carry out their acts of aggression in the name of security, feeling relatively sure that the Arab countries will not follow suit. Israel finally realized the Zionist dream in March 1979. The Balfour Declaration in 1917 was a statement made by a foreigner. By signing a peace treaty with Israel, Sadat turned the Zionist dream and the Balfour Declaration into reality.

Israel succeeded in freezing its southern front, where it faced the biggest and strongest Arab country and demilitarising Sinai. But most importantly of all, Begin achieved the dismantling of the Arab security system, because Egypt was the lynchpin of that system. The only beneficiary of the Camp David agreement has been Israel. The consequences for all other parties to the Middle East conflict have been disastrous, even for Egypt. Although it got back Sinai, its sovereignty over it is limited and Egypt is now isolated in the Arab

rld, which is in itself a threat to its security. The collective
amage done to the Arab world, and the interests of world peace,
comprise a doleful inventory:

1) The Arab collective self-defence system has collapsed. Even
if Egypt rethinks its position and rejoins it, it will require
restoration and replanning.

2) The guarantees the United States has given and continues to
give to Israel offer the Soviet Union the perfect excuse to
respond favourably to any Arab demand for assistance; the level
of polarisation in the Middle East may in the near future reach
unprecedented levels.

3) The presence of units of the American Rapid Deployment
Force in Sinai will encourage the Soviet Union to station troops
in one or more Arab countries.

4) Sadat's decision to go it alone has had and will continue to
have serious repercussions on Egypt's credibility not only in the
Arab–Israeli conflict but also in other political questions
affecting the Arab system.

5) Egypt's various commitments resulting from the peace treaty
challenge its status as a full partner in the Arab system.

6) The Israelis are now more determined than ever to prevent
the creation of a Palestinian state and to annex the West Bank
and Gaza.

The Arabs have only three options: war, an arms race, or
encouraging international pressure on Israel. Two of those options
entail war, either immediately or in the long run. The only peaceful
way out of the present predicament is an international effort to
bring pressure to bear on Israel.

The issues relating to territorial claims or security measures are
and should be governed by international law and reciprocity. They
should therefore not constitute an obstacle to concluding
agreement once the more fundamental problems are dealt with.
The crux of the problem has always been and remains the issue of
Palestine. The Camp David accords were still–born in this regard.
The Arabs' international effort should aim at devising a genuine
and workable substitute for the Camp David accords on full
autonomy for the Palestinians. My suggestion is that they call for a
limited summit conference to discuss and solve the Palestinian
problem. It should not deal with any other problem. It must be

attended by the five permanent members of the United Natio~
Security Council, Israel, the PLO, the Arab confrontation states
and Saudi Arabia as representative of the remaining Arab states. Its
terms of reference would be to agree on a new framework for
solving the Palestinian question based on:

1) A transitional period during which the West Bank, Gaza and
even East Jerusalem would be put under United Nations
administration.
2) The stationing of a UN force to safeguard internal security in
the West Bank and Gaza and on the borders of Israel during this
transitional period.
3) The holding of a referendum after a year of UN
administration to allow all Palestinians, whether they live in the
West Bank, Gaza or abroad as refugees, to exercise their right to
self-determination.
4) The establishment of an independent Palestinian state if the
referendum indicates this is what the Palestinians want. This new
state should be neutral, and it would have limited security forces,
sufficient only for defence purposes.
5) The signing of a peace treaty between Israel and the
Palestinian state on the very same day of the creation of the
latter.

My proposal is very simple and feasible provided Israel acts in
good faith to solve the Palestinian problem in a just way. These
suggestions would ultimately lead to the mutual recognition of
Israel and the Palestinian state and it would provide international
guarantees making the boundaries of both countries secure. If
Israel wants to be accepted by its Arab neighbours as a fully-fledged
state, it must accept a Palestinian state. It cannot continue to apply
a double standard, one for Israel and one for the Arabs. Putting the
West Bank and Gaza under United Nations supervision, pending a
decision on their final status, would guarantee that the Palestinian
issue is solved by peaceful means. It would only require Israel to
withdraw completely from the occupied Arab territories, but it
would also create the proper mechanism leading to the mutual
recognition of Israel and the Palestinian state.

If the above plan is accepted and implemented by Israel and the
Palestinians, Israeli withdrawal from the remaining occupied
territory would not constitute a serious problem, because the

rce of the Middle East conflict would have been removed. Peace
eaties between Israel and Syria, Lebanon and Jordan could follow
smoothly.

The New Peace Plans

Other peace proposals exist and deserve comment. In all candour,
I am amazed by the philosophy behind the Reagan initiative, which
I assume was proposed to solve the Middle East dispute
peacefully. On the one hand it is encouraging that an American
President admits publicly for the first time that the core of the
Middle East crisis is the Palestinian problem, a position the Arabs
have reiterated repeatedly during the last 30 years or more.
However, like many others, I am dismayed that President Reagan
officially and publicly stated that the United States does not support
the establishment of an independent Palestinian state and added
that Washington was not in favour of self-determination for the
Palestinians. Reagan's proposals thus acknowledge the problem
but do not reflect a clear understanding of the reasons for its
existence. They thus become a non-starter. Given the major
deficiency in the American initiative, it will only encourage the
Israelis to be more intransigant in their continuous rejection of self-
determination for the Palestinians and the Palestinian state.

The fact that the Begin government publicly rejected the Reagan
initiative does not in anyway detract from the real purpose of
Reagan's proposal. The Americans and the Israelis knew for sure
that had Begin welcomed Reagan's initiative it would automatically
have led to outright Arab opposition. Begin's outright rejection was
only a tactical move. It was a theatrical gesture meant to give the
false impression to the Arabs that the American initiative was
bearing heavily on the Israeli government. Ultimately, no Israeli
government could seriously reject totally an American initiative.
This is further borne out by the position taken by the Labor Party
(not in power), which wholeheartedly welcomed the proposal and
wasted no opportunity to publicise its support for the new
American proposals. Furthermore, given the American–Israeli
system and their intricate relations, it is unlikely that the Israeli side
was unaware of the philosophy and the details of the Reagan
initiative. If the American side had not consulted with the Israelis
prior to the announcement, it would be violating a firm American

commitment not to propose or support a solution for the Middle East without prior consultation with and approval of the Israeli side.

The Reagan proposals were intentionally timed to divide the Arabs when they met at the summit meeting in Fez. Fortunately, the Arab Heads of State were candid in their reply when they unanimously reiterated the Arab position that the Palestinians should exercise their right to self-determination, that they are entitled to an independent Palestinian state, and that the PLO is the sole legitimate representative of the Palestinians. Moreover, at Fez the Arab Heads of State went further and accepted that all states in the area are entitled to live in peace within international boundaries guaranteed by the UN Security Council.

After Fez, Brezhnev came out with his own initiative. The Soviet leader while emphasising the issue of security for both the Israelis and the Arabs, went further and said in unambiguous terms that no one has the right to negate the legal basis on which Israel itself was recognised as an independent state in 1947. Brezhnev referred to the UN resolution adopted by the UN General Assembly in 1947 which approved the creation of two sovereign states on the former mandated territory of Palestine: an Arab State and a Jewish one. It is also to be noted that Brezhnev's proposal, like any Arab proposal, was based on the basic philosophy behind the Security Council Resolution 242, namely that peace in the Middle East must be based on the very clear principle of the inadmissability of acquiring foreign territory by force. This is why the Brezhnev proposal, while recognising the Israeli right to exist peacefully within international boundaries, applies the same criteria equally to the Palestinian side.

The Threat of Superpower Confrontation

For my own part I remain convinced that in order to cope with the interests of all the parties concerned, there is no other way but to convene an international conference dealing with the core problem – the Palestinian problem. In the meantime, pending the solution of the Palestinian problem, the Middle East will become increasingly polarised and the threat of a new war all the more pressing.

I sincerely hope that this will not come to pass, that the situation will not be allowed to deteriorate to the point of no return, to the int of despair, where the Arabs feel that the only way out is nother bloody confrontation, or Israeli overconfidence leads them to rash acts. If both sides are convinced that a new war is inevitable, they will continue arming themselves, acquiring offensive weapons such as have never been used in the Middle East before. As a result, the fifth Arab-Israeli war will bear no resemblance to the previous ones, but lead to much greater loss of life and to enormous physical destruction.

True, it will take time to reach that point, but it is abundantly clear that the direct result of continued tension will be an arms race. The Arabs and the Israelis will turn to the United States and the Soviet Union for aid. Both Washington and Moscow will have to respond to the demands of their clients – either their present clients or their future ones. Both superpowers will try to take advantage of the continued tension to pursue their strategic interests in the area. As a result of superpower intervention the conflict might well eventually engulf some parts of Asia and Africa.

This dangerous phenomenon started manifesting itself as soon as a separate peace was concluded between Israel and Egypt. This peace has strengthened the long-standing military and traditional relationship between the United States and Israel, which among other things defines almost exactly the division of roles of both countries with regard to Middle East strategy. To camouflage the real purpose of this strategic agreement between Washington and Tel Aviv, the parties declared that the main concern of this unusual and sensitive cooperation was to combat the spread of Soviet influence in the area. This certainly cannot be taken seriously because one can scarcely believe that the small state of Israel would have the resources and capabilities to compete with the Soviet Union in any major confrontation in the Middle East. It was very clear from the outset that with this arrangement the US agreed to grant Israel the function of policeman of the Arab world, pledging full American support to Israeli actions in the area. The invasion of Lebanon was indeed the first operation in implementing this stategic American–Israeli agreement.

Parallel to this we see the United States trying to build a special relationship with Egypt. No one in Washington and certainly no one in Israel imagines that the US–Egyptian relationship will be on a par with the Israeli connection. However, it is true that Egypt has already become heavily dependent on American military and economic aid; such dependence is expected to grow, and unless

unusual events take place this relationship might re.
unprecedented dimensions. The US already has bases or 'facilitie
in Egypt, and units of the American Rapid Deployment Force are
positioned in stategic points on Egyptian soil. It is thus futile to deny
that the US has already succeeded in transforming its relationship
with Egypt into a strategic one.

Consequently, in order to harmonize its policies in the region,
the United States will be forced to develop its strategic plans in the
Middle East to be dependent on both Israel and Egypt.
Consequently, it can be expected that the US strategists will try to
create a strategic triangle, with its apex Israel, and its two sides
Egypt and Lebanon. Through this new mechanism the USA will try
to manipulate events in the Middle East, including the Gulf. The
creation of this new geopolitical, and military triangle will certainly
have serious repercussions on the geopolitics of the entire Middle
East. Furthermore, this triangular relationship will form the basis
for the use of the American Rapid Deployment Force in an
emergency.

America's dependence on the triangular relationship will not
prevent it from working to establish other strategic positions in the
area, particularly in the Gulf states. Such moves by the US are
bound to encourage the Soviet Union to widen its own spheres of
influence in the region. This is already happening to a certain
extent, although the development has not been given enough
attention. Suddenly, for example, Soviet military assistance to
North Yemen is double the level of US assistance. North Yemen
used to be completely out of bounds to the Soviet Union, but now
the Soviet presence is no longer limited to South Yemen but has
extended to the North as well.

This is not an isolated development. The Soviets are also
becoming more involved in Syria. Moreover, it would not be
surprising if Iraq were forced to rely even more on the Soviet
Union, as a result of the war with Iran. If this happens, the Soviet
Union will be able to build a formidable strategic bridge on the basis
of its relationship with Syria and Iraq. Given Iraq's geographical
position on the Gulf, it would not be difficult for the Soviet Union to
close the net around the Gulf states gradually. The potential for
superpower confrontation entailed by such a move becomes clearer
when one remembers that the United States has already claimed the
Gulf as a zone of vital American interest.

There are other points of conflict and tension in the Arab world

The situation in Lebanon remains very bad. The Israelis have pointed themselves custodians of Christians' interests in Lebanon and will continue to seize every excuse for intervening in that country. Begin himself publicly admitted Israel's intentions in Lebanon when he revealed that in the last five years Israel has extended to some Christian factions aid amounting to US$55 million. This alliance between the Israelis and the Christian Lebanese is going to have a far-reaching impact on the future of that country. If there is no concerted Arab action to stop this development, Lebanon will lose its identity even if a final peace is reached in the area. It will fall within the Israeli sphere of influence and will become a springboard from which the Israelis will penetrate the Arab economic system and various other systems.

To be sure, not all these problems are the direct consequence of the Arab–Israeli conflict. They do thrive, however, in the atmosphere of constant crisis prevailing in the Middle East and have been exacerbated by policies pursued by Israel ever since the treaty with Egypt. The outlook for the Middle East would immediately become much less discouraging if that source of tension were removed. The linkage is clearly there. The key is a just and peaceful solution of the Middle East conflict. If this were accomplished, the attempts of the great powers to shape and reshape their spheres of influence in the area could be contained.

Polarisation threatens political stability especially when it involves competition between two superpowers in a particular area. In a strategic region like the Middle East this is particularly true. Throughout the history of the Middle East superpowers have come and gone. I am afraid they will continue to do so unless the governments and people of the Middle East, who are mainly Arabs, act in such a way as to limit the competition between the USA and the Soviet Union.

Polarisation damages the welfare of the Arab people by restricting their freedom to take political decisions and constitutes a serious threat to the Arab system and its security. In recent times polarisation has been synonymous with neo-colonialism. The two superpowers have attempted to divide the sensitive and strategic areas of the world into their own spheres through invasion or by establishing permanent bases or creating new strategies supported by rapid deployment forces. All these policies are directed at the physical control of certain parts of the world by foreign military powers; exactly the same as classical colonialisation in the past. The only difference is the use of new terminologies and theories to conceal the real objective.

My fervent hope is that Arab leaders will give the problem top priority and lessen their dependance on the superpowers. The Arabs must diversify their spheres of cooperation in every possible way. The only guarantee against excessive polarisation in the Arab world lies in the rebuilding of a cohesive Arab system serving Arab aims and safeguarding Arab interests with the Arab people resisting foreign schemes alien to their own philosophy. This is why I fervently hope that the Iran–Iraq war will be handled from within the Arab system. In the Arab world we have a tremendous responsibility with regard to this prolonged dispute, which could threaten the whole Arab peninsula, as well as the Islamic system, if it is not brought to a rapid conclusion.

Egypt has an obligation to play a leading role. The major task facing President Mubarak at the present time is liberating Egypt's freedom of action from the shackles imposed on it, directly or indirectly, by the Egyptian–Israeli peace treaty. The top priority for the new President should be the restoration of whatever is left of the Arab system and of the regional strategy. I hasten to admit that this is not an easy task, and that unless the right steps are taken under the most auspicious circumstances there is a danger that US economic and military aid to Egypt will be curtailed in retaliation. Even if the US government did not believe that Egypt's new policy went against American interests, Israel would certainly object to a rapprochement between Egypt and the other Arab countries and would seek to force US assistance to Egypt to be reduced through the influence of the Jewish lobby on Congress.

Difficult as the task might be, it has to be accomplished, because unless there is a change in Egyptian policy Egypt's influence in the Middle East will wane. Relations between Egypt and the rest of the Arab countries would at best be limited to cooperation in fields such as trade and tourism, but could not extend to political and strategic cooperation. The Egyptian leadership has no choice but to continue rebuilding and strengthening Egypt's military power. There is no way for Egypt to achieve this except by keeping the Egyptian options open. It must diversify its sources for purchase of armaments, and it must rebuild the broken bridges between Egypt and the Arab world to provide Egypt with the financial assistance required to re-establish its armed forces in such a way that Egypt can make its weight felt in the reshaping of the Middle East. A lance of military power between Israel and the Arab world, particularly Egypt, is an indispensable condition for a permanent and stable peace in the region. There is no other choice for Egypt but to follow this course, especially if we take into consideration that by the year 2000 the Egyptian population is expected to reach the staggering figure of almost 70 million.

The impact of the separate Egyptian–Israeli peace on the traditional Egyptian system has been such, as I have clearly explained above, that it can no longer react to international or local political and military developments adequately. Unless Egypt remedies the present position, the old system can no longer solve or even contain temporarily major problems in the Arab world and particularly in the Gulf. It is imperative that Egypt together with the Arab states develop a new Arab–Gulf system capable of coping with the developments expected to take place in the area. This new system must be prepared to deal with foreign intervention and also with domestic upheavals affecting the Gulf states and their leaders.

We cannot ignore the fact that the entire area is threatened, not only because of its own problems but also because of the conflicting interests of the two superpowers. Before polarisation becomes irreversable, it is imperative that the Arab countries, together if possible, try to limit the superpowers' interference in the area. In building their economic and military capabilities, the Arabs should diversify their sources as much as possible, avoiding complete dependence on either superpower. It is only if the interference of the superpowers is decreased that peace and tranquility can be achieved in this fragile area.

It is indeed striking to note that the superpowers' polarisation in the Middle East has no parallel in any other part of the world. This may be due to the fact that the Middle East crisis is not yet settled or to the strategic importance of the area, which encourages the superpowers to play their game of chess at the expense of this troubled region. I will not go as far as suggesting that the superpowers have deliberately prevented the chronic Middle East crisis from being solved. However, there is no doubt that both Moscow and Washington are trying to derive the greatest possible advantage from the instability of the area, competing with each other to establish their political and strategic influence.

It is true that the superpowers have come and gone from specific countries. The Americans lost Libya to the Soviets and the Soviets lost Egypt to the US; Jordan used to be totally in the American sphere of influence but it is now seeking Soviet military help. The United States has lost Iran and the Soviets have lost Somalia. The West is in the process of losing North Yemen. But the United States has gained bases in Oman and Somalia.

Despite the kaleidoscope of changing relations, the presence and interference of the superpowers in the Middle East is a constant, and if it does not cease it is quite possible that certain régimes in the area will disappear. The real losers will be the people of the Middle East, because they will continue to suffer and will be unable to develop their own resources in a healthier climate, without constant superpower intervention.

The Arab people are facing unprecedented challenges in both the domestic and the international sphere, but I am confident that they can mobilise their resources and genius, order their priorities, and rise to the challenge. The Arab world can only succeed with a united strategy and so long as no country again takes unilateral action which threatens the overall system and destroys the sense of collective responsibility. Only if we remain united can we attain a genuine peace, and, more important, peace of soul and mind. It is only if such peace is achieved that the next generation in this region can enjoy a more productive and prosperous existence.

Notes

1. *International Herald Tribune*, 4 October 1982.

CHRONOLOGY

2 November 1917	British Foreign Minister Arthur Balfour writes to Chaim Weizman declaring that Britain views with favour the establishment in Palestine of a national home for the Jewish people
29 November 1947	United Nations Resolution 181/II partitioning Palestine into Jewish and Palestinian states
14 May 1948	Israel declared its independence and the first Arab–Israeli war erupted
29 October 1956	British, French and Israeli forces invade Egypt provoking the second Arab–Israeli war
5 June 1967	Israel attacks Egypt and Syria starting the Six-day War
22 November 1967	Security Council Resolution 242 setting out a basis for peace in the Middle East
19 June 1970	United States Secretary of State William Rogers presents peace proposals known as the 'Rogers Plan'
27 May 1971	President Sadat and President Podgorny sign the Egyptian–Soviet Friendship Treaty
5 May 1972	Symposium at the Centre for Political and Strategic Studies of *Al-Ahram* newspaper
19 July 1972	Sadat expels the Soviet military experts from Egypt
6 October 1973	Egyptian forces cross the Suez Canal starting the October War
17 October 1973	Arab states initiate the first phase of the oil embargo
22 October 1973	Security Council Resolution 338 declaring ceasefire
29 October 1973	Fahmy's first visit to Washington
31 October 1973	Fahmy's first meeting with Nixon
6 November 1973	Kissinger's first visit to Cairo
11 November 1973	Six-point agreement between Egypt and Israel

21 December 1973	Opening of Geneva Peace Conference
18 January 1974	First disengagement agreement between Egypt and Israel
21 January 1974	Fahmy's first visit to Moscow
13–15 February 1974	Egypt–Saudi Arab–Syria–Algeria summit in Algiers decides to end oil embargo
28 February 1974	Egypt and United States re-establish full diplomatic relations
2 March 1974	Soviet Foreign Minister Gromyko visits Egypt
18 March 1974	Arab oil ministers meet in Vienna and officially end the oil embargo
31 May 1974	Syrian–Israeli disengagement agreement
12 June 1974	Nixon visits Egypt
15 October 1974	Fahmy's meeting with Brezhnev in Moscow during which Brezhnev decides to visit Egypt
28 October 1974	Rabat summit recognises the PLO as the sole legitimate representative of the Palestinians
17 November 1974	Yasser Arafat delivers speech to the United Nations General Assembly
22 November 1974	PLO given observer status at UN
29 December 1974	Fahmy and General Gamasy in Moscow meet hospitalised Brezhnev, whose visit to Egypt is postponed
7 March 1975	Kissinger starts shuttle for second disengagement between Egyptian and Israeli forces
1–2 June 1975	Sadat–Ford summit conference in Salzburg, Austria
5 June 1975	Egypt re-opens Suez Canal
1 September 1975	Second disengagement agreement between Egypt and Israel
4 December 1975	United Nations Security Council accords the PLO the privileges of a member nation
March 1976	Egypt unilaterally abrogates Egyptian–Soviet Friendship Treaty
September 1976	Tuhami and Dayan meet secretly in Rabat, Morocco
1 October 1977	USA–USSR Joint Declaration on the Middle East issue
5 October 1977	Fahmy meets President Carter in New York
28 October– 4 November 1977	Sadat and Fahmy visit Rumania, Iran and Riyad

9 November 1977	Sadat declares to the Egyptian Assembly his readiness to visit Jerusalem
12 November 1977	Arab Foreign Ministers' conference in Tunis
17 November 1977	Fahmy resigns
19 November 1977	Sadat visits Jerusalem
17 September 1978	Sadat, Begin and Carter agree to Camp David accords
26 March 1979	Treaty of Peace between Egypt and Israel signed in Washington

Index